NOTES ON LANG

RUSSIA
CHINA
NORTH KOREA
SOUTH KOREA
JAPAN

IN THE YEAR 2000, THE SOUTH KOREAN MINISTRY OF CULTURE AND TOURISM ANNOUNCED A REVISED ROMANIZATION OF THE KOREAN LANGUAGE.

ROMANIZATION MEANS HOW SOMETHING IS CONVERTED FROM A DIFFERENT WRITING SYSTEM TO ROMAN/LATIN CHARACTERS.

FOR EXAMPLE, THE BIG PORT CITY IN THE SOUTH IS CALLED THIS:

IN THE KOREAN ALPHABET, HANGUL: 부산광역시	IN TRADITIONAL CHINESE CHARACTERS, HANJA: 釜山廣城市
IN PRE-2000 ROMANIZATION: PUSAN	IN POST-2000 ROMANIZATION: BUSAN

I SKIP THE ROMANIZATION. IT'S EASIER TO JUST CALL IT 부산광역시

THIS STORY TAKES PLACE LONG BEFORE THE YEAR 2000. THE MAPS, ARTICLES, AND MILITARY HISTORIES OF THIS PERIOD WERE ALL RECORDED IN THE ROMANIZATION OF THAT TIME.

IN THIS BOOK, PRE-2000 ROMANIZATION:	IN SOUTH KOREA TODAY, POST-2000 ROMANIZATION:
INCHON	INCHEON
SEOUL	SEOUL
SUWON	SUWON
CHONAN	CHEONAN
TAEJON	DAEJEON
YONGDONG	YEONGDONG
TAEGU	DAEGU
KWANGJU	GWANGJU
PUSAN	BUSAN

SEOUL AND SUWON STAYED THE SAME!

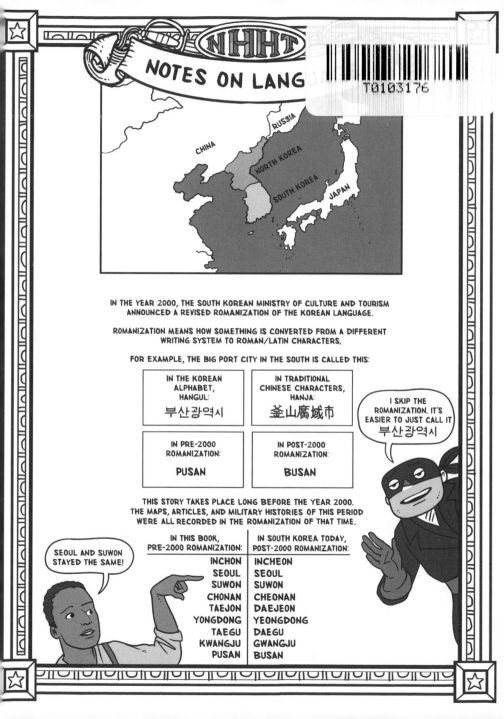

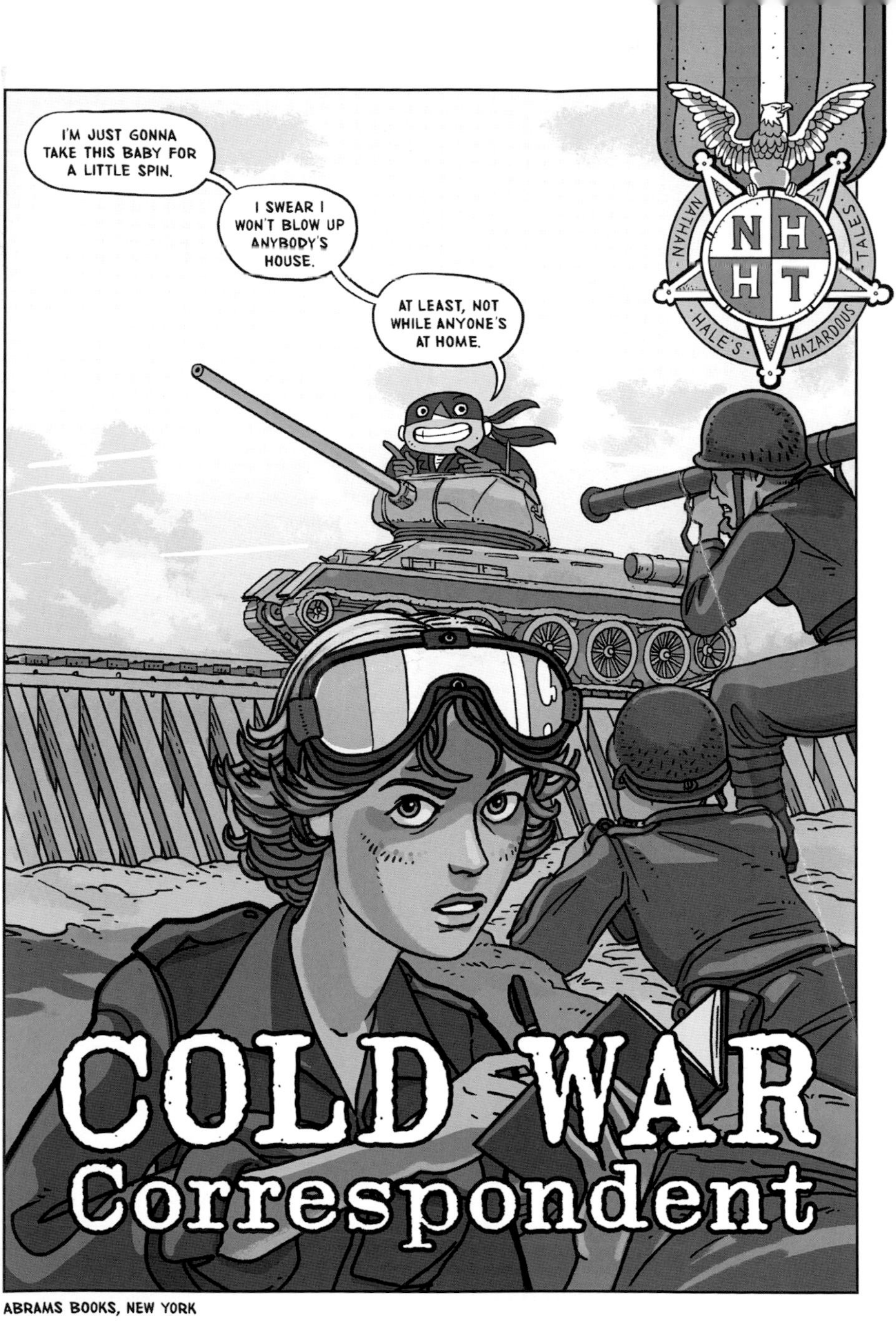
I'M JUST GONNA TAKE THIS BABY FOR A LITTLE SPIN.
I SWEAR I WON'T BLOW UP ANYBODY'S HOUSE.
AT LEAST, NOT WHILE ANYONE'S AT HOME.
NATHAN HALE'S HAZARDOUS TALES
NH HT
COLD WAR
Correspondent

ABRAMS BOOKS, NEW YORK

CATALOGING-IN-PUBLICATION DATA HAS BEEN APPLIED FOR AND MAY BE OBTAINED FROM THE LIBRARY OF CONGRESS.

ISBN 978-1-4197-4951-3

TEXT AND ILLUSTRATIONS COPYRIGHT © 2021 NATHAN HALE
BOOK DESIGN BY NATHAN HALE AND ANDREA MILLER
COLOR ASSISTANT LUCY HALE
KOREAN INTERCULTURAL CONSULTANT MIA KIM

P. 126: TOP: KEYSTONE PRESS / ALAMY STOCK PHOTO; BOTTOM: COURTESY OF THE AUTHOR

P. 127: TOP LEFT: CARL MYDANS / THE LIFE PICTURE COLLECTION VIA GETTY IMAGES; TOP RIGHT: FRANCIS MILLER / THE LIFE PICTURE COLLECTION VIA GETTY IMAGES; BOTTOM: CARL MYDANS / THE LIFE PICTURE COLLECTION VIA GETTY IMAGES

PRINTED AND BOUND IN U.S.A.
10 9 8 7 6 5 4 3 2 1

AMULET BOOKS ARE AVAILABLE AT SPECIAL DISCOUNTS WHEN PURCHASED IN QUANTITY FOR PREMIUMS AND PROMOTIONS AS WELL AS FUNDRAISING OR EDUCATIONAL USE. SPECIAL EDITIONS CAN ALSO BE CREATED TO SPECIFICATION. FOR DETAILS, CONTACT SPECIALSALES@ABRAMSBOOKS.COM OR THE ADDRESS BELOW.

ABRAMS The Art of Books
195 Broadway, New York, NY 10007
abramsbooks.com

FOR MAGGIE, THE EDITOR NOT THE REPORTER,
BUT ALSO FEARLESS IN COMBAT

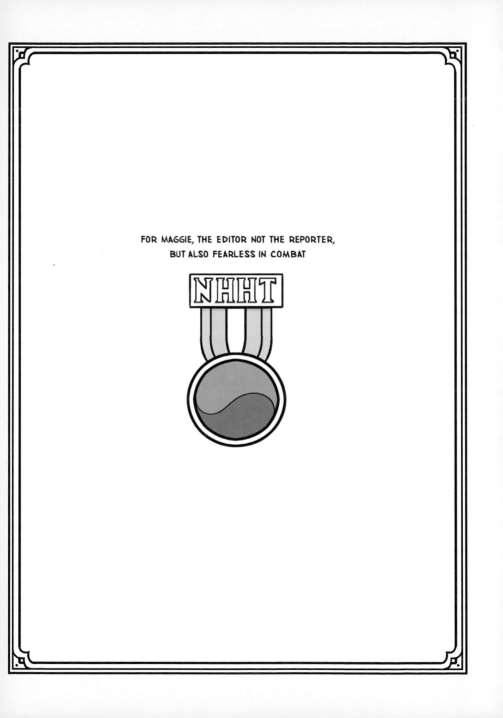

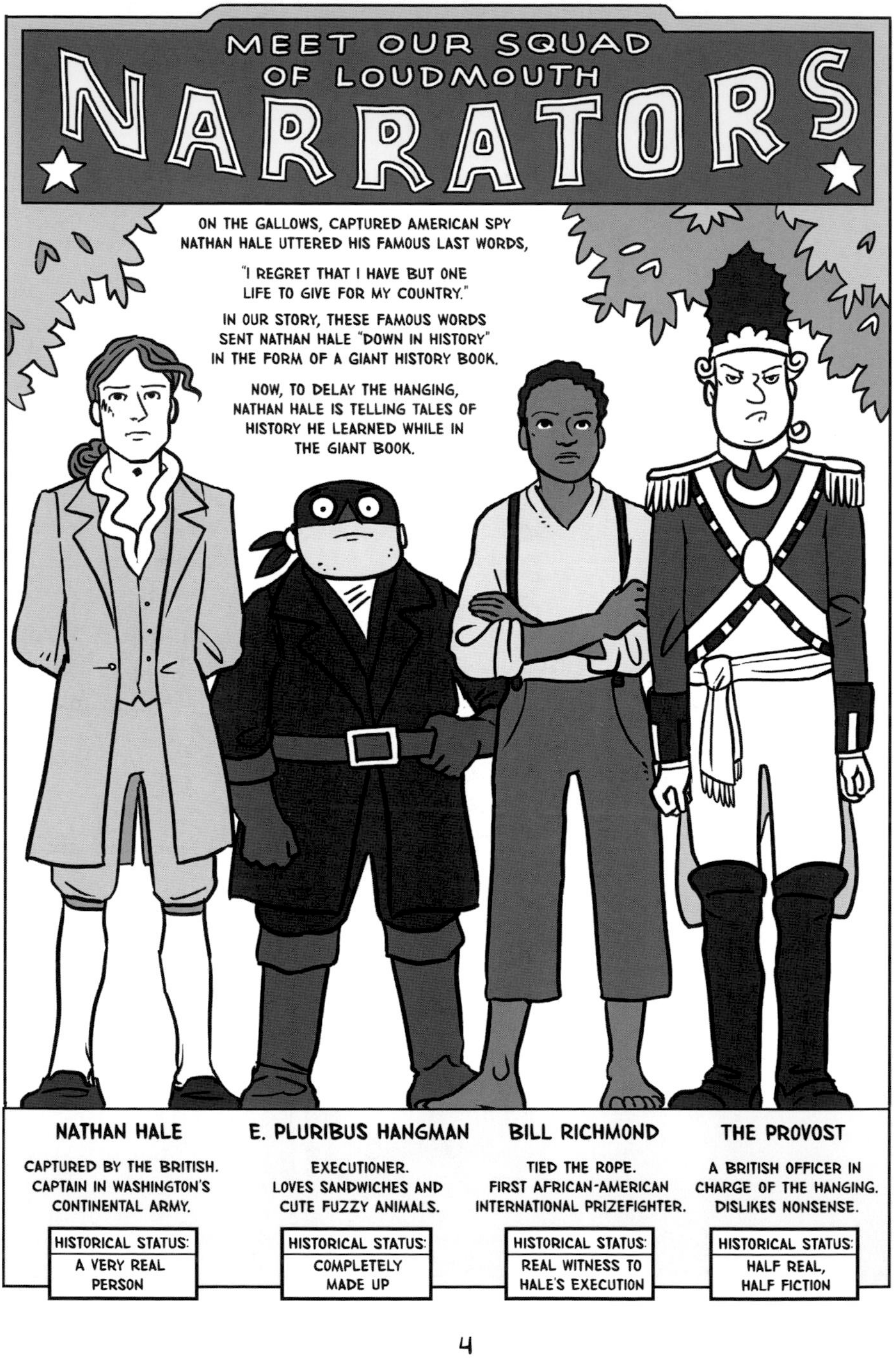
MEET OUR SQUAD OF LOUDMOUTH
NARRATORS
ON THE GALLOWS, CAPTURED AMERICAN SPY NATHAN HALE UTTERED HIS FAMOUS LAST WORDS,
"I REGRET THAT I HAVE BUT ONE LIFE TO GIVE FOR MY COUNTRY."
IN OUR STORY, THESE FAMOUS WORDS SENT NATHAN HALE "DOWN IN HISTORY" IN THE FORM OF A GIANT HISTORY BOOK.
NOW, TO DELAY THE HANGING, NATHAN HALE IS TELLING TALES OF HISTORY HE LEARNED WHILE IN THE GIANT BOOK.
NATHAN HALE
CAPTURED BY THE BRITISH. CAPTAIN IN WASHINGTON'S CONTINENTAL ARMY.
HISTORICAL STATUS: A VERY REAL PERSON
E. PLURIBUS HANGMAN
EXECUTIONER. LOVES SANDWICHES AND CUTE FUZZY ANIMALS.
HISTORICAL STATUS: COMPLETELY MADE UP
BILL RICHMOND
TIED THE ROPE. FIRST AFRICAN-AMERICAN INTERNATIONAL PRIZEFIGHTER.
HISTORICAL STATUS: REAL WITNESS TO HALE'S EXECUTION
THE PROVOST
A BRITISH OFFICER IN CHARGE OF THE HANGING. DISLIKES NONSENSE.
HISTORICAL STATUS: HALF REAL, HALF FICTION

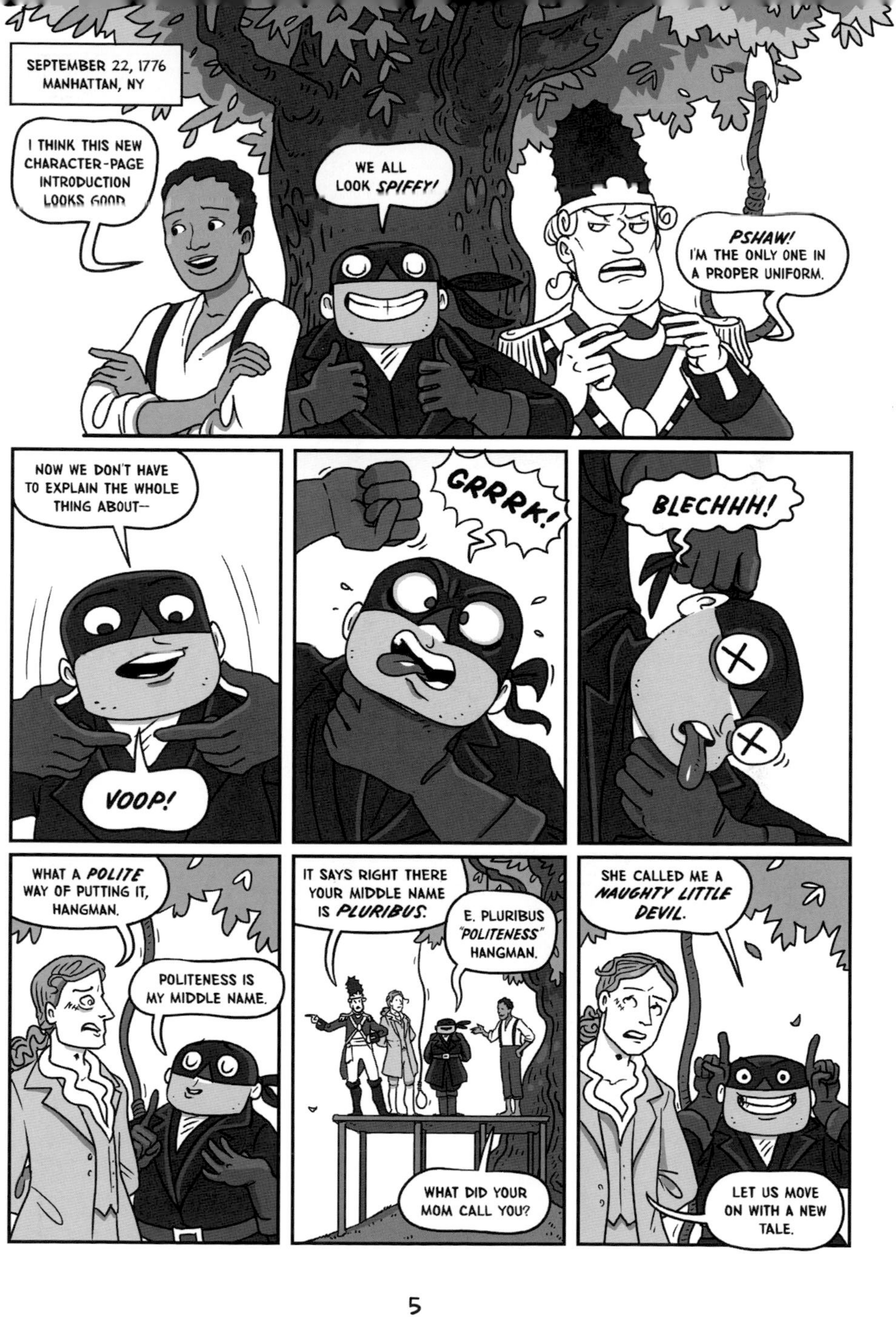

SEPTEMBER 22, 1776
MANHATTAN, NY
I THINK THIS NEW CHARACTER-PAGE INTRODUCTION LOOKS GOOD.
WE ALL LOOK SPIFFY!
PSHAW! I'M THE ONLY ONE IN A PROPER UNIFORM.
NOW WE DON'T HAVE TO EXPLAIN THE WHOLE THING ABOUT--
VOOP!
GRRRK!
BLECHHH!
WHAT A POLITE WAY OF PUTTING IT, HANGMAN.
POLITENESS IS MY MIDDLE NAME.
IT SAYS RIGHT THERE YOUR MIDDLE NAME IS PLURIBUS.
E. PLURIBUS "POLITENESS" HANGMAN.
WHAT DID YOUR MOM CALL YOU?
SHE CALLED ME A NAUGHTY LITTLE DEVIL.
LET US MOVE ON WITH A NEW TALE.

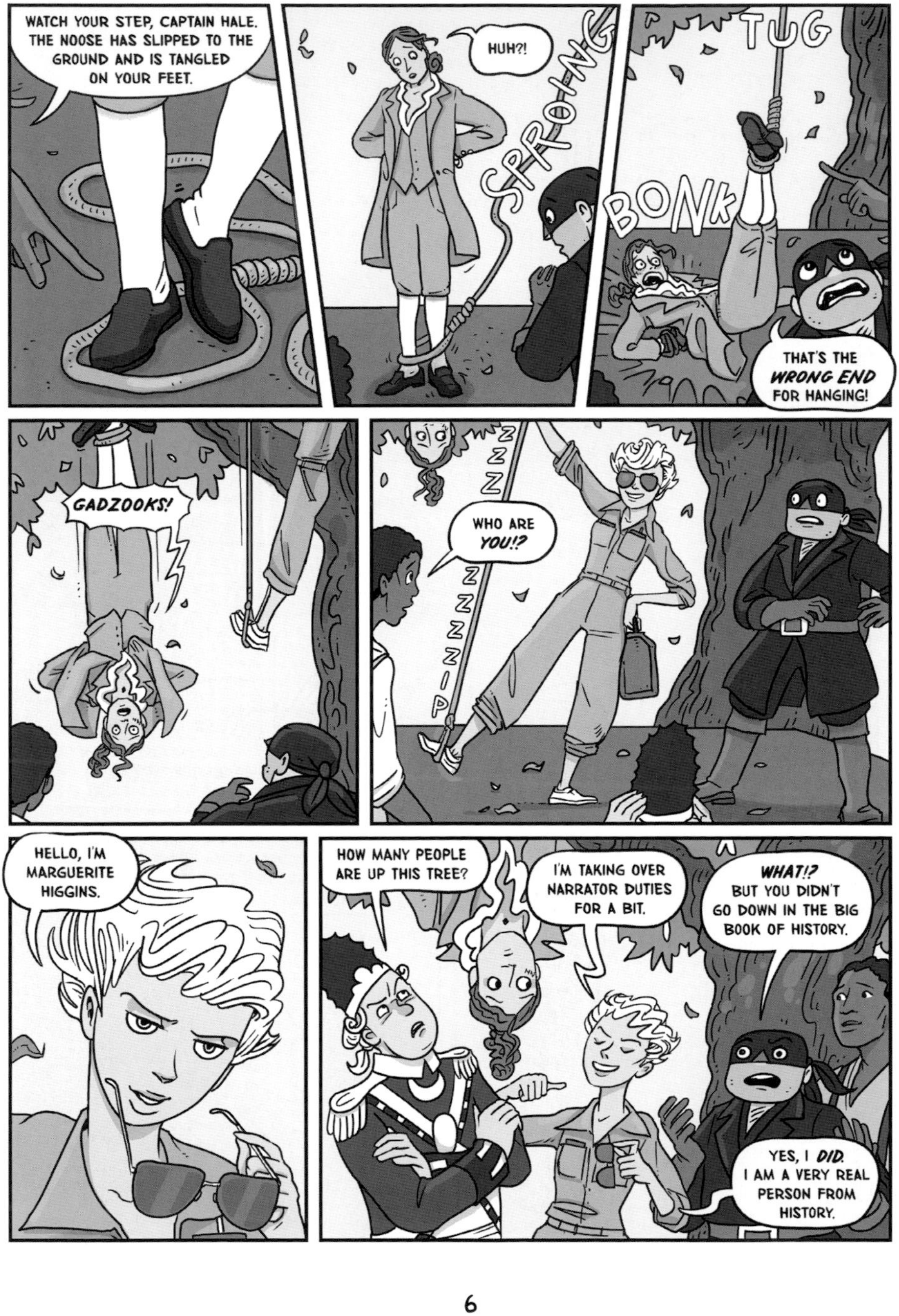
WATCH YOUR STEP, CAPTAIN HALE. THE NOOSE HAS SLIPPED TO THE GROUND AND IS TANGLED ON YOUR FEET.
HUH?!
SPROING
TUG
BONK
THAT'S THE WRONG END FOR HANGING!
GADZOOKS!
WHO ARE YOU!?
ZZZ
ZZZZZZIP
HELLO, I'M MARGUERITE HIGGINS.
HOW MANY PEOPLE ARE UP THIS TREE?
I'M TAKING OVER NARRATOR DUTIES FOR A BIT.
WHAT!? BUT YOU DIDN'T GO DOWN IN THE BIG BOOK OF HISTORY.
YES, I DID. I AM A VERY REAL PERSON FROM HISTORY.

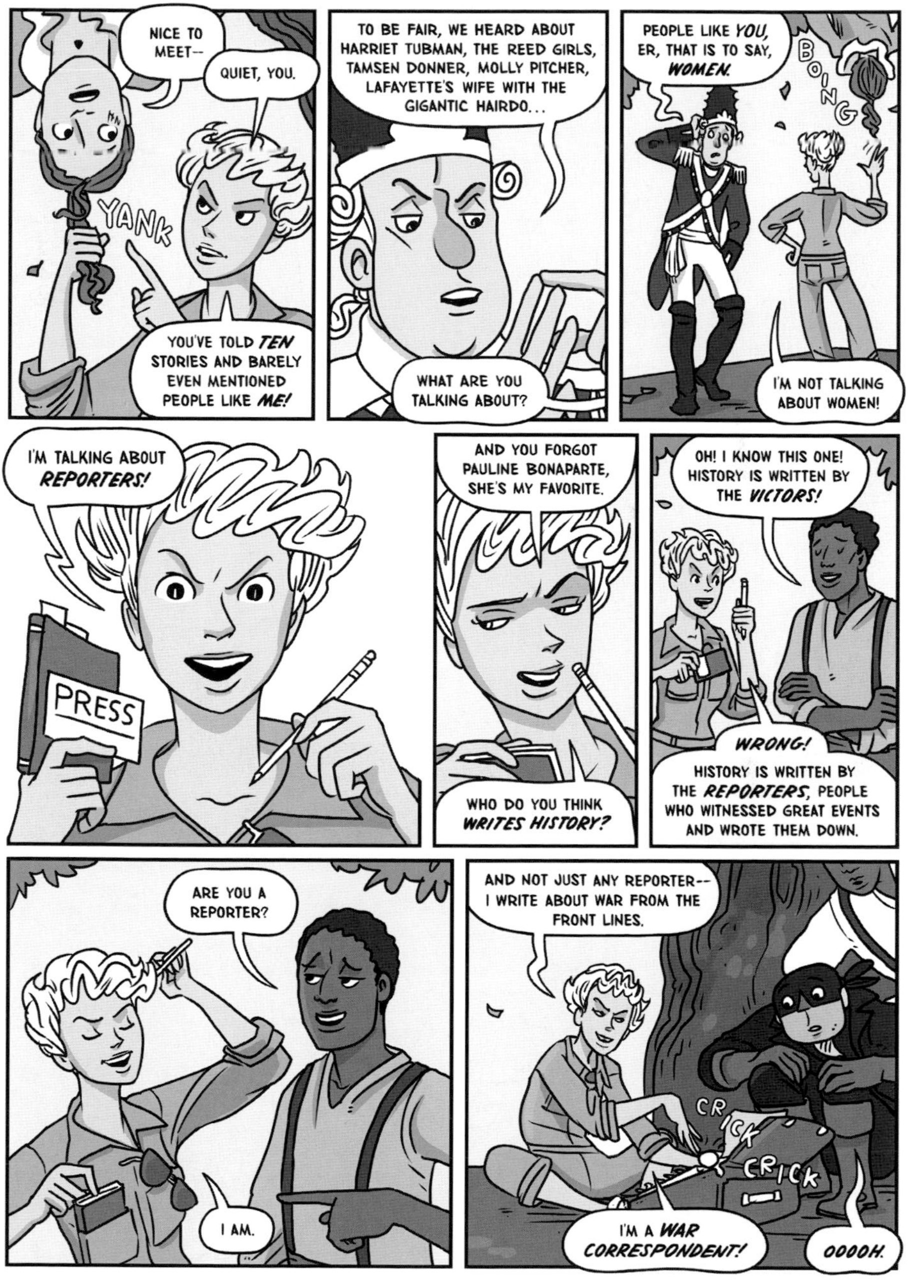
NICE TO MEET--
QUIET, YOU.
YANK
YOU'VE TOLD TEN STORIES AND BARELY EVEN MENTIONED PEOPLE LIKE ME!
TO BE FAIR, WE HEARD ABOUT HARRIET TUBMAN, THE REED GIRLS, TAMSEN DONNER, MOLLY PITCHER, LAFAYETTE'S WIFE WITH THE GIGANTIC HAIRDO...
WHAT ARE YOU TALKING ABOUT?
PEOPLE LIKE YOU, ER, THAT IS TO SAY, WOMEN.
BOING
I'M NOT TALKING ABOUT WOMEN!
I'M TALKING ABOUT REPORTERS!
PRESS
AND YOU FORGOT PAULINE BONAPARTE, SHE'S MY FAVORITE.
WHO DO YOU THINK WRITES HISTORY?
OH! I KNOW THIS ONE! HISTORY IS WRITTEN BY THE VICTORS!
WRONG!
HISTORY IS WRITTEN BY THE REPORTERS, PEOPLE WHO WITNESSED GREAT EVENTS AND WROTE THEM DOWN.
ARE YOU A REPORTER?
I AM.
AND NOT JUST ANY REPORTER-- I WRITE ABOUT WAR FROM THE FRONT LINES.
CRICK
CRICK
I'M A WAR CORRESPONDENT!
OOOOH.

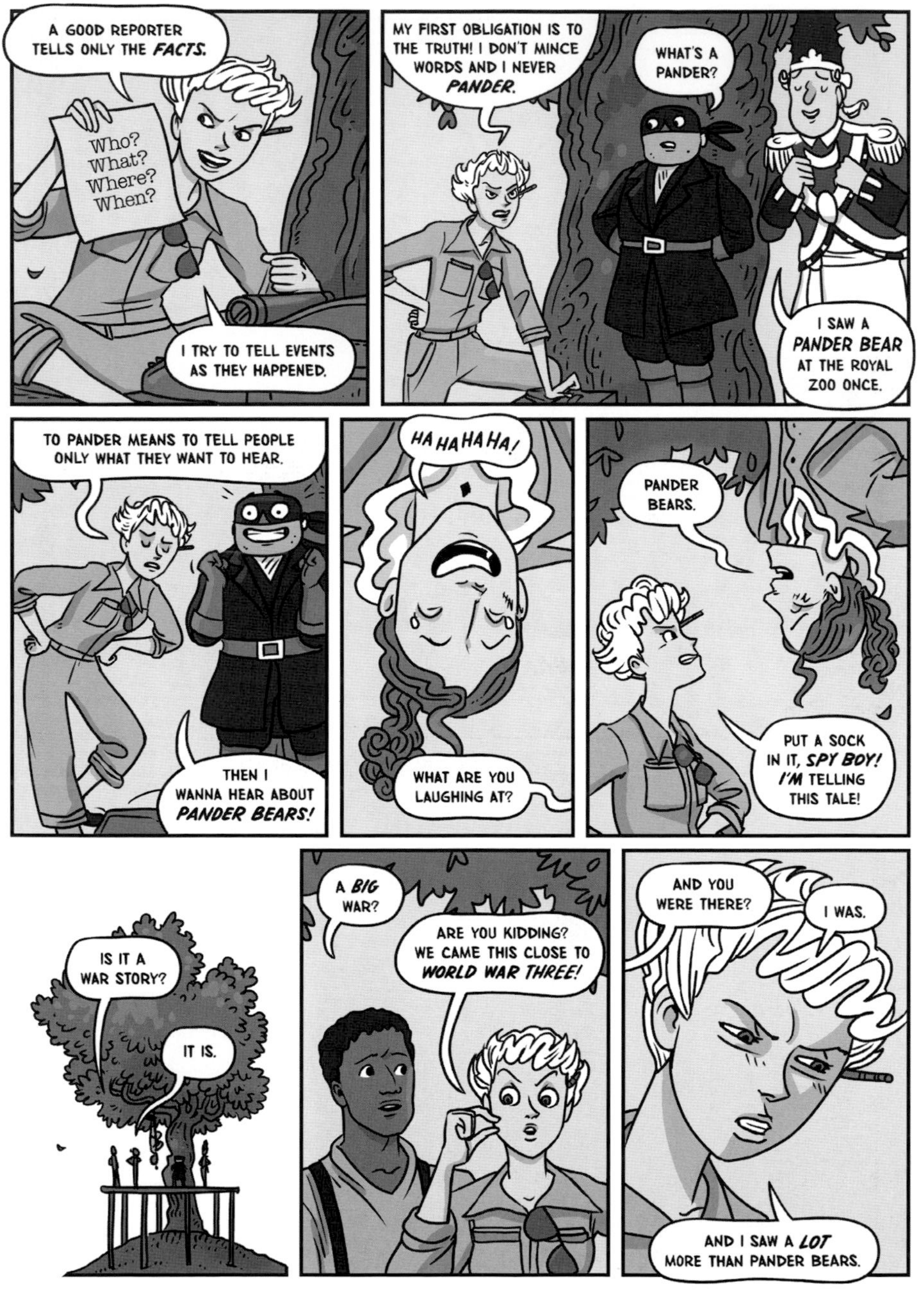
A GOOD REPORTER TELLS ONLY THE *FACTS.*
Who? What? Where? When?
I TRY TO TELL EVENTS AS THEY HAPPENED.
MY FIRST OBLIGATION IS TO THE TRUTH! I DON'T MINCE WORDS AND I NEVER *PANDER.*
WHAT'S A PANDER?
I SAW A *PANDER BEAR* AT THE ROYAL ZOO ONCE.
TO PANDER MEANS TO TELL PEOPLE ONLY WHAT THEY WANT TO HEAR.
THEN I WANNA HEAR ABOUT *PANDER BEARS!*
HA HA HA HA HA!
WHAT ARE YOU LAUGHING AT?
PANDER BEARS.
PUT A SOCK IN IT, *SPY BOY! I'M* TELLING THIS TALE!
IS IT A WAR STORY?
IT IS.
A *BIG* WAR?
ARE YOU KIDDING? WE CAME THIS CLOSE TO *WORLD WAR THREE!*
AND YOU WERE THERE?
I WAS.
AND I SAW A *LOT* MORE THAN PANDER BEARS.

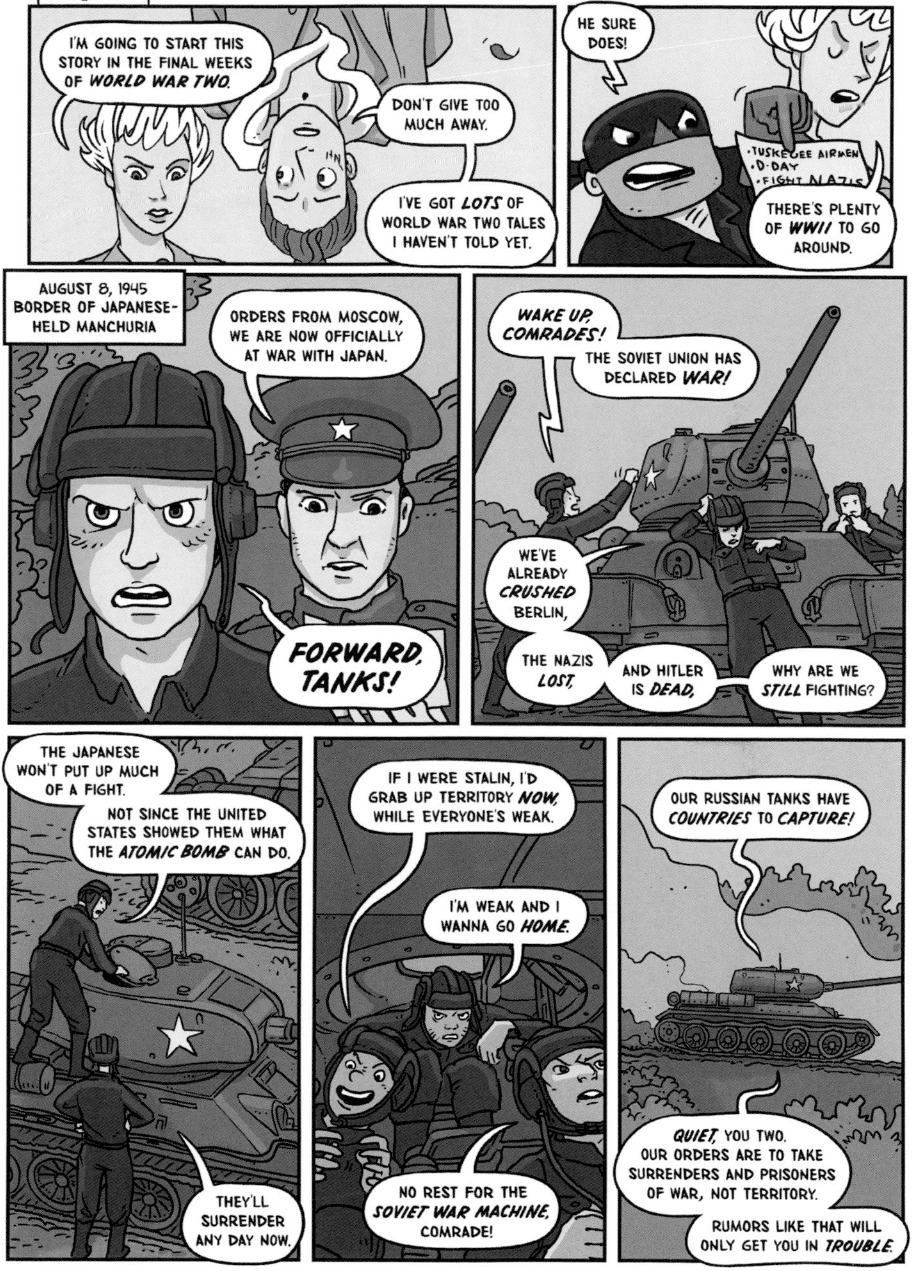
I'M GOING TO START THIS STORY IN THE FINAL WEEKS OF WORLD WAR TWO.
DON'T GIVE TOO MUCH AWAY.
I'VE GOT LOTS OF WORLD WAR TWO TALES I HAVEN'T TOLD YET.
HE SURE DOES!
•TUSKEGEE AIRMEN •D-DAY •FIGHT NAZIS
THERE'S PLENTY OF WWII TO GO AROUND.
AUGUST 8, 1945 BORDER OF JAPANESE-HELD MANCHURIA
ORDERS FROM MOSCOW, WE ARE NOW OFFICIALLY AT WAR WITH JAPAN.
FORWARD, TANKS!
WAKE UP, COMRADES!
THE SOVIET UNION HAS DECLARED WAR!
WE'VE ALREADY CRUSHED BERLIN,
THE NAZIS LOST,
AND HITLER IS DEAD,
WHY ARE WE STILL FIGHTING?
THE JAPANESE WON'T PUT UP MUCH OF A FIGHT.
NOT SINCE THE UNITED STATES SHOWED THEM WHAT THE ATOMIC BOMB CAN DO.
THEY'LL SURRENDER ANY DAY NOW.
IF I WERE STALIN, I'D GRAB UP TERRITORY NOW, WHILE EVERYONE'S WEAK.
I'M WEAK AND I WANNA GO HOME.
NO REST FOR THE SOVIET WAR MACHINE, COMRADE!
OUR RUSSIAN TANKS HAVE COUNTRIES TO CAPTURE!
QUIET, YOU TWO. OUR ORDERS ARE TO TAKE SURRENDERS AND PRISONERS OF WAR, NOT TERRITORY.
RUMORS LIKE THAT WILL ONLY GET YOU IN TROUBLE.

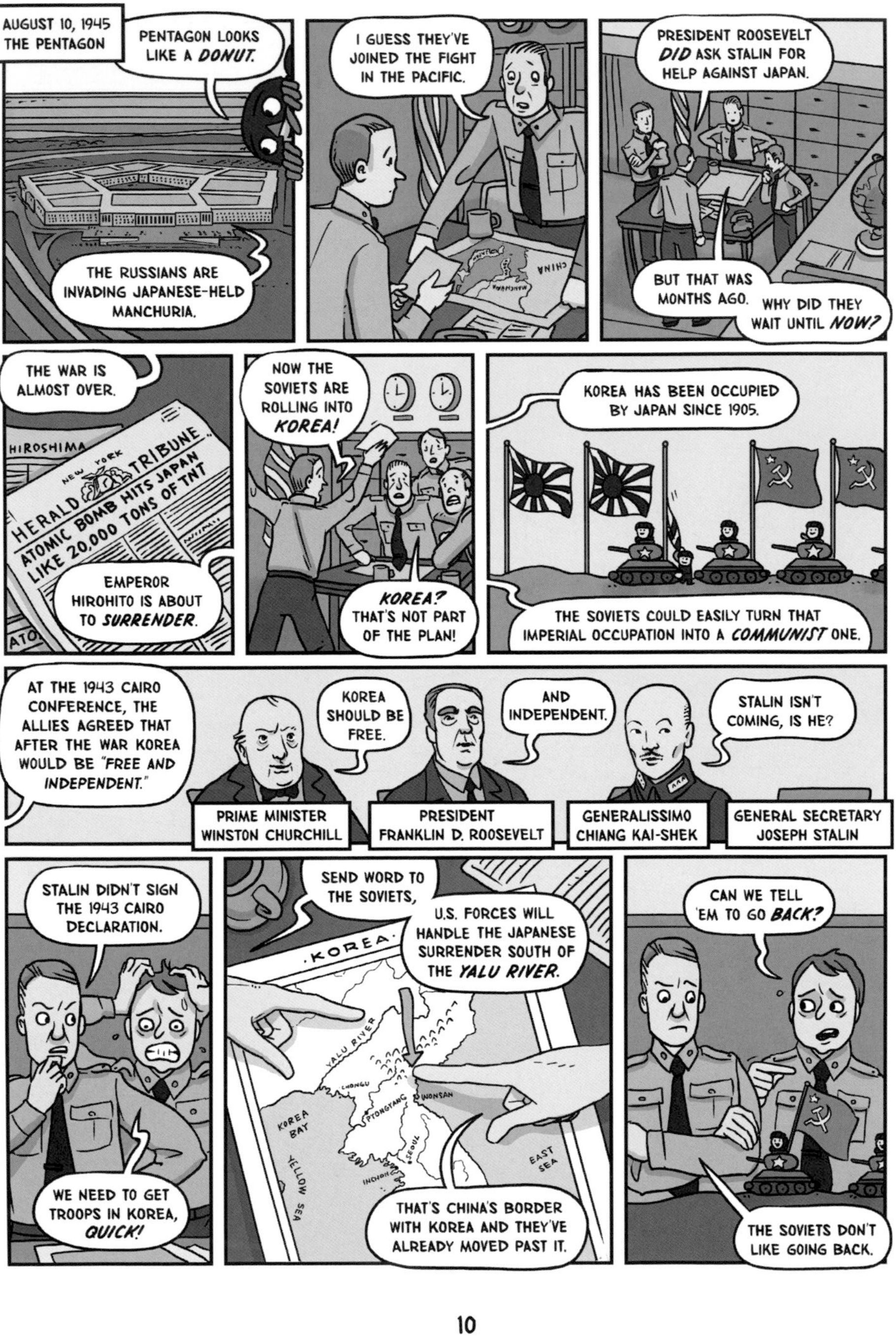

AUGUST 10, 1945
THE PENTAGON
PENTAGON LOOKS LIKE A *DONUT.*
THE RUSSIANS ARE INVADING JAPANESE-HELD MANCHURIA.
I GUESS THEY'VE JOINED THE FIGHT IN THE PACIFIC.
PRESIDENT ROOSEVELT *DID* ASK STALIN FOR HELP AGAINST JAPAN.
BUT THAT WAS MONTHS AGO.
WHY DID THEY WAIT UNTIL *NOW?*
THE WAR IS ALMOST OVER.
HIROSHIMA
NEW YORK HERALD TRIBUNE
ATOMIC BOMB HITS JAPAN LIKE 20,000 TONS OF TNT
EMPEROR HIROHITO IS ABOUT TO *SURRENDER.*
NOW THE SOVIETS ARE ROLLING INTO *KOREA!*
KOREA? THAT'S NOT PART OF THE PLAN!
KOREA HAS BEEN OCCUPIED BY JAPAN SINCE 1905.
THE SOVIETS COULD EASILY TURN THAT IMPERIAL OCCUPATION INTO A *COMMUNIST* ONE.
AT THE 1943 CAIRO CONFERENCE, THE ALLIES AGREED THAT AFTER THE WAR KOREA WOULD BE *"FREE AND INDEPENDENT."*
KOREA SHOULD BE FREE.
AND INDEPENDENT.
STALIN ISN'T COMING, IS HE?
PRIME MINISTER WINSTON CHURCHILL
PRESIDENT FRANKLIN D. ROOSEVELT
GENERALISSIMO CHIANG KAI-SHEK
GENERAL SECRETARY JOSEPH STALIN
STALIN DIDN'T SIGN THE 1943 CAIRO DECLARATION.
WE NEED TO GET TROOPS IN KOREA, *QUICK!*
SEND WORD TO THE SOVIETS,
U.S. FORCES WILL HANDLE THE JAPANESE SURRENDER SOUTH OF THE *YALU RIVER.*
KOREA
YALU RIVER
PYONGYANG
WONSAN
KOREA BAY
SEOUL
INCHON
YELLOW SEA
EAST SEA
THAT'S CHINA'S BORDER WITH KOREA AND THEY'VE ALREADY MOVED PAST IT.
CAN WE TELL 'EM TO GO *BACK?*
THE SOVIETS DON'T LIKE GOING BACK.

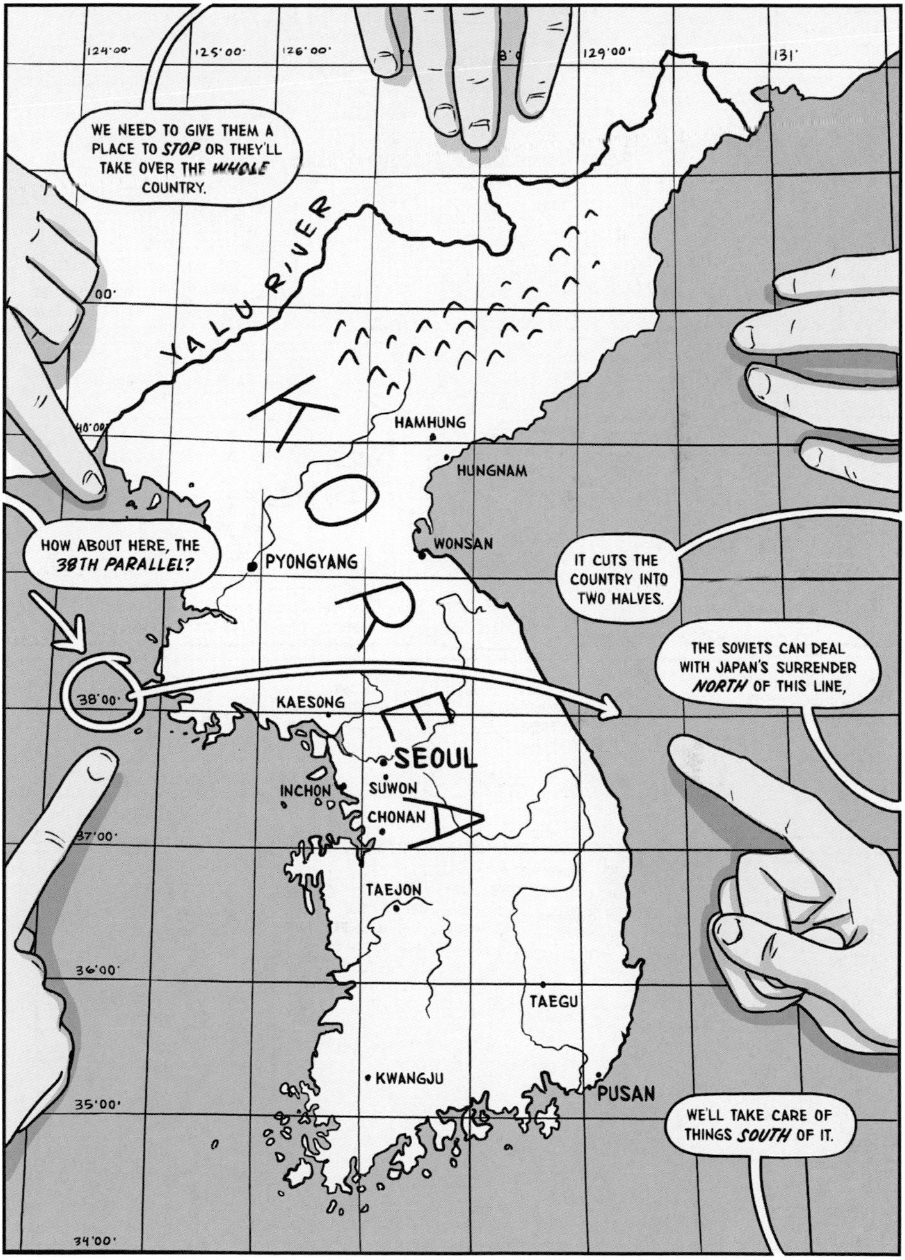
WE NEED TO GIVE THEM A PLACE TO STOP OR THEY'LL TAKE OVER THE WHOLE COUNTRY.
HOW ABOUT HERE, THE 38TH PARALLEL?
IT CUTS THE COUNTRY INTO TWO HALVES.
THE SOVIETS CAN DEAL WITH JAPAN'S SURRENDER NORTH OF THIS LINE,
WE'LL TAKE CARE OF THINGS SOUTH OF IT.
124°00'
125°00'
126°00'
129°00'
131°
YALU RIVER
KOREA
HAMHUNG
HUNGNAM
WONSAN
PYONGYANG
38°00'
KAESONG
SEOUL
INCHON
SUWON
CHONAN
37°00'
TAEJON
36°00'
TAEGU
KWANGJU
PUSAN
35°00'
34°00'

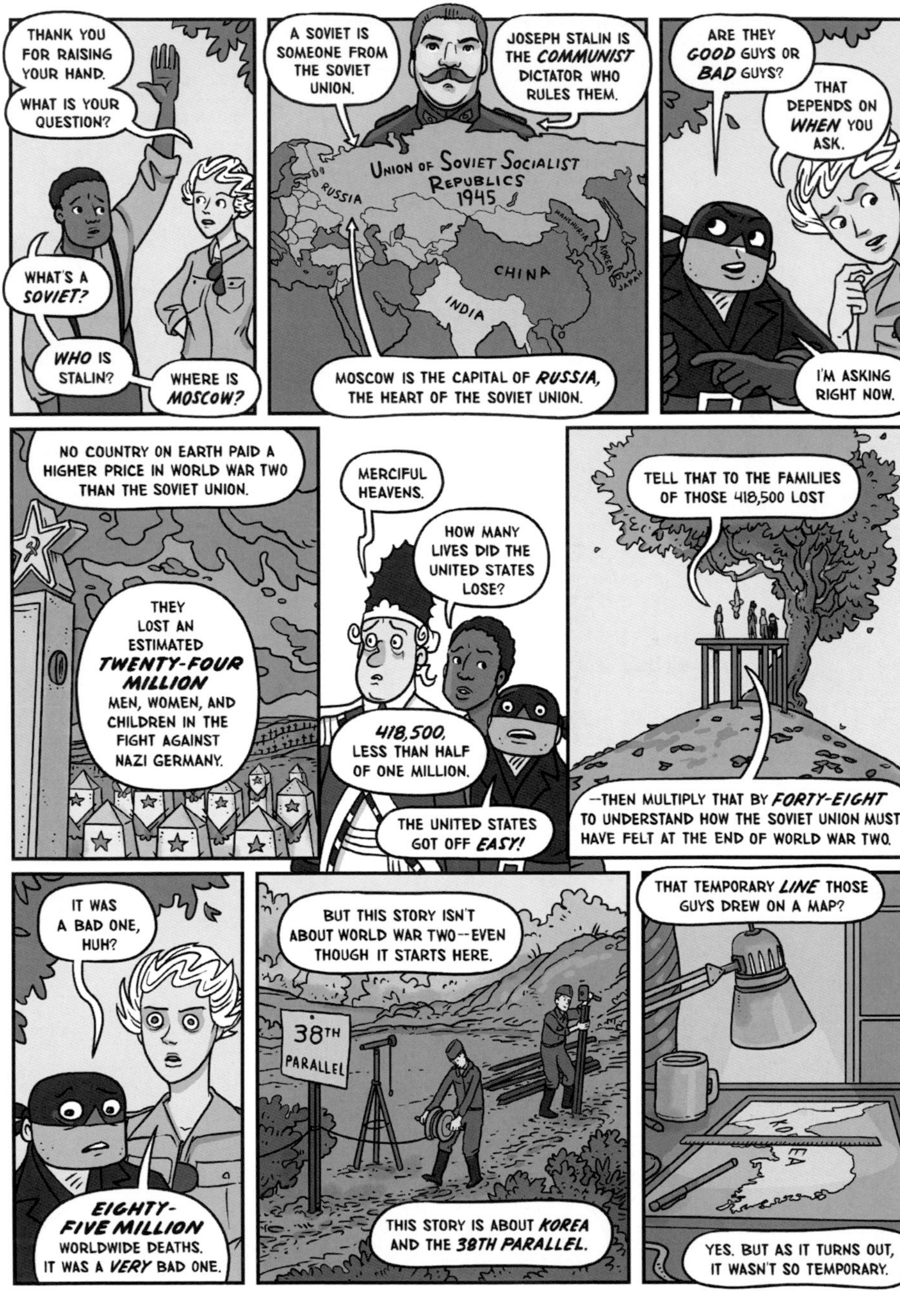

THANK YOU FOR RAISING YOUR HAND.
WHAT IS YOUR QUESTION?
WHAT'S A *SOVIET?*
WHO IS STALIN?
WHERE IS *MOSCOW?*
A SOVIET IS SOMEONE FROM THE SOVIET UNION.
JOSEPH STALIN IS THE *COMMUNIST* DICTATOR WHO RULES THEM.
UNION OF SOVIET SOCIALIST REPUBLICS 1945
RUSSIA
MANCHURIA
KOREA
JAPAN
CHINA
INDIA
MOSCOW IS THE CAPITAL OF *RUSSIA,* THE HEART OF THE SOVIET UNION.
ARE THEY *GOOD* GUYS OR *BAD* GUYS?
THAT DEPENDS ON *WHEN* YOU ASK.
I'M ASKING RIGHT NOW.
NO COUNTRY ON EARTH PAID A HIGHER PRICE IN WORLD WAR TWO THAN THE SOVIET UNION.
THEY LOST AN ESTIMATED ***TWENTY-FOUR MILLION*** MEN, WOMEN, AND CHILDREN IN THE FIGHT AGAINST NAZI GERMANY.
MERCIFUL HEAVENS.
HOW MANY LIVES DID THE UNITED STATES LOSE?
418,500, LESS THAN HALF OF ONE MILLION.
THE UNITED STATES GOT OFF *EASY!*
TELL THAT TO THE FAMILIES OF THOSE 418,500 LOST
--THEN MULTIPLY THAT BY *FORTY-EIGHT* TO UNDERSTAND HOW THE SOVIET UNION MUST HAVE FELT AT THE END OF WORLD WAR TWO.
IT WAS A BAD ONE, HUH?
EIGHTY-FIVE MILLION WORLDWIDE DEATHS. IT WAS A *VERY* BAD ONE.
BUT THIS STORY ISN'T ABOUT WORLD WAR TWO--EVEN THOUGH IT STARTS HERE.
38TH PARALLEL
THIS STORY IS ABOUT *KOREA* AND THE *38TH PARALLEL.*
THAT TEMPORARY *LINE* THOSE GUYS DREW ON A MAP?
YES. BUT AS IT TURNS OUT, IT WASN'T SO TEMPORARY.

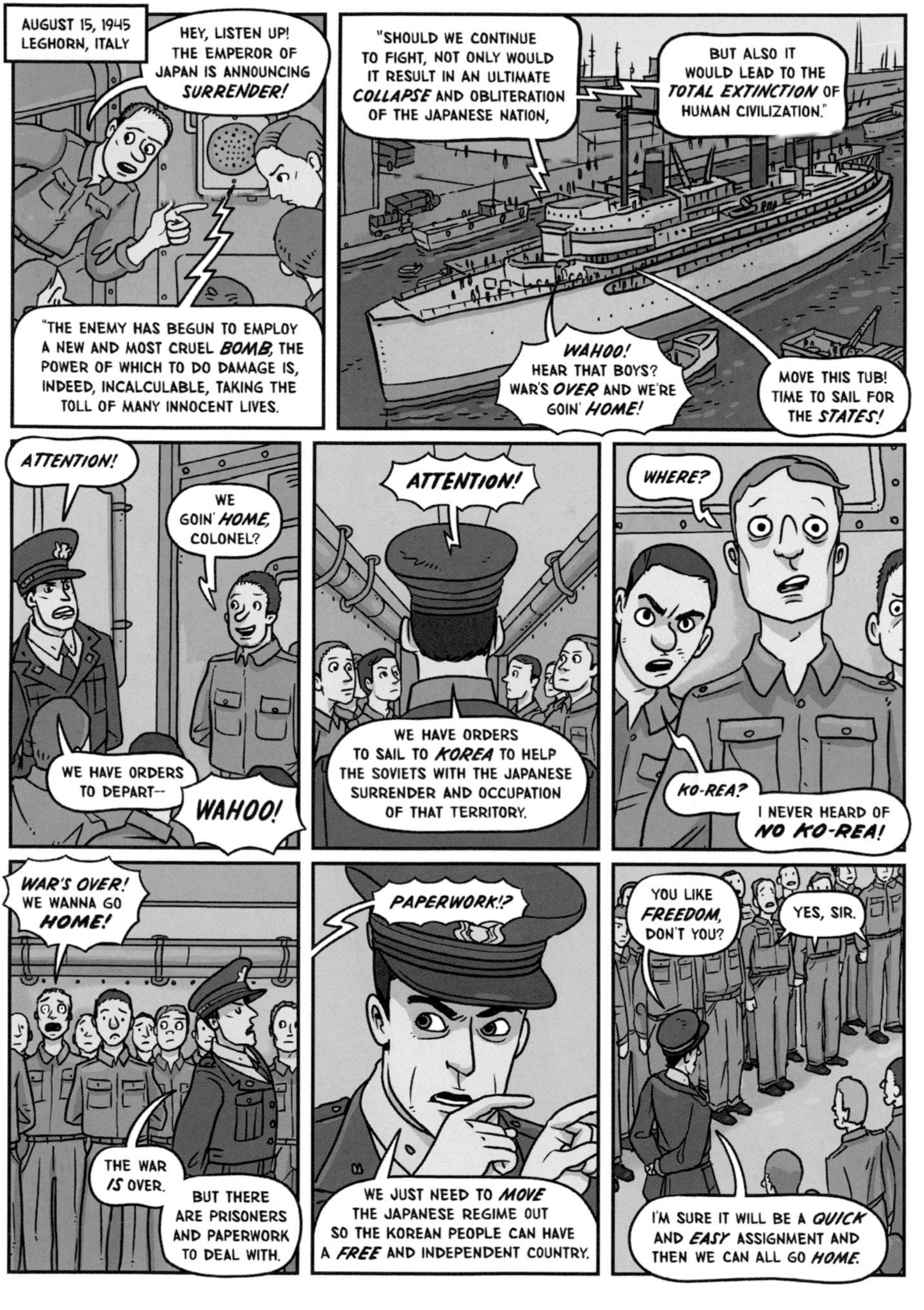
AUGUST 15, 1945
LEGHORN, ITALY
HEY, LISTEN UP! THE EMPEROR OF JAPAN IS ANNOUNCING SURRENDER!
"THE ENEMY HAS BEGUN TO EMPLOY A NEW AND MOST CRUEL BOMB, THE POWER OF WHICH TO DO DAMAGE IS, INDEED, INCALCULABLE, TAKING THE TOLL OF MANY INNOCENT LIVES.
"SHOULD WE CONTINUE TO FIGHT, NOT ONLY WOULD IT RESULT IN AN ULTIMATE COLLAPSE AND OBLITERATION OF THE JAPANESE NATION,
BUT ALSO IT WOULD LEAD TO THE TOTAL EXTINCTION OF HUMAN CIVILIZATION."
WAHOO! HEAR THAT BOYS? WAR'S OVER AND WE'RE GOIN' HOME!
MOVE THIS TUB! TIME TO SAIL FOR THE STATES!
ATTENTION!
WE GOIN' HOME, COLONEL?
WE HAVE ORDERS TO DEPART--
WAHOO!
ATTENTION!
WE HAVE ORDERS TO SAIL TO KOREA TO HELP THE SOVIETS WITH THE JAPANESE SURRENDER AND OCCUPATION OF THAT TERRITORY.
WHERE?
KO-REA?
I NEVER HEARD OF NO KO-REA!
WAR'S OVER! WE WANNA GO HOME!
THE WAR IS OVER.
BUT THERE ARE PRISONERS AND PAPERWORK TO DEAL WITH.
PAPERWORK!?
WE JUST NEED TO MOVE THE JAPANESE REGIME OUT SO THE KOREAN PEOPLE CAN HAVE A FREE AND INDEPENDENT COUNTRY.
YOU LIKE FREEDOM, DON'T YOU?
YES, SIR.
I'M SURE IT WILL BE A QUICK AND EASY ASSIGNMENT AND THEN WE CAN ALL GO HOME.

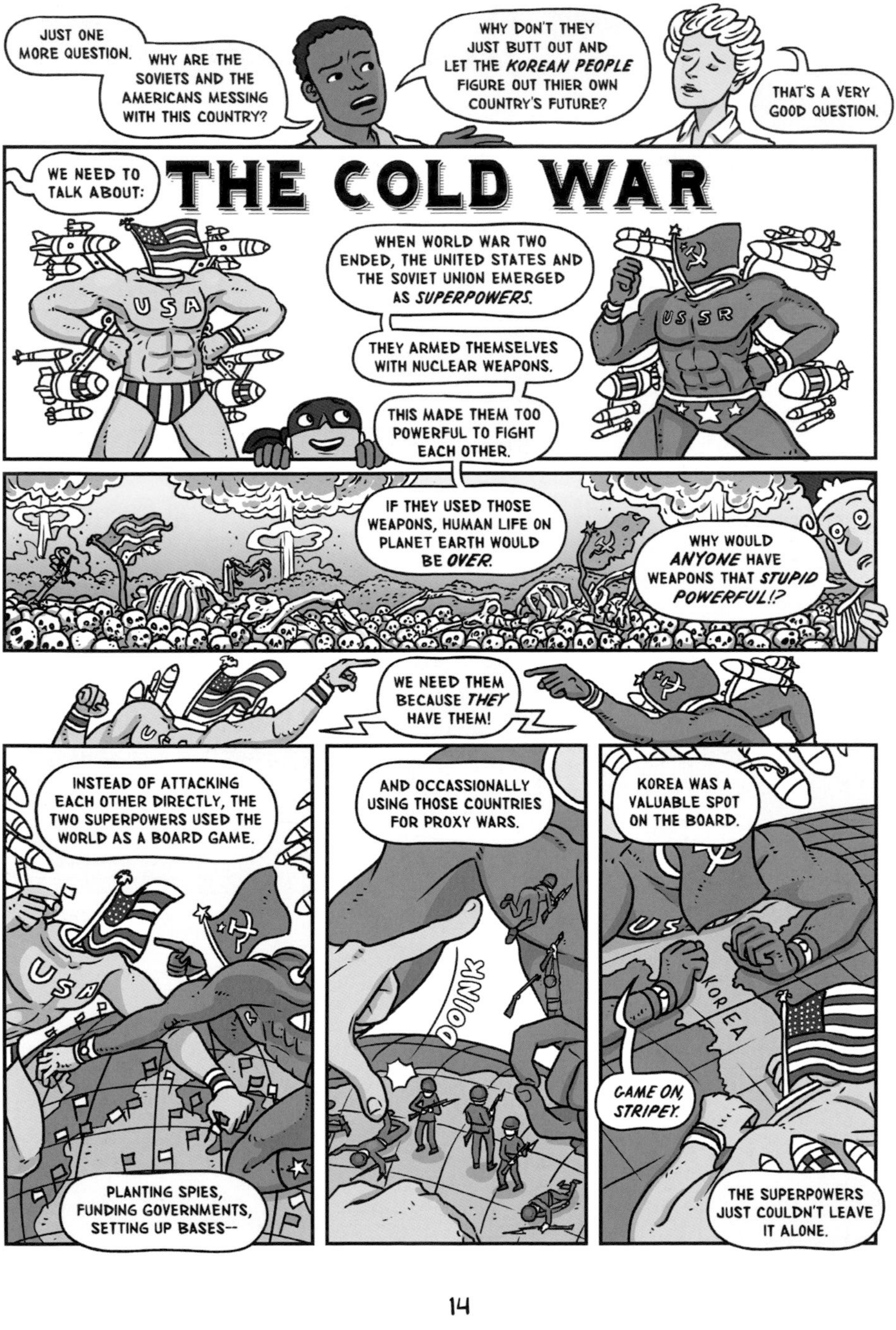
JUST ONE MORE QUESTION.
WHY ARE THE SOVIETS AND THE AMERICANS MESSING WITH THIS COUNTRY?
WHY DON'T THEY JUST BUTT OUT AND LET THE KOREAN PEOPLE FIGURE OUT THIER OWN COUNTRY'S FUTURE?
THAT'S A VERY GOOD QUESTION.
WE NEED TO TALK ABOUT:
THE COLD WAR
USA
USSR
WHEN WORLD WAR TWO ENDED, THE UNITED STATES AND THE SOVIET UNION EMERGED AS SUPERPOWERS.
THEY ARMED THEMSELVES WITH NUCLEAR WEAPONS.
THIS MADE THEM TOO POWERFUL TO FIGHT EACH OTHER.
IF THEY USED THOSE WEAPONS, HUMAN LIFE ON PLANET EARTH WOULD BE OVER.
WHY WOULD ANYONE HAVE WEAPONS THAT STUPID POWERFUL!?
WE NEED THEM BECAUSE THEY HAVE THEM!
INSTEAD OF ATTACKING EACH OTHER DIRECTLY, THE TWO SUPERPOWERS USED THE WORLD AS A BOARD GAME.
USA
PLANTING SPIES, FUNDING GOVERNMENTS, SETTING UP BASES--
AND OCCASSIONALLY USING THOSE COUNTRIES FOR PROXY WARS.
DOINK
KOREA WAS A VALUABLE SPOT ON THE BOARD.
KOREA
GAME ON, STRIPEY.
THE SUPERPOWERS JUST COULDN'T LEAVE IT ALONE.

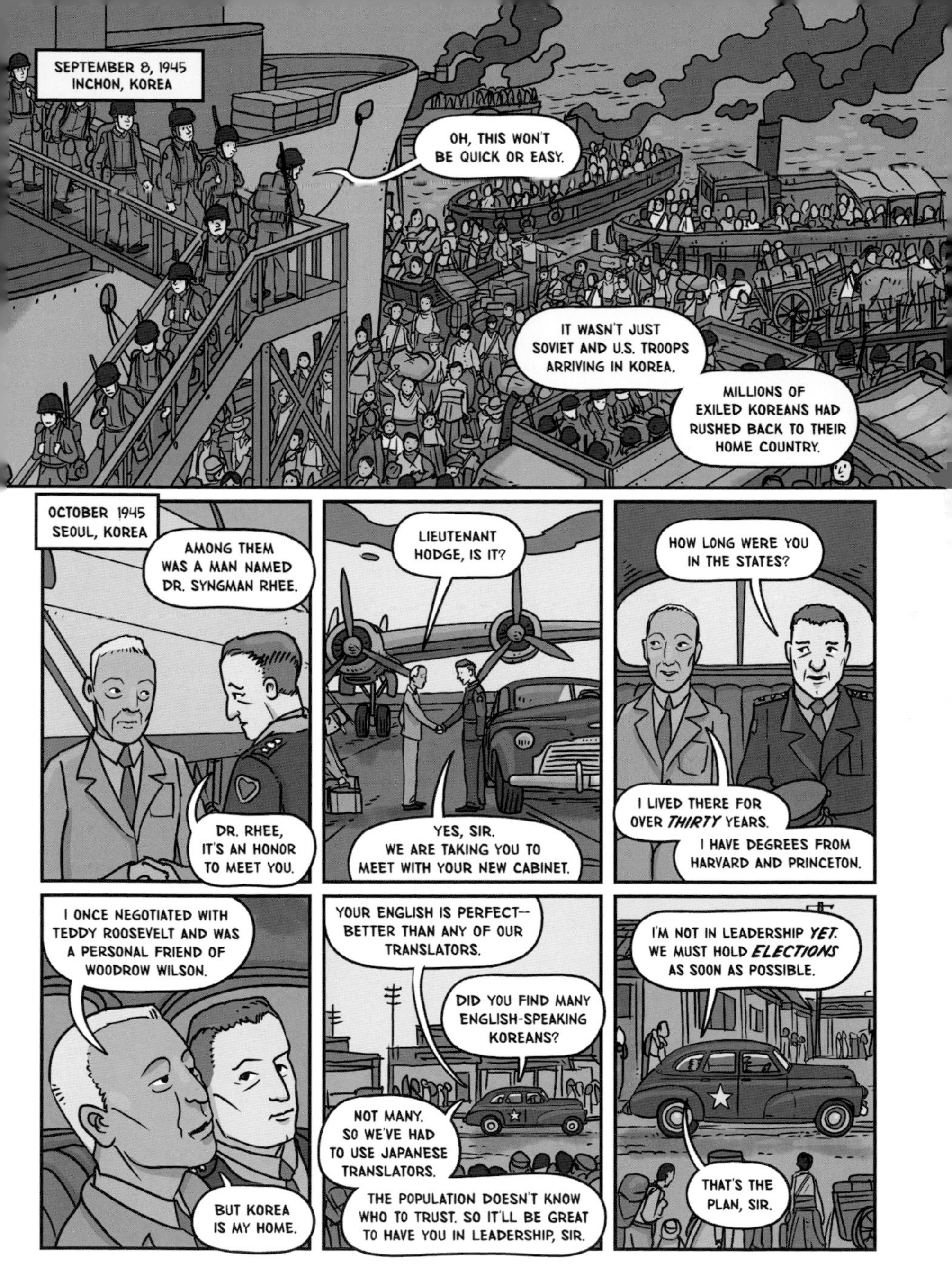
SEPTEMBER 8, 1945
INCHON, KOREA
OH, THIS WON'T BE QUICK OR EASY.
IT WASN'T JUST SOVIET AND U.S. TROOPS ARRIVING IN KOREA.
MILLIONS OF EXILED KOREANS HAD RUSHED BACK TO THEIR HOME COUNTRY.
OCTOBER 1945
SEOUL, KOREA
AMONG THEM WAS A MAN NAMED DR. SYNGMAN RHEE.
DR. RHEE, IT'S AN HONOR TO MEET YOU.
LIEUTENANT HODGE, IS IT?
YES, SIR. WE ARE TAKING YOU TO MEET WITH YOUR NEW CABINET.
HOW LONG WERE YOU IN THE STATES?
I LIVED THERE FOR OVER *THIRTY* YEARS.
I HAVE DEGREES FROM HARVARD AND PRINCETON.
I ONCE NEGOTIATED WITH TEDDY ROOSEVELT AND WAS A PERSONAL FRIEND OF WOODROW WILSON.
BUT KOREA IS MY HOME.
YOUR ENGLISH IS PERFECT-- BETTER THAN ANY OF OUR TRANSLATORS.
DID YOU FIND MANY ENGLISH-SPEAKING KOREANS?
NOT MANY. SO WE'VE HAD TO USE JAPANESE TRANSLATORS.
THE POPULATION DOESN'T KNOW WHO TO TRUST. SO IT'LL BE GREAT TO HAVE YOU IN LEADERSHIP, SIR.
I'M NOT IN LEADERSHIP *YET.* WE MUST HOLD *ELECTIONS* AS SOON AS POSSIBLE.
THAT'S THE PLAN, SIR.

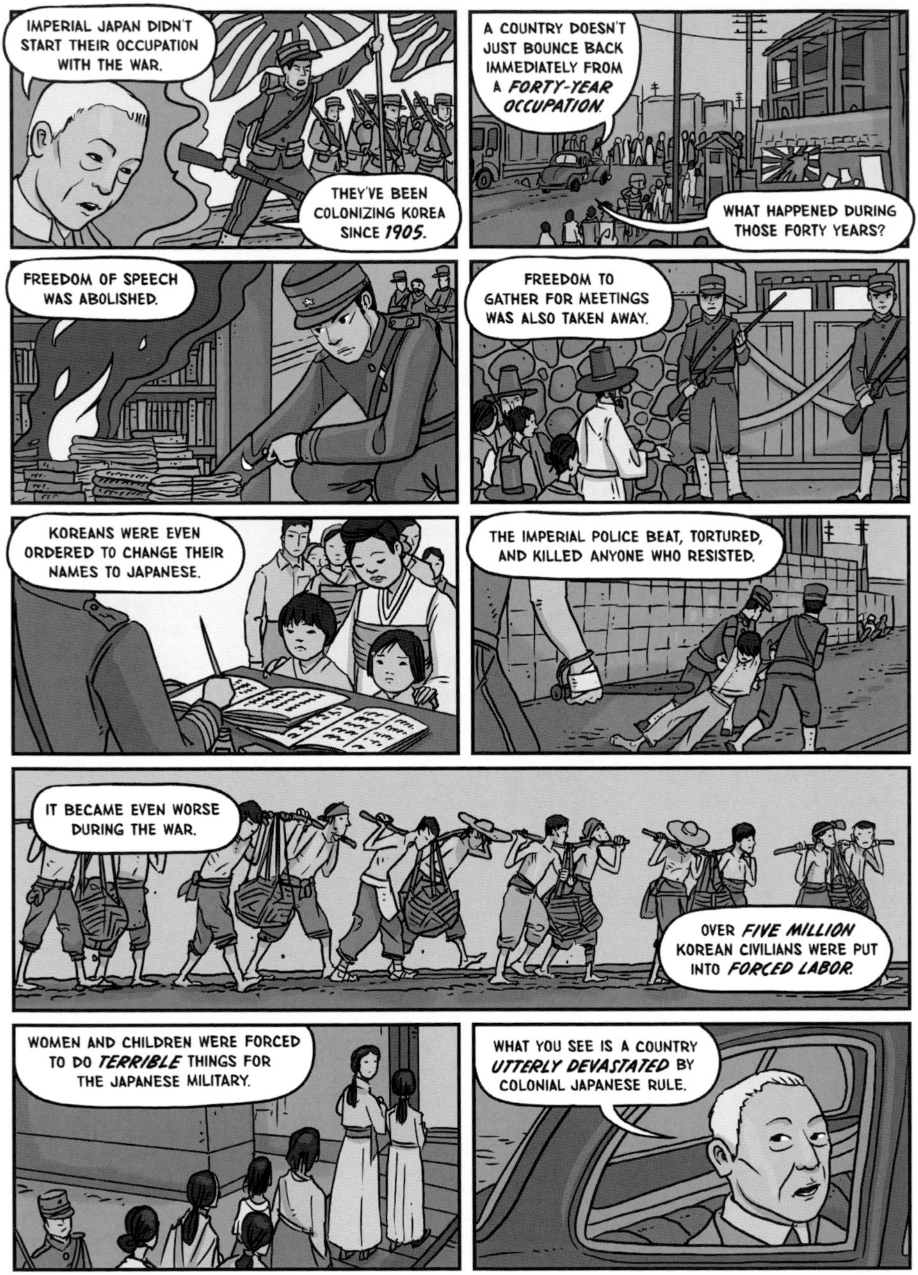
IMPERIAL JAPAN DIDN'T START THEIR OCCUPATION WITH THE WAR.
THEY'VE BEEN COLONIZING KOREA SINCE *1905*.
A COUNTRY DOESN'T JUST BOUNCE BACK IMMEDIATELY FROM A *FORTY-YEAR OCCUPATION*.
WHAT HAPPENED DURING THOSE FORTY YEARS?
FREEDOM OF SPEECH WAS ABOLISHED.
FREEDOM TO GATHER FOR MEETINGS WAS ALSO TAKEN AWAY.
KOREANS WERE EVEN ORDERED TO CHANGE THEIR NAMES TO JAPANESE.
THE IMPERIAL POLICE BEAT, TORTURED, AND KILLED ANYONE WHO RESISTED.
IT BECAME EVEN WORSE DURING THE WAR.
OVER *FIVE MILLION* KOREAN CIVILIANS WERE PUT INTO *FORCED LABOR*.
WOMEN AND CHILDREN WERE FORCED TO DO *TERRIBLE* THINGS FOR THE JAPANESE MILITARY.
WHAT YOU SEE IS A COUNTRY *UTTERLY DEVASTATED* BY COLONIAL JAPANESE RULE.

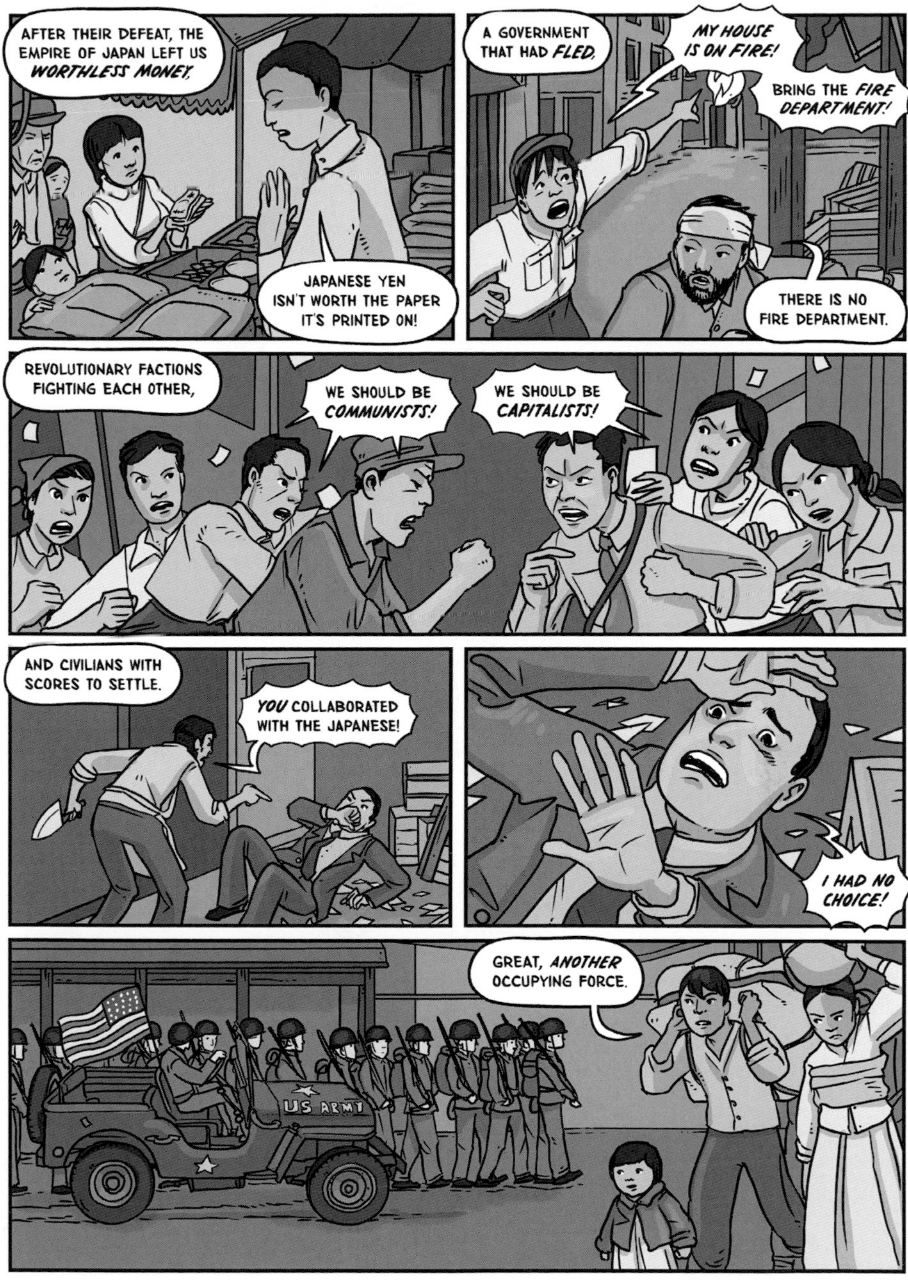
AFTER THEIR DEFEAT, THE EMPIRE OF JAPAN LEFT US *WORTHLESS MONEY,*
JAPANESE YEN ISN'T WORTH THE PAPER IT'S PRINTED ON!
A GOVERNMENT THAT HAD *FLED,*
MY HOUSE IS ON FIRE!
BRING THE *FIRE DEPARTMENT!*
THERE IS NO FIRE DEPARTMENT.
REVOLUTIONARY FACTIONS FIGHTING EACH OTHER,
WE SHOULD BE *COMMUNISTS!*
WE SHOULD BE *CAPITALISTS!*
AND CIVILIANS WITH SCORES TO SETTLE.
YOU COLLABORATED WITH THE JAPANESE!
I HAD NO CHOICE!
GREAT, *ANOTHER* OCCUPYING FORCE.
US ARMY

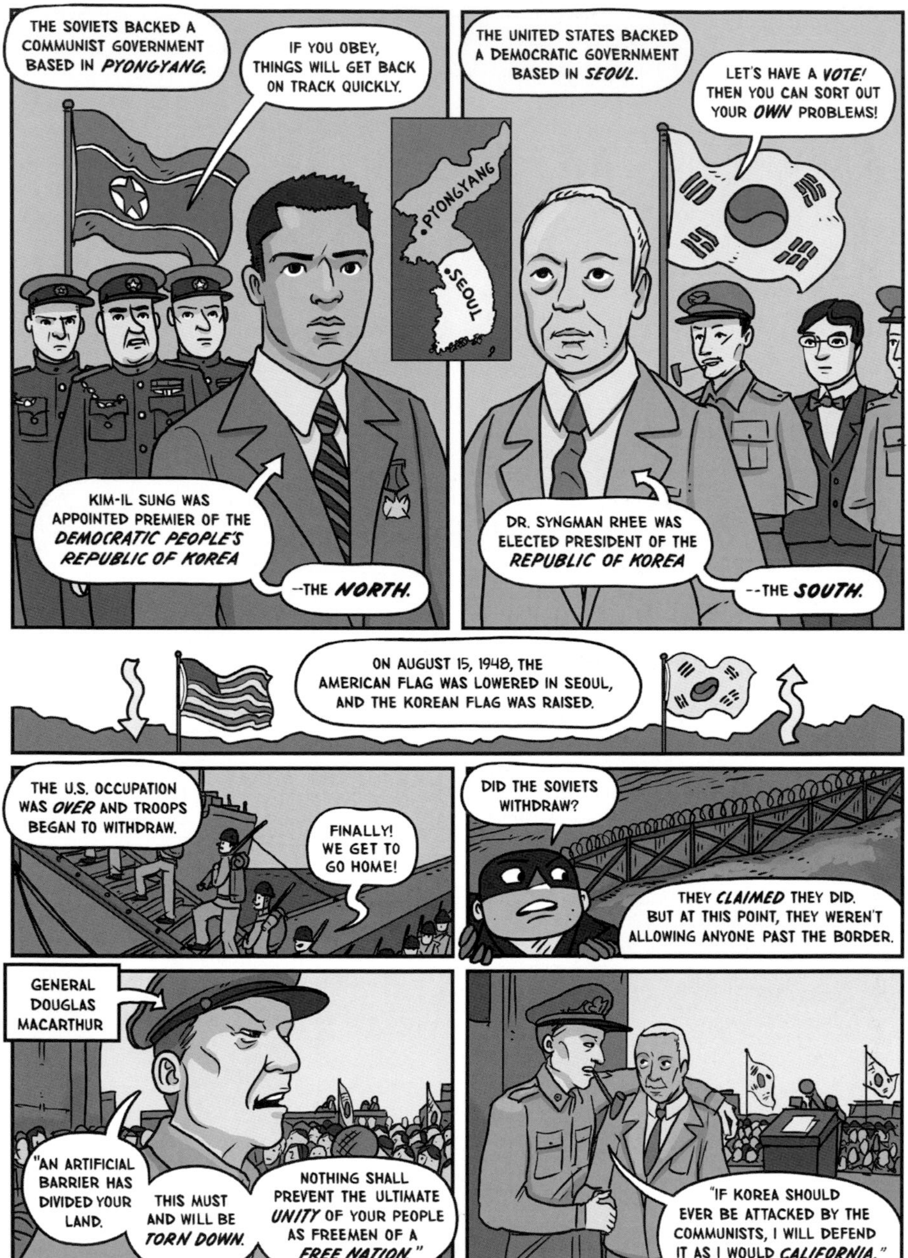
THE SOVIETS BACKED A COMMUNIST GOVERNMENT BASED IN PYONGYANG.
IF YOU OBEY, THINGS WILL GET BACK ON TRACK QUICKLY.
PYONGYANG
SEOUL
KIM-IL SUNG WAS APPOINTED PREMIER OF THE DEMOCRATIC PEOPLE'S REPUBLIC OF KOREA
--THE NORTH.
THE UNITED STATES BACKED A DEMOCRATIC GOVERNMENT BASED IN SEOUL.
LET'S HAVE A VOTE! THEN YOU CAN SORT OUT YOUR OWN PROBLEMS!
DR. SYNGMAN RHEE WAS ELECTED PRESIDENT OF THE REPUBLIC OF KOREA
--THE SOUTH.
ON AUGUST 15, 1948, THE AMERICAN FLAG WAS LOWERED IN SEOUL, AND THE KOREAN FLAG WAS RAISED.
THE U.S. OCCUPATION WAS OVER AND TROOPS BEGAN TO WITHDRAW.
FINALLY! WE GET TO GO HOME!
DID THE SOVIETS WITHDRAW?
THEY CLAIMED THEY DID. BUT AT THIS POINT, THEY WEREN'T ALLOWING ANYONE PAST THE BORDER.
GENERAL DOUGLAS MACARTHUR
"AN ARTIFICIAL BARRIER HAS DIVIDED YOUR LAND.
THIS MUST AND WILL BE TORN DOWN.
NOTHING SHALL PREVENT THE ULTIMATE UNITY OF YOUR PEOPLE AS FREEMEN OF A FREE NATION."
"IF KOREA SHOULD EVER BE ATTACKED BY THE COMMUNISTS, I WILL DEFEND IT AS I WOULD CALIFORNIA."

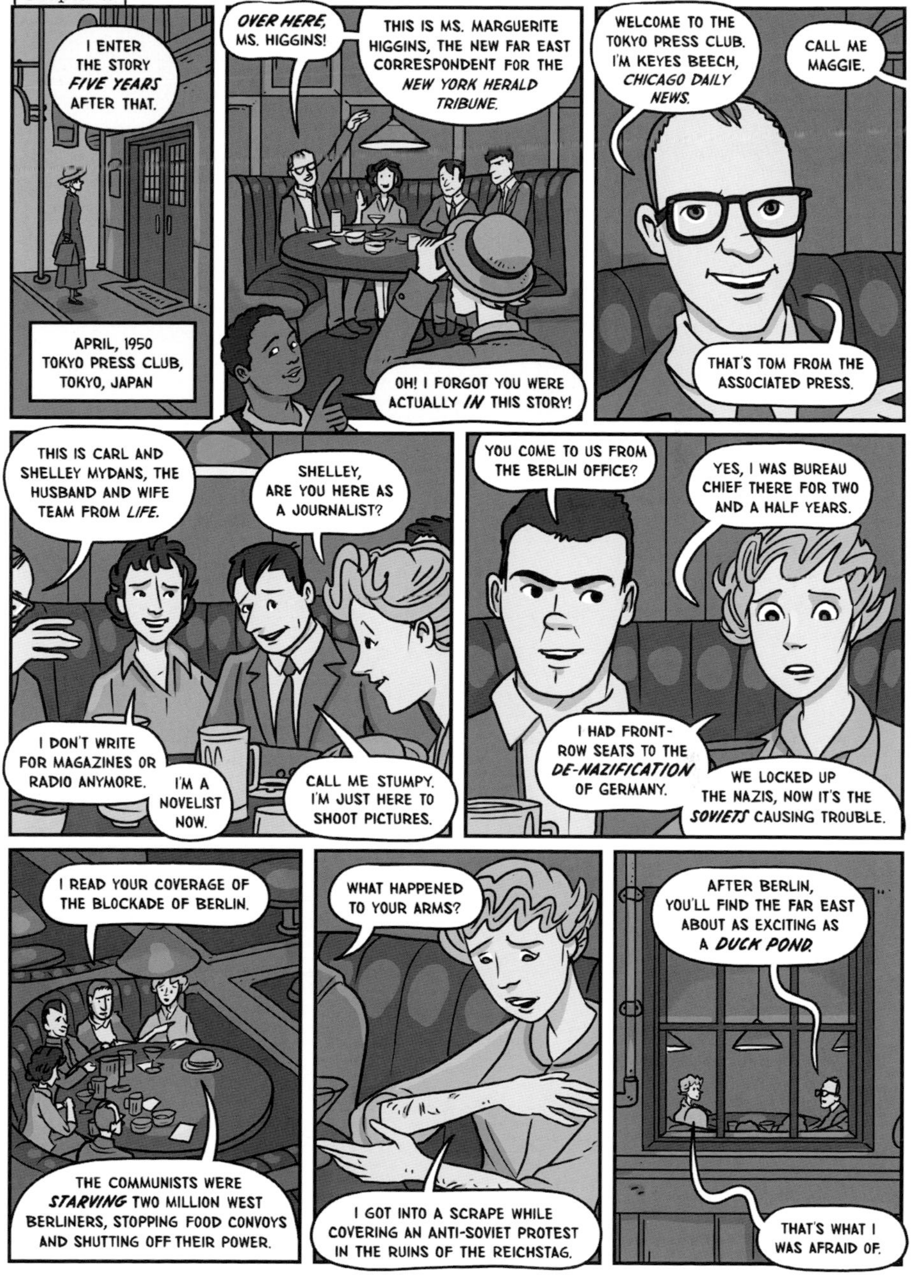
I ENTER THE STORY *FIVE YEARS* AFTER THAT.
APRIL, 1950
TOKYO PRESS CLUB,
TOKYO, JAPAN
OVER HERE, MS. HIGGINS!
THIS IS MS. MARGUERITE HIGGINS, THE NEW FAR EAST CORRESPONDENT FOR THE *NEW YORK HERALD TRIBUNE.*
OH! I FORGOT YOU WERE ACTUALLY *IN* THIS STORY!
WELCOME TO THE TOKYO PRESS CLUB. I'M KEYES BEECH, *CHICAGO DAILY NEWS.*
CALL ME MAGGIE.
THAT'S TOM FROM THE ASSOCIATED PRESS.
THIS IS CARL AND SHELLEY MYDANS, THE HUSBAND AND WIFE TEAM FROM *LIFE.*
SHELLEY, ARE YOU HERE AS A JOURNALIST?
I DON'T WRITE FOR MAGAZINES OR RADIO ANYMORE.
I'M A NOVELIST NOW.
CALL ME STUMPY. I'M JUST HERE TO SHOOT PICTURES.
YOU COME TO US FROM THE BERLIN OFFICE?
YES, I WAS BUREAU CHIEF THERE FOR TWO AND A HALF YEARS.
I HAD FRONT-ROW SEATS TO THE *DE-NAZIFICATION* OF GERMANY.
WE LOCKED UP THE NAZIS, NOW IT'S THE *SOVIETS* CAUSING TROUBLE.
I READ YOUR COVERAGE OF THE BLOCKADE OF BERLIN.
THE COMMUNISTS WERE *STARVING* TWO MILLION WEST BERLINERS, STOPPING FOOD CONVOYS AND SHUTTING OFF THEIR POWER.
WHAT HAPPENED TO YOUR ARMS?
I GOT INTO A SCRAPE WHILE COVERING AN ANTI-SOVIET PROTEST IN THE RUINS OF THE REICHSTAG.
AFTER BERLIN, YOU'LL FIND THE FAR EAST ABOUT AS EXCITING AS A *DUCK POND.*
THAT'S WHAT I WAS AFRAID OF.

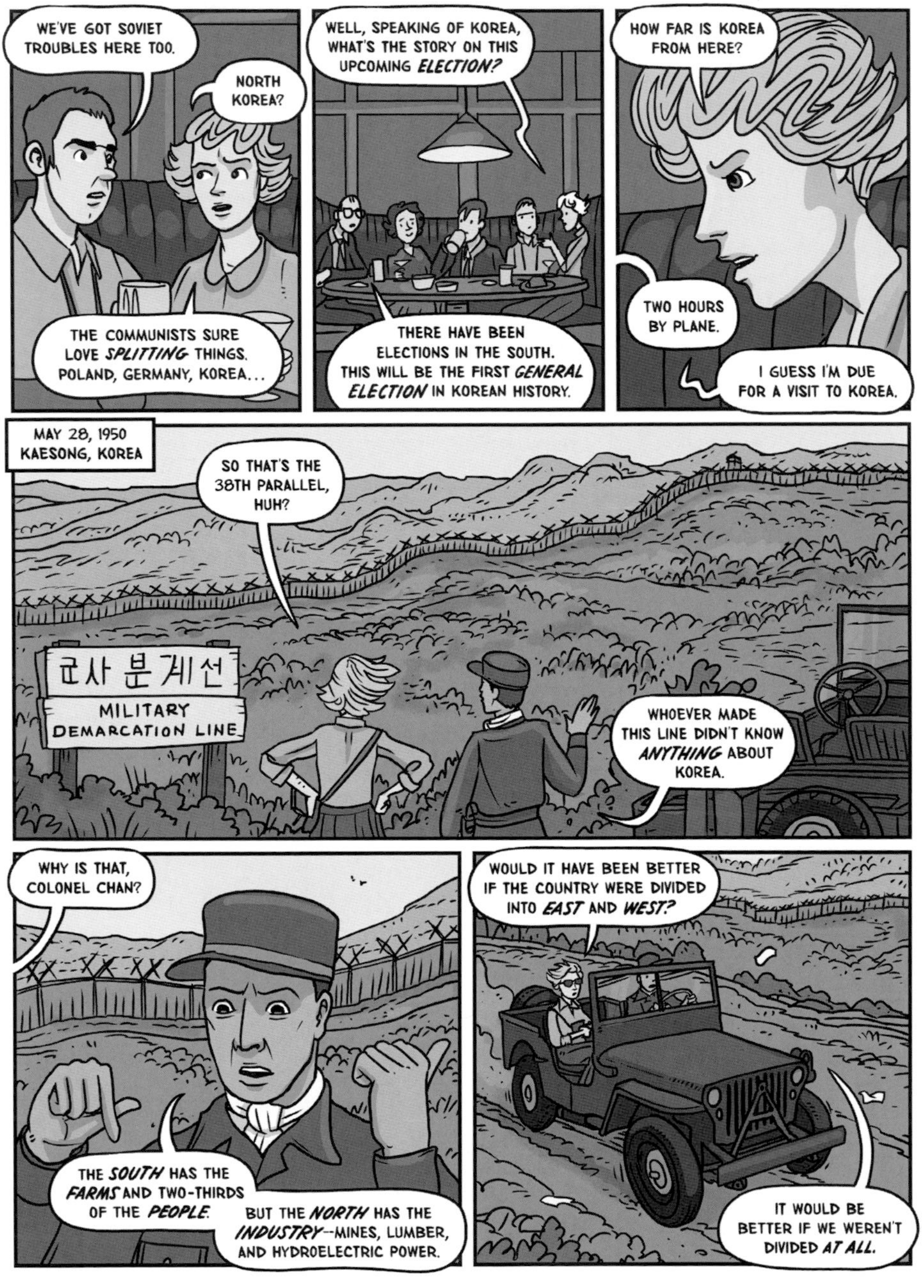
WE'VE GOT SOVIET TROUBLES HERE TOO.
NORTH KOREA?
THE COMMUNISTS SURE LOVE *SPLITTING* THINGS. POLAND, GERMANY, KOREA...
WELL, SPEAKING OF KOREA, WHAT'S THE STORY ON THIS UPCOMING *ELECTION?*
THERE HAVE BEEN ELECTIONS IN THE SOUTH. THIS WILL BE THE FIRST *GENERAL ELECTION* IN KOREAN HISTORY.
HOW FAR IS KOREA FROM HERE?
TWO HOURS BY PLANE.
I GUESS I'M DUE FOR A VISIT TO KOREA.
MAY 28, 1950 KAESONG, KOREA
SO THAT'S THE 38TH PARALLEL, HUH?
군사 분계선
MILITARY DEMARCATION LINE
WHOEVER MADE THIS LINE DIDN'T KNOW *ANYTHING* ABOUT KOREA.
WHY IS THAT, COLONEL CHAN?
THE *SOUTH* HAS THE *FARMS* AND TWO-THIRDS OF THE *PEOPLE*.
BUT THE *NORTH* HAS THE *INDUSTRY*--MINES, LUMBER, AND HYDROELECTRIC POWER.
WOULD IT HAVE BEEN BETTER IF THE COUNTRY WERE DIVIDED INTO *EAST* AND *WEST?*
IT WOULD BE BETTER IF WE WEREN'T DIVIDED *AT ALL*.

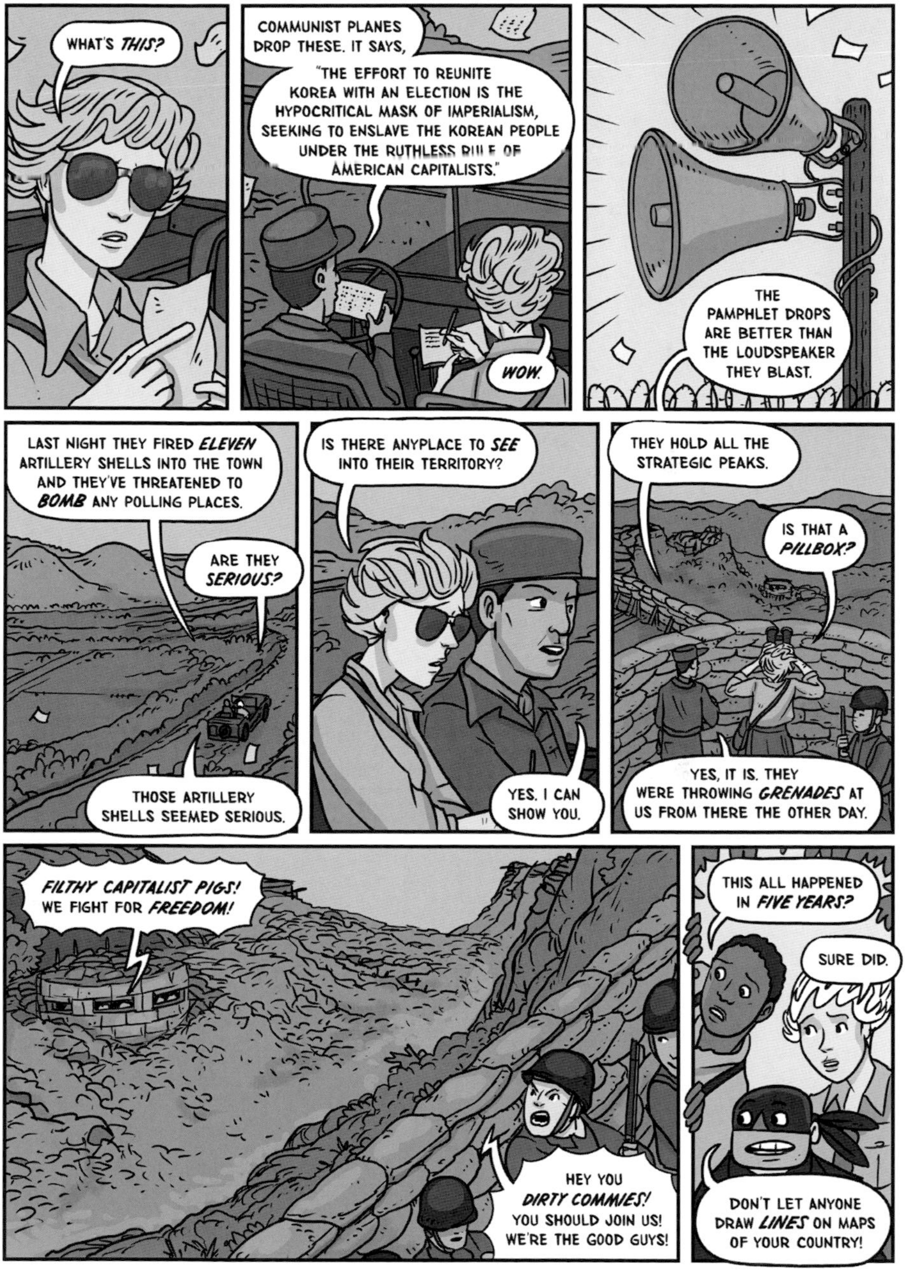
WHAT'S *THIS?*
COMMUNIST PLANES DROP THESE. IT SAYS,
"THE EFFORT TO REUNITE KOREA WITH AN ELECTION IS THE HYPOCRITICAL MASK OF IMPERIALISM, SEEKING TO ENSLAVE THE KOREAN PEOPLE UNDER THE RUTHLESS RULE OF AMERICAN CAPITALISTS."
WOW.
THE PAMPHLET DROPS ARE BETTER THAN THE LOUDSPEAKER THEY BLAST.
LAST NIGHT THEY FIRED *ELEVEN* ARTILLERY SHELLS INTO THE TOWN AND THEY'VE THREATENED TO *BOMB* ANY POLLING PLACES.
ARE THEY *SERIOUS?*
THOSE ARTILLERY SHELLS SEEMED SERIOUS.
IS THERE ANYPLACE TO *SEE* INTO THEIR TERRITORY?
YES. I CAN SHOW YOU.
THEY HOLD ALL THE STRATEGIC PEAKS.
IS THAT A *PILLBOX?*
YES, IT IS. THEY WERE THROWING *GRENADES* AT US FROM THERE THE OTHER DAY.
FILTHY CAPITALIST PIGS! WE FIGHT FOR *FREEDOM!*
HEY YOU *DIRTY COMMIES!* YOU SHOULD JOIN US! WE'RE THE GOOD GUYS!
THIS ALL HAPPENED IN *FIVE YEARS?*
SURE DID.
DON'T LET ANYONE DRAW *LINES* ON MAPS OF YOUR COUNTRY!

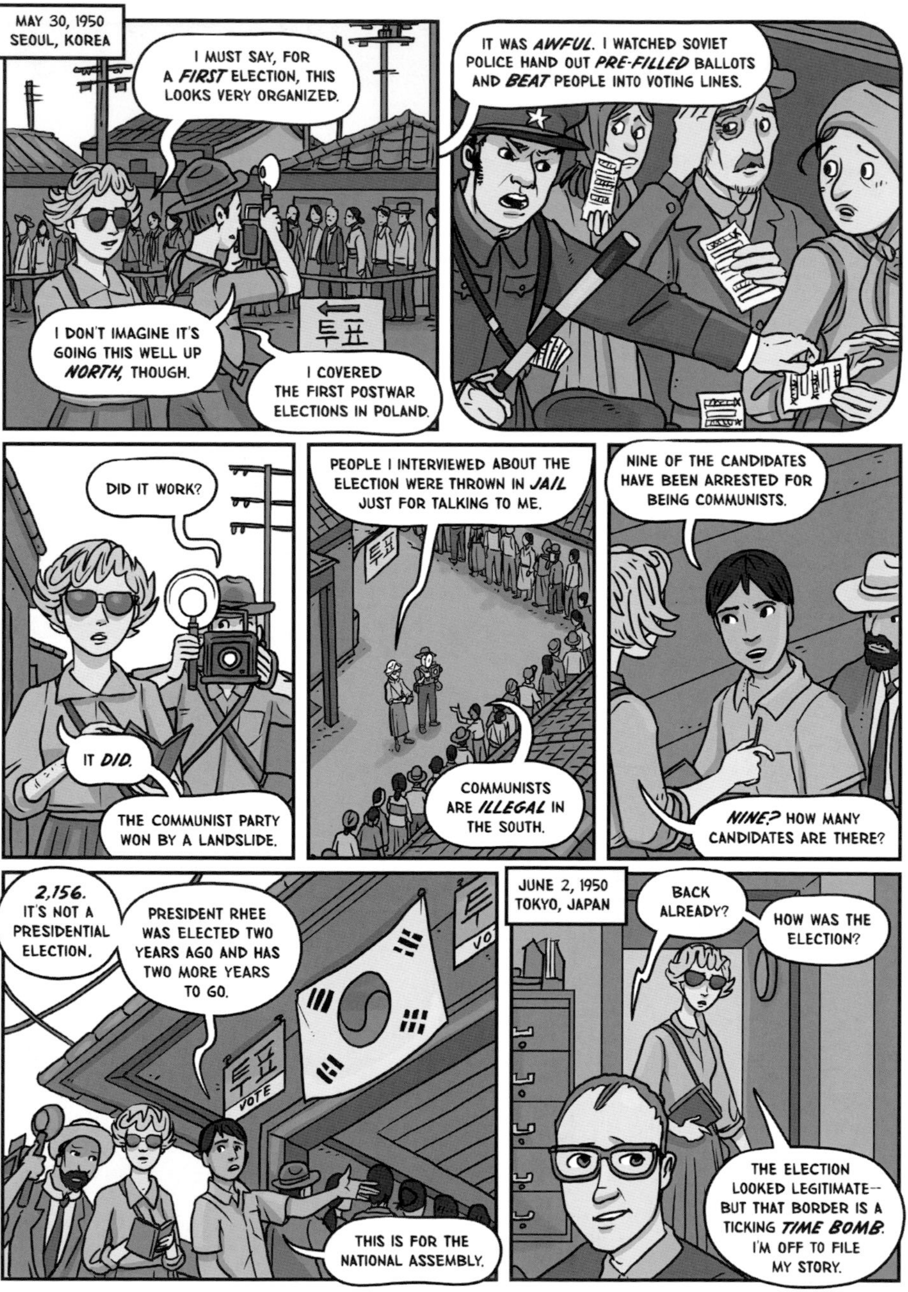
MAY 30, 1950 SEOUL, KOREA
I MUST SAY, FOR A FIRST ELECTION, THIS LOOKS VERY ORGANIZED.
투표
I DON'T IMAGINE IT'S GOING THIS WELL UP NORTH, THOUGH.
I COVERED THE FIRST POSTWAR ELECTIONS IN POLAND.
IT WAS AWFUL. I WATCHED SOVIET POLICE HAND OUT PRE-FILLED BALLOTS AND BEAT PEOPLE INTO VOTING LINES.
DID IT WORK?
IT DID.
THE COMMUNIST PARTY WON BY A LANDSLIDE.
PEOPLE I INTERVIEWED ABOUT THE ELECTION WERE THROWN IN JAIL JUST FOR TALKING TO ME.
투표
COMMUNISTS ARE ILLEGAL IN THE SOUTH.
NINE OF THE CANDIDATES HAVE BEEN ARRESTED FOR BEING COMMUNISTS.
NINE? HOW MANY CANDIDATES ARE THERE?
2,156. IT'S NOT A PRESIDENTIAL ELECTION.
PRESIDENT RHEE WAS ELECTED TWO YEARS AGO AND HAS TWO MORE YEARS TO GO.
투표
VOTE
THIS IS FOR THE NATIONAL ASSEMBLY.
JUNE 2, 1950 TOKYO, JAPAN
BACK ALREADY?
HOW WAS THE ELECTION?
THE ELECTION LOOKED LEGITIMATE-- BUT THAT BORDER IS A TICKING TIME BOMB. I'M OFF TO FILE MY STORY.

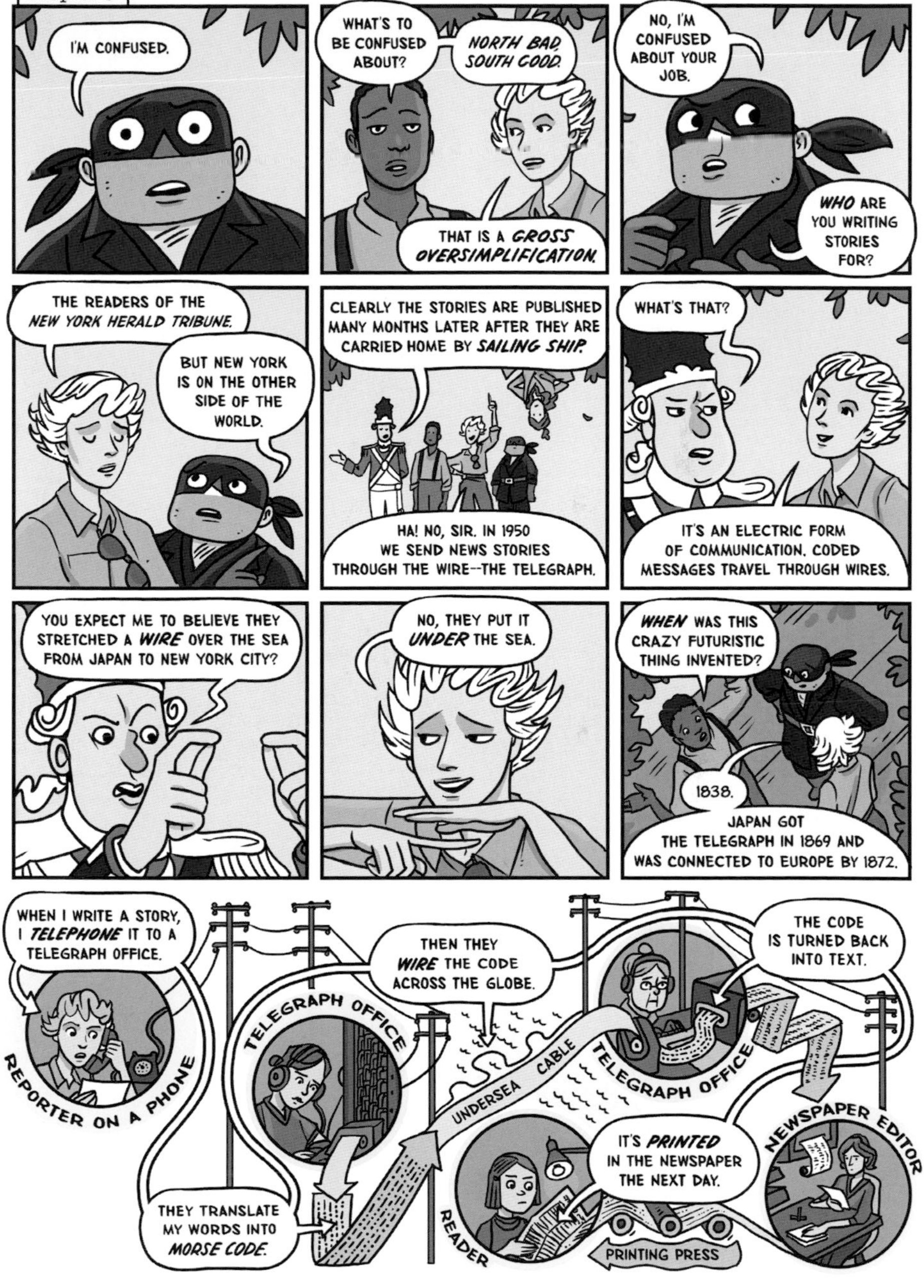
I'M CONFUSED.
WHAT'S TO BE CONFUSED ABOUT?
NORTH BAD. SOUTH GOOD.
THAT IS A GROSS OVERSIMPLIFICATION.
NO, I'M CONFUSED ABOUT YOUR JOB.
WHO ARE YOU WRITING STORIES FOR?
THE READERS OF THE NEW YORK HERALD TRIBUNE.
BUT NEW YORK IS ON THE OTHER SIDE OF THE WORLD.
CLEARLY THE STORIES ARE PUBLISHED MANY MONTHS LATER AFTER THEY ARE CARRIED HOME BY SAILING SHIP.
HA! NO, SIR. IN 1950 WE SEND NEWS STORIES THROUGH THE WIRE--THE TELEGRAPH.
WHAT'S THAT?
IT'S AN ELECTRIC FORM OF COMMUNICATION. CODED MESSAGES TRAVEL THROUGH WIRES.
YOU EXPECT ME TO BELIEVE THEY STRETCHED A WIRE OVER THE SEA FROM JAPAN TO NEW YORK CITY?
NO, THEY PUT IT UNDER THE SEA.
WHEN WAS THIS CRAZY FUTURISTIC THING INVENTED?
1838.
JAPAN GOT THE TELEGRAPH IN 1869 AND WAS CONNECTED TO EUROPE BY 1872.
WHEN I WRITE A STORY, I TELEPHONE IT TO A TELEGRAPH OFFICE.
REPORTER ON A PHONE
TELEGRAPH OFFICE
THEY TRANSLATE MY WORDS INTO MORSE CODE.
THEN THEY WIRE THE CODE ACROSS THE GLOBE.
UNDERSEA CABLE
TELEGRAPH OFFICE
THE CODE IS TURNED BACK INTO TEXT.
NEWSPAPER EDITOR
PRINTING PRESS
IT'S PRINTED IN THE NEWSPAPER THE NEXT DAY.
READER

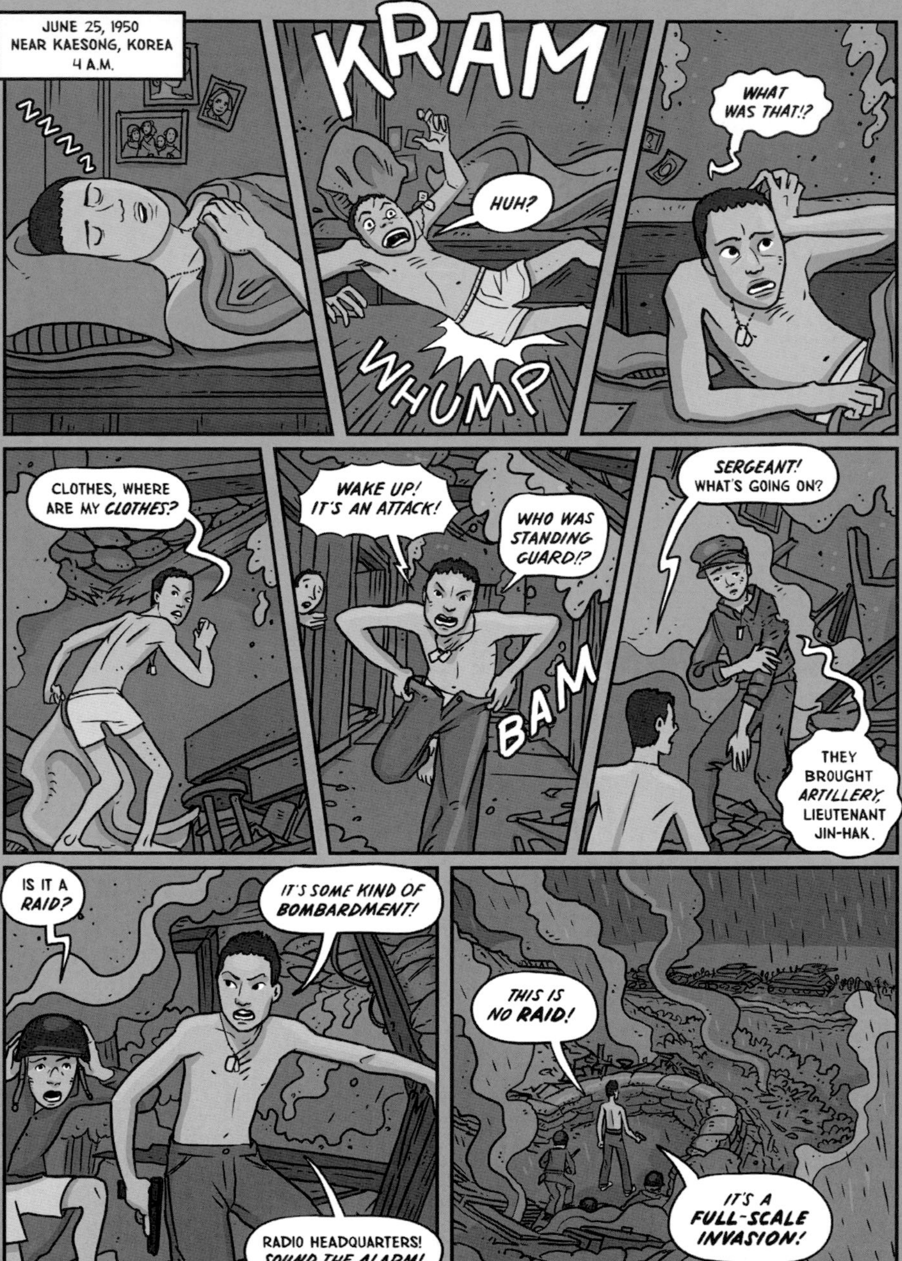
JUNE 25, 1950
NEAR KAESONG, KOREA
4 A.M.
ZZZZ
KRAM
HUH?
WHUMP
WHAT WAS THAT!?
CLOTHES, WHERE ARE MY CLOTHES?
WAKE UP! IT'S AN ATTACK!
WHO WAS STANDING GUARD!?
BAM
SERGEANT! WHAT'S GOING ON?
THEY BROUGHT ARTILLERY, LIEUTENANT JIN-HAK.
IS IT A RAID?
IT'S SOME KIND OF BOMBARDMENT!
RADIO HEADQUARTERS! SOUND THE ALARM!
THIS IS NO RAID!
IT'S A FULL-SCALE INVASION!

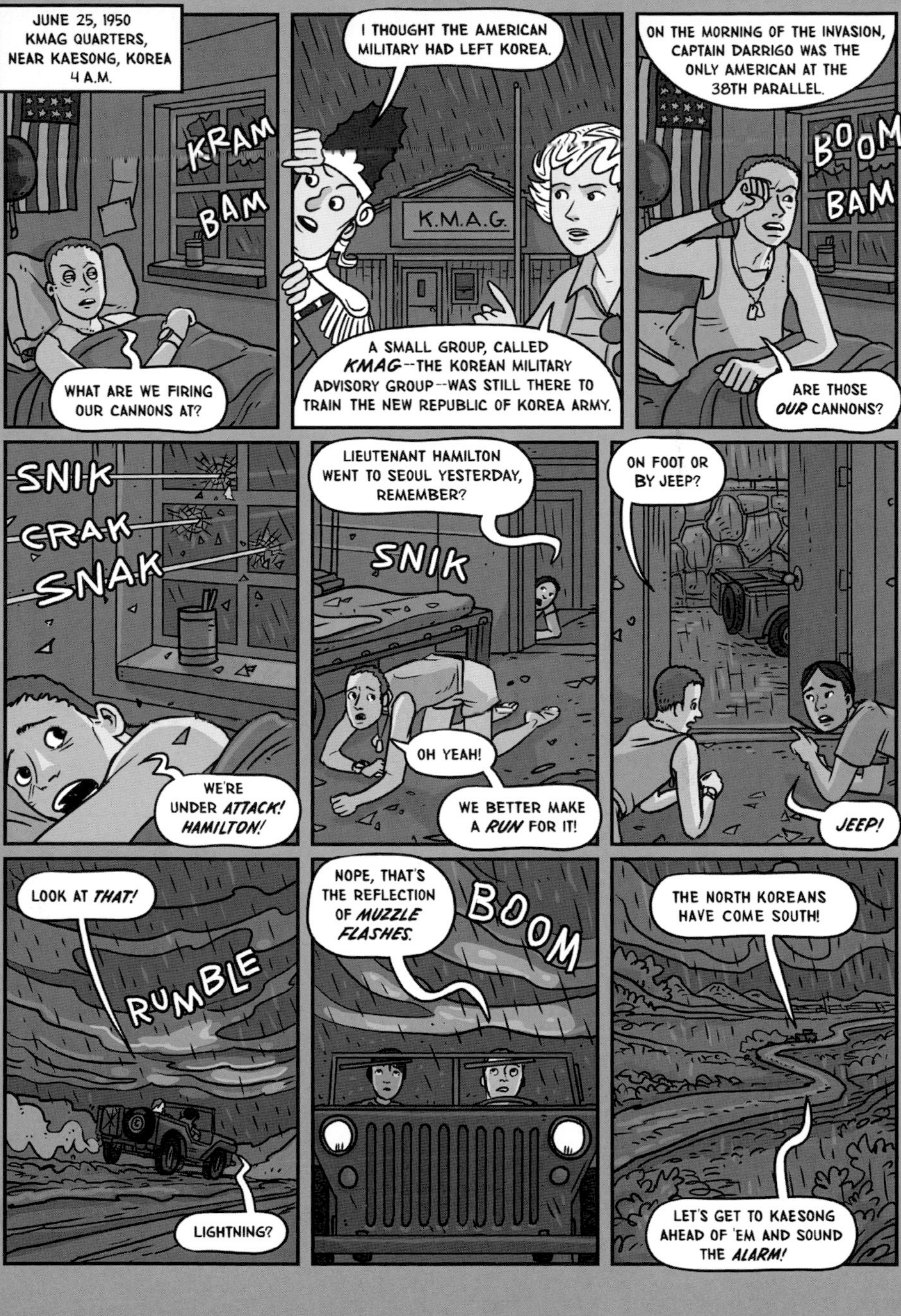
JUNE 25, 1950
KMAG QUARTERS, NEAR KAESONG, KOREA
4 A.M.
KRAM
BAM
WHAT ARE WE FIRING OUR CANNONS AT?
I THOUGHT THE AMERICAN MILITARY HAD LEFT KOREA.
K.M.A.G.
A SMALL GROUP, CALLED *KMAG*--THE KOREAN MILITARY ADVISORY GROUP--WAS STILL THERE TO TRAIN THE NEW REPUBLIC OF KOREA ARMY.
ON THE MORNING OF THE INVASION, CAPTAIN DARRIGO WAS THE ONLY AMERICAN AT THE 38TH PARALLEL.
BOOM
BAM
ARE THOSE *OUR* CANNONS?
SNIK
CRAK
SNAK
WE'RE UNDER *ATTACK! HAMILTON!*
LIEUTENANT HAMILTON WENT TO SEOUL YESTERDAY, REMEMBER?
SNIK
OH YEAH!
WE BETTER MAKE A *RUN* FOR IT!
ON FOOT OR BY JEEP?
JEEP!
LOOK AT *THAT!*
RUMBLE
LIGHTNING?
NOPE, THAT'S THE REFLECTION OF *MUZZLE FLASHES.*
BOOM
THE NORTH KOREANS HAVE COME SOUTH!
LET'S GET TO KAESONG AHEAD OF 'EM AND SOUND THE *ALARM!*

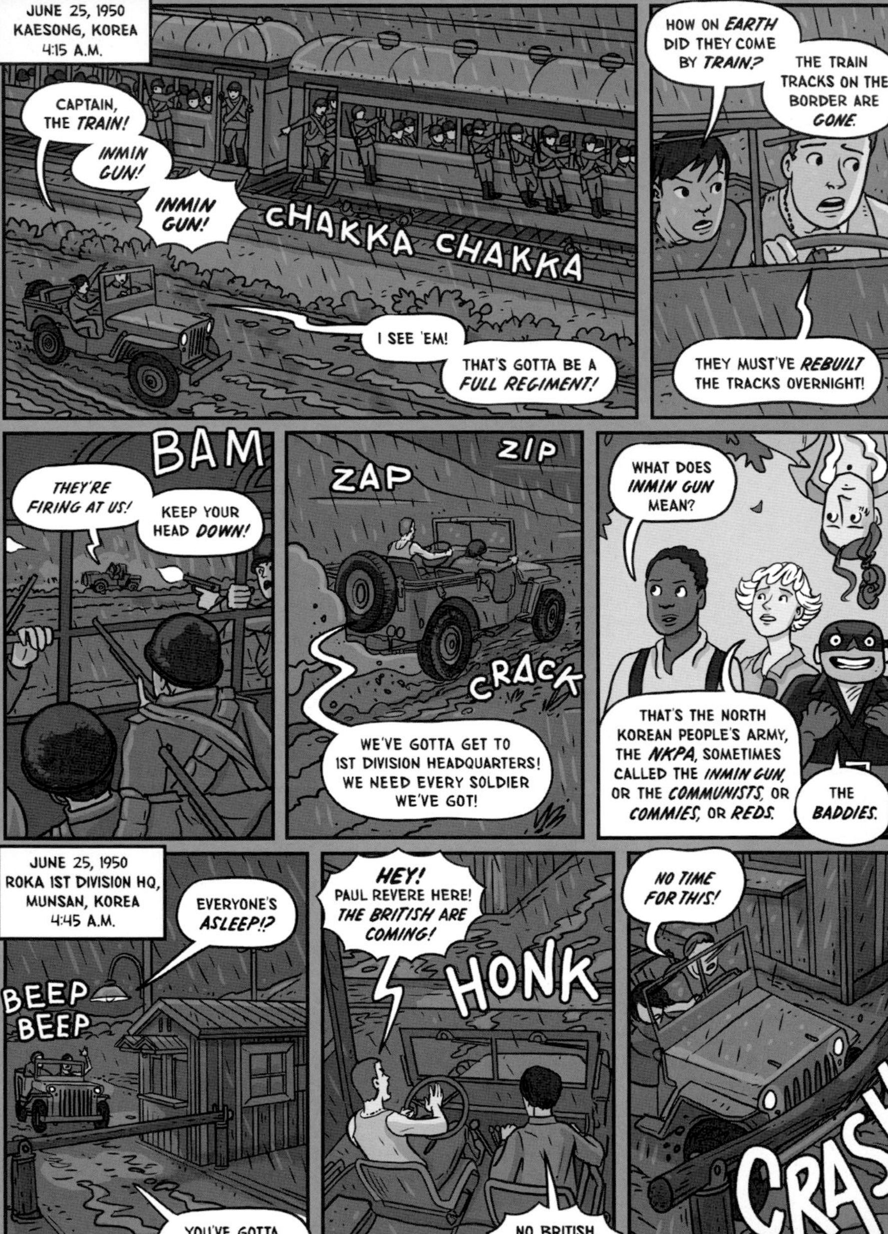
JUNE 25, 1950
KAESONG, KOREA
4:15 A.M.
CAPTAIN, THE *TRAIN!*
INMIN GUN!
INMIN GUN!
CHAKKA CHAKKA
I SEE 'EM!
THAT'S GOTTA BE A *FULL REGIMENT!*
HOW ON *EARTH* DID THEY COME BY *TRAIN?*
THE TRAIN TRACKS ON THE BORDER ARE *GONE.*
THEY MUST'VE *REBUILT* THE TRACKS OVERNIGHT!
BAM
THEY'RE FIRING AT US!
KEEP YOUR HEAD *DOWN!*
ZIP
ZAP
CRACK
WE'VE GOTTA GET TO 1ST DIVISION HEADQUARTERS! WE NEED EVERY SOLDIER WE'VE GOT!
WHAT DOES *INMIN GUN* MEAN?
THAT'S THE NORTH KOREAN PEOPLE'S ARMY, THE *NKPA,* SOMETIMES CALLED THE *INMIN GUN,* OR THE *COMMUNISTS,* OR *COMMIES,* OR *REDS.*
THE *BADDIES.*
JUNE 25, 1950
ROKA 1ST DIVISION HQ,
MUNSAN, KOREA
4:45 A.M.
EVERYONE'S *ASLEEP!?*
BEEP BEEP
YOU'VE GOTTA BE KIDDING ME.
HEY! PAUL REVERE HERE! *THE BRITISH ARE COMING!*
HONK
NO BRITISH, *INMIN GUN!*
NO TIME FOR THIS!
CRASH

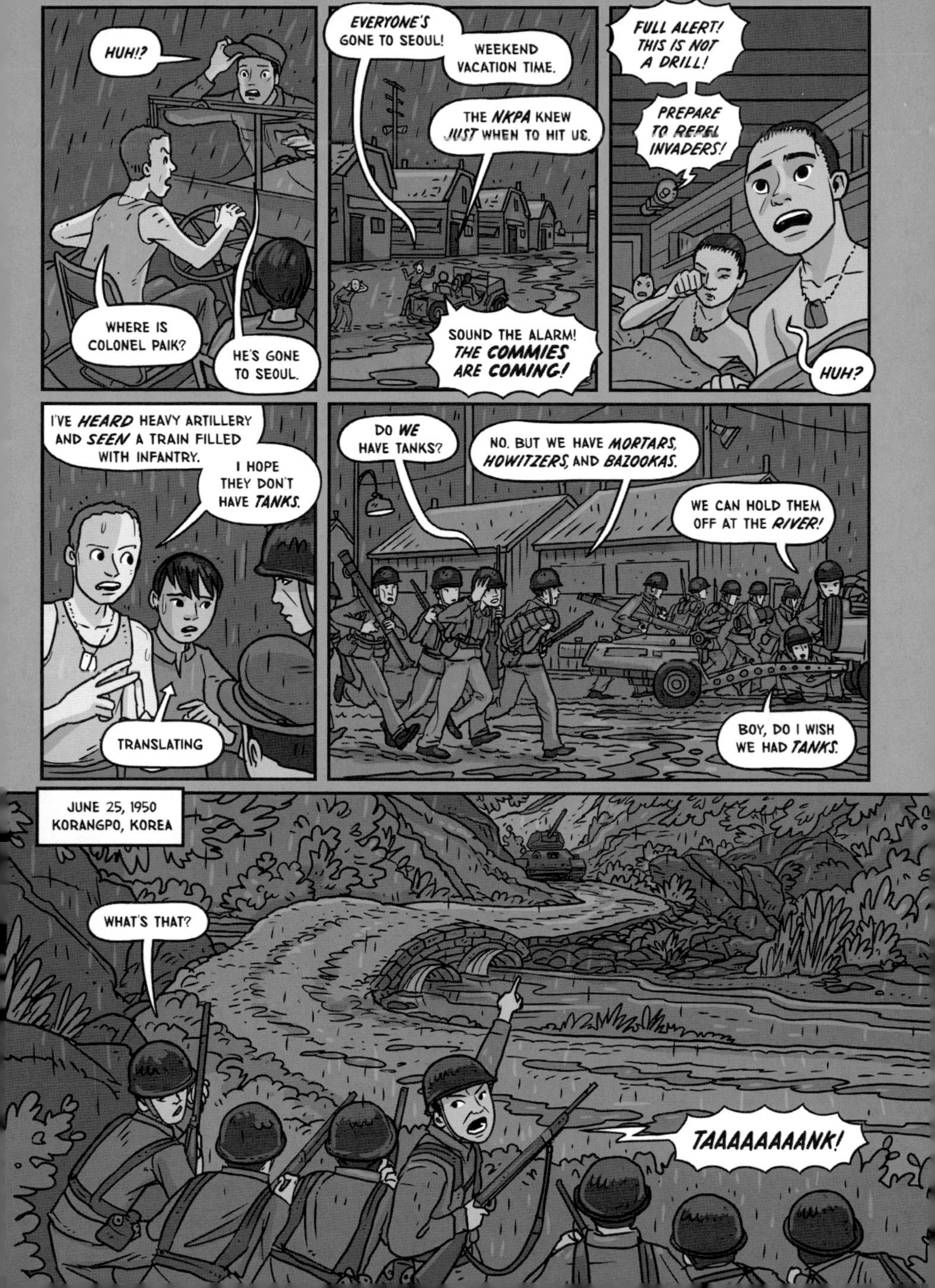
HUH!?
WHERE IS COLONEL PAIK?
HE'S GONE TO SEOUL.
EVERYONE'S GONE TO SEOUL!
WEEKEND VACATION TIME.
THE NKPA KNEW JUST WHEN TO HIT US.
SOUND THE ALARM! THE COMMIES ARE COMING!
FULL ALERT! THIS IS NOT A DRILL!
PREPARE TO REPEL INVADERS!
HUH?
I'VE HEARD HEAVY ARTILLERY AND SEEN A TRAIN FILLED WITH INFANTRY.
I HOPE THEY DON'T HAVE TANKS.
TRANSLATING
DO WE HAVE TANKS?
NO. BUT WE HAVE MORTARS, HOWITZERS, AND BAZOOKAS.
WE CAN HOLD THEM OFF AT THE RIVER!
BOY, DO I WISH WE HAD TANKS.
JUNE 25, 1950 KORANGPO, KOREA
WHAT'S THAT?
TAAAAAAAANK!

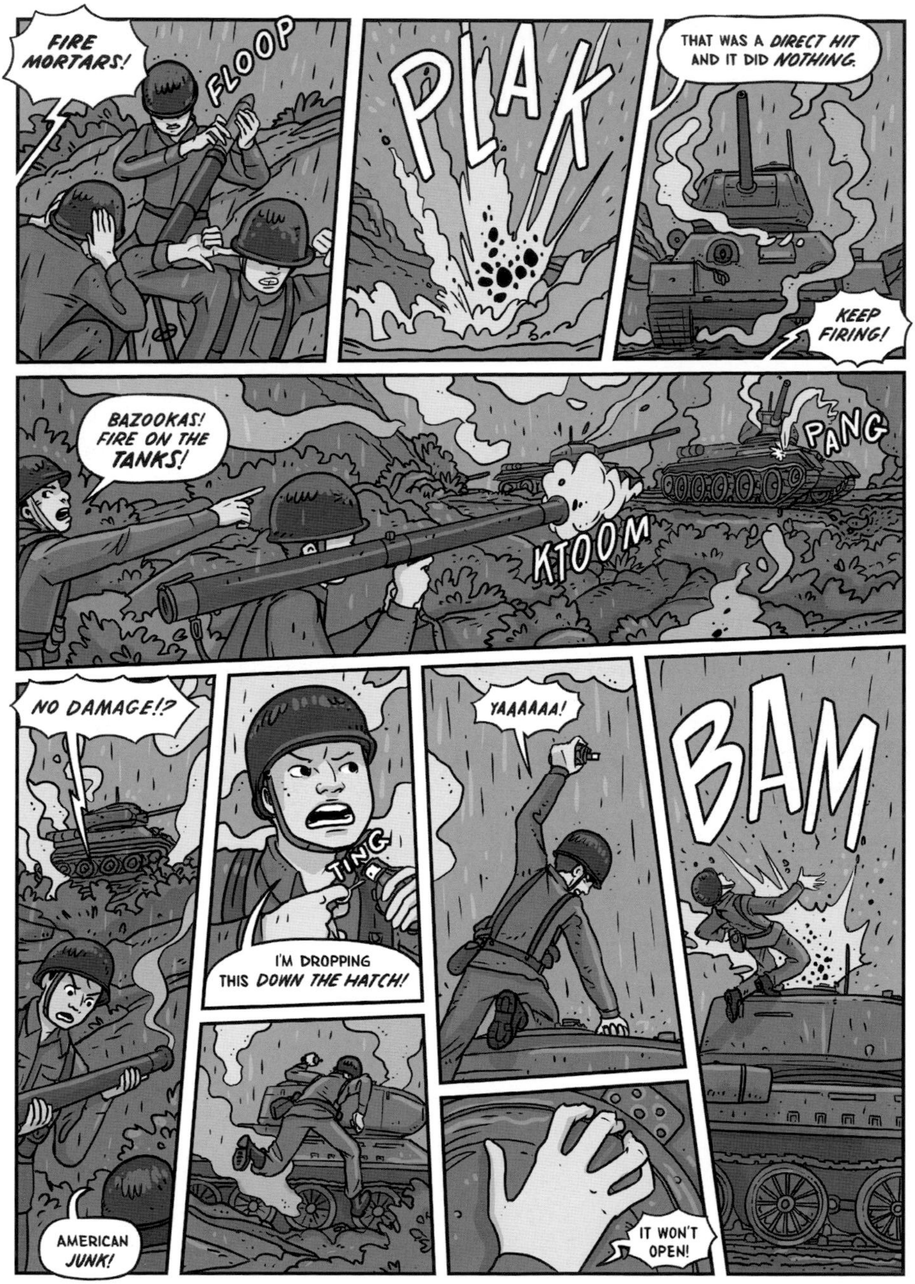
FIRE MORTARS!
FLOOP
PLAK
THAT WAS A DIRECT HIT AND IT DID NOTHING.
KEEP FIRING!
BAZOOKAS! FIRE ON THE TANKS!
KTOOM
PANG
NO DAMAGE!?
AMERICAN JUNK!
TING
I'M DROPPING THIS DOWN THE HATCH!
YAAAAAA!
IT WON'T OPEN!
BAM

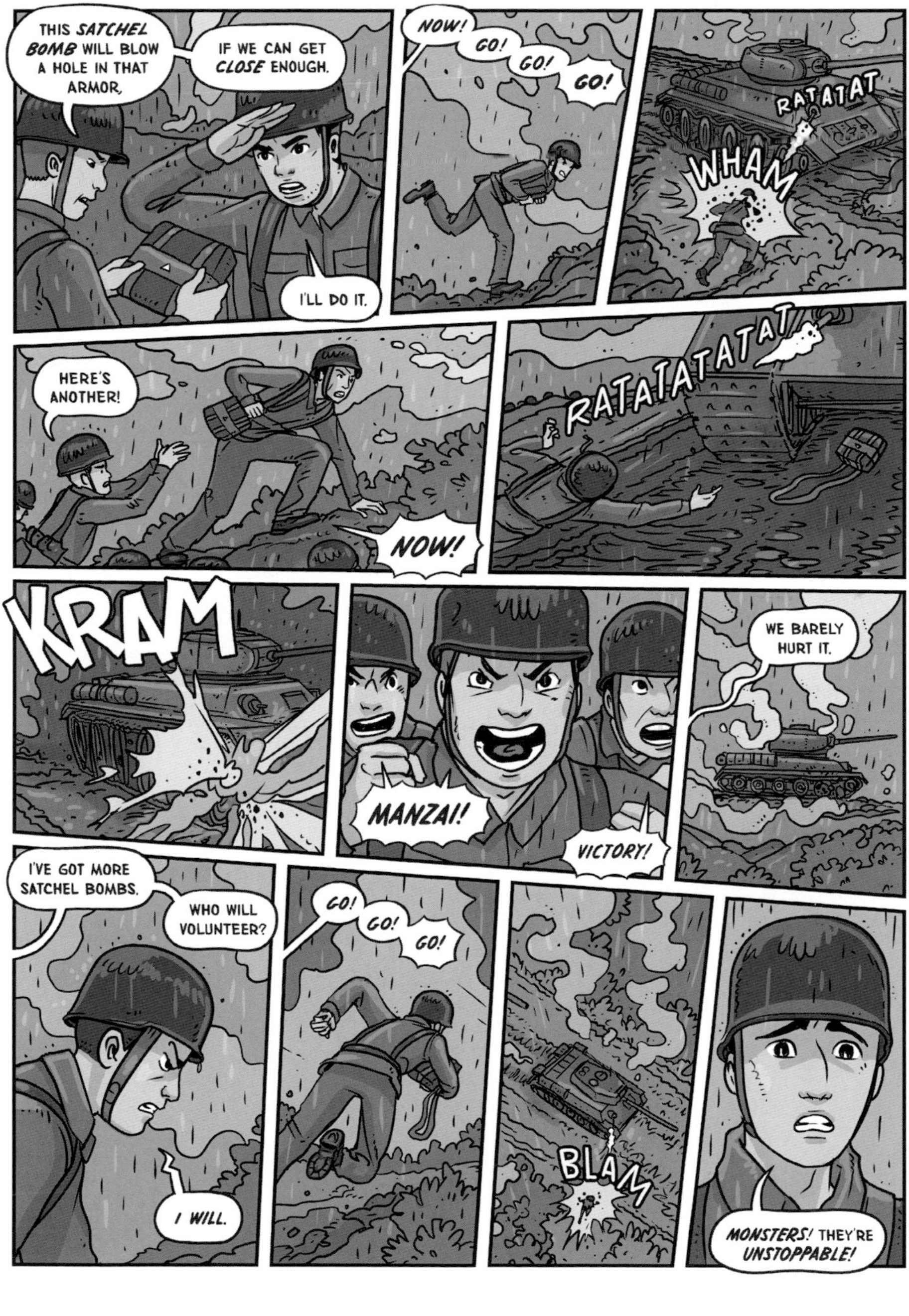
THIS SATCHEL BOMB WILL BLOW A HOLE IN THAT ARMOR,
IF WE CAN GET CLOSE ENOUGH.
I'LL DO IT.
NOW!
GO!
GO!
GO!
RATATAT
WHAM
HERE'S ANOTHER!
NOW!
RATATATATATAT
KRAM
MANZAI!
VICTORY!
WE BARELY HURT IT.
I'VE GOT MORE SATCHEL BOMBS.
WHO WILL VOLUNTEER?
I WILL.
GO!
GO!
GO!
BLAM
MONSTERS! THEY'RE UNSTOPPABLE!

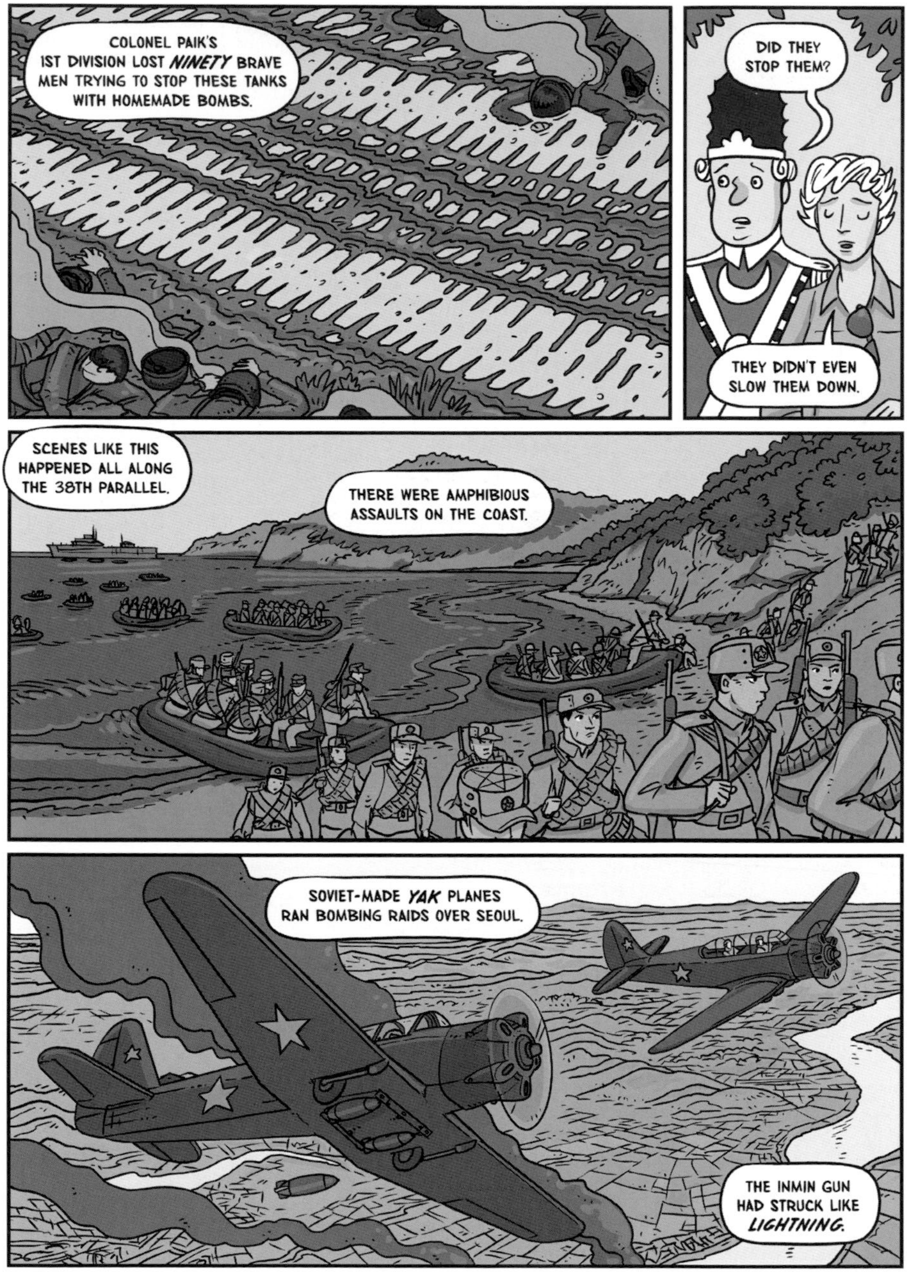
COLONEL PAIK'S 1ST DIVISION LOST NINETY BRAVE MEN TRYING TO STOP THESE TANKS WITH HOMEMADE BOMBS.
DID THEY STOP THEM?
THEY DIDN'T EVEN SLOW THEM DOWN.
SCENES LIKE THIS HAPPENED ALL ALONG THE 38TH PARALLEL.
THERE WERE AMPHIBIOUS ASSAULTS ON THE COAST.
SOVIET-MADE YAK PLANES RAN BOMBING RAIDS OVER SEOUL.
THE INMIN GUN HAD STRUCK LIKE LIGHTNING.

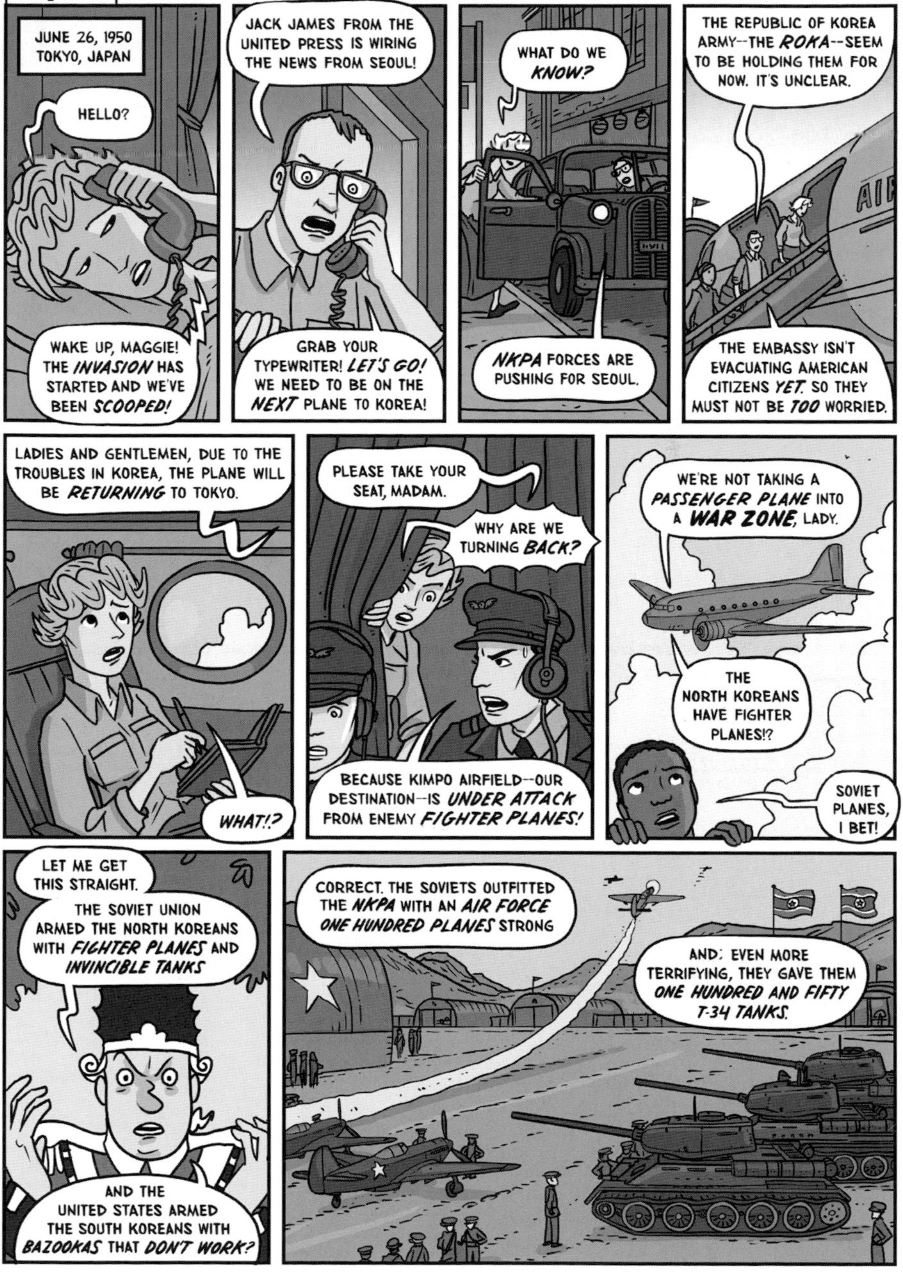
JUNE 26, 1950
TOKYO, JAPAN
HELLO?
WAKE UP, MAGGIE! THE INVASION HAS STARTED AND WE'VE BEEN SCOOPED!
JACK JAMES FROM THE UNITED PRESS IS WIRING THE NEWS FROM SEOUL!
GRAB YOUR TYPEWRITER! LET'S GO! WE NEED TO BE ON THE NEXT PLANE TO KOREA!
WHAT DO WE KNOW?
NKPA FORCES ARE PUSHING FOR SEOUL.
THE REPUBLIC OF KOREA ARMY--THE ROKA--SEEM TO BE HOLDING THEM FOR NOW. IT'S UNCLEAR.
THE EMBASSY ISN'T EVACUATING AMERICAN CITIZENS YET. SO THEY MUST NOT BE TOO WORRIED.
LADIES AND GENTLEMEN, DUE TO THE TROUBLES IN KOREA, THE PLANE WILL BE RETURNING TO TOKYO.
WHAT!?
PLEASE TAKE YOUR SEAT, MADAM.
WHY ARE WE TURNING BACK?
BECAUSE KIMPO AIRFIELD--OUR DESTINATION--IS UNDER ATTACK FROM ENEMY FIGHTER PLANES!
WE'RE NOT TAKING A PASSENGER PLANE INTO A WAR ZONE, LADY.
THE NORTH KOREANS HAVE FIGHTER PLANES!?
SOVIET PLANES, I BET!
LET ME GET THIS STRAIGHT.
THE SOVIET UNION ARMED THE NORTH KOREANS WITH FIGHTER PLANES AND INVINCIBLE TANKS
AND THE UNITED STATES ARMED THE SOUTH KOREANS WITH BAZOOKAS THAT DON'T WORK?
CORRECT. THE SOVIETS OUTFITTED THE NKPA WITH AN AIR FORCE ONE HUNDRED PLANES STRONG
AND: EVEN MORE TERRIFYING, THEY GAVE THEM ONE HUNDRED AND FIFTY T-34 TANKS.

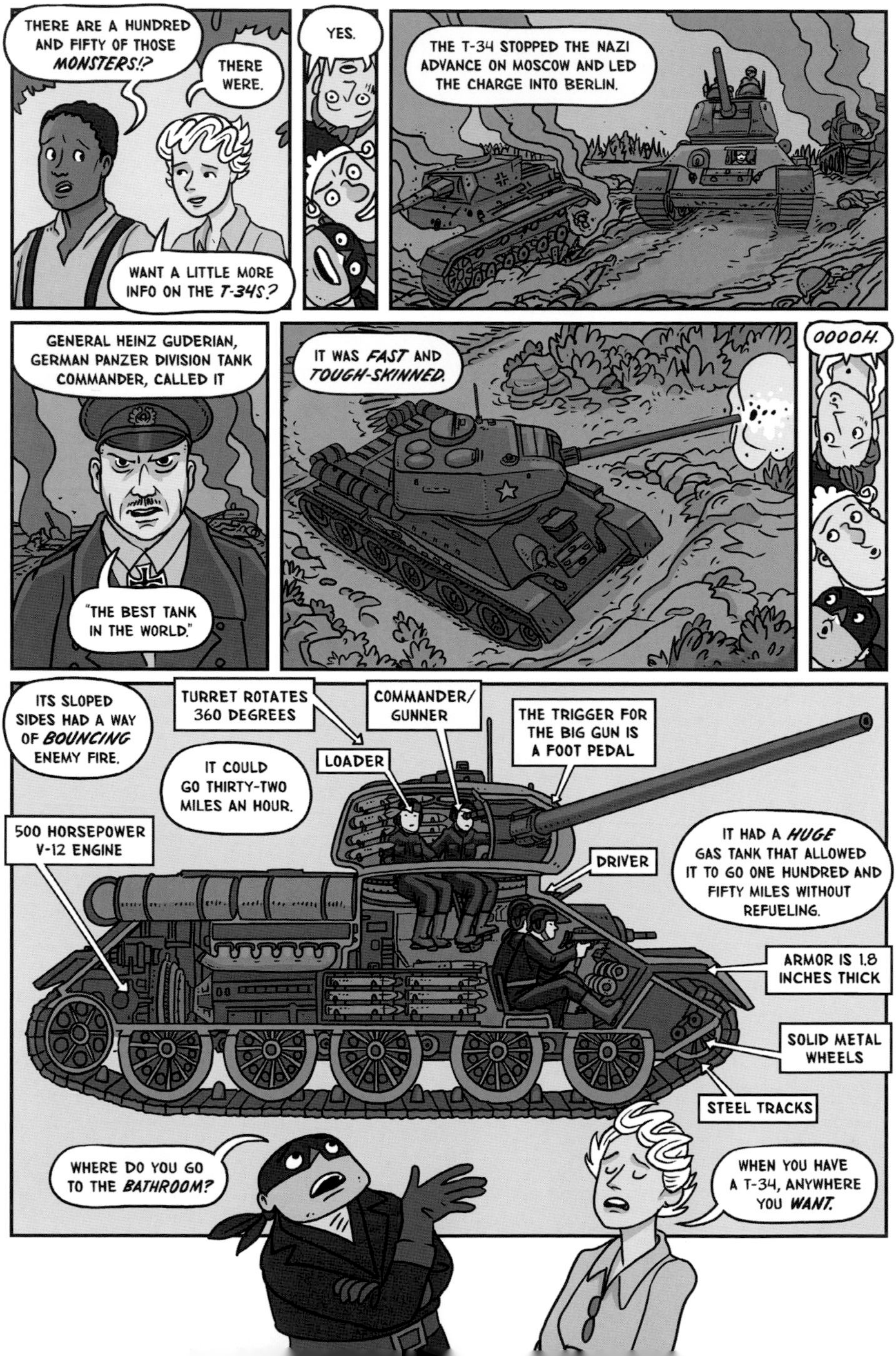
THERE ARE A HUNDRED AND FIFTY OF THOSE MONSTERS!?
THERE WERE.
WANT A LITTLE MORE INFO ON THE T-34S?
YES.
THE T-34 STOPPED THE NAZI ADVANCE ON MOSCOW AND LED THE CHARGE INTO BERLIN.
GENERAL HEINZ GUDERIAN, GERMAN PANZER DIVISION TANK COMMANDER, CALLED IT
"THE BEST TANK IN THE WORLD."
IT WAS FAST AND TOUGH-SKINNED.
OOOOH.
ITS SLOPED SIDES HAD A WAY OF BOUNCING ENEMY FIRE.
TURRET ROTATES 360 DEGREES
COMMANDER/ GUNNER
THE TRIGGER FOR THE BIG GUN IS A FOOT PEDAL
LOADER
IT COULD GO THIRTY-TWO MILES AN HOUR.
500 HORSEPOWER V-12 ENGINE
DRIVER
IT HAD A HUGE GAS TANK THAT ALLOWED IT TO GO ONE HUNDRED AND FIFTY MILES WITHOUT REFUELING.
ARMOR IS 1.8 INCHES THICK
SOLID METAL WHEELS
STEEL TRACKS
WHERE DO YOU GO TO THE BATHROOM?
WHEN YOU HAVE A T-34, ANYWHERE YOU WANT.

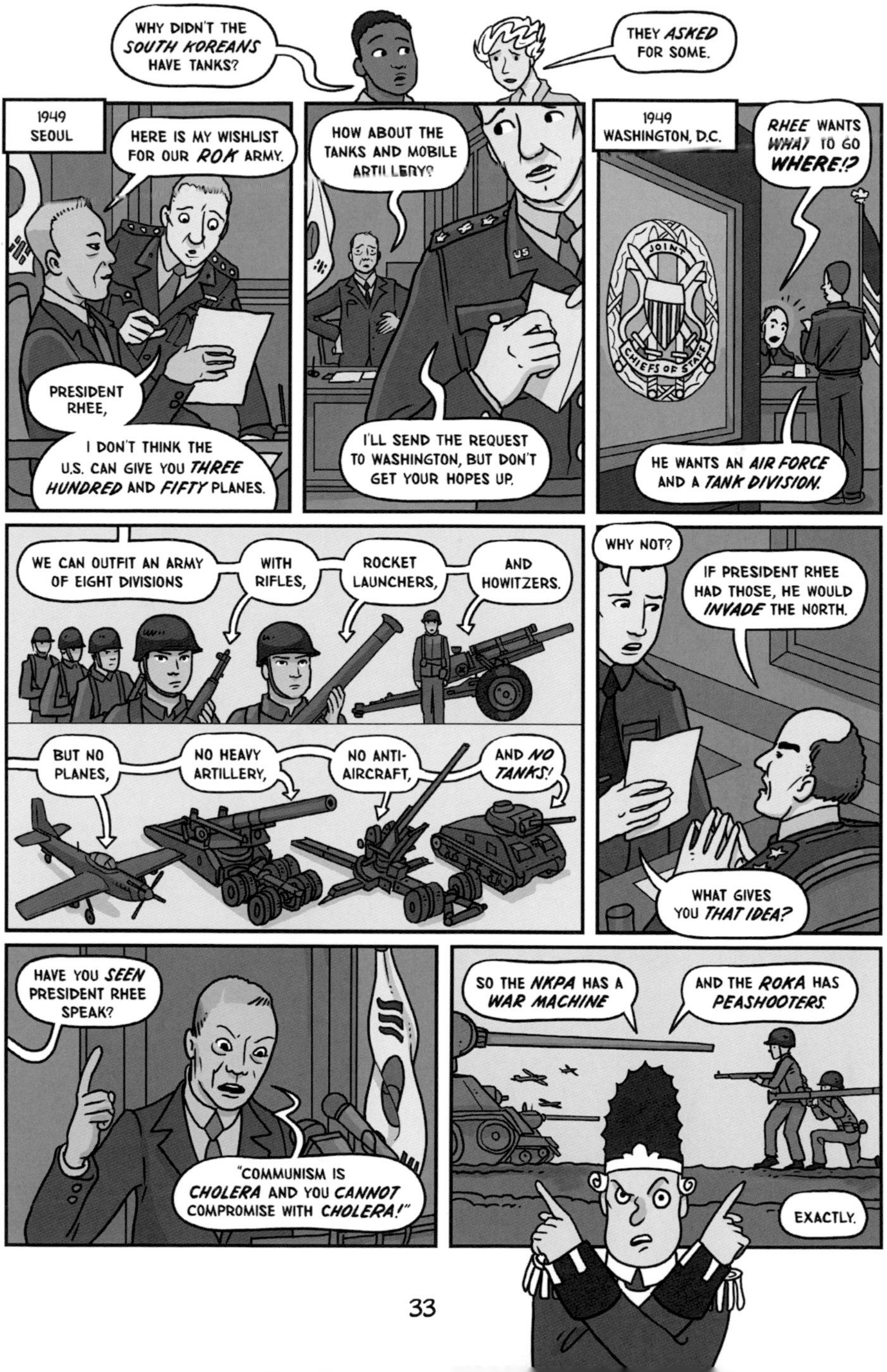

WHY DIDN'T THE SOUTH KOREANS HAVE TANKS?
THEY ASKED FOR SOME.
1949 SEOUL
HERE IS MY WISHLIST FOR OUR ROK ARMY.
PRESIDENT RHEE,
I DON'T THINK THE U.S. CAN GIVE YOU THREE HUNDRED AND FIFTY PLANES.
HOW ABOUT THE TANKS AND MOBILE ARTILLERY?
I'LL SEND THE REQUEST TO WASHINGTON, BUT DON'T GET YOUR HOPES UP.
1949 WASHINGTON, D.C.
RHEE WANTS WHAT TO GO WHERE!?
HE WANTS AN AIR FORCE AND A TANK DIVISION.
WE CAN OUTFIT AN ARMY OF EIGHT DIVISIONS
WITH RIFLES,
ROCKET LAUNCHERS,
AND HOWITZERS.
BUT NO PLANES,
NO HEAVY ARTILLERY,
NO ANTI-AIRCRAFT,
AND NO TANKS!
WHY NOT?
IF PRESIDENT RHEE HAD THOSE, HE WOULD INVADE THE NORTH.
WHAT GIVES YOU THAT IDEA?
HAVE YOU SEEN PRESIDENT RHEE SPEAK?
"COMMUNISM IS CHOLERA AND YOU CANNOT COMPROMISE WITH CHOLERA!"
SO THE NKPA HAS A WAR MACHINE
AND THE ROKA HAS PEASHOOTERS.
EXACTLY.

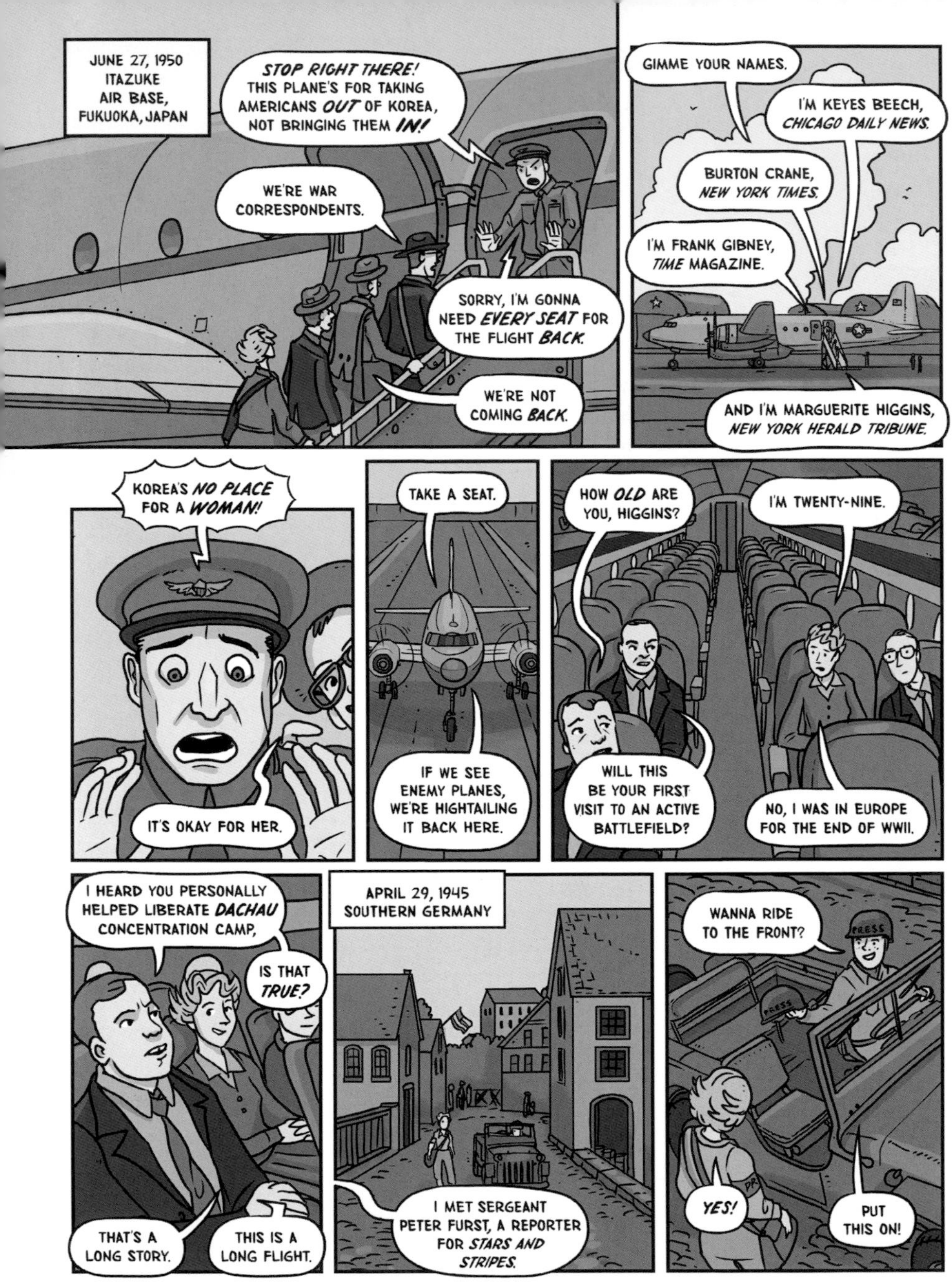

JUNE 27, 1950 ITAZUKE AIR BASE, FUKUOKA, JAPAN
STOP RIGHT THERE! THIS PLANE'S FOR TAKING AMERICANS OUT OF KOREA, NOT BRINGING THEM IN!
WE'RE WAR CORRESPONDENTS.
SORRY, I'M GONNA NEED EVERY SEAT FOR THE FLIGHT BACK.
WE'RE NOT COMING BACK.
GIMME YOUR NAMES.
I'M KEYES BEECH, CHICAGO DAILY NEWS.
BURTON CRANE, NEW YORK TIMES.
I'M FRANK GIBNEY, TIME MAGAZINE.
AND I'M MARGUERITE HIGGINS, NEW YORK HERALD TRIBUNE.
KOREA'S NO PLACE FOR A WOMAN!
IT'S OKAY FOR HER.
TAKE A SEAT.
IF WE SEE ENEMY PLANES, WE'RE HIGHTAILING IT BACK HERE.
HOW OLD ARE YOU, HIGGINS?
I'M TWENTY-NINE.
WILL THIS BE YOUR FIRST VISIT TO AN ACTIVE BATTLEFIELD?
NO, I WAS IN EUROPE FOR THE END OF WWII.
I HEARD YOU PERSONALLY HELPED LIBERATE DACHAU CONCENTRATION CAMP,
IS THAT TRUE?
THAT'S A LONG STORY.
THIS IS A LONG FLIGHT.
APRIL 29, 1945 SOUTHERN GERMANY
I MET SERGEANT PETER FURST, A REPORTER FOR STARS AND STRIPES.
WANNA RIDE TO THE FRONT?
PRESS
YES!
PUT THIS ON!

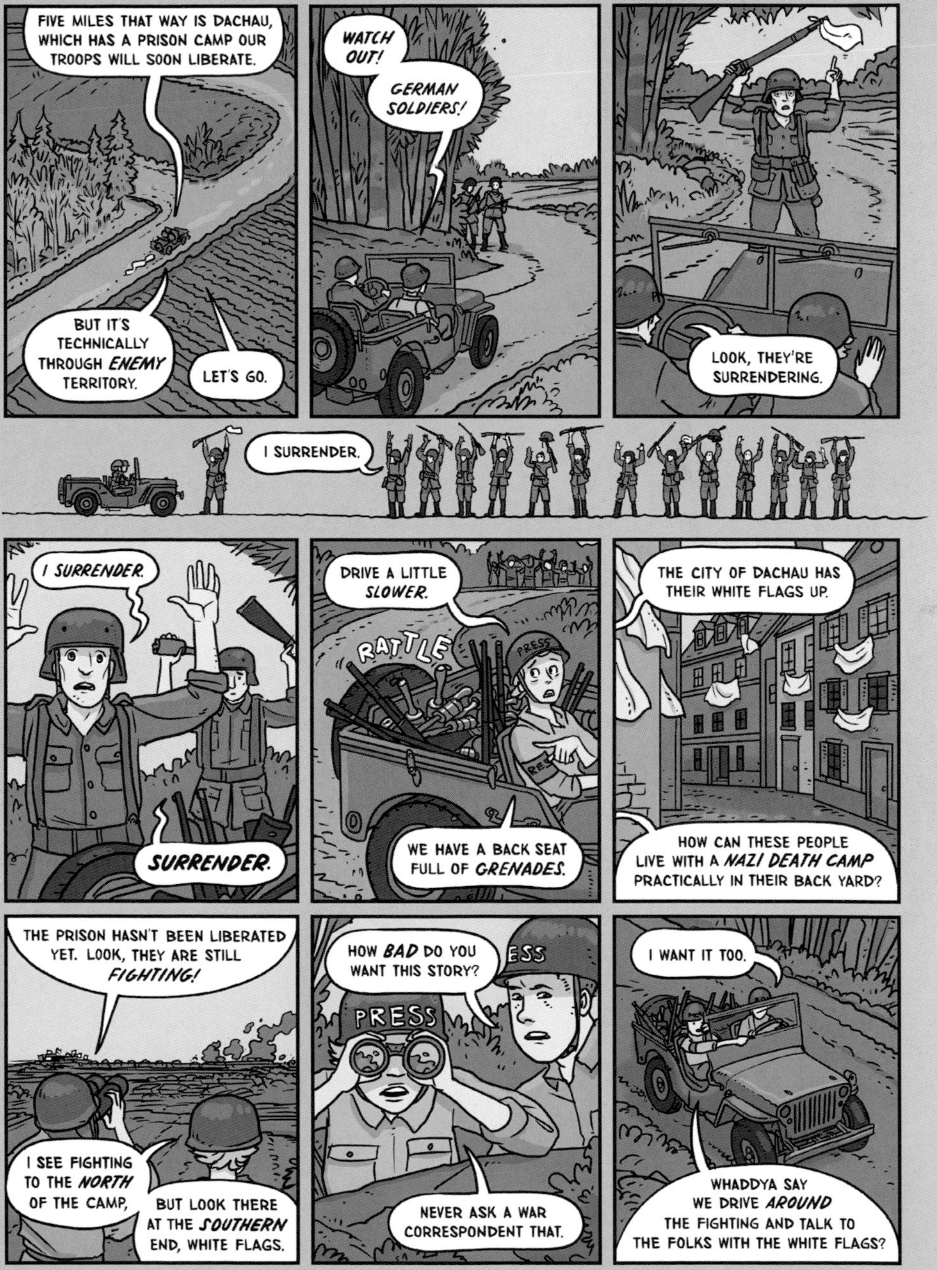
FIVE MILES THAT WAY IS DACHAU, WHICH HAS A PRISON CAMP OUR TROOPS WILL SOON LIBERATE.
BUT IT'S TECHNICALLY THROUGH ENEMY TERRITORY.
LET'S GO.
WATCH OUT!
GERMAN SOLDIERS!
LOOK, THEY'RE SURRENDERING.
I SURRENDER.
I SURRENDER.
SURRENDER.
DRIVE A LITTLE SLOWER.
RATTLE
PRESS
WE HAVE A BACK SEAT FULL OF GRENADES.
THE CITY OF DACHAU HAS THEIR WHITE FLAGS UP.
HOW CAN THESE PEOPLE LIVE WITH A NAZI DEATH CAMP PRACTICALLY IN THEIR BACK YARD?
THE PRISON HASN'T BEEN LIBERATED YET. LOOK, THEY ARE STILL FIGHTING!
I SEE FIGHTING TO THE NORTH OF THE CAMP,
BUT LOOK THERE AT THE SOUTHERN END, WHITE FLAGS.
HOW BAD DO YOU WANT THIS STORY?
PRESS
NEVER ASK A WAR CORRESPONDENT THAT.
I WANT IT TOO.
WHADDYA SAY WE DRIVE AROUND THE FIGHTING AND TALK TO THE FOLKS WITH THE WHITE FLAGS?

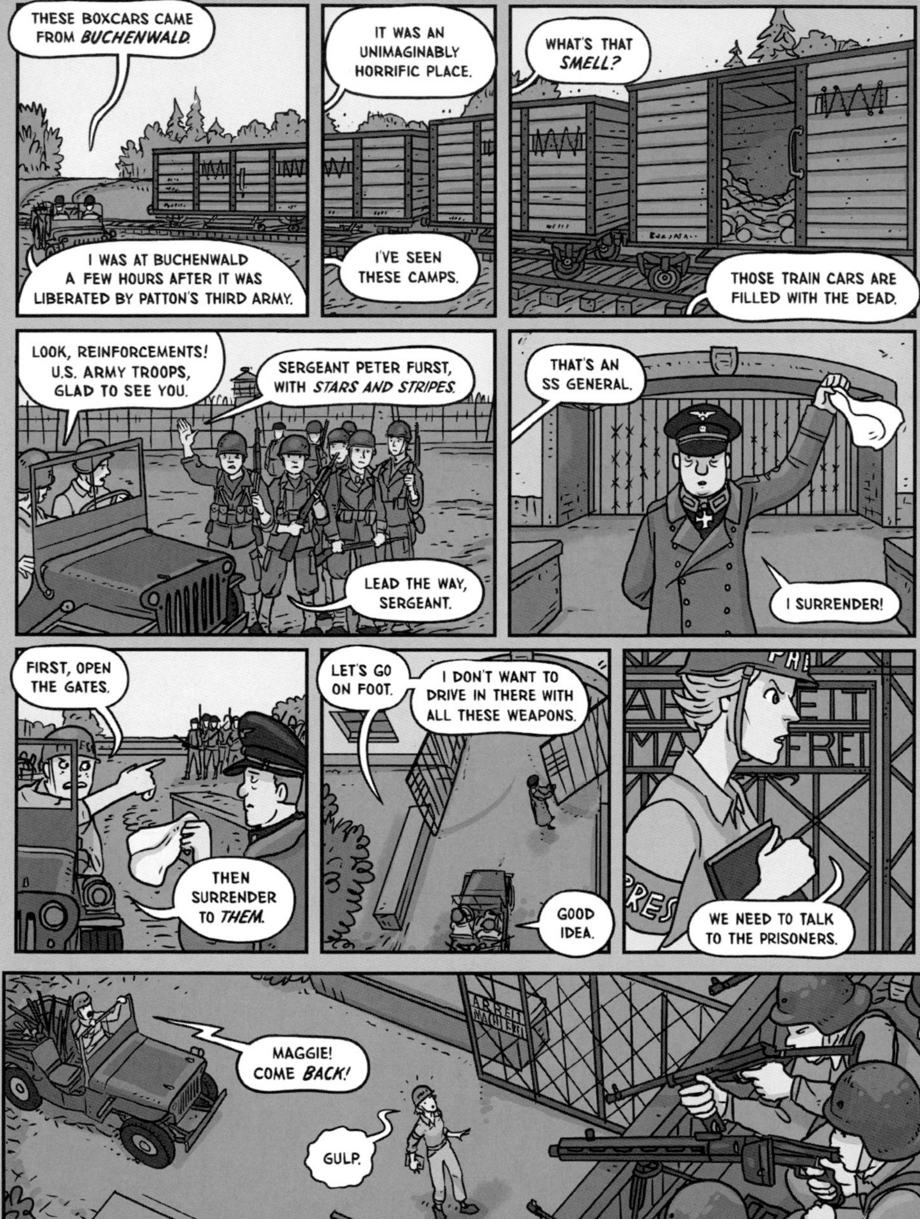

THESE BOXCARS CAME FROM BUCHENWALD.
I WAS AT BUCHENWALD A FEW HOURS AFTER IT WAS LIBERATED BY PATTON'S THIRD ARMY.
IT WAS AN UNIMAGINABLY HORRIFIC PLACE.
I'VE SEEN THESE CAMPS.
WHAT'S THAT SMELL?
THOSE TRAIN CARS ARE FILLED WITH THE DEAD.
LOOK, REINFORCEMENTS! U.S. ARMY TROOPS, GLAD TO SEE YOU.
SERGEANT PETER FURST, WITH STARS AND STRIPES.
LEAD THE WAY, SERGEANT.
THAT'S AN SS GENERAL.
I SURRENDER!
FIRST, OPEN THE GATES.
THEN SURRENDER TO THEM.
LET'S GO ON FOOT.
I DON'T WANT TO DRIVE IN THERE WITH ALL THESE WEAPONS.
GOOD IDEA.
WE NEED TO TALK TO THE PRISONERS.
MAGGIE! COME BACK!
GULP.

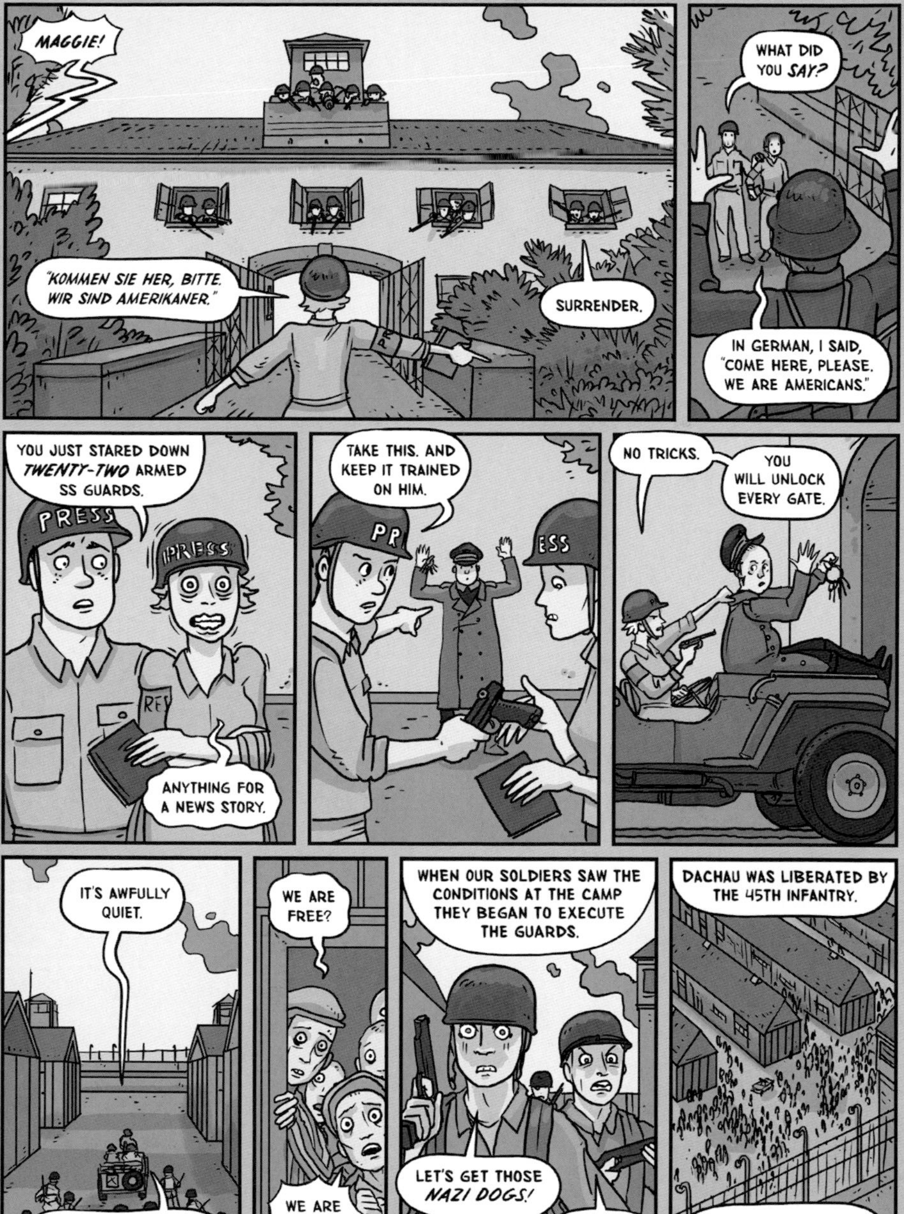
MAGGIE!
"KOMMEN SIE HER, BITTE. WIR SIND AMERIKANER."
SURRENDER.
WHAT DID YOU SAY?
IN GERMAN, I SAID, "COME HERE, PLEASE. WE ARE AMERICANS."
YOU JUST STARED DOWN TWENTY-TWO ARMED SS GUARDS.
PRESS
PRESS
ANYTHING FOR A NEWS STORY.
TAKE THIS. AND KEEP IT TRAINED ON HIM.
NO TRICKS.
YOU WILL UNLOCK EVERY GATE.
IT'S AWFULLY QUIET.
"SIE SIND FREI. DIE AMERIKANER SIND HIER."
WE ARE FREE?
WE ARE FREE!?
WHEN OUR SOLDIERS SAW THE CONDITIONS AT THE CAMP THEY BEGAN TO EXECUTE THE GUARDS.
LET'S GET THOSE NAZI DOGS!
LEAVE NO SS ALIVE!
DACHAU WAS LIBERATED BY THE 45TH INFANTRY.
BUT I WAS THERE TO WITNESS AND REPORT.

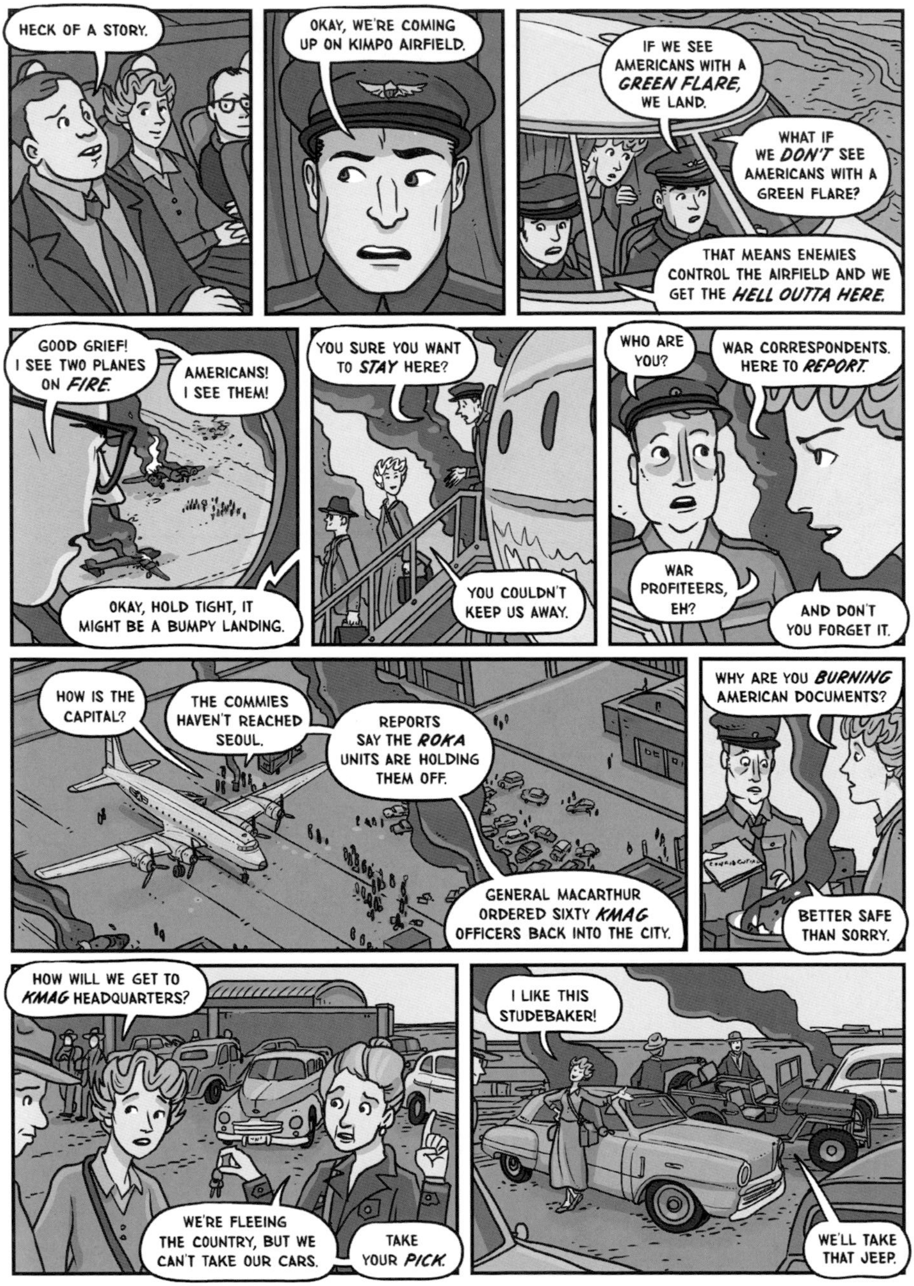
HECK OF A STORY.
OKAY, WE'RE COMING UP ON KIMPO AIRFIELD.
IF WE SEE AMERICANS WITH A *GREEN FLARE,* WE LAND.
WHAT IF WE *DON'T* SEE AMERICANS WITH A GREEN FLARE?
THAT MEANS ENEMIES CONTROL THE AIRFIELD AND WE GET THE *HELL OUTTA HERE.*
GOOD GRIEF! I SEE TWO PLANES ON *FIRE.*
AMERICANS! I SEE THEM!
OKAY, HOLD TIGHT, IT MIGHT BE A BUMPY LANDING.
YOU SURE YOU WANT TO *STAY* HERE?
YOU COULDN'T KEEP US AWAY.
WHO ARE YOU?
WAR CORRESPONDENTS. HERE TO *REPORT.*
WAR PROFITEERS, EH?
AND DON'T YOU FORGET IT.
HOW IS THE CAPITAL?
THE COMMIES HAVEN'T REACHED SEOUL.
REPORTS SAY THE *ROKA* UNITS ARE HOLDING THEM OFF.
GENERAL MACARTHUR ORDERED SIXTY *KMAG* OFFICERS BACK INTO THE CITY.
WHY ARE YOU *BURNING* AMERICAN DOCUMENTS?
BETTER SAFE THAN SORRY.
HOW WILL WE GET TO *KMAG* HEADQUARTERS?
WE'RE FLEEING THE COUNTRY, BUT WE CAN'T TAKE OUR CARS.
TAKE YOUR *PICK.*
I LIKE THIS STUDEBAKER!
WE'LL TAKE THAT JEEP.

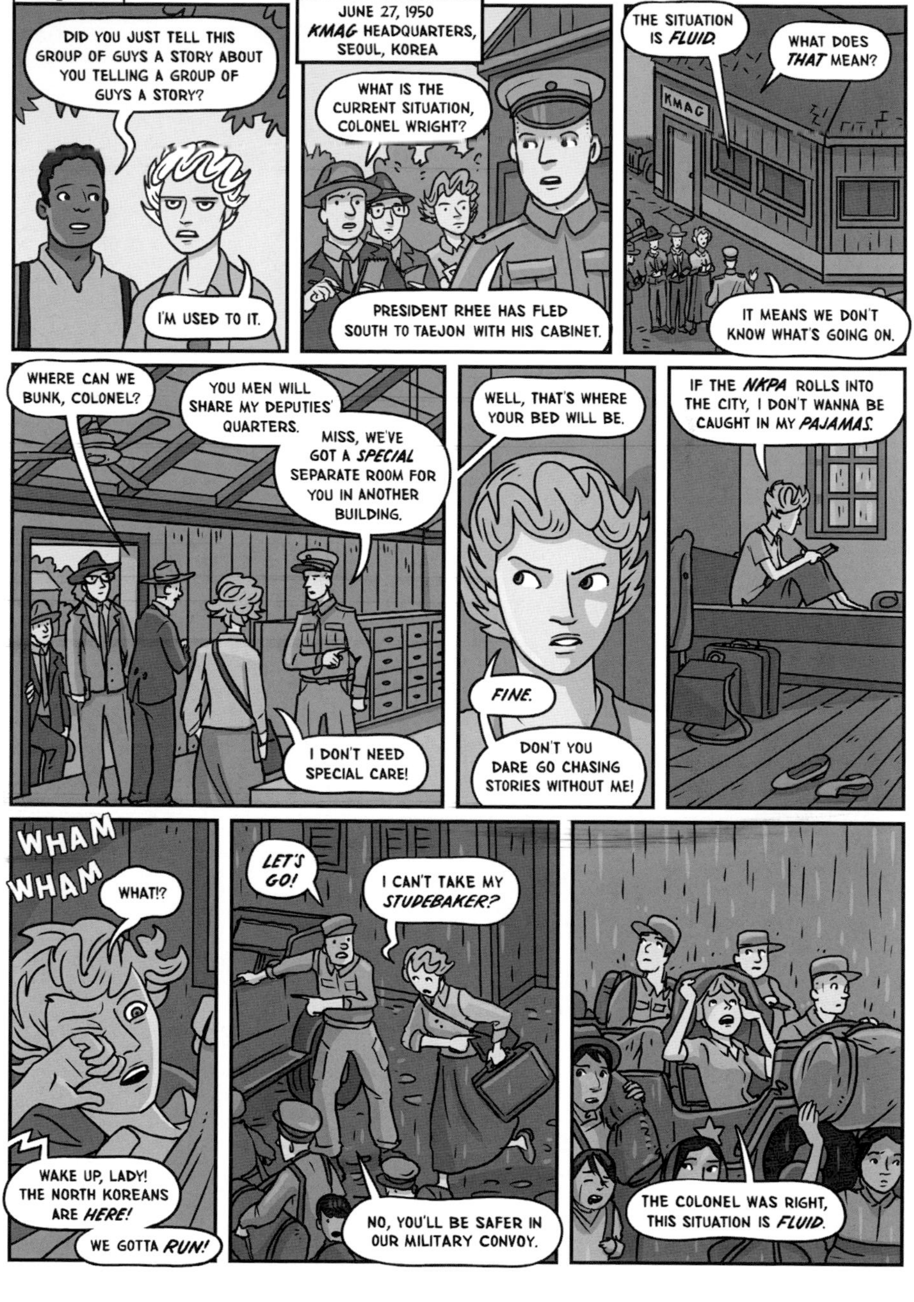
DID YOU JUST TELL THIS GROUP OF GUYS A STORY ABOUT YOU TELLING A GROUP OF GUYS A STORY?
I'M USED TO IT.
JUNE 27, 1950 KMAG HEADQUARTERS, SEOUL, KOREA
WHAT IS THE CURRENT SITUATION, COLONEL WRIGHT?
PRESIDENT RHEE HAS FLED SOUTH TO TAEJON WITH HIS CABINET.
KMAG
THE SITUATION IS FLUID.
WHAT DOES THAT MEAN?
IT MEANS WE DON'T KNOW WHAT'S GOING ON.
WHERE CAN WE BUNK, COLONEL?
YOU MEN WILL SHARE MY DEPUTIES' QUARTERS.
MISS, WE'VE GOT A SPECIAL SEPARATE ROOM FOR YOU IN ANOTHER BUILDING.
I DON'T NEED SPECIAL CARE!
WELL, THAT'S WHERE YOUR BED WILL BE.
FINE.
DON'T YOU DARE GO CHASING STORIES WITHOUT ME!
IF THE NKPA ROLLS INTO THE CITY, I DON'T WANNA BE CAUGHT IN MY PAJAMAS.
WHAM
WHAM
WHAT!?
WAKE UP, LADY! THE NORTH KOREANS ARE HERE!
WE GOTTA RUN!
LET'S GO!
I CAN'T TAKE MY STUDEBAKER?
NO, YOU'LL BE SAFER IN OUR MILITARY CONVOY.
THE COLONEL WAS RIGHT, THIS SITUATION IS FLUID.

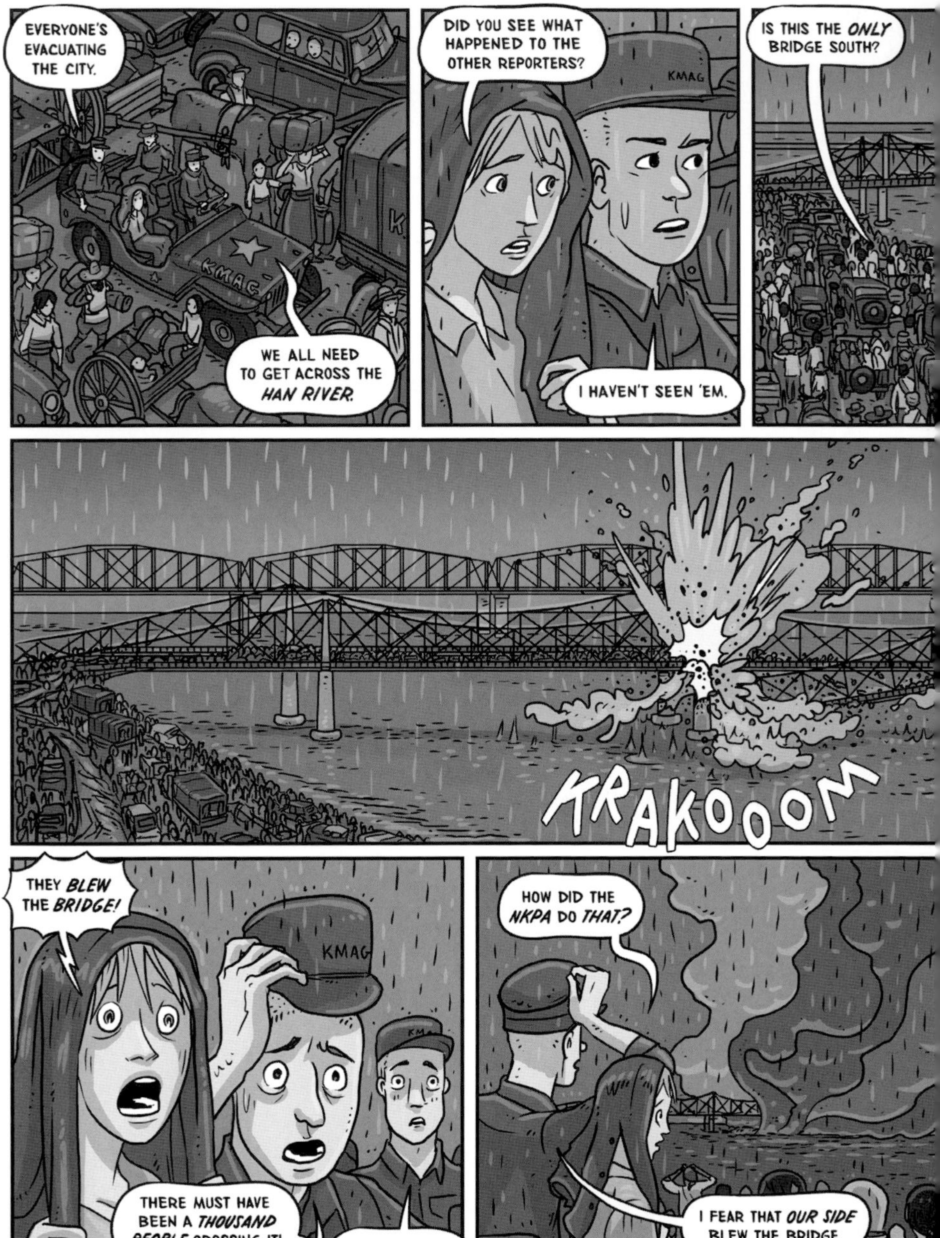

EVERYONE'S EVACUATING THE CITY.
WE ALL NEED TO GET ACROSS THE *HAN RIVER.*
KMAG
DID YOU SEE WHAT HAPPENED TO THE OTHER REPORTERS?
I HAVEN'T SEEN 'EM.
IS THIS THE *ONLY* BRIDGE SOUTH?
KRAKOOOM
THEY *BLEW* THE *BRIDGE!*
THERE MUST HAVE BEEN A *THOUSAND PEOPLE* CROSSING IT!
NOT ANYMORE.
HOW DID THE *NKPA* DO *THAT?*
I FEAR THAT *OUR SIDE* BLEW THE BRIDGE.

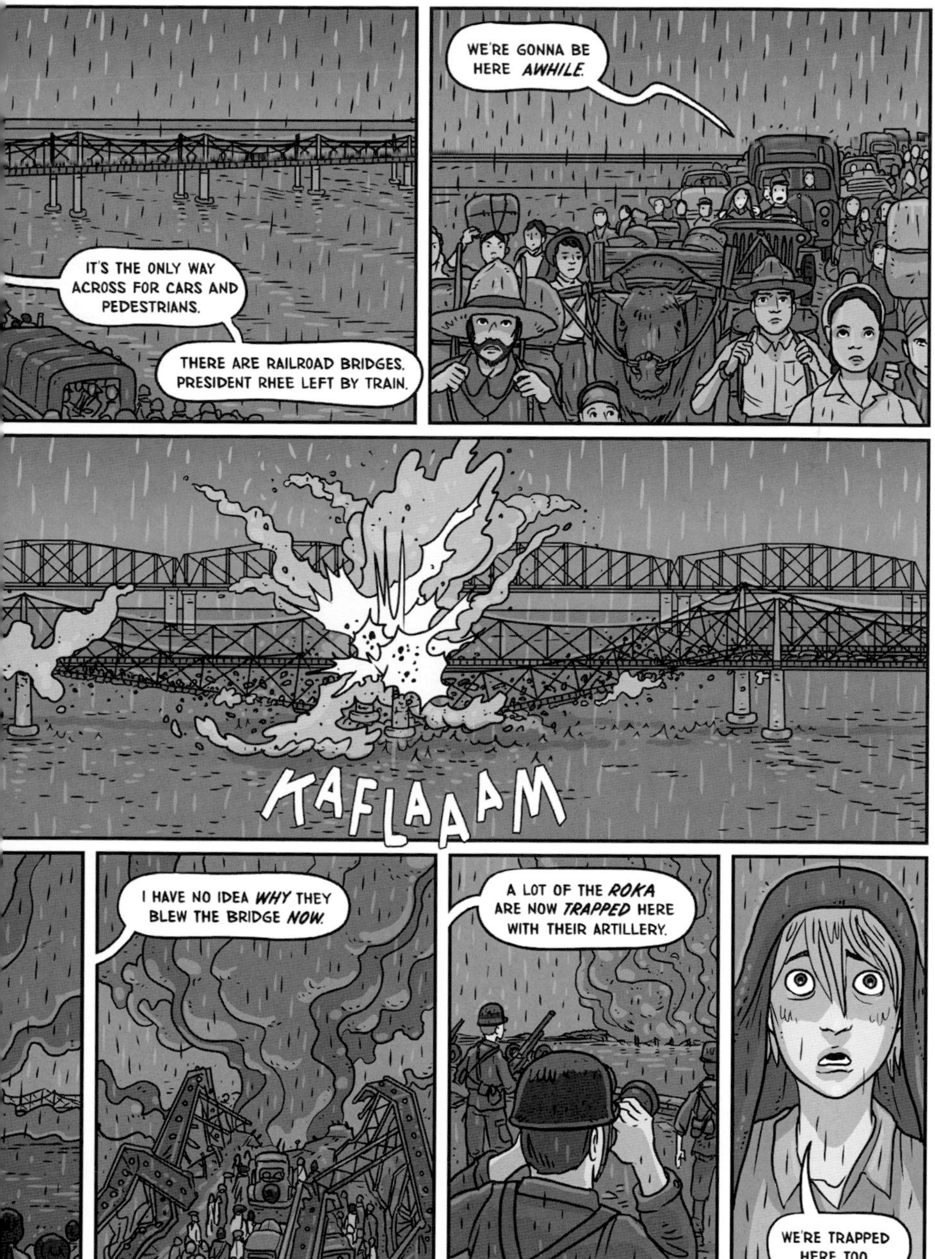
IT'S THE ONLY WAY ACROSS FOR CARS AND PEDESTRIANS.
THERE ARE RAILROAD BRIDGES. PRESIDENT RHEE LEFT BY TRAIN.
WE'RE GONNA BE HERE AWHILE.
KAFLAAAM
I HAVE NO IDEA WHY THEY BLEW THE BRIDGE NOW.
A LOT OF THE ROKA ARE NOW TRAPPED HERE WITH THEIR ARTILLERY.
WE'RE TRAPPED HERE TOO.

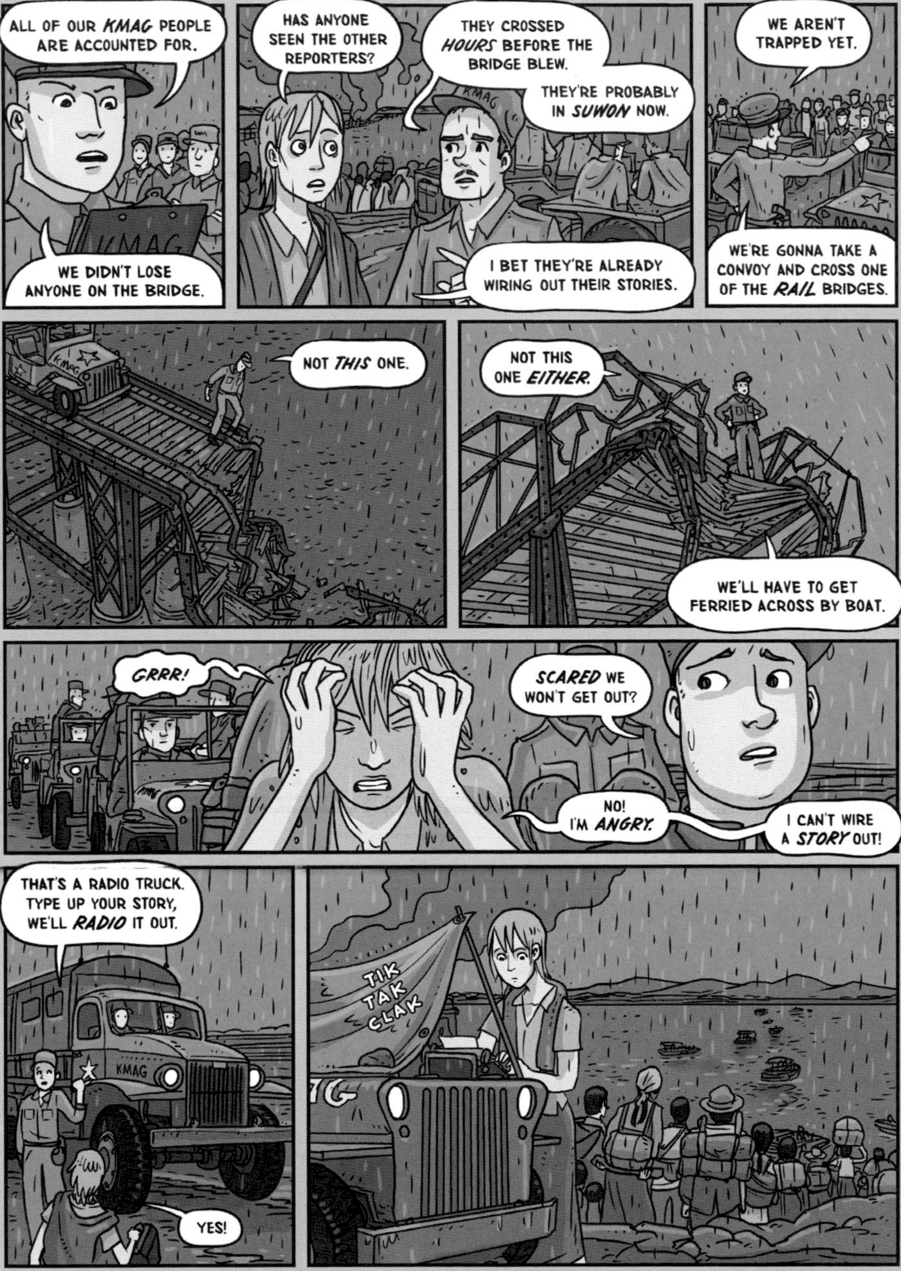
ALL OF OUR KMAG PEOPLE ARE ACCOUNTED FOR.
WE DIDN'T LOSE ANYONE ON THE BRIDGE.
HAS ANYONE SEEN THE OTHER REPORTERS?
THEY CROSSED HOURS BEFORE THE BRIDGE BLEW.
THEY'RE PROBABLY IN SUWON NOW.
I BET THEY'RE ALREADY WIRING OUT THEIR STORIES.
WE AREN'T TRAPPED YET.
WE'RE GONNA TAKE A CONVOY AND CROSS ONE OF THE RAIL BRIDGES.
NOT THIS ONE.
NOT THIS ONE EITHER.
WE'LL HAVE TO GET FERRIED ACROSS BY BOAT.
GRRR!
SCARED WE WON'T GET OUT?
NO! I'M ANGRY.
I CAN'T WIRE A STORY OUT!
THAT'S A RADIO TRUCK. TYPE UP YOUR STORY, WE'LL RADIO IT OUT.
YES!
TIK TAK CLAK

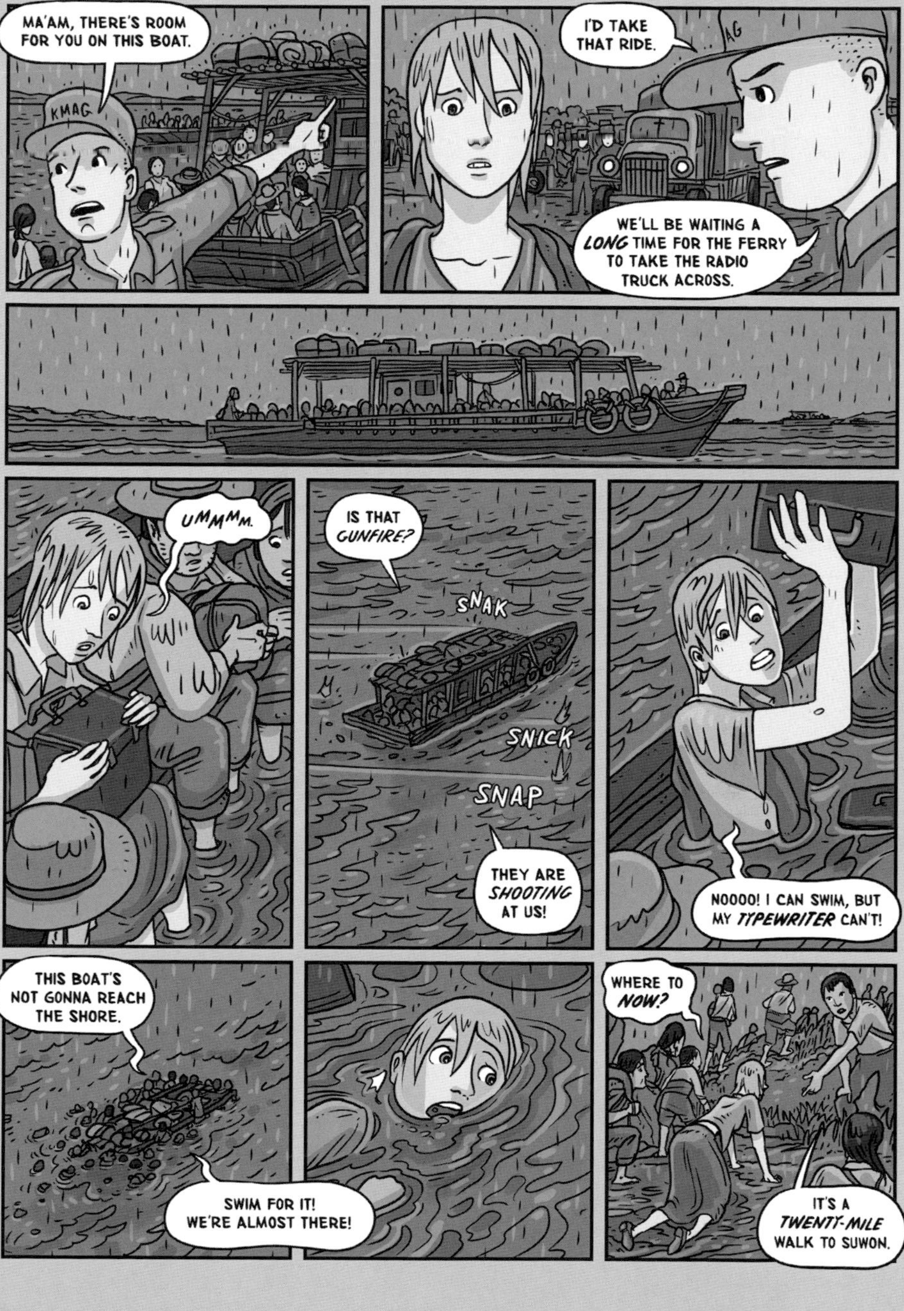
MA'AM, THERE'S ROOM FOR YOU ON THIS BOAT.
KMAG
I'D TAKE THAT RIDE.
WE'LL BE WAITING A *LONG* TIME FOR THE FERRY TO TAKE THE RADIO TRUCK ACROSS.
UMMMM.
IS THAT *GUNFIRE?*
SNAK
SNICK
SNAP
THEY ARE *SHOOTING* AT US!
NOOOO! I CAN SWIM, BUT MY *TYPEWRITER* CAN'T!
THIS BOAT'S NOT GONNA REACH THE SHORE.
SWIM FOR IT! WE'RE ALMOST THERE!
WHERE TO *NOW?*
IT'S A *TWENTY-MILE* WALK TO SUWON.

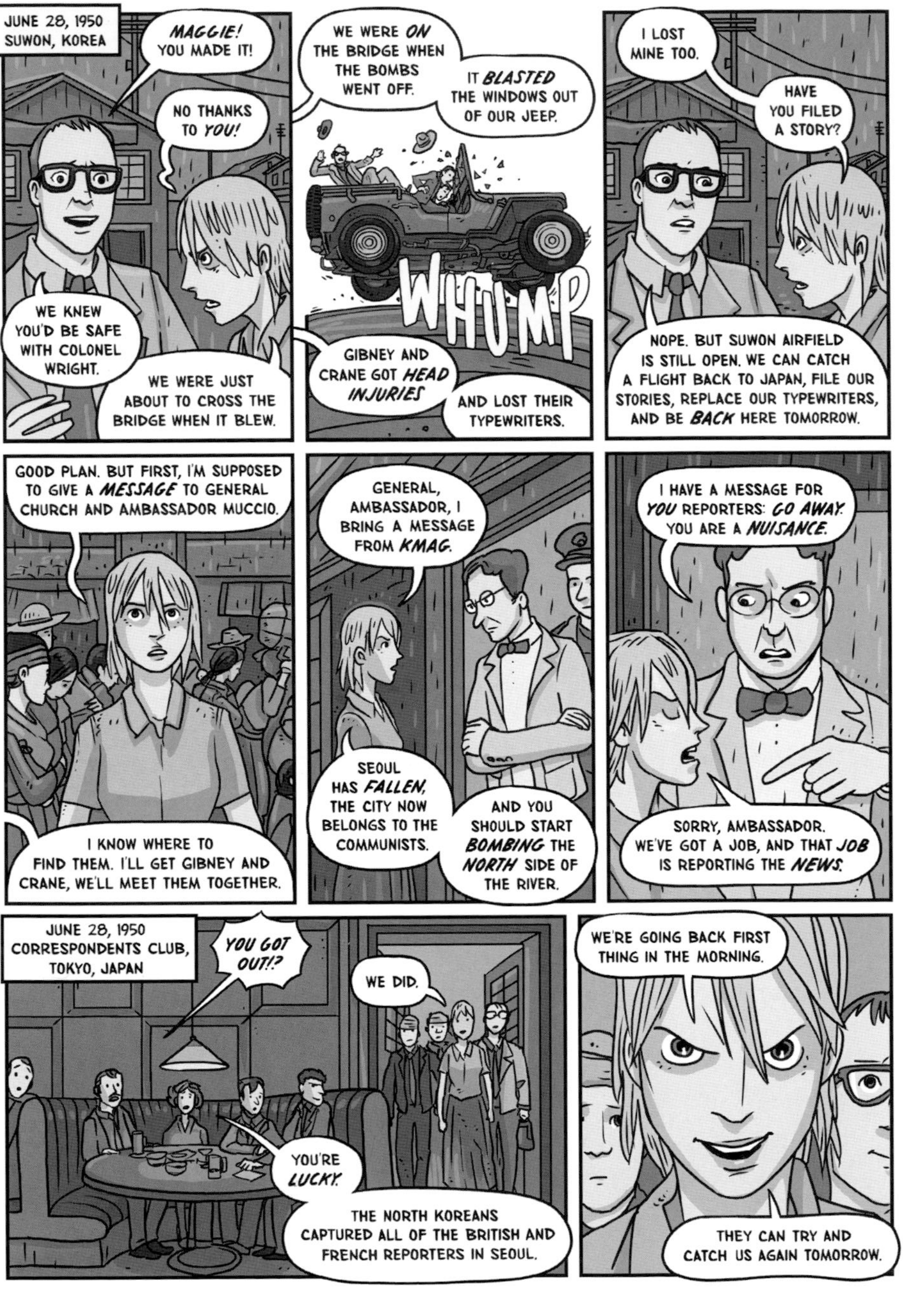

JUNE 28, 1950
SUWON, KOREA
MAGGIE! YOU MADE IT!
NO THANKS TO YOU!
WE KNEW YOU'D BE SAFE WITH COLONEL WRIGHT.
WE WERE JUST ABOUT TO CROSS THE BRIDGE WHEN IT BLEW.
WE WERE ON THE BRIDGE WHEN THE BOMBS WENT OFF.
IT BLASTED THE WINDOWS OUT OF OUR JEEP.
WHUMP
GIBNEY AND CRANE GOT HEAD INJURIES
AND LOST THEIR TYPEWRITERS.
I LOST MINE TOO.
HAVE YOU FILED A STORY?
NOPE. BUT SUWON AIRFIELD IS STILL OPEN. WE CAN CATCH A FLIGHT BACK TO JAPAN, FILE OUR STORIES, REPLACE OUR TYPEWRITERS, AND BE BACK HERE TOMORROW.
GOOD PLAN. BUT FIRST, I'M SUPPOSED TO GIVE A MESSAGE TO GENERAL CHURCH AND AMBASSADOR MUCCIO.
I KNOW WHERE TO FIND THEM. I'LL GET GIBNEY AND CRANE, WE'LL MEET THEM TOGETHER.
GENERAL, AMBASSADOR, I BRING A MESSAGE FROM KMAG.
SEOUL HAS FALLEN, THE CITY NOW BELONGS TO THE COMMUNISTS.
AND YOU SHOULD START BOMBING THE NORTH SIDE OF THE RIVER.
I HAVE A MESSAGE FOR YOU REPORTERS: GO AWAY. YOU ARE A NUISANCE.
SORRY, AMBASSADOR. WE'VE GOT A JOB, AND THAT JOB IS REPORTING THE NEWS.
JUNE 28, 1950
CORRESPONDENTS CLUB, TOKYO, JAPAN
YOU GOT OUT!?
WE DID.
YOU'RE LUCKY.
THE NORTH KOREANS CAPTURED ALL OF THE BRITISH AND FRENCH REPORTERS IN SEOUL.
WE'RE GOING BACK FIRST THING IN THE MORNING.
THEY CAN TRY AND CATCH US AGAIN TOMORROW.

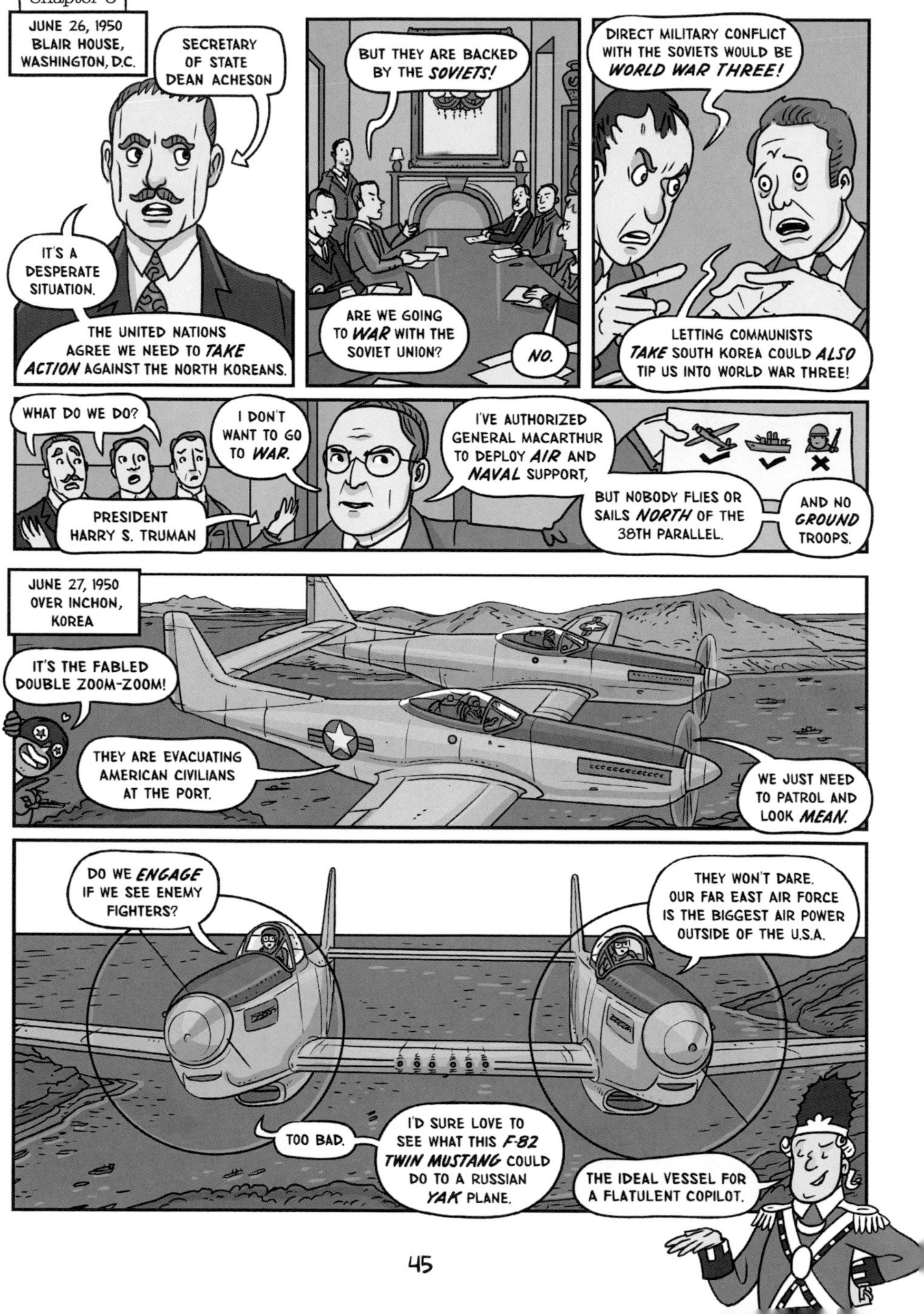
JUNE 26, 1950
BLAIR HOUSE, WASHINGTON, D.C.
SECRETARY OF STATE DEAN ACHESON
IT'S A DESPERATE SITUATION.
THE UNITED NATIONS AGREE WE NEED TO TAKE ACTION AGAINST THE NORTH KOREANS.
BUT THEY ARE BACKED BY THE SOVIETS!
ARE WE GOING TO WAR WITH THE SOVIET UNION?
NO.
DIRECT MILITARY CONFLICT WITH THE SOVIETS WOULD BE WORLD WAR THREE!
LETTING COMMUNISTS TAKE SOUTH KOREA COULD ALSO TIP US INTO WORLD WAR THREE!
WHAT DO WE DO?
I DON'T WANT TO GO TO WAR.
PRESIDENT HARRY S. TRUMAN
I'VE AUTHORIZED GENERAL MACARTHUR TO DEPLOY AIR AND NAVAL SUPPORT,
BUT NOBODY FLIES OR SAILS NORTH OF THE 38TH PARALLEL.
AND NO GROUND TROOPS.
JUNE 27, 1950
OVER INCHON, KOREA
IT'S THE FABLED DOUBLE ZOOM-ZOOM!
THEY ARE EVACUATING AMERICAN CIVILIANS AT THE PORT.
WE JUST NEED TO PATROL AND LOOK MEAN.
DO WE ENGAGE IF WE SEE ENEMY FIGHTERS?
THEY WON'T DARE. OUR FAR EAST AIR FORCE IS THE BIGGEST AIR POWER OUTSIDE OF THE U.S.A.
TOO BAD.
I'D SURE LOVE TO SEE WHAT THIS F-82 TWIN MUSTANG COULD DO TO A RUSSIAN YAK PLANE.
THE IDEAL VESSEL FOR A FLATULENT COPILOT.

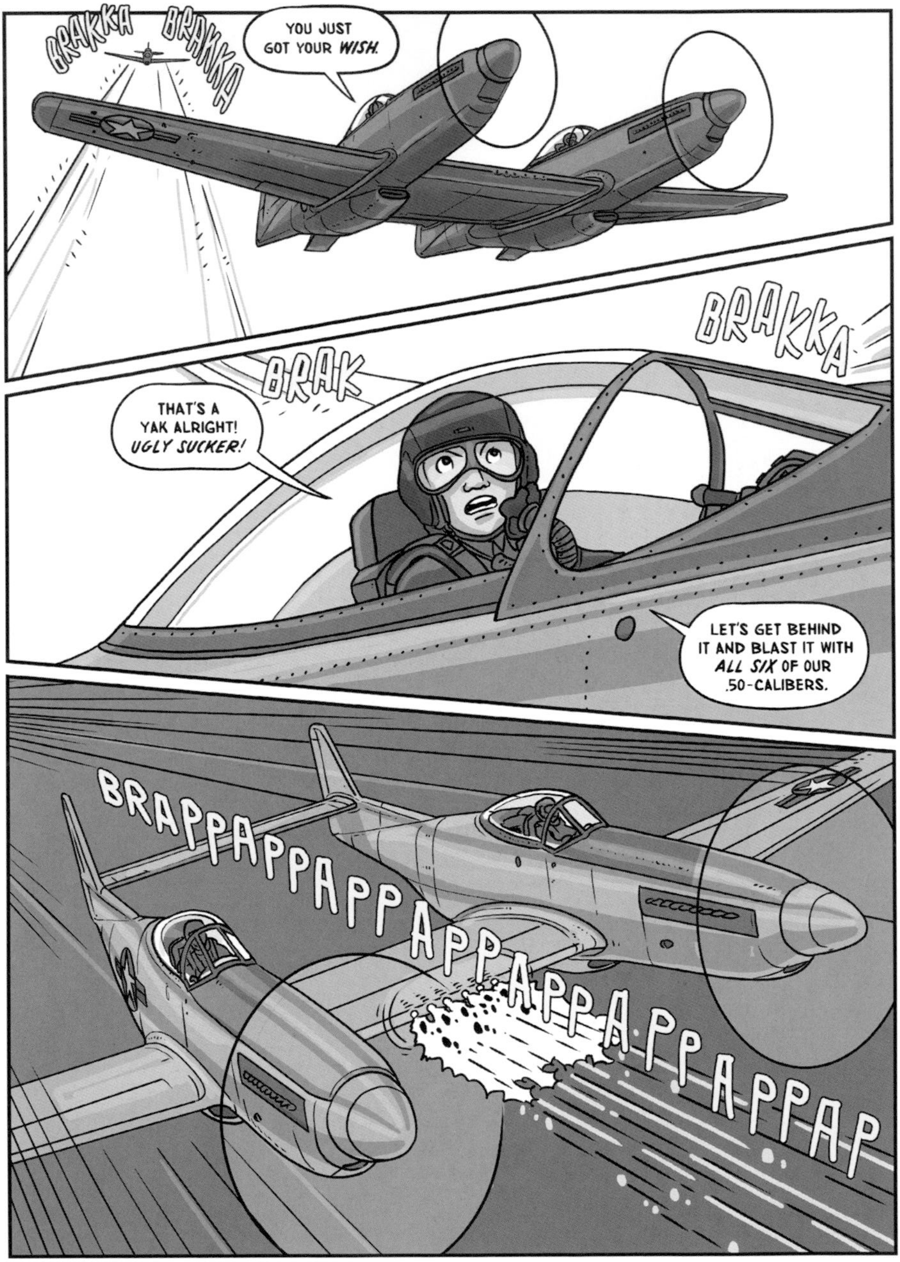
BRAKKA BRAKKA
YOU JUST GOT YOUR *WISH.*
BRAK
BRAKKA
THAT'S A YAK ALRIGHT! *UGLY SUCKER!*
LET'S GET BEHIND IT AND BLAST IT WITH *ALL SIX* OF OUR .50-CALIBERS.
BRAPPAPPAPPAPPAPPAPPAPPAPPAP

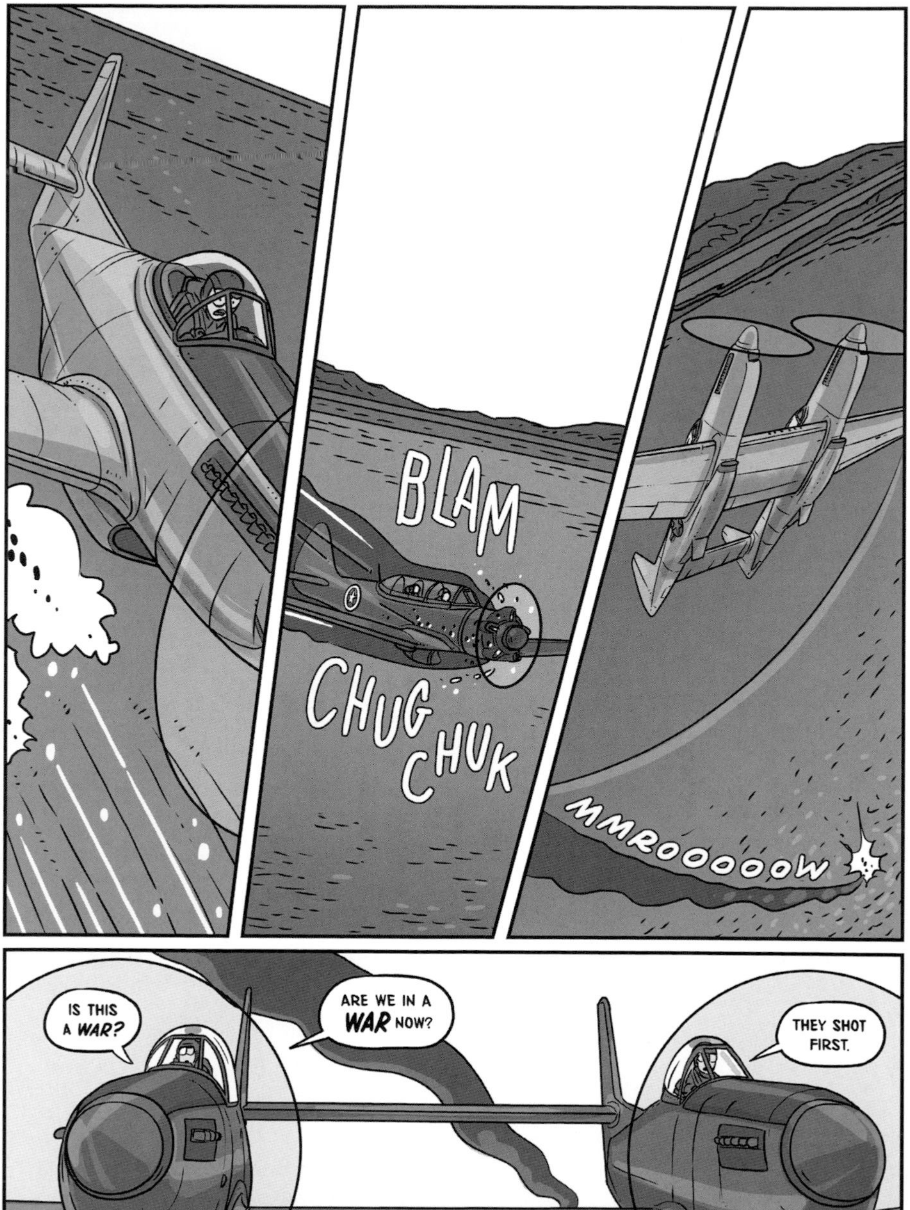
BLAM
CHUG
CHUK
MMROOOOOOW
IS THIS A WAR?
ARE WE IN A WAR NOW?
THEY SHOT FIRST.

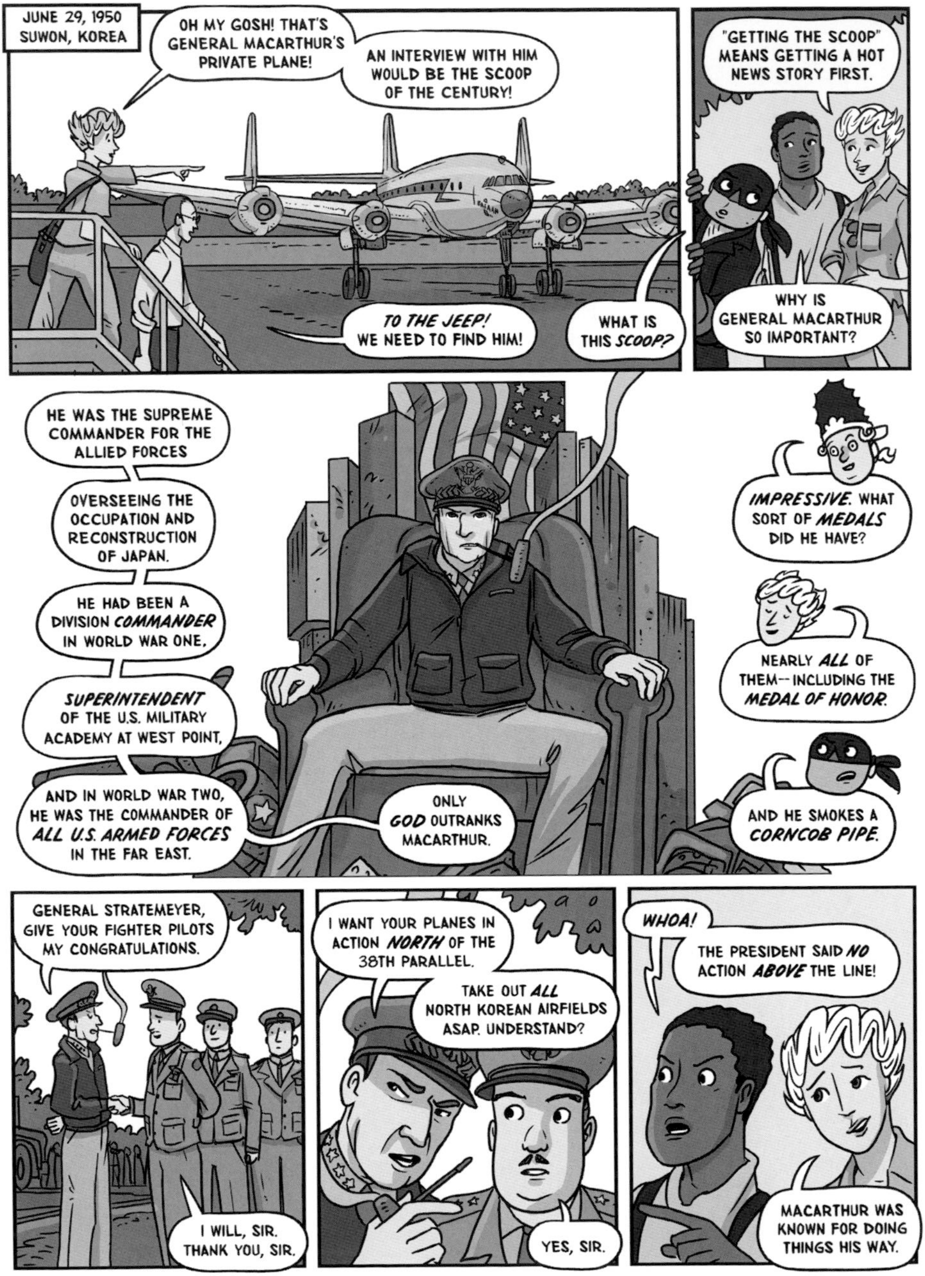
JUNE 29, 1950
SUWON, KOREA
OH MY GOSH! THAT'S GENERAL MACARTHUR'S PRIVATE PLANE!
AN INTERVIEW WITH HIM WOULD BE THE SCOOP OF THE CENTURY!
TO THE JEEP! WE NEED TO FIND HIM!
WHAT IS THIS SCOOP?
"GETTING THE SCOOP" MEANS GETTING A HOT NEWS STORY FIRST.
WHY IS GENERAL MACARTHUR SO IMPORTANT?
HE WAS THE SUPREME COMMANDER FOR THE ALLIED FORCES
OVERSEEING THE OCCUPATION AND RECONSTRUCTION OF JAPAN.
HE HAD BEEN A DIVISION COMMANDER IN WORLD WAR ONE,
SUPERINTENDENT OF THE U.S. MILITARY ACADEMY AT WEST POINT,
AND IN WORLD WAR TWO, HE WAS THE COMMANDER OF ALL U.S. ARMED FORCES IN THE FAR EAST.
ONLY GOD OUTRANKS MACARTHUR.
IMPRESSIVE. WHAT SORT OF MEDALS DID HE HAVE?
NEARLY ALL OF THEM-- INCLUDING THE MEDAL OF HONOR.
AND HE SMOKES A CORNCOB PIPE.
GENERAL STRATEMEYER, GIVE YOUR FIGHTER PILOTS MY CONGRATULATIONS.
I WILL, SIR. THANK YOU, SIR.
I WANT YOUR PLANES IN ACTION NORTH OF THE 38TH PARALLEL.
TAKE OUT ALL NORTH KOREAN AIRFIELDS ASAP. UNDERSTAND?
YES, SIR.
WHOA!
THE PRESIDENT SAID NO ACTION ABOVE THE LINE!
MACARTHUR WAS KNOWN FOR DOING THINGS HIS WAY.

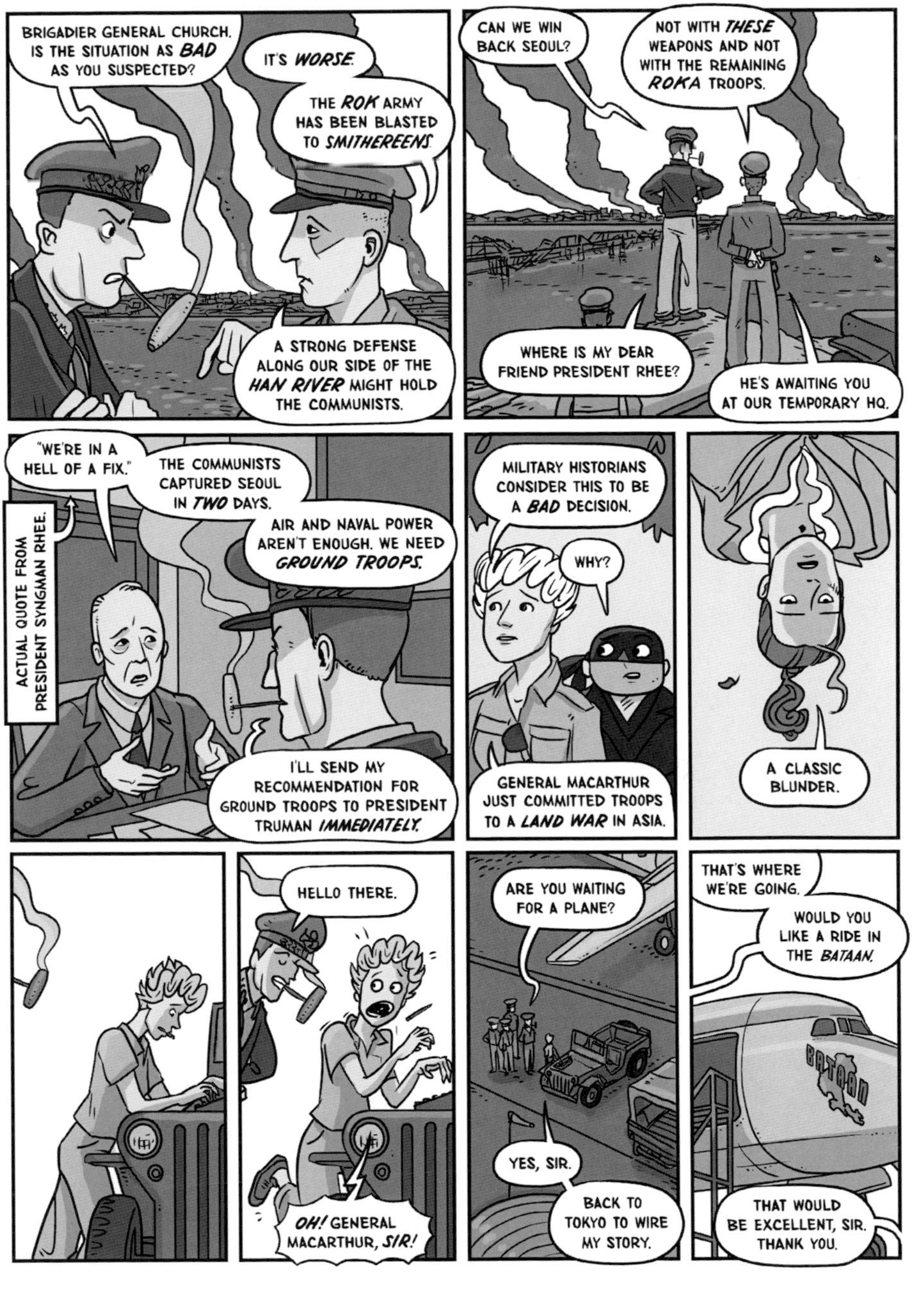
BRIGADIER GENERAL CHURCH. IS THE SITUATION AS BAD AS YOU SUSPECTED?
IT'S WORSE.
THE ROK ARMY HAS BEEN BLASTED TO SMITHEREENS.
A STRONG DEFENSE ALONG OUR SIDE OF THE HAN RIVER MIGHT HOLD THE COMMUNISTS.
CAN WE WIN BACK SEOUL?
NOT WITH THESE WEAPONS AND NOT WITH THE REMAINING ROKA TROOPS.
WHERE IS MY DEAR FRIEND PRESIDENT RHEE?
HE'S AWAITING YOU AT OUR TEMPORARY HQ.
"WE'RE IN A HELL OF A FIX."
ACTUAL QUOTE FROM PRESIDENT SYNGMAN RHEE.
THE COMMUNISTS CAPTURED SEOUL IN TWO DAYS.
AIR AND NAVAL POWER AREN'T ENOUGH. WE NEED GROUND TROOPS.
I'LL SEND MY RECOMMENDATION FOR GROUND TROOPS TO PRESIDENT TRUMAN IMMEDIATELY.
MILITARY HISTORIANS CONSIDER THIS TO BE A BAD DECISION.
WHY?
GENERAL MACARTHUR JUST COMMITTED TROOPS TO A LAND WAR IN ASIA.
A CLASSIC BLUNDER.
HELLO THERE.
OH! GENERAL MACARTHUR, SIR!
ARE YOU WAITING FOR A PLANE?
YES, SIR.
BACK TO TOKYO TO WIRE MY STORY.
THAT'S WHERE WE'RE GOING.
WOULD YOU LIKE A RIDE IN THE BATAAN.
BATAAN
THAT WOULD BE EXCELLENT, SIR. THANK YOU.

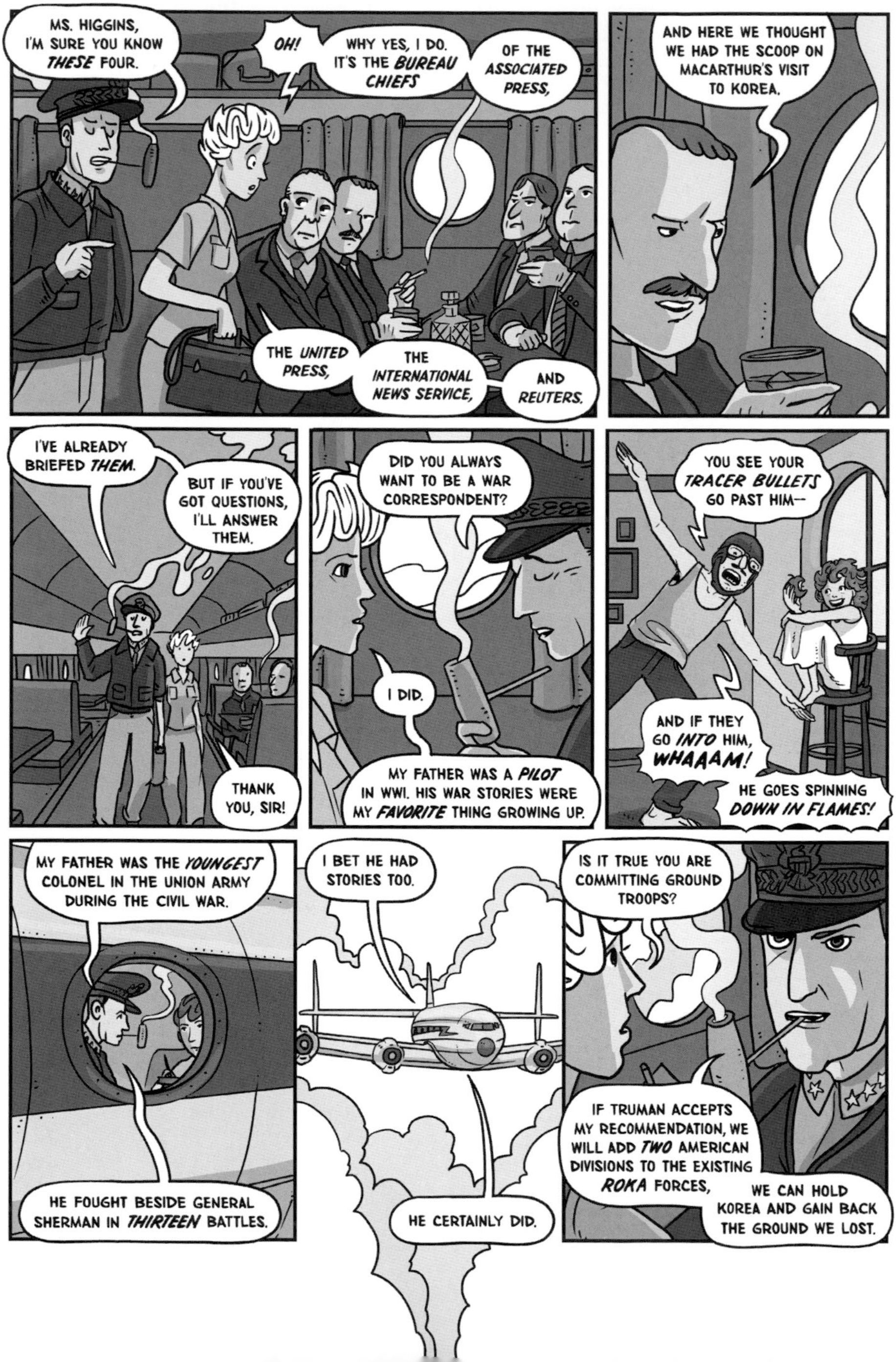

MS. HIGGINS, I'M SURE YOU KNOW *THESE* FOUR.
OH!
WHY YES, I DO. IT'S THE *BUREAU CHIEFS*
OF THE *ASSOCIATED PRESS,*
THE *UNITED PRESS,*
THE *INTERNATIONAL NEWS SERVICE,*
AND *REUTERS.*
AND HERE WE THOUGHT WE HAD THE SCOOP ON MACARTHUR'S VISIT TO KOREA.
I'VE ALREADY BRIEFED *THEM.*
BUT IF YOU'VE GOT QUESTIONS, I'LL ANSWER THEM.
THANK YOU, SIR!
DID YOU ALWAYS WANT TO BE A WAR CORRESPONDENT?
I DID.
MY FATHER WAS A *PILOT* IN WWI. HIS WAR STORIES WERE MY *FAVORITE* THING GROWING UP.
YOU SEE YOUR *TRACER BULLETS* GO PAST HIM--
AND IF THEY GO *INTO* HIM, *WHAAAM!*
HE GOES SPINNING *DOWN IN FLAMES!*
MY FATHER WAS THE *YOUNGEST* COLONEL IN THE UNION ARMY DURING THE CIVIL WAR.
HE FOUGHT BESIDE GENERAL SHERMAN IN *THIRTEEN* BATTLES.
I BET HE HAD STORIES TOO.
HE CERTAINLY DID.
IS IT TRUE YOU ARE COMMITTING GROUND TROOPS?
IF TRUMAN ACCEPTS MY RECOMMENDATION, WE WILL ADD *TWO* AMERICAN DIVISIONS TO THE EXISTING *ROKA* FORCES,
WE CAN HOLD KOREA AND GAIN BACK THE GROUND WE LOST.

Chapter 7

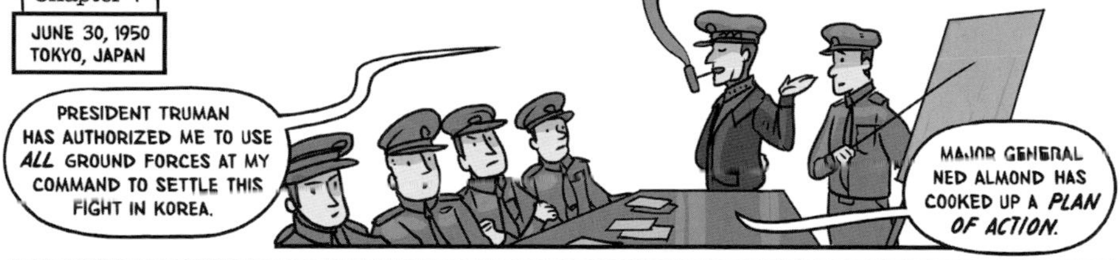
JUNE 30, 1950
TOKYO, JAPAN
PRESIDENT TRUMAN HAS AUTHORIZED ME TO USE ALL GROUND FORCES AT MY COMMAND TO SETTLE THIS FIGHT IN KOREA.
MAJOR GENERAL NED ALMOND HAS COOKED UP A PLAN OF ACTION.

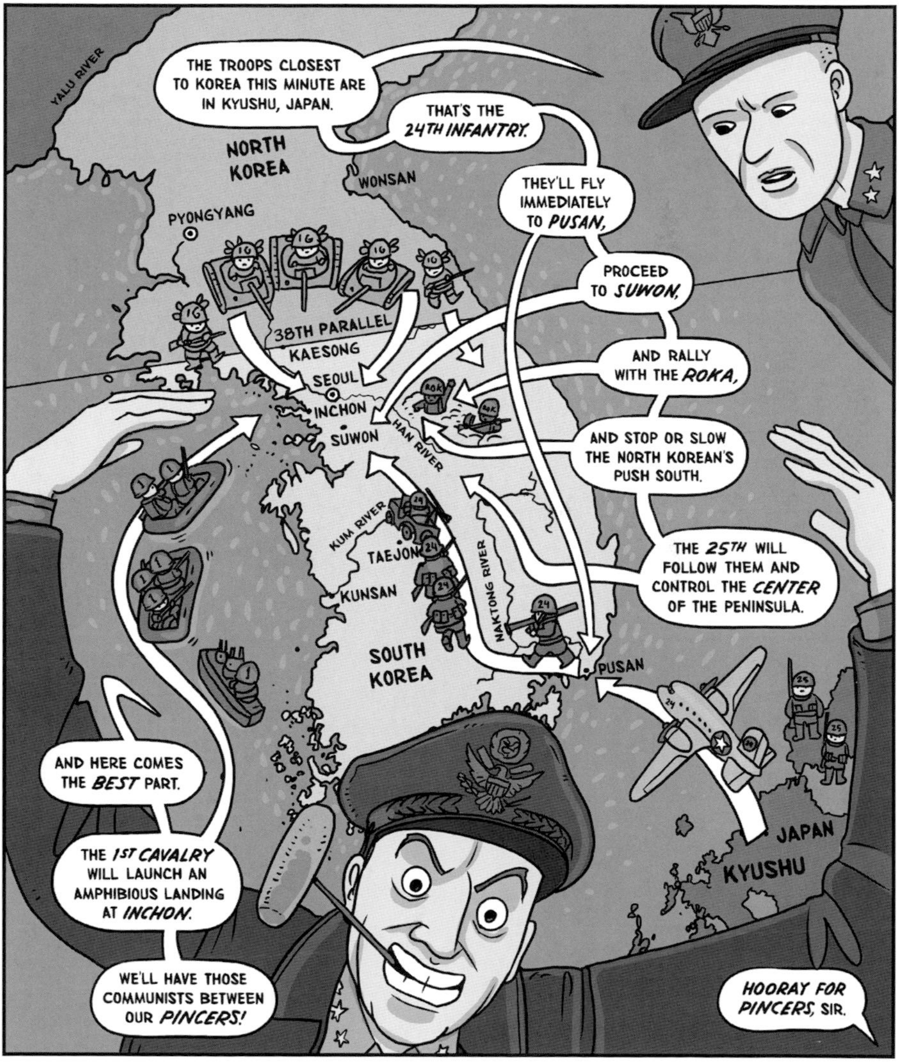
YALU RIVER
NORTH KOREA
WONSAN
PYONGYANG
38TH PARALLEL
KAESONG
SEOUL
INCHON
SUWON
HAN RIVER
KUM RIVER
TAEJON
KUNSAN
NAKTONG RIVER
SOUTH KOREA
PUSAN
JAPAN
KYUSHU
THE TROOPS CLOSEST TO KOREA THIS MINUTE ARE IN KYUSHU, JAPAN.
THAT'S THE 24TH INFANTRY.
THEY'LL FLY IMMEDIATELY TO PUSAN,
PROCEED TO SUWON,
AND RALLY WITH THE ROKA,
AND STOP OR SLOW THE NORTH KOREAN'S PUSH SOUTH.
THE 25TH WILL FOLLOW THEM AND CONTROL THE CENTER OF THE PENINSULA.
AND HERE COMES THE BEST PART.
THE 1ST CAVALRY WILL LAUNCH AN AMPHIBIOUS LANDING AT INCHON.
WE'LL HAVE THOSE COMMUNISTS BETWEEN OUR PINCERS!
HOORAY FOR PINCERS, SIR.

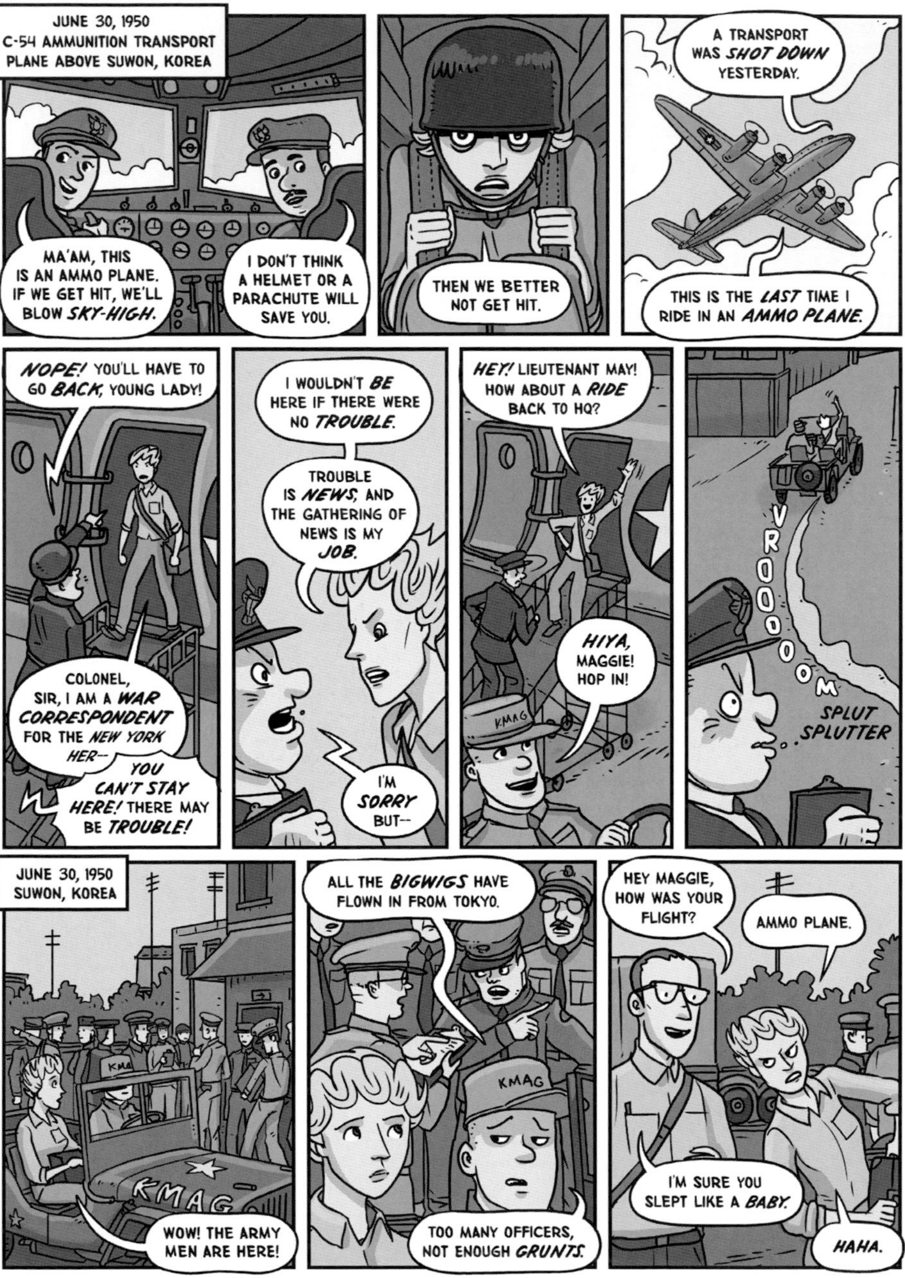
JUNE 30, 1950
C-54 AMMUNITION TRANSPORT PLANE ABOVE SUWON, KOREA
MA'AM, THIS IS AN AMMO PLANE. IF WE GET HIT, WE'LL BLOW SKY-HIGH.
I DON'T THINK A HELMET OR A PARACHUTE WILL SAVE YOU.
THEN WE BETTER NOT GET HIT.
A TRANSPORT WAS SHOT DOWN YESTERDAY.
THIS IS THE LAST TIME I RIDE IN AN AMMO PLANE.
NOPE! YOU'LL HAVE TO GO BACK, YOUNG LADY!
COLONEL, SIR, I AM A WAR CORRESPONDENT FOR THE NEW YORK HER--
YOU CAN'T STAY HERE! THERE MAY BE TROUBLE!
I WOULDN'T BE HERE IF THERE WERE NO TROUBLE.
TROUBLE IS NEWS, AND THE GATHERING OF NEWS IS MY JOB.
I'M SORRY BUT--
HEY! LIEUTENANT MAY! HOW ABOUT A RIDE BACK TO HQ?
HIYA, MAGGIE! HOP IN!
KMAG
VROOOOOOM
SPLUT SPLUTTER
JUNE 30, 1950
SUWON, KOREA
KMAG
KMAG
WOW! THE ARMY MEN ARE HERE!
ALL THE BIGWIGS HAVE FLOWN IN FROM TOKYO.
KMAG
TOO MANY OFFICERS, NOT ENOUGH GRUNTS.
HEY MAGGIE, HOW WAS YOUR FLIGHT?
AMMO PLANE.
I'M SURE YOU SLEPT LIKE A BABY.
HAHA.

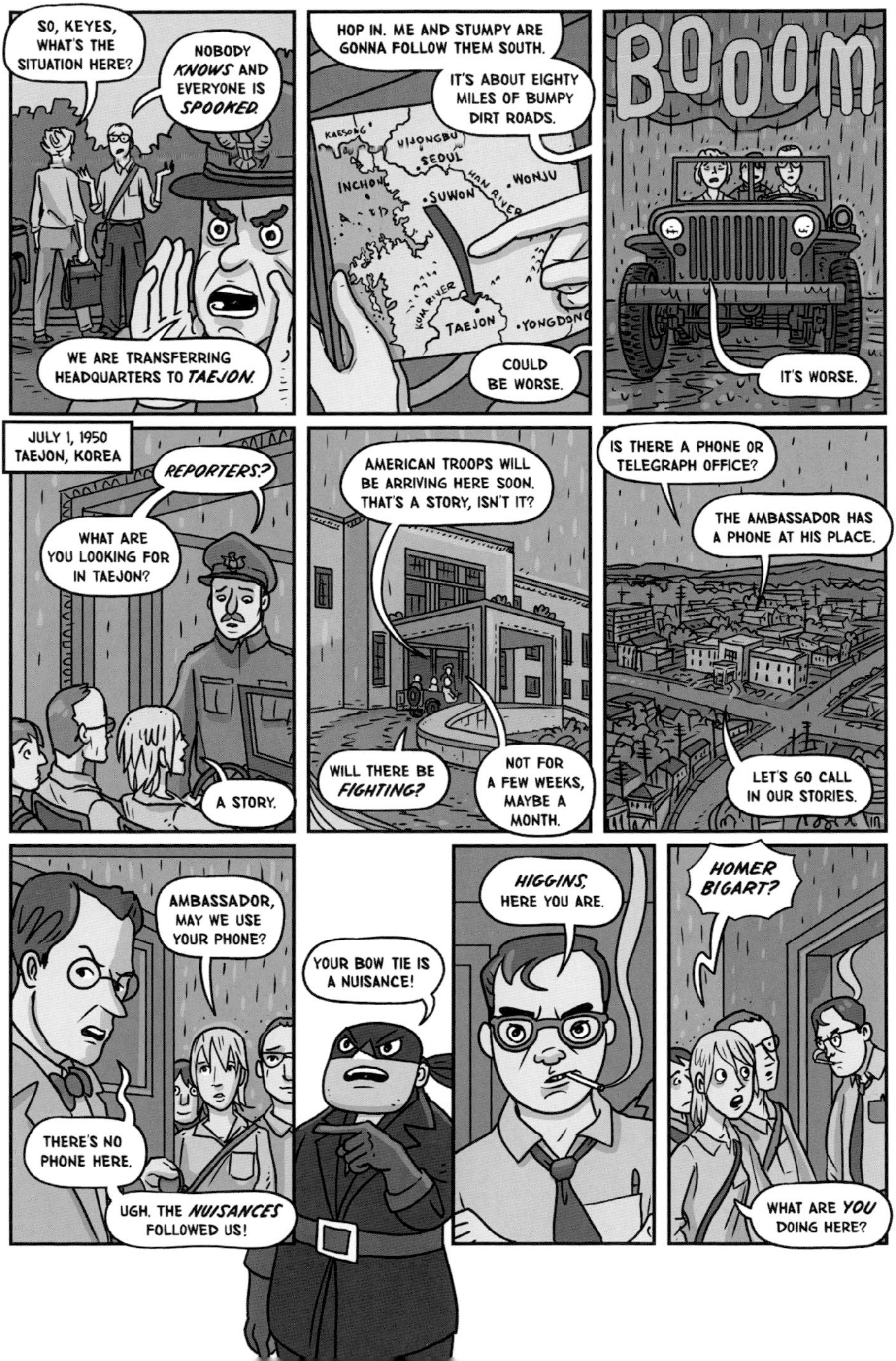
SO, KEYES, WHAT'S THE SITUATION HERE?
NOBODY KNOWS AND EVERYONE IS SPOOKED.
WE ARE TRANSFERRING HEADQUARTERS TO TAEJON.
HOP IN. ME AND STUMPY ARE GONNA FOLLOW THEM SOUTH.
IT'S ABOUT EIGHTY MILES OF BUMPY DIRT ROADS.
KAESONG
UIJONGBU
SEOUL
INCHON
SUWON
HAN RIVER
WONJU
KUM RIVER
TAEJON
YONGDONG
COULD BE WORSE.
BOOOM
IT'S WORSE.
JULY 1, 1950
TAEJON, KOREA
REPORTERS?
WHAT ARE YOU LOOKING FOR IN TAEJON?
A STORY.
AMERICAN TROOPS WILL BE ARRIVING HERE SOON. THAT'S A STORY, ISN'T IT?
WILL THERE BE FIGHTING?
NOT FOR A FEW WEEKS, MAYBE A MONTH.
IS THERE A PHONE OR TELEGRAPH OFFICE?
THE AMBASSADOR HAS A PHONE AT HIS PLACE.
LET'S GO CALL IN OUR STORIES.
AMBASSADOR, MAY WE USE YOUR PHONE?
THERE'S NO PHONE HERE.
UGH. THE NUISANCES FOLLOWED US!
YOUR BOW TIE IS A NUISANCE!
HIGGINS, HERE YOU ARE.
HOMER BIGART?
WHAT ARE YOU DOING HERE?

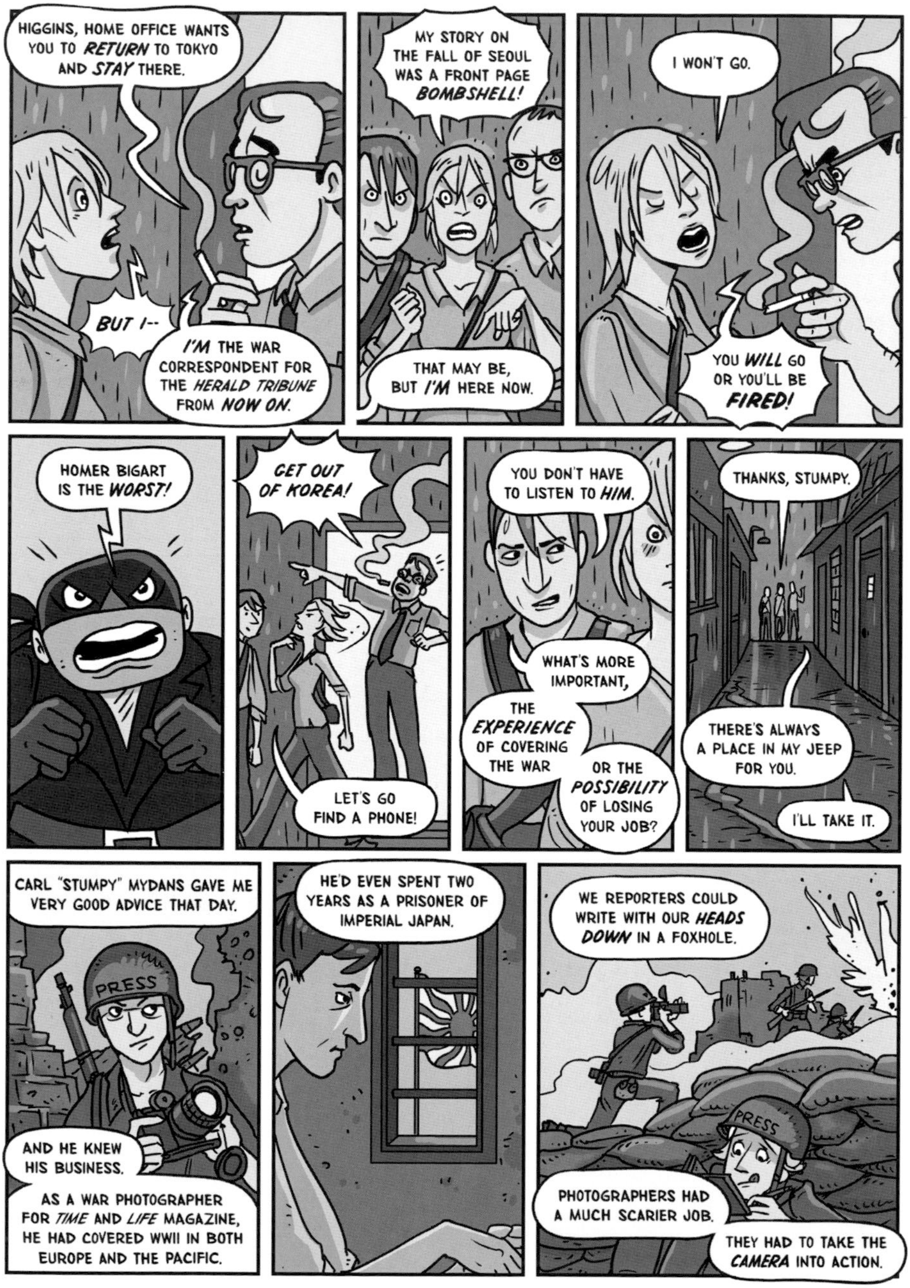
HIGGINS, HOME OFFICE WANTS YOU TO *RETURN* TO TOKYO AND *STAY* THERE.
BUT I--
I'M THE WAR CORRESPONDENT FOR THE *HERALD TRIBUNE* FROM *NOW ON*.
MY STORY ON THE FALL OF SEOUL WAS A FRONT PAGE *BOMBSHELL!*
THAT MAY BE, BUT *I'M* HERE NOW.
I WON'T GO.
YOU *WILL* GO OR YOU'LL BE *FIRED!*
HOMER BIGART IS THE *WORST!*
GET OUT OF KOREA!
LET'S GO FIND A PHONE!
YOU DON'T HAVE TO LISTEN TO *HIM*.
WHAT'S MORE IMPORTANT,
THE *EXPERIENCE* OF COVERING THE WAR
OR THE *POSSIBILITY* OF LOSING YOUR JOB?
THANKS, STUMPY.
THERE'S ALWAYS A PLACE IN MY JEEP FOR YOU.
I'LL TAKE IT.
CARL "STUMPY" MYDANS GAVE ME VERY GOOD ADVICE THAT DAY.
PRESS
AND HE KNEW HIS BUSINESS.
AS A WAR PHOTOGRAPHER FOR *TIME* AND *LIFE* MAGAZINE, HE HAD COVERED WWII IN BOTH EUROPE AND THE PACIFIC.
HE'D EVEN SPENT TWO YEARS AS A PRISONER OF IMPERIAL JAPAN.
WE REPORTERS COULD WRITE WITH OUR *HEADS DOWN* IN A FOXHOLE.
PRESS
PHOTOGRAPHERS HAD A MUCH SCARIER JOB.
THEY HAD TO TAKE THE *CAMERA* INTO ACTION.

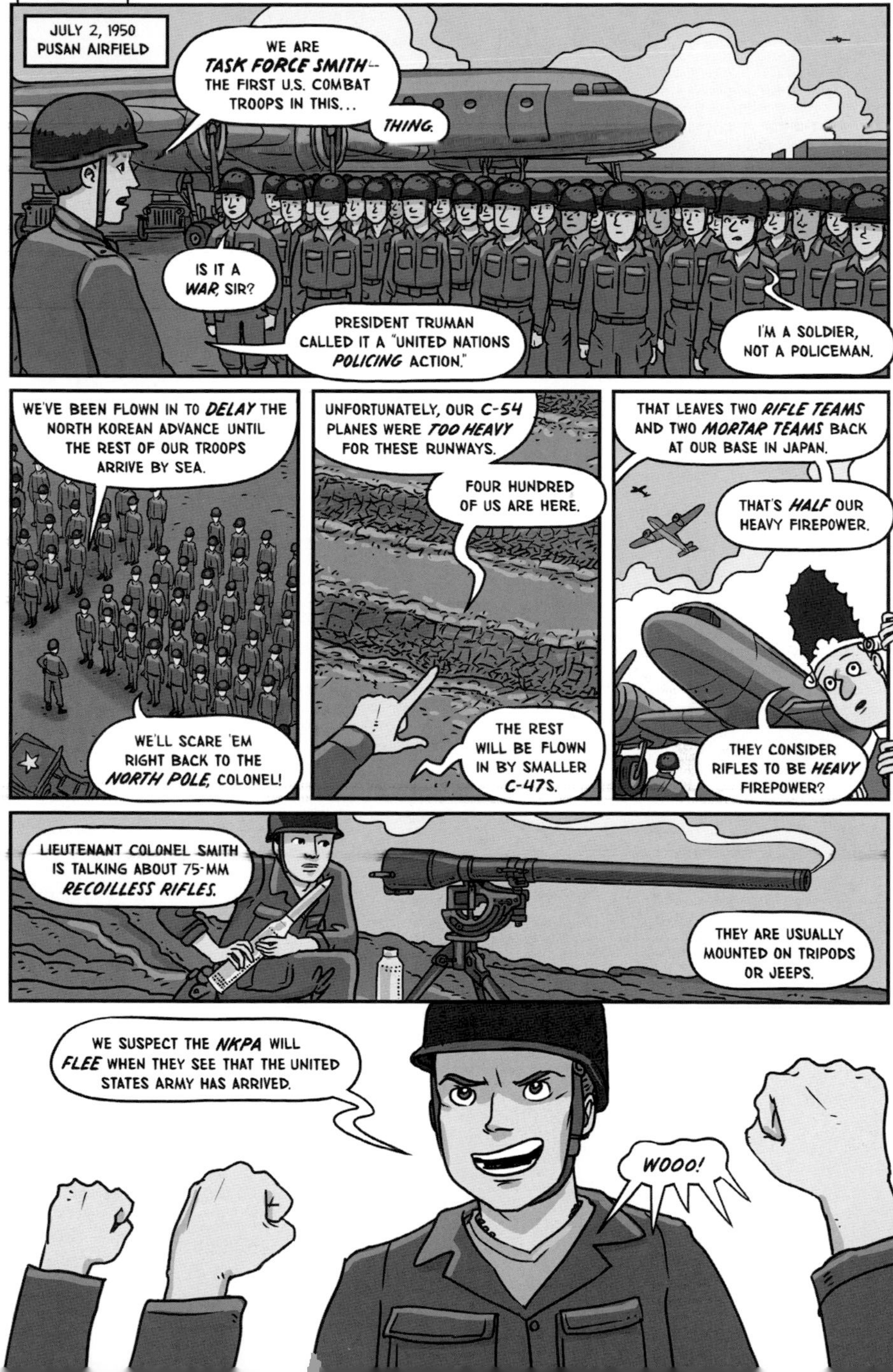
JULY 2, 1950
PUSAN AIRFIELD
WE ARE TASK FORCE SMITH-- THE FIRST U.S. COMBAT TROOPS IN THIS...
THING.
IS IT A WAR, SIR?
PRESIDENT TRUMAN CALLED IT A "UNITED NATIONS POLICING ACTION."
I'M A SOLDIER, NOT A POLICEMAN.
WE'VE BEEN FLOWN IN TO DELAY THE NORTH KOREAN ADVANCE UNTIL THE REST OF OUR TROOPS ARRIVE BY SEA.
WE'LL SCARE 'EM RIGHT BACK TO THE NORTH POLE, COLONEL!
UNFORTUNATELY, OUR C-54 PLANES WERE TOO HEAVY FOR THESE RUNWAYS.
FOUR HUNDRED OF US ARE HERE.
THE REST WILL BE FLOWN IN BY SMALLER C-47S.
THAT LEAVES TWO RIFLE TEAMS AND TWO MORTAR TEAMS BACK AT OUR BASE IN JAPAN.
THAT'S HALF OUR HEAVY FIREPOWER.
THEY CONSIDER RIFLES TO BE HEAVY FIREPOWER?
LIEUTENANT COLONEL SMITH IS TALKING ABOUT 75-MM RECOILLESS RIFLES.
THEY ARE USUALLY MOUNTED ON TRIPODS OR JEEPS.
WE SUSPECT THE NKPA WILL FLEE WHEN THEY SEE THAT THE UNITED STATES ARMY HAS ARRIVED.
WOOO!

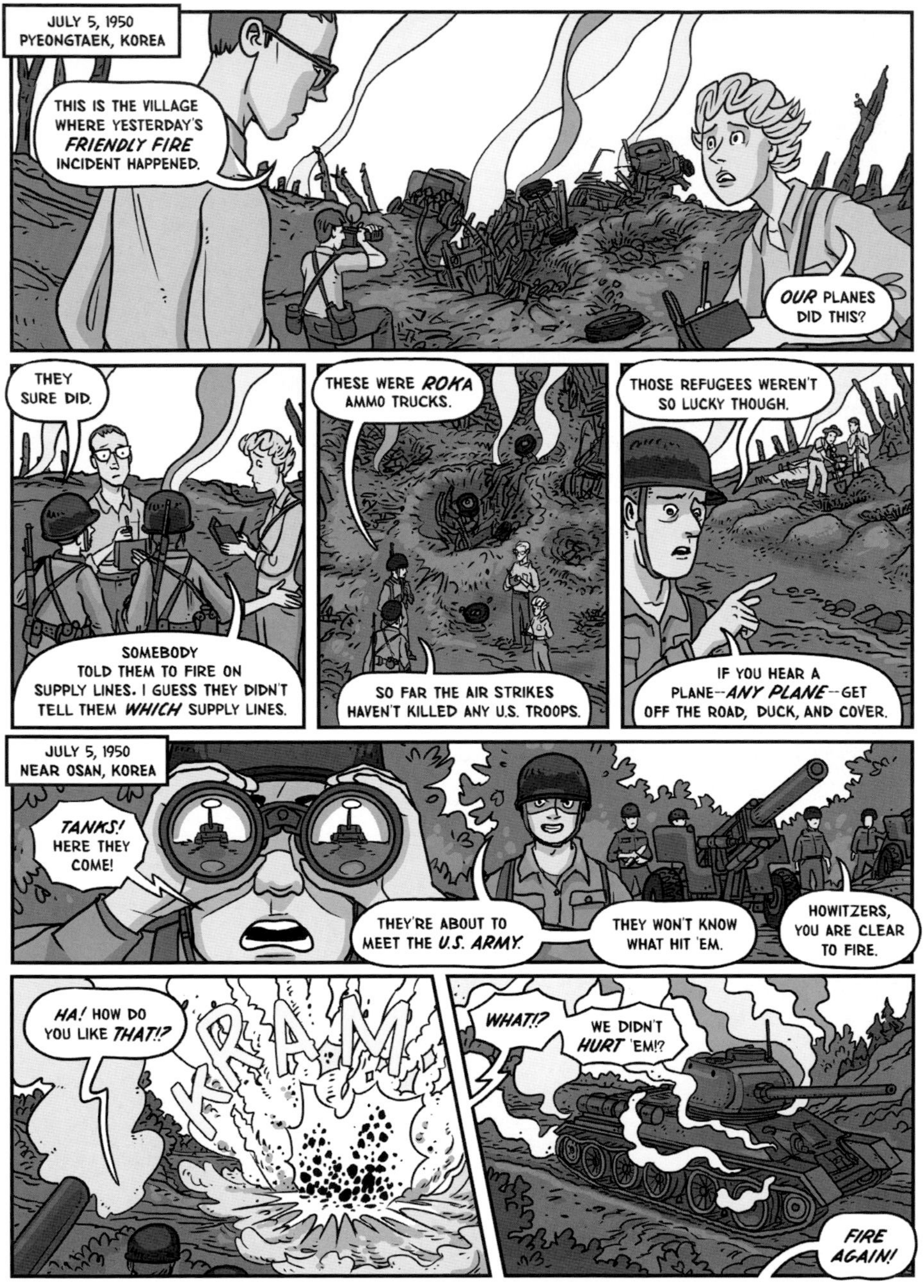
JULY 5, 1950
PYEONGTAEK, KOREA
THIS IS THE VILLAGE WHERE YESTERDAY'S FRIENDLY FIRE INCIDENT HAPPENED.
OUR PLANES DID THIS?
THEY SURE DID.
SOMEBODY TOLD THEM TO FIRE ON SUPPLY LINES. I GUESS THEY DIDN'T TELL THEM WHICH SUPPLY LINES.
THESE WERE ROKA AMMO TRUCKS.
SO FAR THE AIR STRIKES HAVEN'T KILLED ANY U.S. TROOPS.
THOSE REFUGEES WEREN'T SO LUCKY THOUGH.
IF YOU HEAR A PLANE--ANY PLANE--GET OFF THE ROAD, DUCK, AND COVER.
JULY 5, 1950
NEAR OSAN, KOREA
TANKS! HERE THEY COME!
THEY'RE ABOUT TO MEET THE U.S. ARMY.
THEY WON'T KNOW WHAT HIT 'EM.
HOWITZERS, YOU ARE CLEAR TO FIRE.
HA! HOW DO YOU LIKE THAT!?
KRAM
WHAT!?
WE DIDN'T HURT 'EM!?
FIRE AGAIN!

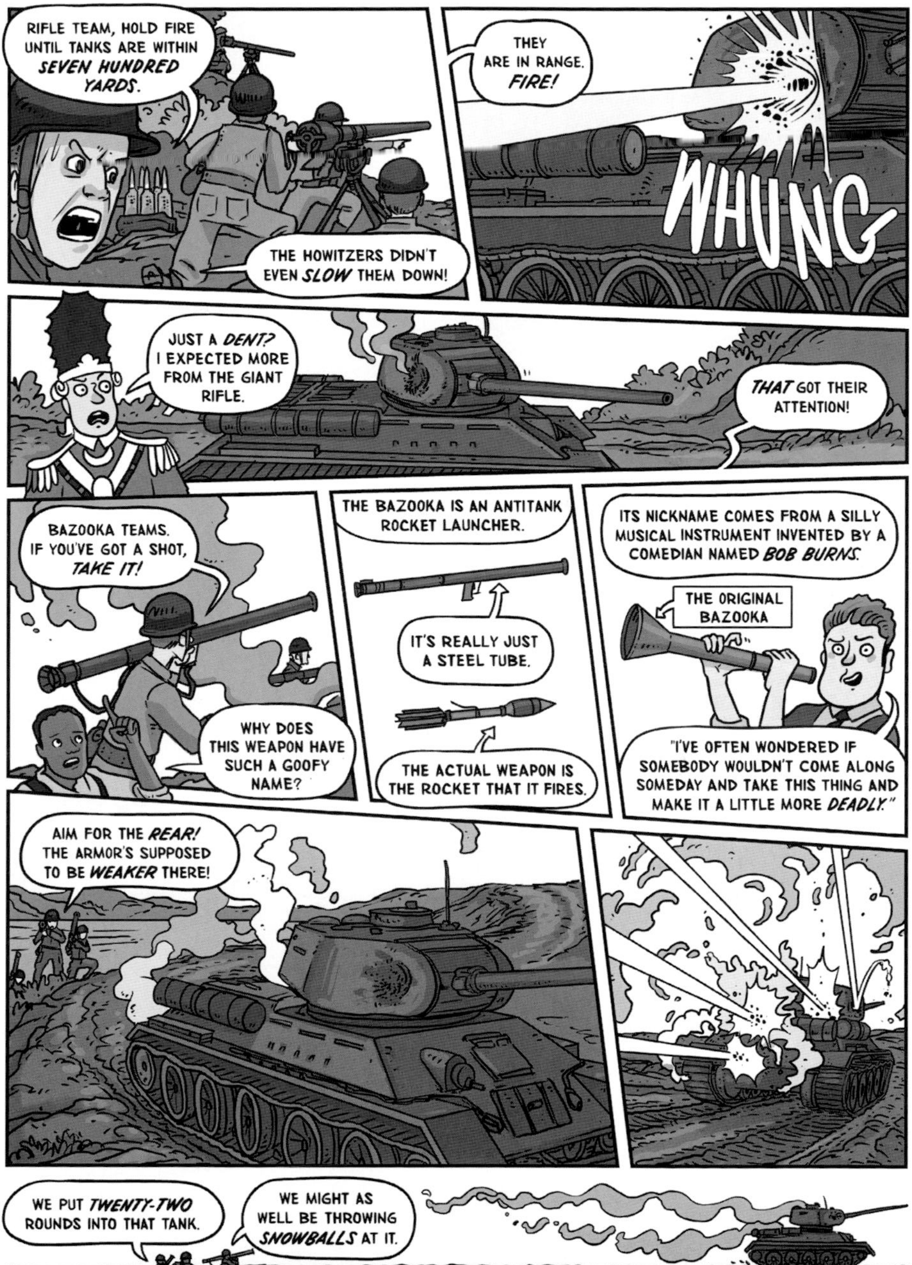
RIFLE TEAM, HOLD FIRE UNTIL TANKS ARE WITHIN SEVEN HUNDRED YARDS.
THE HOWITZERS DIDN'T EVEN SLOW THEM DOWN!
THEY ARE IN RANGE. FIRE!
WHUNG
JUST A DENT? I EXPECTED MORE FROM THE GIANT RIFLE.
THAT GOT THEIR ATTENTION!
BAZOOKA TEAMS. IF YOU'VE GOT A SHOT, TAKE IT!
WHY DOES THIS WEAPON HAVE SUCH A GOOFY NAME?
THE BAZOOKA IS AN ANTITANK ROCKET LAUNCHER.
IT'S REALLY JUST A STEEL TUBE.
THE ACTUAL WEAPON IS THE ROCKET THAT IT FIRES.
ITS NICKNAME COMES FROM A SILLY MUSICAL INSTRUMENT INVENTED BY A COMEDIAN NAMED BOB BURNS.
THE ORIGINAL BAZOOKA
"I'VE OFTEN WONDERED IF SOMEBODY WOULDN'T COME ALONG SOMEDAY AND TAKE THIS THING AND MAKE IT A LITTLE MORE DEADLY."
AIM FOR THE REAR! THE ARMOR'S SUPPOSED TO BE WEAKER THERE!
WE PUT TWENTY-TWO ROUNDS INTO THAT TANK.
WE MIGHT AS WELL BE THROWING SNOWBALLS AT IT.

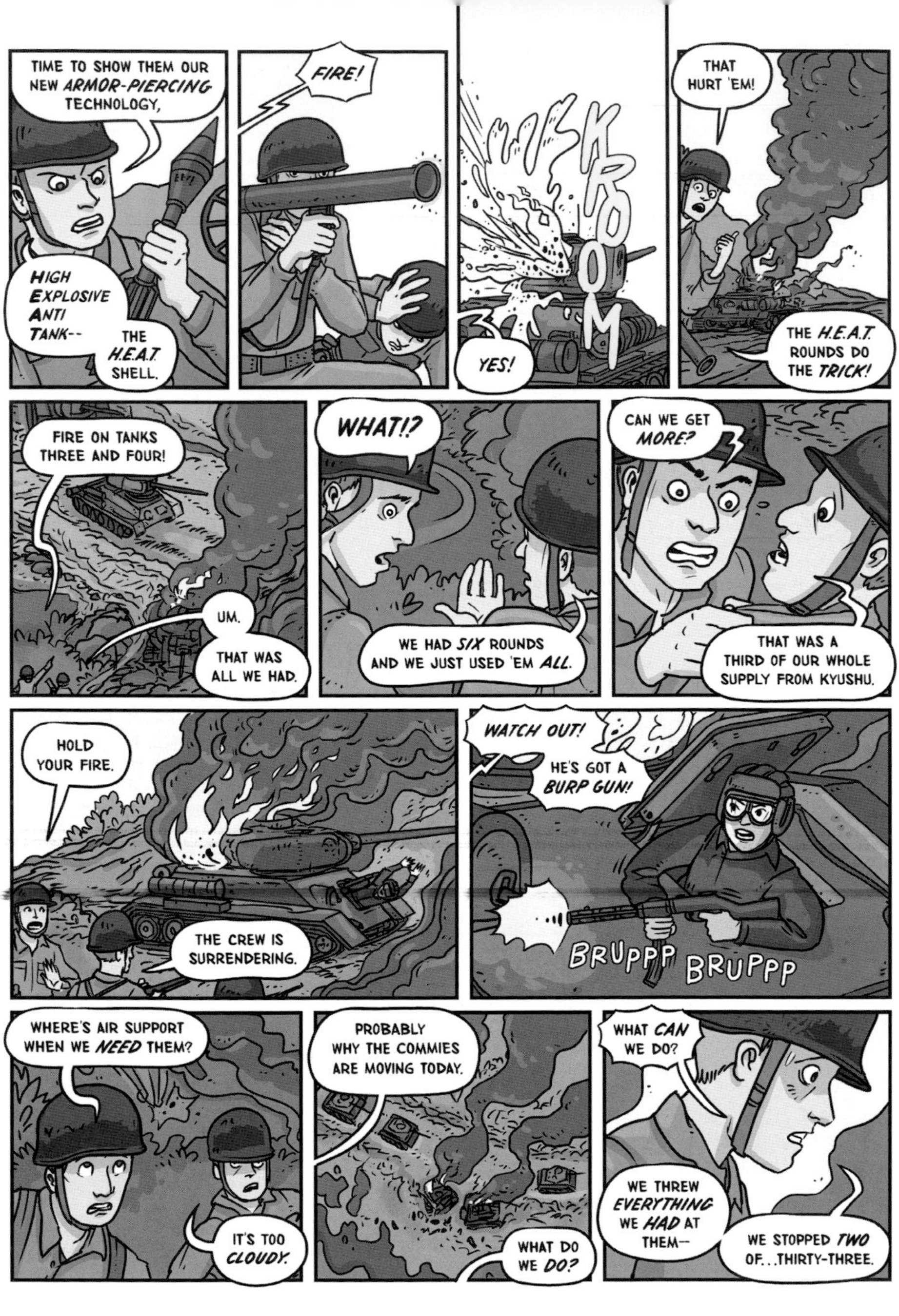
TIME TO SHOW THEM OUR NEW *ARMOR-PIERCING* TECHNOLOGY,
HIGH **E**XPLOSIVE **A**NTI **T**ANK--
THE *H.E.A.T.* SHELL.
FIRE!
KROOM
YES!
THAT HURT 'EM!
THE *H.E.A.T.* ROUNDS DO THE *TRICK!*
FIRE ON TANKS THREE AND FOUR!
UM.
THAT WAS ALL WE HAD.
WHAT!?
WE HAD *SIX* ROUNDS AND WE JUST USED 'EM *ALL.*
CAN WE GET *MORE?*
THAT WAS A THIRD OF OUR WHOLE SUPPLY FROM KYUSHU.
HOLD YOUR FIRE.
THE CREW IS SURRENDERING.
WATCH OUT!
HE'S GOT A *BURP GUN!*
BRUPPP BRUPPP
WHERE'S AIR SUPPORT WHEN WE *NEED* THEM?
IT'S TOO *CLOUDY.*
PROBABLY WHY THE COMMIES ARE MOVING TODAY.
WHAT DO WE *DO?*
WHAT *CAN* WE DO?
WE THREW *EVERYTHING* WE *HAD* AT THEM--
WE STOPPED *TWO* OF. . .THIRTY-THREE.

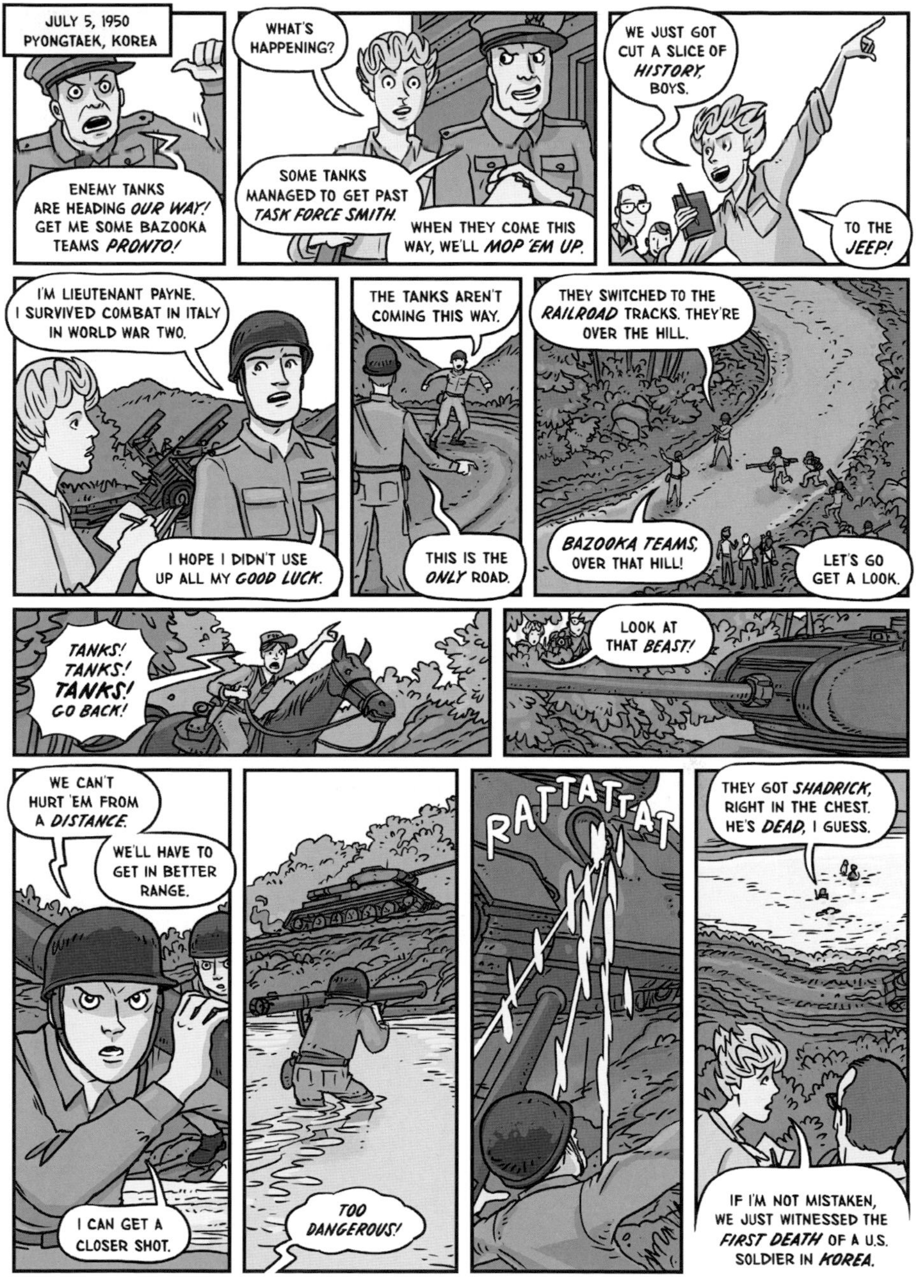
JULY 5, 1950
PYONGTAEK, KOREA
ENEMY TANKS ARE HEADING OUR WAY! GET ME SOME BAZOOKA TEAMS PRONTO!
WHAT'S HAPPENING?
SOME TANKS MANAGED TO GET PAST TASK FORCE SMITH.
WHEN THEY COME THIS WAY, WE'LL MOP 'EM UP.
WE JUST GOT CUT A SLICE OF HISTORY, BOYS.
TO THE JEEP!
I'M LIEUTENANT PAYNE. I SURVIVED COMBAT IN ITALY IN WORLD WAR TWO.
I HOPE I DIDN'T USE UP ALL MY GOOD LUCK.
THE TANKS AREN'T COMING THIS WAY.
THIS IS THE ONLY ROAD.
THEY SWITCHED TO THE RAILROAD TRACKS. THEY'RE OVER THE HILL.
BAZOOKA TEAMS, OVER THAT HILL!
LET'S GO GET A LOOK.
TANKS! TANKS! TANKS! GO BACK!
LOOK AT THAT BEAST!
WE CAN'T HURT 'EM FROM A DISTANCE.
WE'LL HAVE TO GET IN BETTER RANGE.
I CAN GET A CLOSER SHOT.
TOO DANGEROUS!
RATTATTAT
THEY GOT SHADRICK, RIGHT IN THE CHEST. HE'S DEAD, I GUESS.
IF I'M NOT MISTAKEN, WE JUST WITNESSED THE FIRST DEATH OF A U.S. SOLDIER IN KOREA.

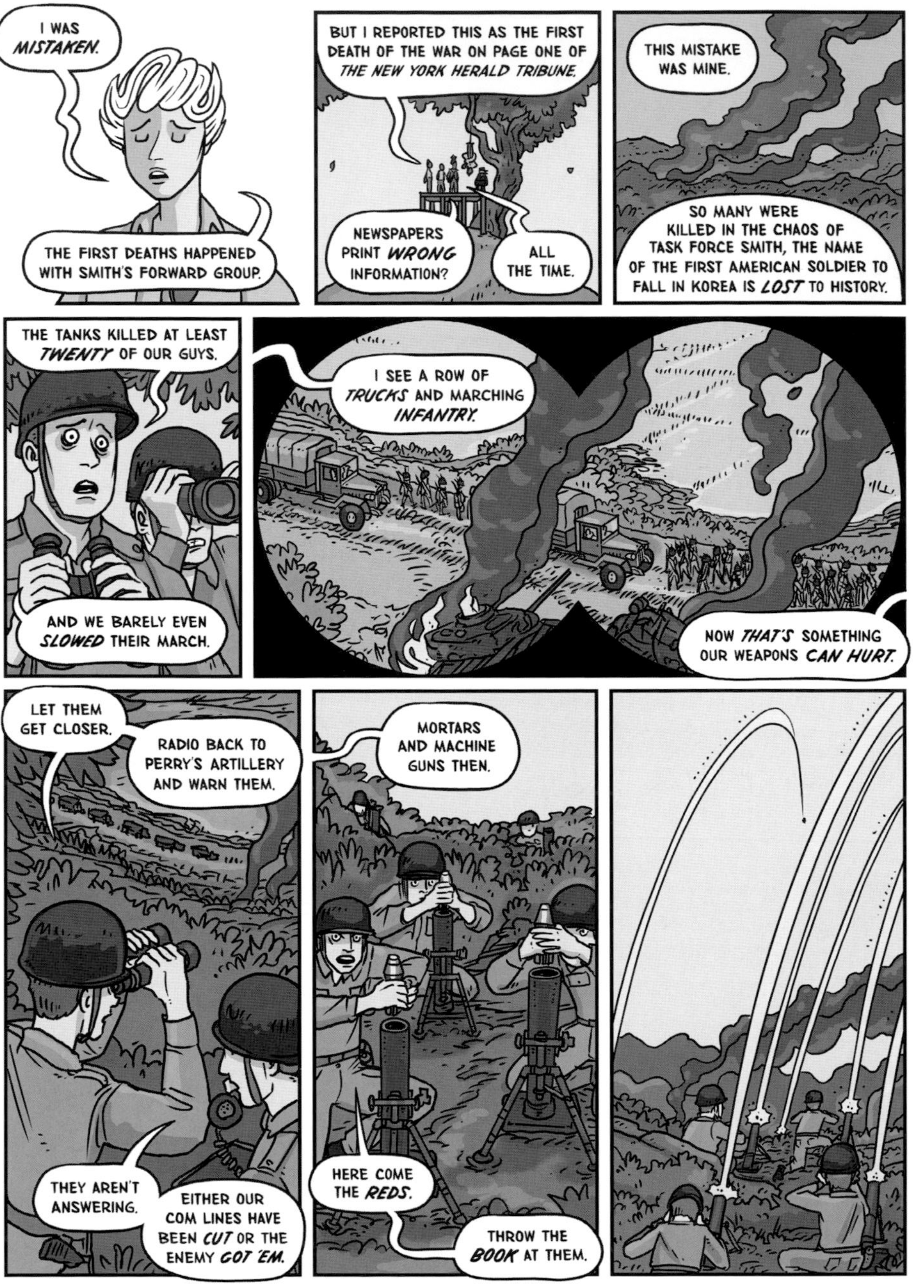
I WAS *MISTAKEN.*
THE FIRST DEATHS HAPPENED WITH SMITH'S FORWARD GROUP.
BUT I REPORTED THIS AS THE FIRST DEATH OF THE WAR ON PAGE ONE OF *THE NEW YORK HERALD TRIBUNE.*
NEWSPAPERS PRINT *WRONG* INFORMATION?
ALL THE TIME.
THIS MISTAKE WAS MINE.
SO MANY WERE KILLED IN THE CHAOS OF TASK FORCE SMITH, THE NAME OF THE FIRST AMERICAN SOLDIER TO FALL IN KOREA IS *LOST* TO HISTORY.
THE TANKS KILLED AT LEAST *TWENTY* OF OUR GUYS.
AND WE BARELY EVEN *SLOWED* THEIR MARCH.
I SEE A ROW OF *TRUCKS* AND MARCHING *INFANTRY.*
NOW *THAT'S* SOMETHING OUR WEAPONS *CAN HURT.*
LET THEM GET CLOSER.
RADIO BACK TO PERRY'S ARTILLERY AND WARN THEM.
THEY AREN'T ANSWERING.
EITHER OUR COM LINES HAVE BEEN *CUT* OR THE ENEMY *GOT 'EM.*
MORTARS AND MACHINE GUNS THEN.
HERE COME THE *REDS.*
THROW THE *BOOK* AT THEM.

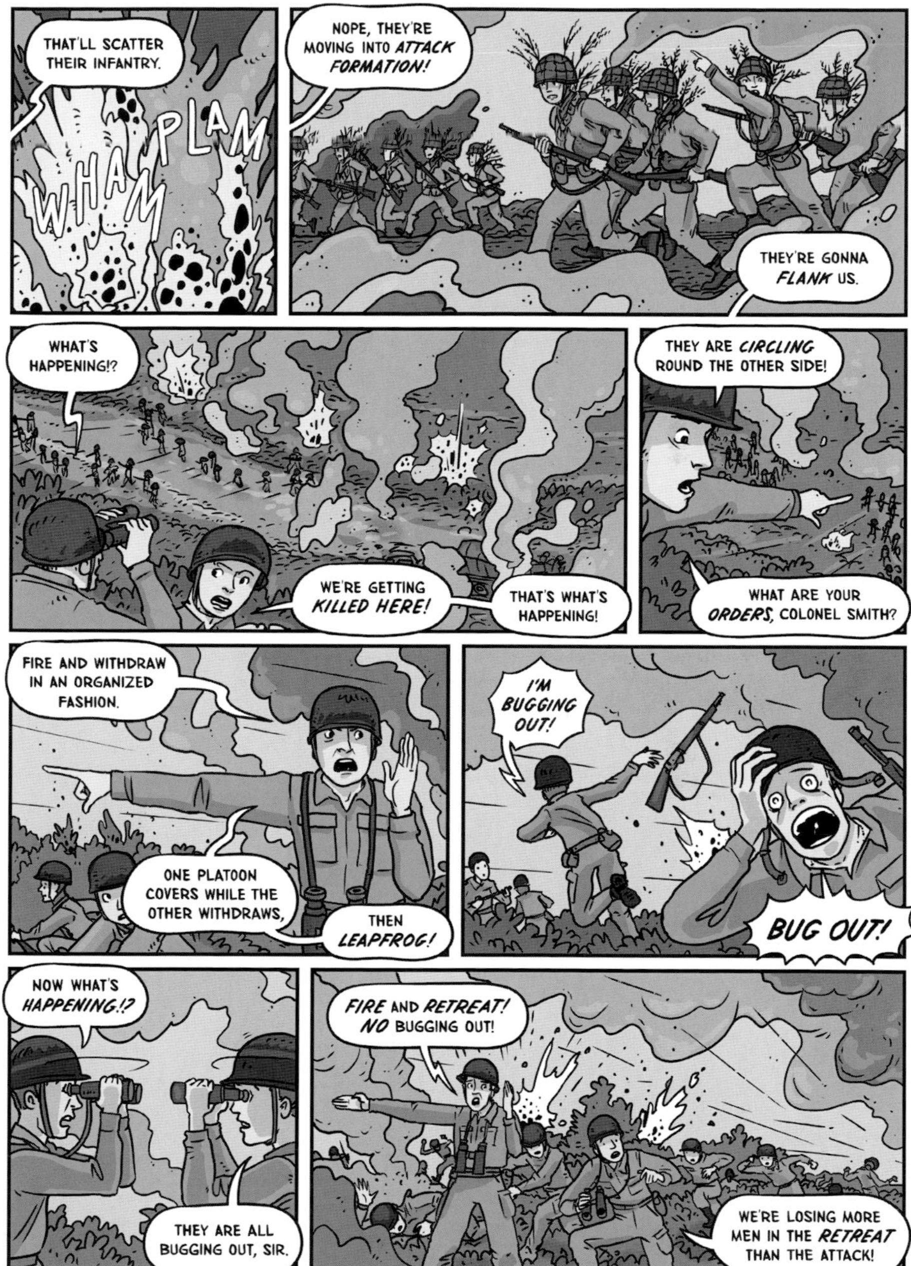
THAT'LL SCATTER THEIR INFANTRY.
WHAM PLAM
NOPE, THEY'RE MOVING INTO ATTACK FORMATION!
THEY'RE GONNA FLANK US.
WHAT'S HAPPENING!?
WE'RE GETTING KILLED HERE!
THAT'S WHAT'S HAPPENING!
THEY ARE CIRCLING ROUND THE OTHER SIDE!
WHAT ARE YOUR ORDERS, COLONEL SMITH?
FIRE AND WITHDRAW IN AN ORGANIZED FASHION.
ONE PLATOON COVERS WHILE THE OTHER WITHDRAWS,
THEN LEAPFROG!
I'M BUGGING OUT!
BUG OUT!
NOW WHAT'S HAPPENING!?
THEY ARE ALL BUGGING OUT, SIR.
FIRE AND RETREAT! NO BUGGING OUT!
WE'RE LOSING MORE MEN IN THE RETREAT THAN THE ATTACK!

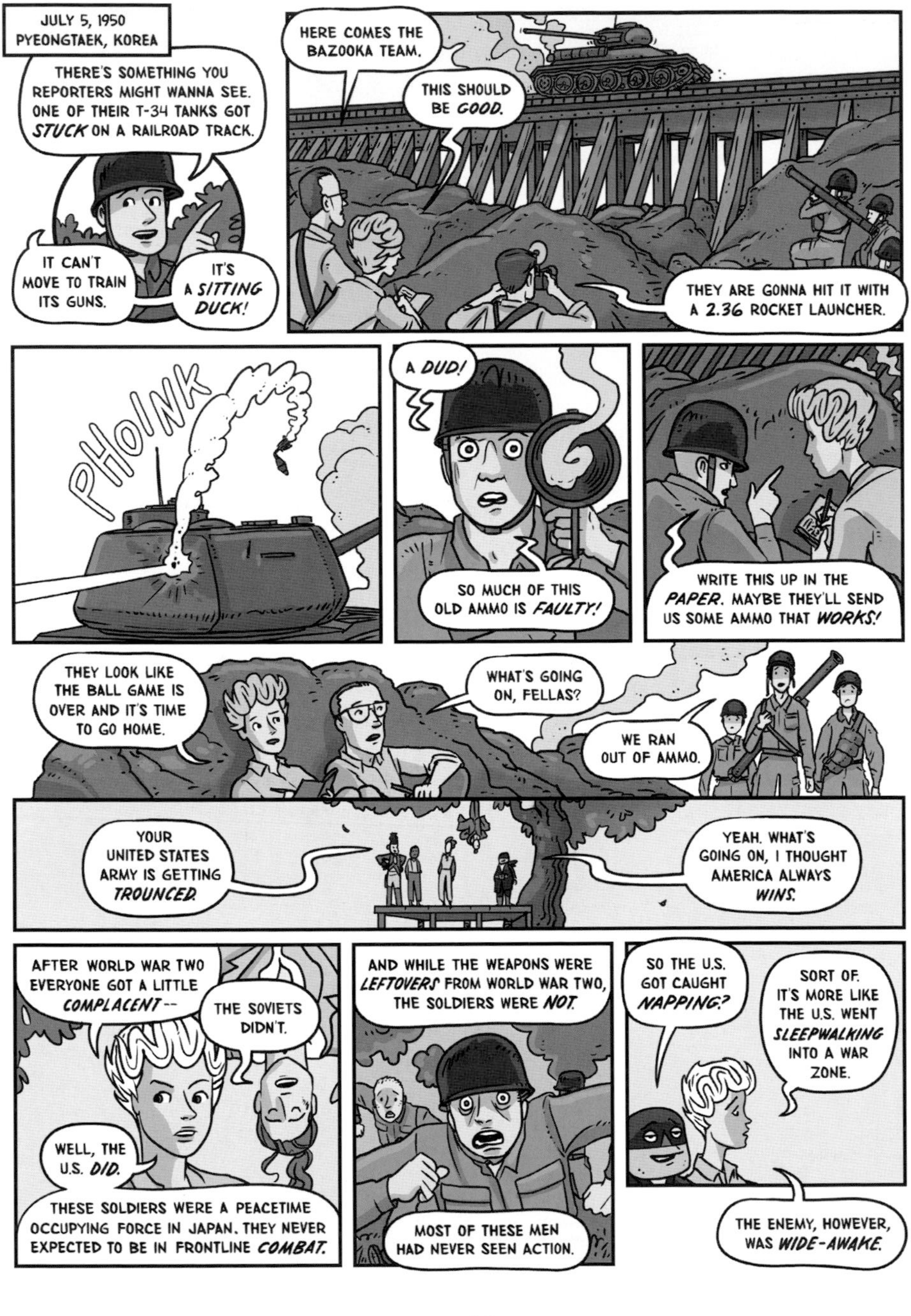
JULY 5, 1950
PYEONGTAEK, KOREA
THERE'S SOMETHING YOU REPORTERS MIGHT WANNA SEE. ONE OF THEIR T-34 TANKS GOT STUCK ON A RAILROAD TRACK.
IT CAN'T MOVE TO TRAIN ITS GUNS.
IT'S A SITTING DUCK!
HERE COMES THE BAZOOKA TEAM.
THIS SHOULD BE GOOD.
THEY ARE GONNA HIT IT WITH A 2.36 ROCKET LAUNCHER.
PHOINK
A DUD!
SO MUCH OF THIS OLD AMMO IS FAULTY!
WRITE THIS UP IN THE PAPER. MAYBE THEY'LL SEND US SOME AMMO THAT WORKS!
THEY LOOK LIKE THE BALL GAME IS OVER AND IT'S TIME TO GO HOME.
WHAT'S GOING ON, FELLAS?
WE RAN OUT OF AMMO.
YOUR UNITED STATES ARMY IS GETTING TROUNCED.
YEAH. WHAT'S GOING ON, I THOUGHT AMERICA ALWAYS WINS.
AFTER WORLD WAR TWO EVERYONE GOT A LITTLE COMPLACENT--
THE SOVIETS DIDN'T.
WELL, THE U.S. DID.
THESE SOLDIERS WERE A PEACETIME OCCUPYING FORCE IN JAPAN. THEY NEVER EXPECTED TO BE IN FRONTLINE COMBAT.
AND WHILE THE WEAPONS WERE LEFTOVERS FROM WORLD WAR TWO, THE SOLDIERS WERE NOT.
MOST OF THESE MEN HAD NEVER SEEN ACTION.
SO THE U.S. GOT CAUGHT NAPPING?
SORT OF. IT'S MORE LIKE THE U.S. WENT SLEEPWALKING INTO A WAR ZONE.
THE ENEMY, HOWEVER, WAS WIDE-AWAKE.

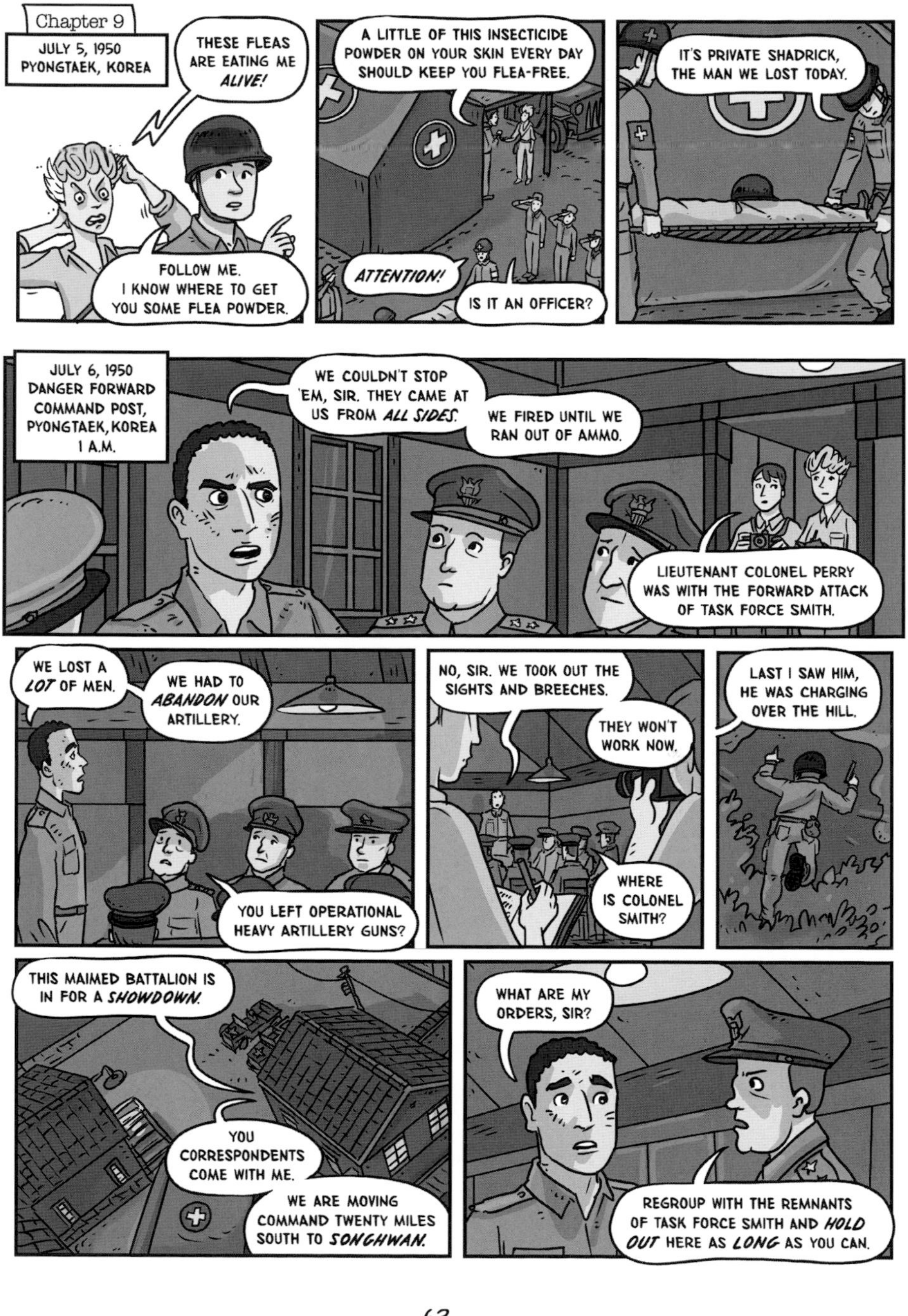
Chapter 9
JULY 5, 1950 PYONGTAEK, KOREA
THESE FLEAS ARE EATING ME *ALIVE!*
FOLLOW ME. I KNOW WHERE TO GET YOU SOME FLEA POWDER.
A LITTLE OF THIS INSECTICIDE POWDER ON YOUR SKIN EVERY DAY SHOULD KEEP YOU FLEA-FREE.
ATTENTION!
IS IT AN OFFICER?
IT'S PRIVATE SHADRICK, THE MAN WE LOST TODAY.
JULY 6, 1950 DANGER FORWARD COMMAND POST, PYONGTAEK, KOREA 1 A.M.
WE COULDN'T STOP 'EM, SIR. THEY CAME AT US FROM *ALL SIDES.*
WE FIRED UNTIL WE RAN OUT OF AMMO.
LIEUTENANT COLONEL PERRY WAS WITH THE FORWARD ATTACK OF TASK FORCE SMITH.
WE LOST A *LOT* OF MEN.
WE HAD TO *ABANDON* OUR ARTILLERY.
YOU LEFT OPERATIONAL HEAVY ARTILLERY GUNS?
NO, SIR. WE TOOK OUT THE SIGHTS AND BREECHES.
THEY WON'T WORK NOW.
WHERE IS COLONEL SMITH?
LAST I SAW HIM, HE WAS CHARGING OVER THE HILL.
THIS MAIMED BATTALION IS IN FOR A *SHOWDOWN.*
YOU CORRESPONDENTS COME WITH ME.
WE ARE MOVING COMMAND TWENTY MILES SOUTH TO *SONGHWAN.*
WHAT ARE MY ORDERS, SIR?
REGROUP WITH THE REMNANTS OF TASK FORCE SMITH AND *HOLD OUT* HERE AS *LONG* AS YOU CAN.

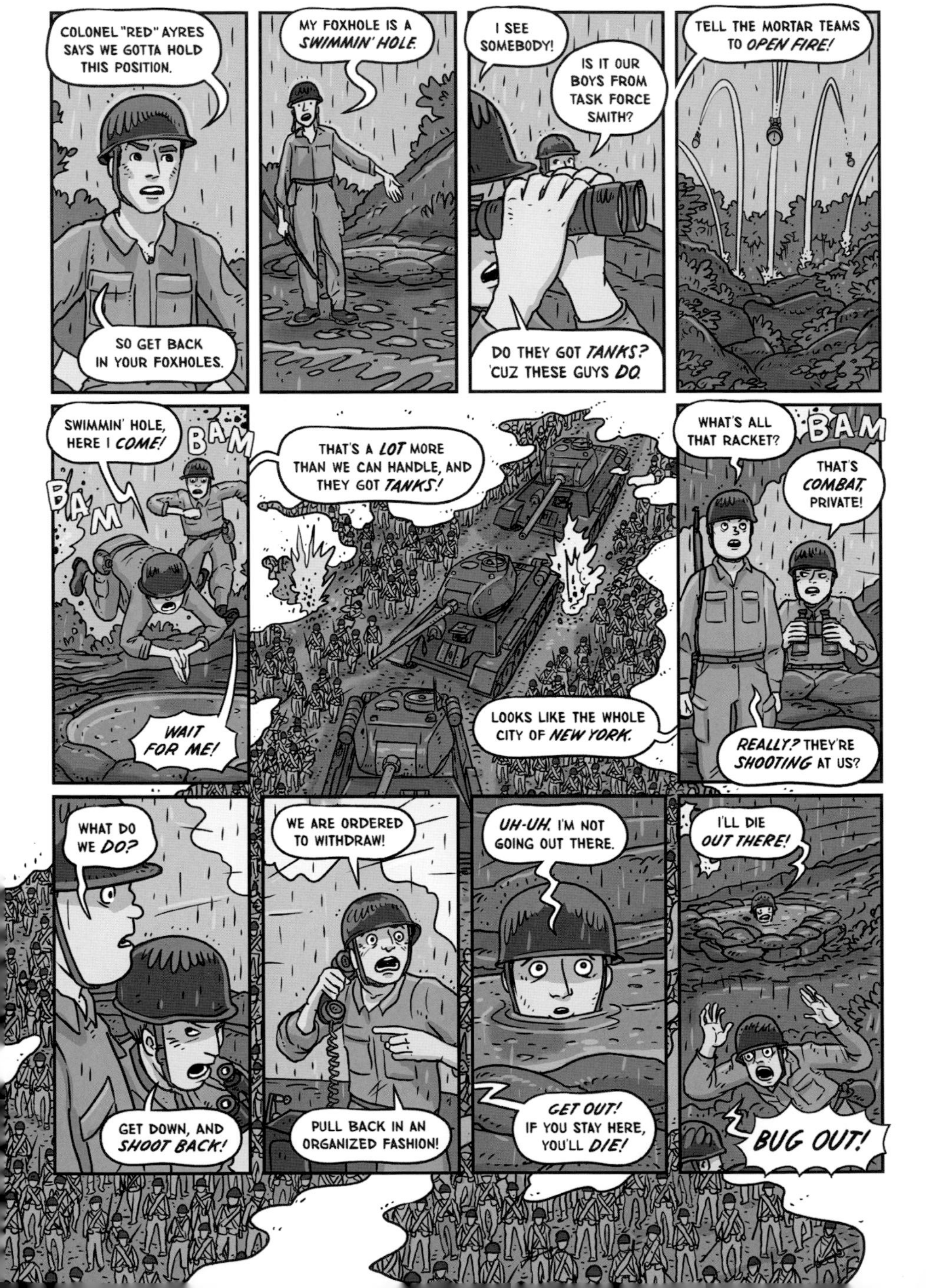
COLONEL "RED" AYRES SAYS WE GOTTA HOLD THIS POSITION.
SO GET BACK IN YOUR FOXHOLES.
MY FOXHOLE IS A SWIMMIN' HOLE.
I SEE SOMEBODY!
IS IT OUR BOYS FROM TASK FORCE SMITH?
DO THEY GOT TANKS? 'CUZ THESE GUYS DO.
TELL THE MORTAR TEAMS TO OPEN FIRE!
SWIMMIN' HOLE, HERE I COME!
BAM
BAM
WAIT FOR ME!
THAT'S A LOT MORE THAN WE CAN HANDLE, AND THEY GOT TANKS!
LOOKS LIKE THE WHOLE CITY OF NEW YORK.
WHAT'S ALL THAT RACKET?
BAM
THAT'S COMBAT, PRIVATE!
REALLY? THEY'RE SHOOTING AT US?
WHAT DO WE DO?
GET DOWN, AND SHOOT BACK!
WE ARE ORDERED TO WITHDRAW!
PULL BACK IN AN ORGANIZED FASHION!
UH-UH. I'M NOT GOING OUT THERE.
GET OUT! IF YOU STAY HERE, YOU'LL DIE!
I'LL DIE OUT THERE!
BUG OUT!

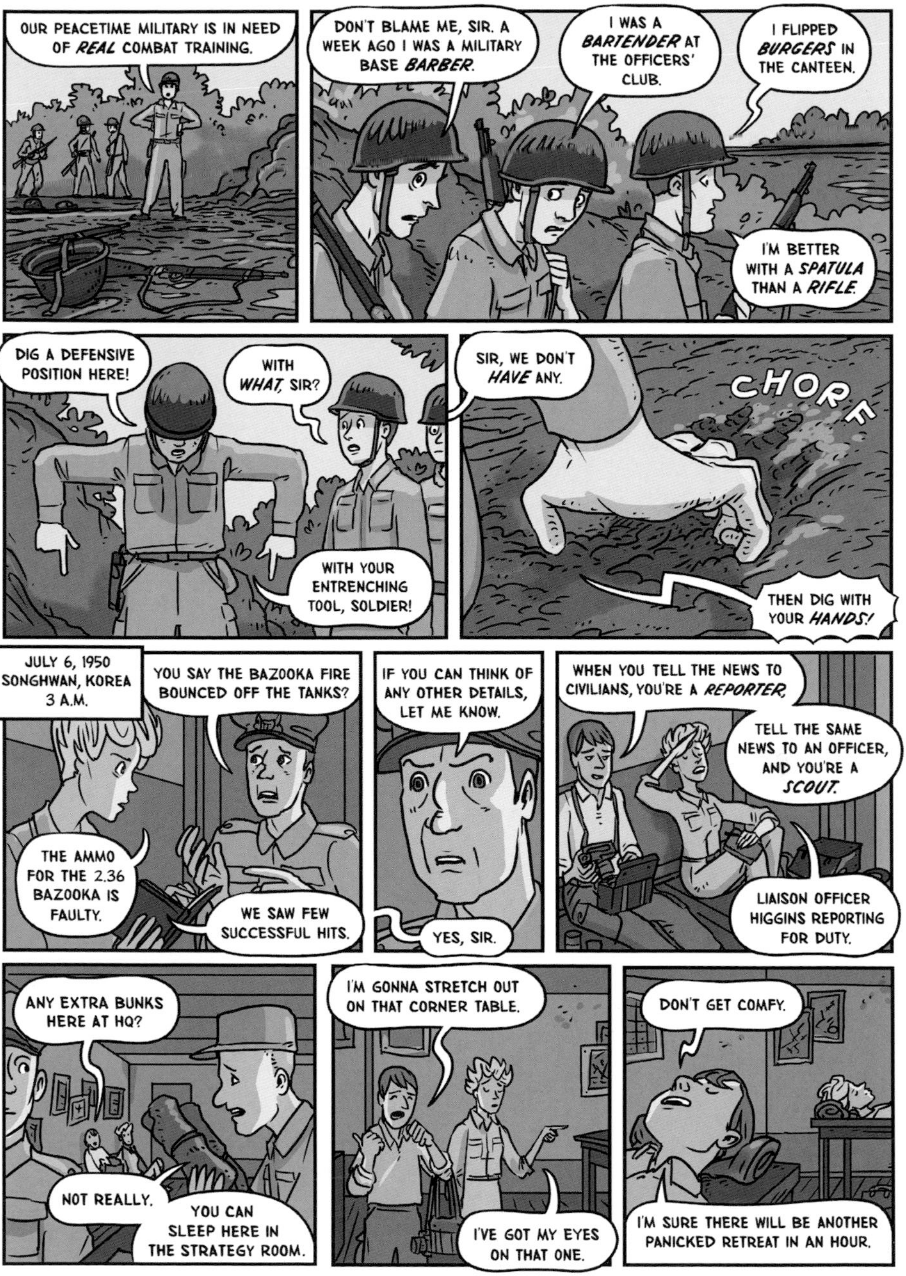
OUR PEACETIME MILITARY IS IN NEED OF *REAL* COMBAT TRAINING.
DON'T BLAME ME, SIR. A WEEK AGO I WAS A MILITARY BASE *BARBER*.
I WAS A *BARTENDER* AT THE OFFICERS' CLUB.
I FLIPPED *BURGERS* IN THE CANTEEN.
I'M BETTER WITH A *SPATULA* THAN A *RIFLE*.
DIG A DEFENSIVE POSITION HERE!
WITH *WHAT*, SIR?
WITH YOUR ENTRENCHING TOOL, SOLDIER!
SIR, WE DON'T *HAVE* ANY.
CHORF
THEN DIG WITH YOUR *HANDS!*
JULY 6, 1950 SONGHWAN, KOREA 3 A.M.
YOU SAY THE BAZOOKA FIRE BOUNCED OFF THE TANKS?
THE AMMO FOR THE 2.36 BAZOOKA IS FAULTY.
WE SAW FEW SUCCESSFUL HITS.
IF YOU CAN THINK OF ANY OTHER DETAILS, LET ME KNOW.
YES, SIR.
WHEN YOU TELL THE NEWS TO CIVILIANS, YOU'RE A *REPORTER*.
TELL THE SAME NEWS TO AN OFFICER, AND YOU'RE A *SCOUT*.
LIAISON OFFICER HIGGINS REPORTING FOR DUTY.
ANY EXTRA BUNKS HERE AT HQ?
NOT REALLY.
YOU CAN SLEEP HERE IN THE STRATEGY ROOM.
I'M GONNA STRETCH OUT ON THAT CORNER TABLE.
I'VE GOT MY EYES ON THAT ONE.
DON'T GET COMFY.
I'M SURE THERE WILL BE ANOTHER PANICKED RETREAT IN AN HOUR.

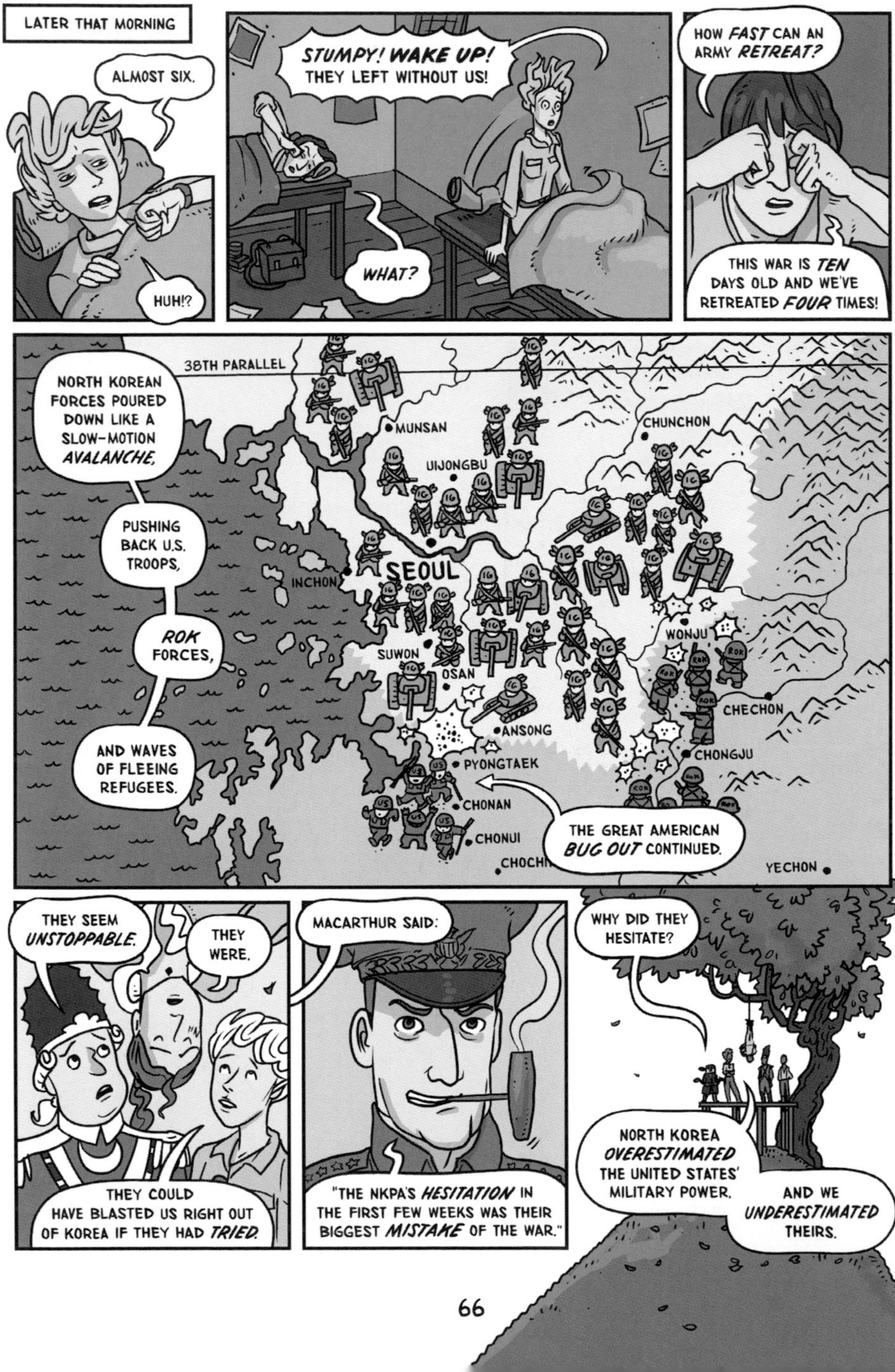
LATER THAT MORNING
ALMOST SIX.
HUH!?
STUMPY! WAKE UP! THEY LEFT WITHOUT US!
WHAT?
HOW FAST CAN AN ARMY RETREAT?
THIS WAR IS TEN DAYS OLD AND WE'VE RETREATED FOUR TIMES!
38TH PARALLEL
NORTH KOREAN FORCES POURED DOWN LIKE A SLOW-MOTION AVALANCHE,
PUSHING BACK U.S. TROOPS,
ROK FORCES,
AND WAVES OF FLEEING REFUGEES.
MUNSAN
UIJONGBU
CHUNCHON
SEOUL
INCHON
WONJU
SUWON
OSAN
CHECHON
ANSONG
CHONGJU
PYONGTAEK
CHONAN
CHONUI
YECHON
THE GREAT AMERICAN BUG OUT CONTINUED.
THEY SEEM UNSTOPPABLE.
THEY WERE.
THEY COULD HAVE BLASTED US RIGHT OUT OF KOREA IF THEY HAD TRIED.
MACARTHUR SAID:
"THE NKPA'S HESITATION IN THE FIRST FEW WEEKS WAS THEIR BIGGEST MISTAKE OF THE WAR."
WHY DID THEY HESITATE?
NORTH KOREA OVERESTIMATED THE UNITED STATES' MILITARY POWER.
AND WE UNDERESTIMATED THEIRS.

Chapter 10

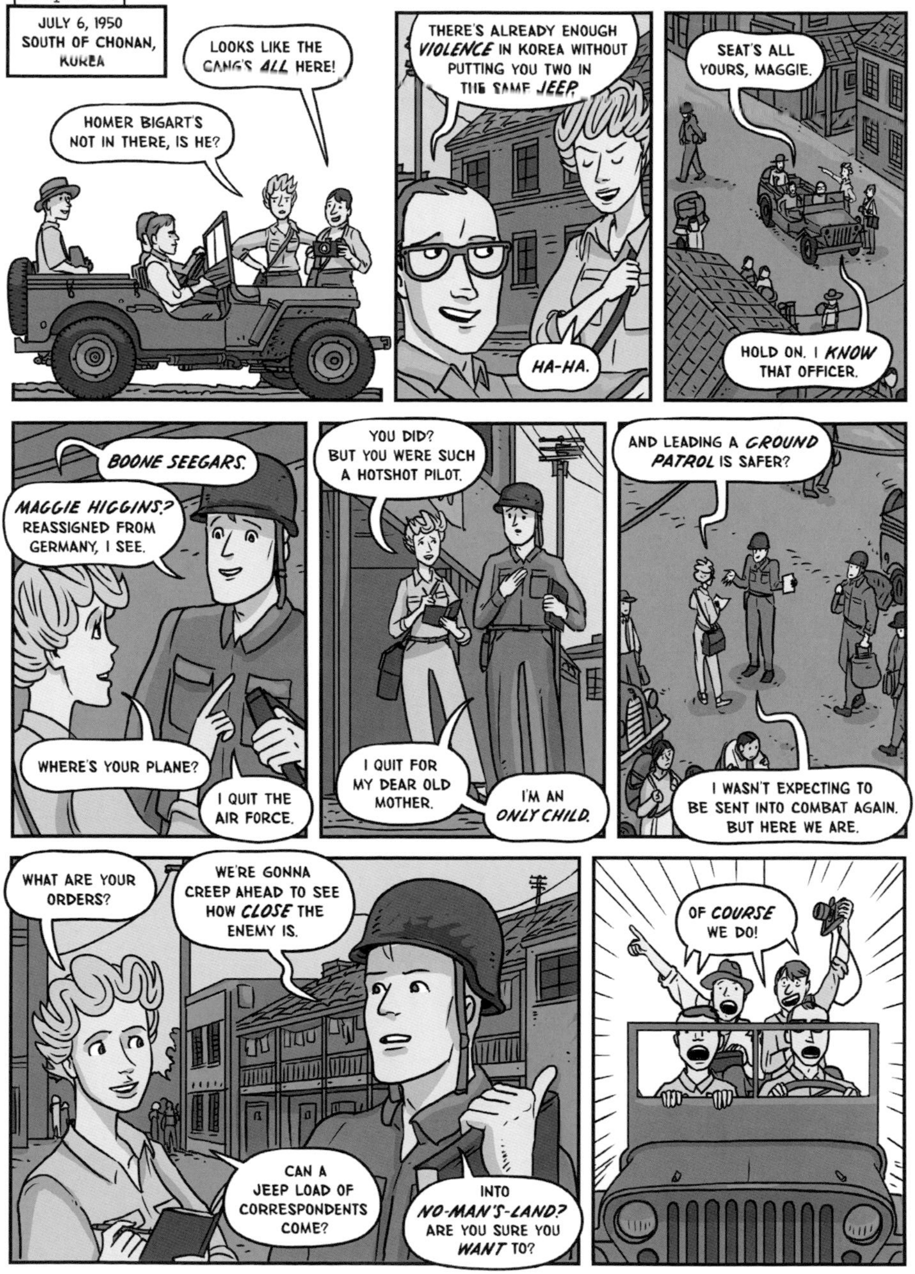

JULY 6, 1950
SOUTH OF CHONAN, KOREA
LOOKS LIKE THE GANG'S ALL HERE!
HOMER BIGART'S NOT IN THERE, IS HE?
THERE'S ALREADY ENOUGH VIOLENCE IN KOREA WITHOUT PUTTING YOU TWO IN THE SAME JEEP.
HA-HA.
SEAT'S ALL YOURS, MAGGIE.
HOLD ON. I KNOW THAT OFFICER.
BOONE SEEGARS.
MAGGIE HIGGINS? REASSIGNED FROM GERMANY, I SEE.
WHERE'S YOUR PLANE?
I QUIT THE AIR FORCE.
YOU DID? BUT YOU WERE SUCH A HOTSHOT PILOT.
I QUIT FOR MY DEAR OLD MOTHER.
I'M AN ONLY CHILD.
AND LEADING A GROUND PATROL IS SAFER?
I WASN'T EXPECTING TO BE SENT INTO COMBAT AGAIN. BUT HERE WE ARE.
WHAT ARE YOUR ORDERS?
WE'RE GONNA CREEP AHEAD TO SEE HOW CLOSE THE ENEMY IS.
CAN A JEEP LOAD OF CORRESPONDENTS COME?
INTO NO-MAN'S-LAND? ARE YOU SURE YOU WANT TO?
OF COURSE WE DO!

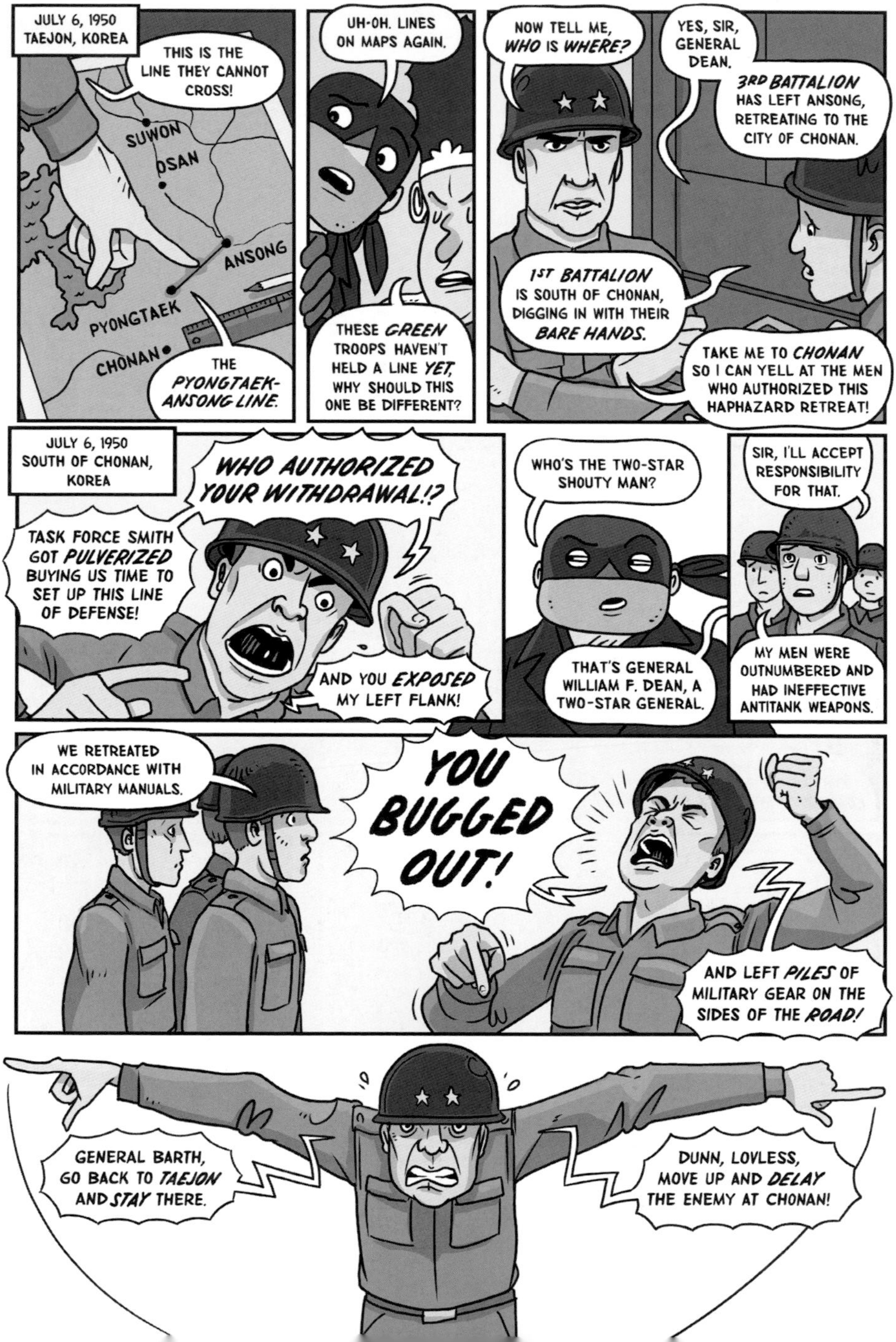
JULY 6, 1950
TAEJON, KOREA
THIS IS THE LINE THEY CANNOT CROSS!
SUWON
OSAN
ANSONG
PYONGTAEK
CHONAN
THE PYONGTAEK-ANSONG LINE.
UH-OH. LINES ON MAPS AGAIN.
THESE GREEN TROOPS HAVEN'T HELD A LINE YET, WHY SHOULD THIS ONE BE DIFFERENT?
NOW TELL ME, WHO IS WHERE?
YES, SIR, GENERAL DEAN.
3RD BATTALION HAS LEFT ANSONG, RETREATING TO THE CITY OF CHONAN.
1ST BATTALION IS SOUTH OF CHONAN, DIGGING IN WITH THEIR BARE HANDS.
TAKE ME TO CHONAN SO I CAN YELL AT THE MEN WHO AUTHORIZED THIS HAPHAZARD RETREAT!
JULY 6, 1950
SOUTH OF CHONAN, KOREA
WHO AUTHORIZED YOUR WITHDRAWAL!?
TASK FORCE SMITH GOT PULVERIZED BUYING US TIME TO SET UP THIS LINE OF DEFENSE!
AND YOU EXPOSED MY LEFT FLANK!
WHO'S THE TWO-STAR SHOUTY MAN?
THAT'S GENERAL WILLIAM F. DEAN, A TWO-STAR GENERAL.
SIR, I'LL ACCEPT RESPONSIBILITY FOR THAT.
MY MEN WERE OUTNUMBERED AND HAD INEFFECTIVE ANTITANK WEAPONS.
WE RETREATED IN ACCORDANCE WITH MILITARY MANUALS.
YOU BUGGED OUT!
AND LEFT PILES OF MILITARY GEAR ON THE SIDES OF THE ROAD!
GENERAL BARTH, GO BACK TO TAEJON AND STAY THERE.
DUNN, LOVLESS, MOVE UP AND DELAY THE ENEMY AT CHONAN!

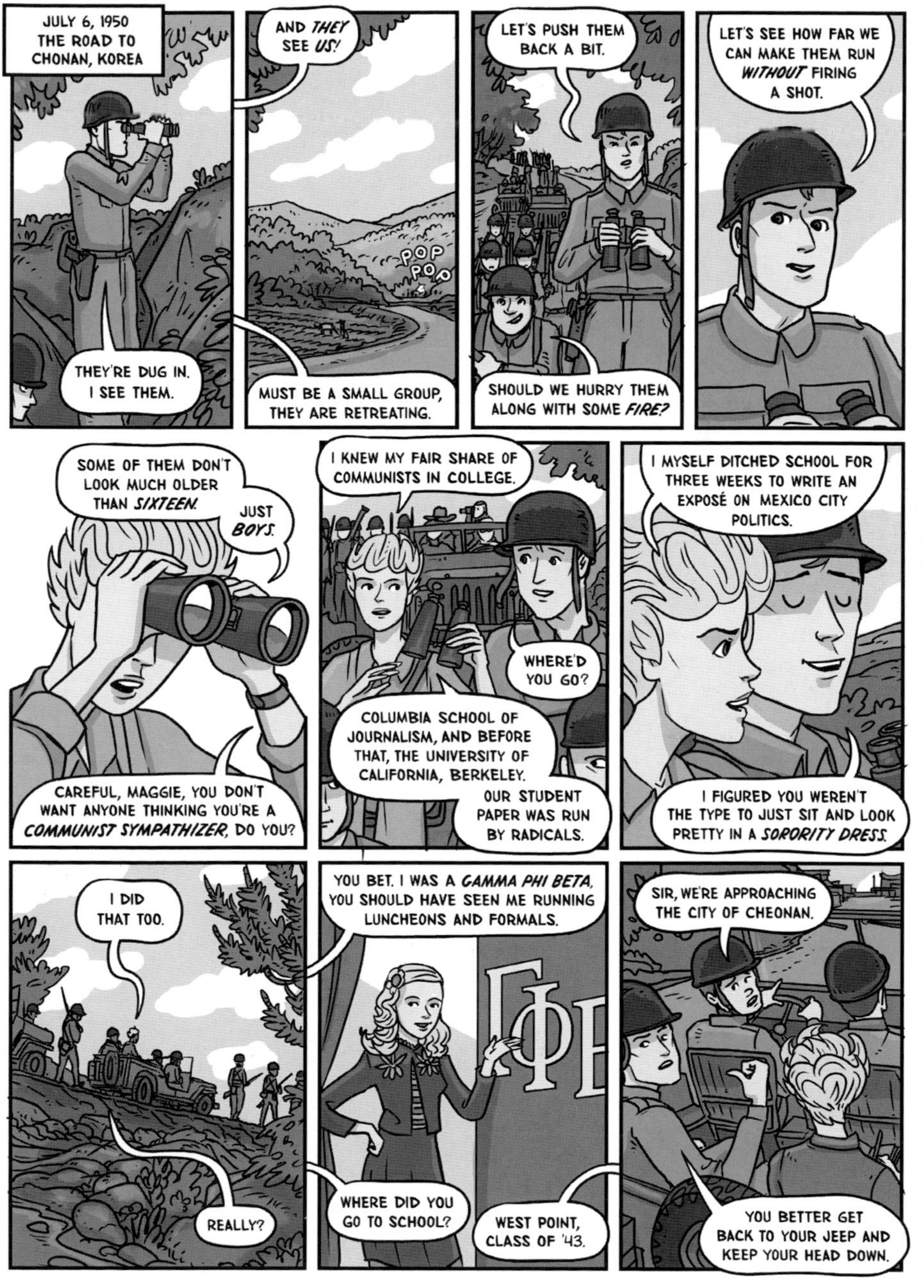
JULY 6, 1950 THE ROAD TO CHONAN, KOREA
THEY'RE DUG IN. I SEE THEM.
AND *THEY* SEE *US!*
POP POP
MUST BE A SMALL GROUP, THEY ARE RETREATING.
LET'S PUSH THEM BACK A BIT.
SHOULD WE HURRY THEM ALONG WITH SOME *FIRE?*
LET'S SEE HOW FAR WE CAN MAKE THEM RUN *WITHOUT* FIRING A SHOT.
SOME OF THEM DON'T LOOK MUCH OLDER THAN *SIXTEEN.*
JUST *BOYS.*
CAREFUL, MAGGIE, YOU DON'T WANT ANYONE THINKING YOU'RE A *COMMUNIST SYMPATHIZER,* DO YOU?
I KNEW MY FAIR SHARE OF COMMUNISTS IN COLLEGE.
WHERE'D YOU GO?
COLUMBIA SCHOOL OF JOURNALISM, AND BEFORE THAT, THE UNIVERSITY OF CALIFORNIA, BERKELEY.
OUR STUDENT PAPER WAS RUN BY RADICALS.
I MYSELF DITCHED SCHOOL FOR THREE WEEKS TO WRITE AN EXPOSÉ ON MEXICO CITY POLITICS.
I FIGURED YOU WEREN'T THE TYPE TO JUST SIT AND LOOK PRETTY IN A *SORORITY DRESS.*
I DID THAT TOO.
REALLY?
YOU BET. I WAS A *GAMMA PHI BETA,* YOU SHOULD HAVE SEEN ME RUNNING LUNCHEONS AND FORMALS.
ΓΦΒ
WHERE DID YOU GO TO SCHOOL?
WEST POINT, CLASS OF '43.
SIR, WE'RE APPROACHING THE CITY OF CHEONAN.
YOU BETTER GET BACK TO YOUR JEEP AND KEEP YOUR HEAD DOWN.

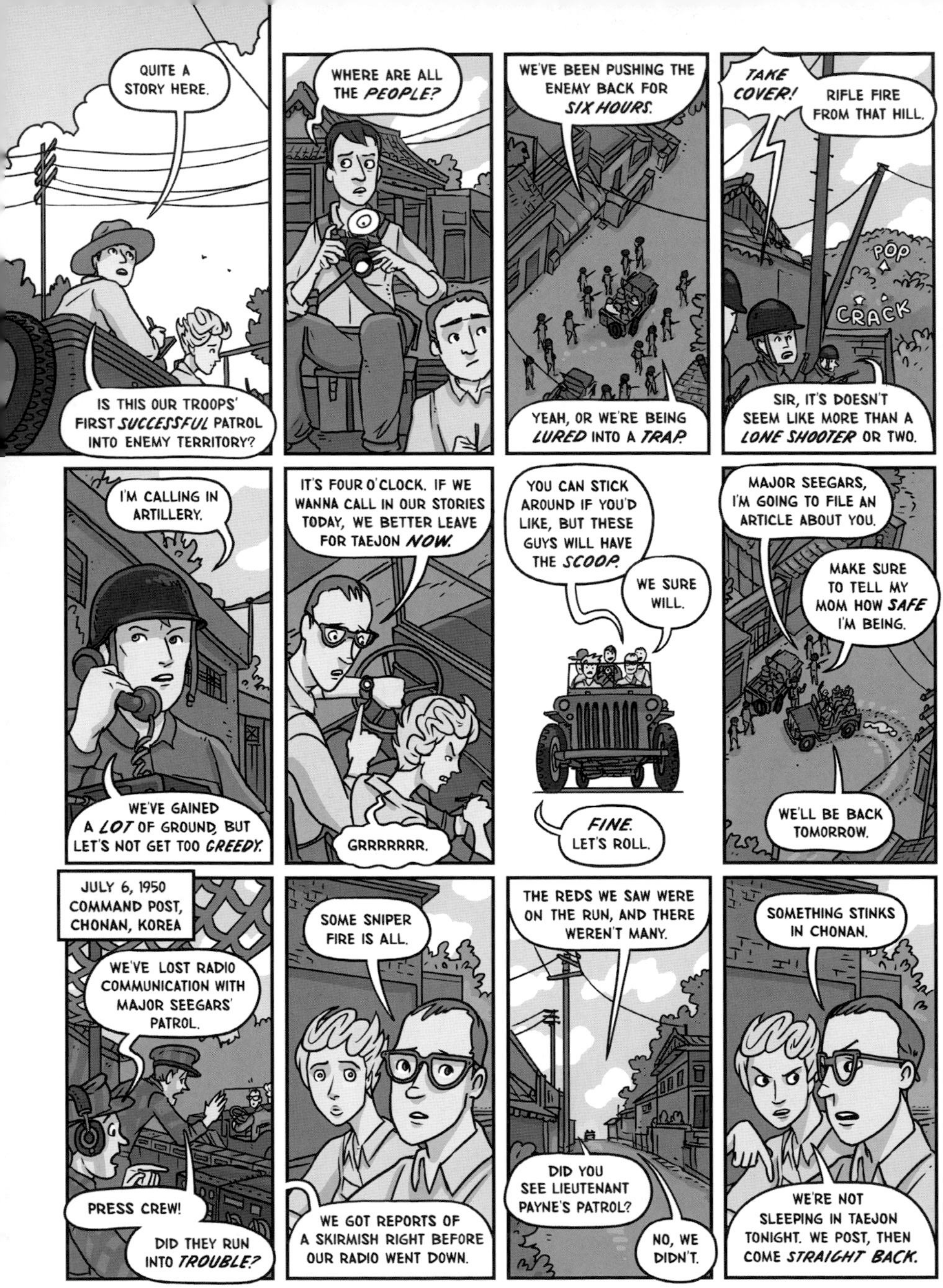
QUITE A STORY HERE.
IS THIS OUR TROOPS' FIRST SUCCESSFUL PATROL INTO ENEMY TERRITORY?
WHERE ARE ALL THE PEOPLE?
WE'VE BEEN PUSHING THE ENEMY BACK FOR SIX HOURS.
YEAH, OR WE'RE BEING LURED INTO A TRAP.
TAKE COVER!
RIFLE FIRE FROM THAT HILL.
POP
CRACK
SIR, IT'S DOESN'T SEEM LIKE MORE THAN A LONE SHOOTER OR TWO.
I'M CALLING IN ARTILLERY.
WE'VE GAINED A LOT OF GROUND, BUT LET'S NOT GET TOO GREEDY.
IT'S FOUR O'CLOCK. IF WE WANNA CALL IN OUR STORIES TODAY, WE BETTER LEAVE FOR TAEJON NOW.
GRRRRRRR.
YOU CAN STICK AROUND IF YOU'D LIKE, BUT THESE GUYS WILL HAVE THE SCOOP.
WE SURE WILL.
FINE. LET'S ROLL.
MAJOR SEEGARS, I'M GOING TO FILE AN ARTICLE ABOUT YOU.
MAKE SURE TO TELL MY MOM HOW SAFE I'M BEING.
WE'LL BE BACK TOMORROW.
JULY 6, 1950 COMMAND POST, CHONAN, KOREA
WE'VE LOST RADIO COMMUNICATION WITH MAJOR SEEGARS' PATROL.
PRESS CREW!
DID THEY RUN INTO TROUBLE?
SOME SNIPER FIRE IS ALL.
WE GOT REPORTS OF A SKIRMISH RIGHT BEFORE OUR RADIO WENT DOWN.
THE REDS WE SAW WERE ON THE RUN, AND THERE WEREN'T MANY.
DID YOU SEE LIEUTENANT PAYNE'S PATROL?
NO, WE DIDN'T.
SOMETHING STINKS IN CHONAN.
WE'RE NOT SLEEPING IN TAEJON TONIGHT. WE POST, THEN COME STRAIGHT BACK.

Chapter 11

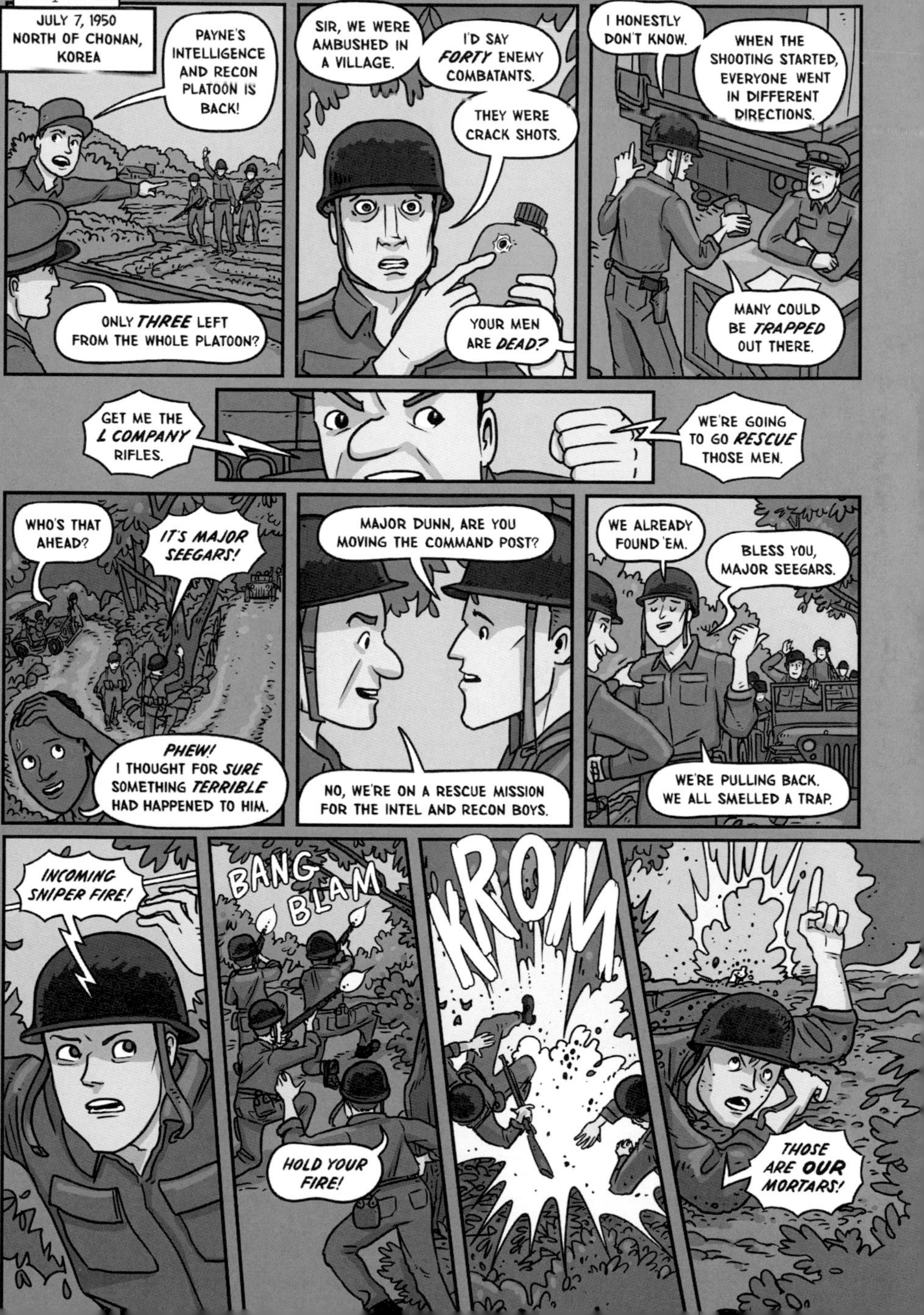
JULY 7, 1950
NORTH OF CHONAN, KOREA
PAYNE'S INTELLIGENCE AND RECON PLATOON IS BACK!
ONLY THREE LEFT FROM THE WHOLE PLATOON?
SIR, WE WERE AMBUSHED IN A VILLAGE.
I'D SAY FORTY ENEMY COMBATANTS.
THEY WERE CRACK SHOTS.
YOUR MEN ARE DEAD?
I HONESTLY DON'T KNOW.
WHEN THE SHOOTING STARTED, EVERYONE WENT IN DIFFERENT DIRECTIONS.
MANY COULD BE TRAPPED OUT THERE.
GET ME THE L COMPANY RIFLES.
WE'RE GOING TO GO RESCUE THOSE MEN.
WHO'S THAT AHEAD?
IT'S MAJOR SEEGARS!
PHEW! I THOUGHT FOR SURE SOMETHING TERRIBLE HAD HAPPENED TO HIM.
MAJOR DUNN, ARE YOU MOVING THE COMMAND POST?
NO, WE'RE ON A RESCUE MISSION FOR THE INTEL AND RECON BOYS.
WE ALREADY FOUND 'EM.
BLESS YOU, MAJOR SEEGARS.
WE'RE PULLING BACK. WE ALL SMELLED A TRAP.
INCOMING SNIPER FIRE!
BANG
BLAM
HOLD YOUR FIRE!
KROM
THOSE ARE OUR MORTARS!

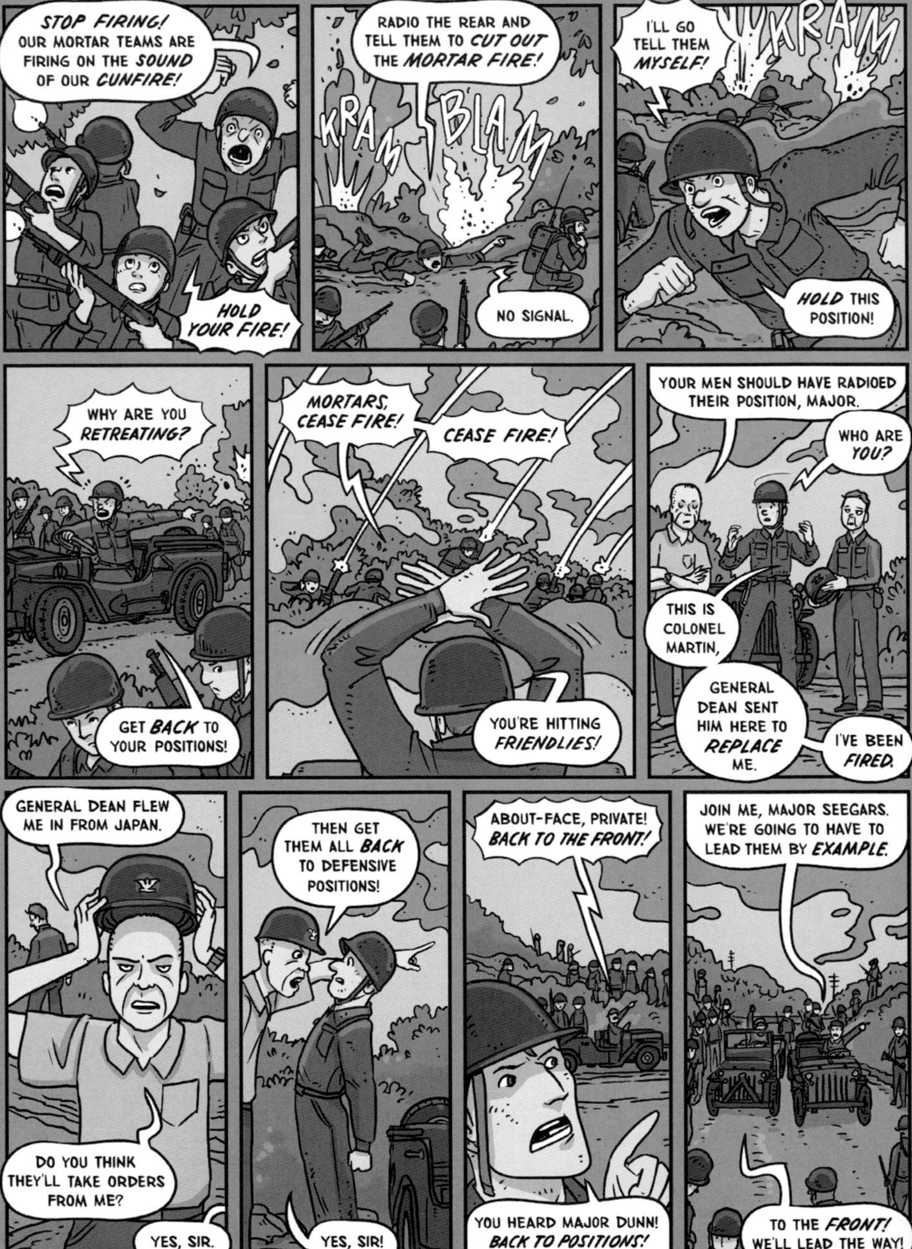
STOP FIRING! OUR MORTAR TEAMS ARE FIRING ON THE SOUND OF OUR GUNFIRE!
HOLD YOUR FIRE!
RADIO THE REAR AND TELL THEM TO CUT OUT THE MORTAR FIRE!
KRAM
BLAM
NO SIGNAL.
I'LL GO TELL THEM MYSELF!
KRAM
HOLD THIS POSITION!
WHY ARE YOU RETREATING?
GET BACK TO YOUR POSITIONS!
MORTARS, CEASE FIRE!
CEASE FIRE!
YOU'RE HITTING FRIENDLIES!
YOUR MEN SHOULD HAVE RADIOED THEIR POSITION, MAJOR.
WHO ARE YOU?
THIS IS COLONEL MARTIN,
GENERAL DEAN SENT HIM HERE TO REPLACE ME.
I'VE BEEN FIRED.
GENERAL DEAN FLEW ME IN FROM JAPAN.
DO YOU THINK THEY'LL TAKE ORDERS FROM ME?
YES, SIR.
THEN GET THEM ALL BACK TO DEFENSIVE POSITIONS!
YES, SIR!
ABOUT-FACE, PRIVATE! BACK TO THE FRONT!
YOU HEARD MAJOR DUNN! BACK TO POSITIONS!
JOIN ME, MAJOR SEEGARS. WE'RE GOING TO HAVE TO LEAD THEM BY EXAMPLE.
TO THE FRONT! WE'LL LEAD THE WAY!

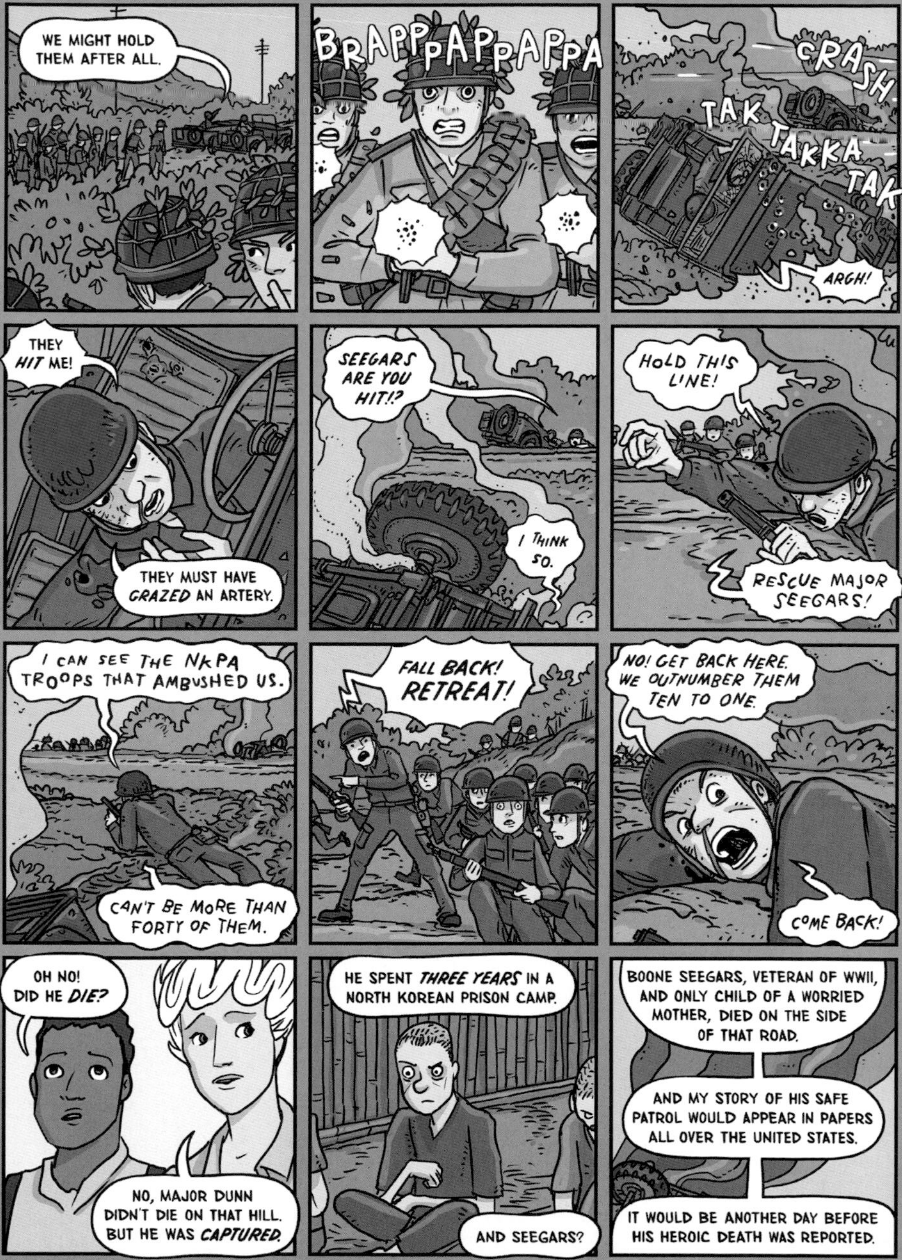
WE MIGHT HOLD THEM AFTER ALL.
BRAPPPAPPPAPPA
CRASH
TAK TAKKA TAK
ARGH!
THEY HIT ME!
THEY MUST HAVE GRAZED AN ARTERY.
SEEGARS ARE YOU HIT!?
I THINK SO.
HOLD THIS LINE!
RESCUE MAJOR SEEGARS!
I CAN SEE THE NKPA TROOPS THAT AMBUSHED US.
CAN'T BE MORE THAN FORTY OF THEM.
FALL BACK! RETREAT!
NO! GET BACK HERE. WE OUTNUMBER THEM TEN TO ONE.
COME BACK!
OH NO! DID HE DIE?
NO, MAJOR DUNN DIDN'T DIE ON THAT HILL. BUT HE WAS CAPTURED.
HE SPENT THREE YEARS IN A NORTH KOREAN PRISON CAMP.
AND SEEGARS?
BOONE SEEGARS, VETERAN OF WWII, AND ONLY CHILD OF A WORRIED MOTHER, DIED ON THE SIDE OF THAT ROAD.
AND MY STORY OF HIS SAFE PATROL WOULD APPEAR IN PAPERS ALL OVER THE UNITED STATES.
IT WOULD BE ANOTHER DAY BEFORE HIS HEROIC DEATH WAS REPORTED.

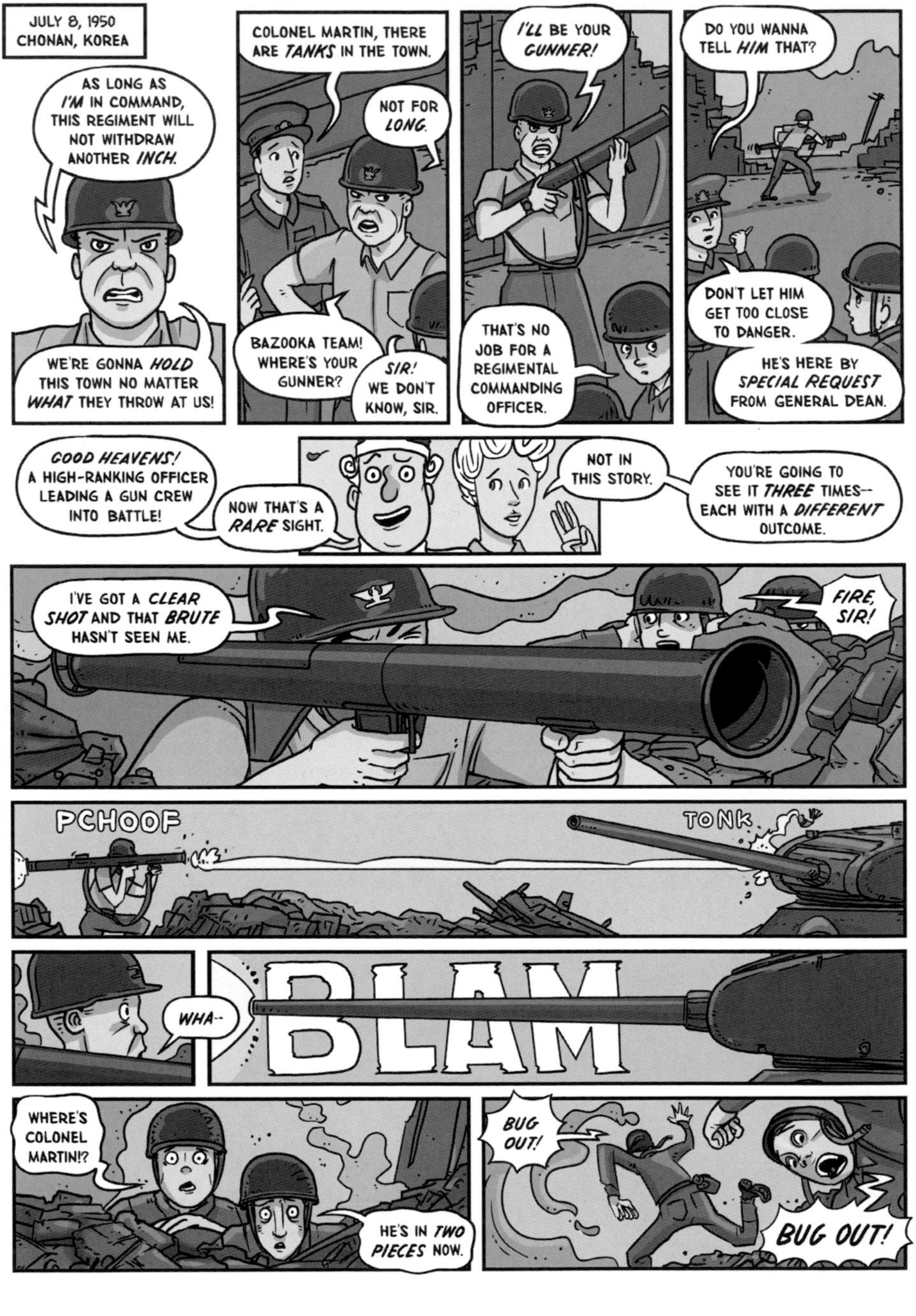
JULY 8, 1950
CHONAN, KOREA
AS LONG AS I'M IN COMMAND, THIS REGIMENT WILL NOT WITHDRAW ANOTHER INCH.
WE'RE GONNA HOLD THIS TOWN NO MATTER WHAT THEY THROW AT US!
COLONEL MARTIN, THERE ARE TANKS IN THE TOWN.
NOT FOR LONG.
BAZOOKA TEAM! WHERE'S YOUR GUNNER?
SIR! WE DON'T KNOW, SIR.
I'LL BE YOUR GUNNER!
THAT'S NO JOB FOR A REGIMENTAL COMMANDING OFFICER.
DO YOU WANNA TELL HIM THAT?
DON'T LET HIM GET TOO CLOSE TO DANGER.
HE'S HERE BY SPECIAL REQUEST FROM GENERAL DEAN.
GOOD HEAVENS! A HIGH-RANKING OFFICER LEADING A GUN CREW INTO BATTLE!
NOW THAT'S A RARE SIGHT.
NOT IN THIS STORY.
YOU'RE GOING TO SEE IT THREE TIMES-- EACH WITH A DIFFERENT OUTCOME.
I'VE GOT A CLEAR SHOT AND THAT BRUTE HASN'T SEEN ME.
FIRE, SIR!
PCHOOF
TONK
WHA--
BLAM
WHERE'S COLONEL MARTIN!?
HE'S IN TWO PIECES NOW.
BUG OUT!
BUG OUT!

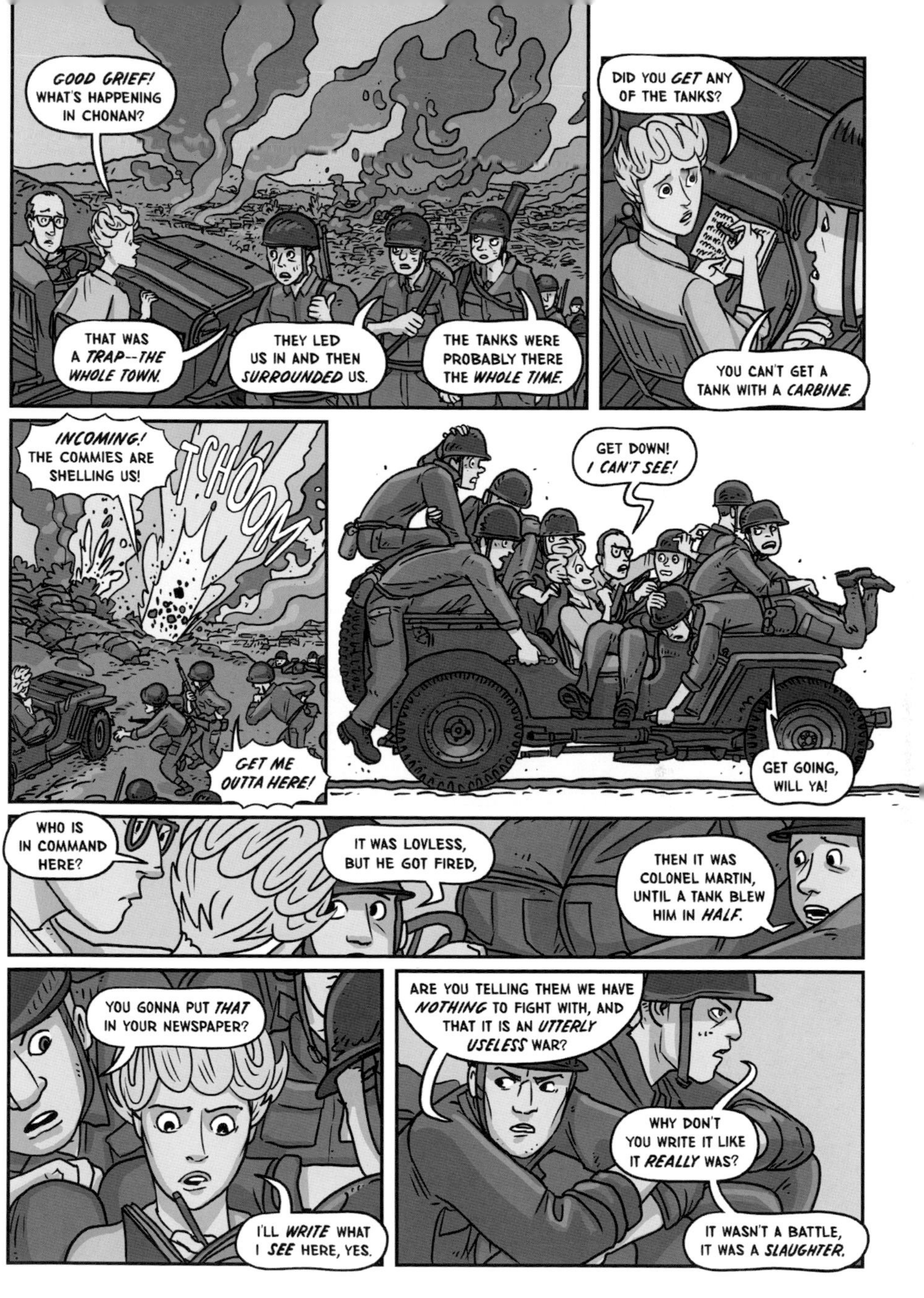
GOOD GRIEF! WHAT'S HAPPENING IN CHONAN?
THAT WAS A TRAP--THE WHOLE TOWN.
THEY LED US IN AND THEN SURROUNDED US.
THE TANKS WERE PROBABLY THERE THE WHOLE TIME.
DID YOU GET ANY OF THE TANKS?
YOU CAN'T GET A TANK WITH A CARBINE.
INCOMING! THE COMMIES ARE SHELLING US!
TCHOOM
GET ME OUTTA HERE!
GET DOWN! I CAN'T SEE!
GET GOING, WILL YA!
WHO IS IN COMMAND HERE?
IT WAS LOVLESS, BUT HE GOT FIRED,
THEN IT WAS COLONEL MARTIN, UNTIL A TANK BLEW HIM IN HALF.
YOU GONNA PUT THAT IN YOUR NEWSPAPER?
I'LL WRITE WHAT I SEE HERE, YES.
ARE YOU TELLING THEM WE HAVE NOTHING TO FIGHT WITH, AND THAT IT IS AN UTTERLY USELESS WAR?
WHY DON'T YOU WRITE IT LIKE IT REALLY WAS?
IT WASN'T A BATTLE, IT WAS A SLAUGHTER.

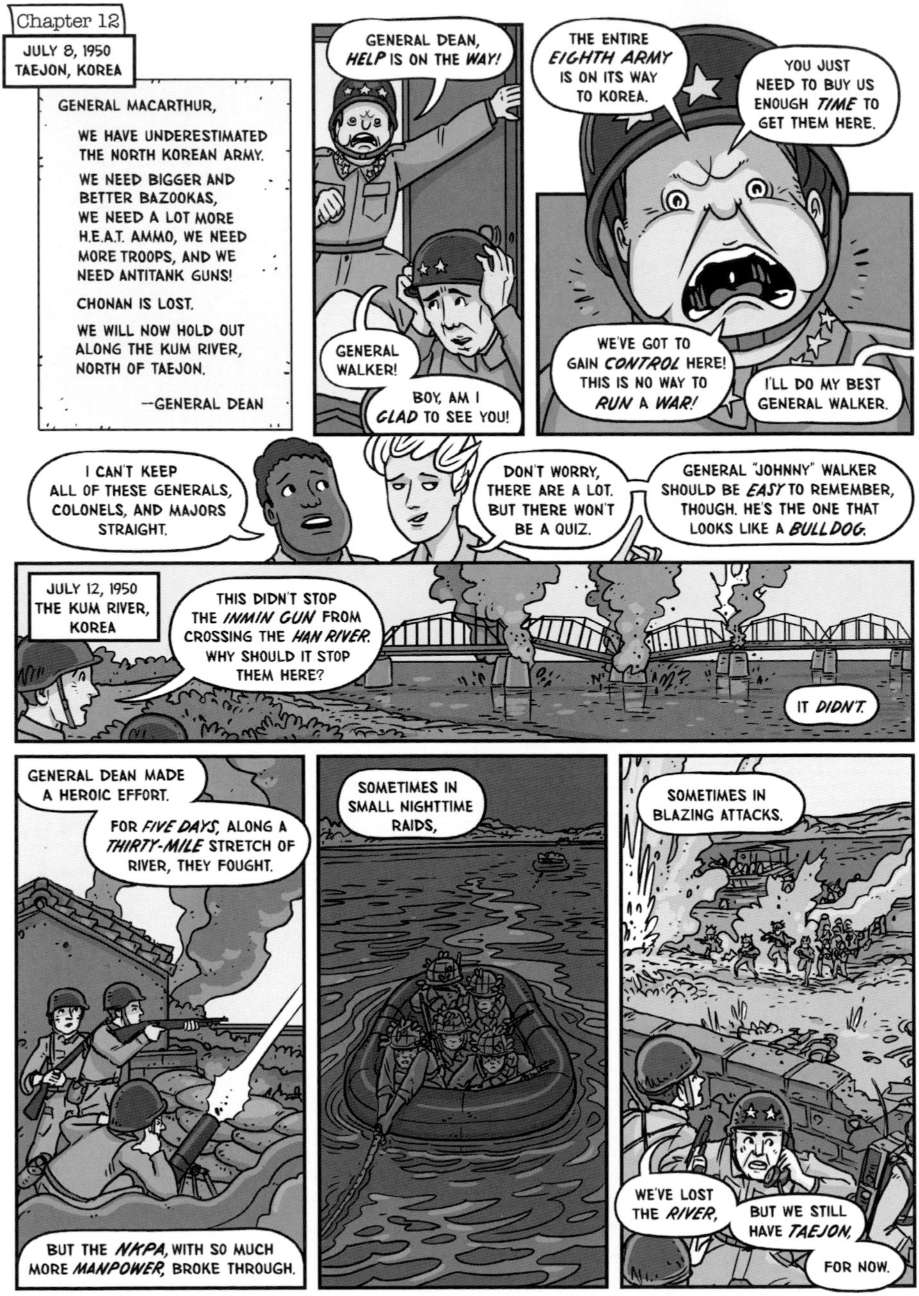
Chapter 12
JULY 8, 1950
TAEJON, KOREA
GENERAL MACARTHUR,
WE HAVE UNDERESTIMATED THE NORTH KOREAN ARMY.
WE NEED BIGGER AND BETTER BAZOOKAS, WE NEED A LOT MORE H.E.A.T. AMMO, WE NEED MORE TROOPS, AND WE NEED ANTITANK GUNS!
CHONAN IS LOST.
WE WILL NOW HOLD OUT ALONG THE KUM RIVER, NORTH OF TAEJON.
--GENERAL DEAN
GENERAL DEAN, HELP IS ON THE WAY!
GENERAL WALKER!
BOY, AM I GLAD TO SEE YOU!
THE ENTIRE EIGHTH ARMY IS ON ITS WAY TO KOREA.
YOU JUST NEED TO BUY US ENOUGH TIME TO GET THEM HERE.
WE'VE GOT TO GAIN CONTROL HERE! THIS IS NO WAY TO RUN A WAR!
I'LL DO MY BEST GENERAL WALKER.
I CAN'T KEEP ALL OF THESE GENERALS, COLONELS, AND MAJORS STRAIGHT.
DON'T WORRY, THERE ARE A LOT. BUT THERE WON'T BE A QUIZ.
GENERAL "JOHNNY" WALKER SHOULD BE EASY TO REMEMBER, THOUGH. HE'S THE ONE THAT LOOKS LIKE A BULLDOG.
JULY 12, 1950
THE KUM RIVER, KOREA
THIS DIDN'T STOP THE INMIN GUN FROM CROSSING THE HAN RIVER. WHY SHOULD IT STOP THEM HERE?
IT DIDN'T.
GENERAL DEAN MADE A HEROIC EFFORT.
FOR FIVE DAYS, ALONG A THIRTY-MILE STRETCH OF RIVER, THEY FOUGHT.
BUT THE NKPA, WITH SO MUCH MORE MANPOWER, BROKE THROUGH.
SOMETIMES IN SMALL NIGHTTIME RAIDS,
SOMETIMES IN BLAZING ATTACKS.
WE'VE LOST THE RIVER,
BUT WE STILL HAVE TAEJON,
FOR NOW.

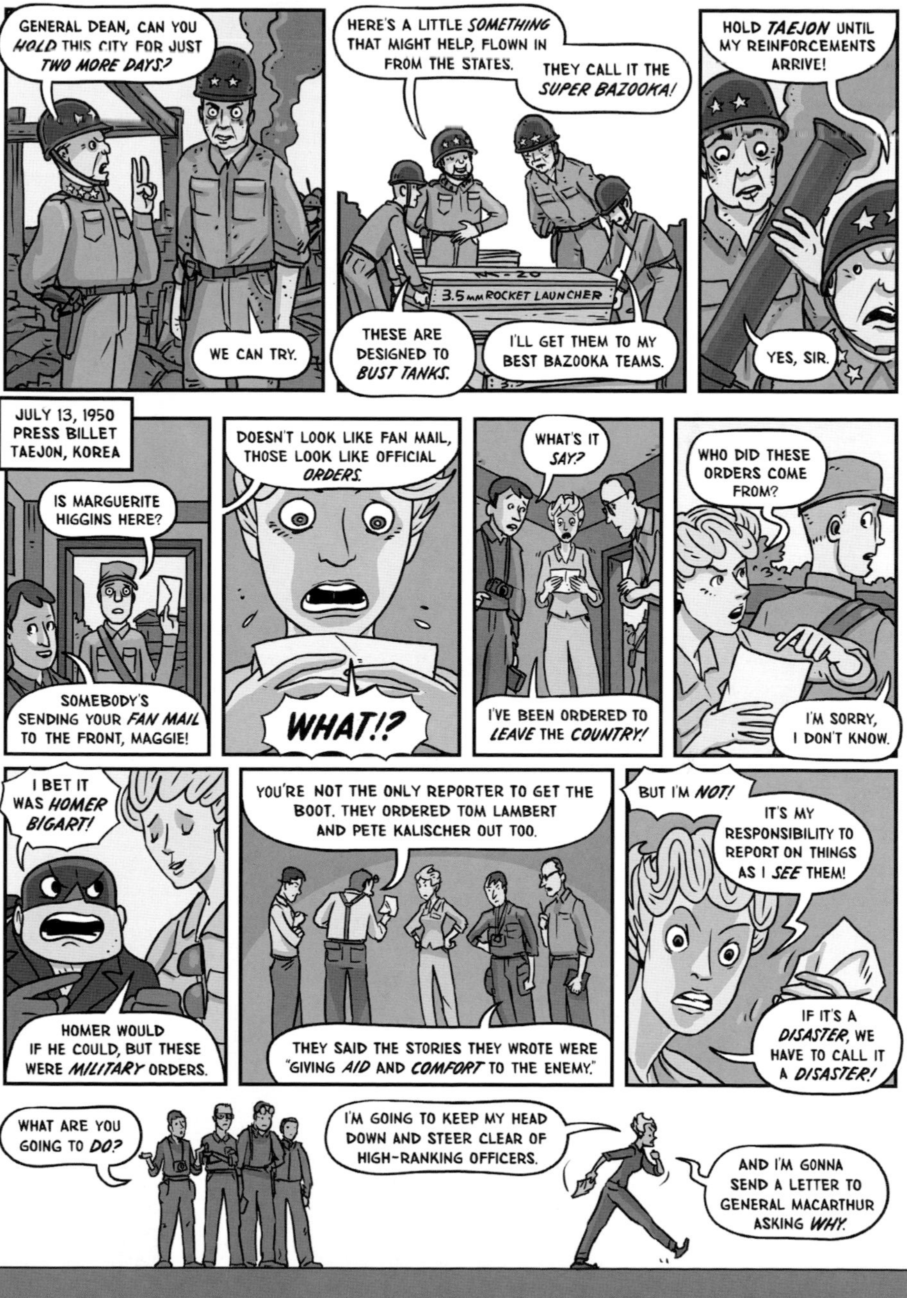

GENERAL DEAN, CAN YOU HOLD THIS CITY FOR JUST TWO MORE DAYS?
WE CAN TRY.
HERE'S A LITTLE SOMETHING THAT MIGHT HELP, FLOWN IN FROM THE STATES.
THEY CALL IT THE SUPER BAZOOKA!
M-20
3.5 MM ROCKET LAUNCHER
THESE ARE DESIGNED TO BUST TANKS.
I'LL GET THEM TO MY BEST BAZOOKA TEAMS.
HOLD TAEJON UNTIL MY REINFORCEMENTS ARRIVE!
YES, SIR.
JULY 13, 1950 PRESS BILLET TAEJON, KOREA
IS MARGUERITE HIGGINS HERE?
SOMEBODY'S SENDING YOUR FAN MAIL TO THE FRONT, MAGGIE!
DOESN'T LOOK LIKE FAN MAIL, THOSE LOOK LIKE OFFICIAL ORDERS.
WHAT!?
WHAT'S IT SAY?
I'VE BEEN ORDERED TO LEAVE THE COUNTRY!
WHO DID THESE ORDERS COME FROM?
I'M SORRY, I DON'T KNOW.
I BET IT WAS HOMER BIGART!
HOMER WOULD IF HE COULD, BUT THESE WERE MILITARY ORDERS.
YOU'RE NOT THE ONLY REPORTER TO GET THE BOOT. THEY ORDERED TOM LAMBERT AND PETE KALISCHER OUT TOO.
THEY SAID THE STORIES THEY WROTE WERE "GIVING AID AND COMFORT TO THE ENEMY."
BUT I'M NOT!
IT'S MY RESPONSIBILITY TO REPORT ON THINGS AS I SEE THEM!
IF IT'S A DISASTER, WE HAVE TO CALL IT A DISASTER!
WHAT ARE YOU GOING TO DO?
I'M GOING TO KEEP MY HEAD DOWN AND STEER CLEAR OF HIGH-RANKING OFFICERS.
AND I'M GONNA SEND A LETTER TO GENERAL MACARTHUR ASKING WHY.

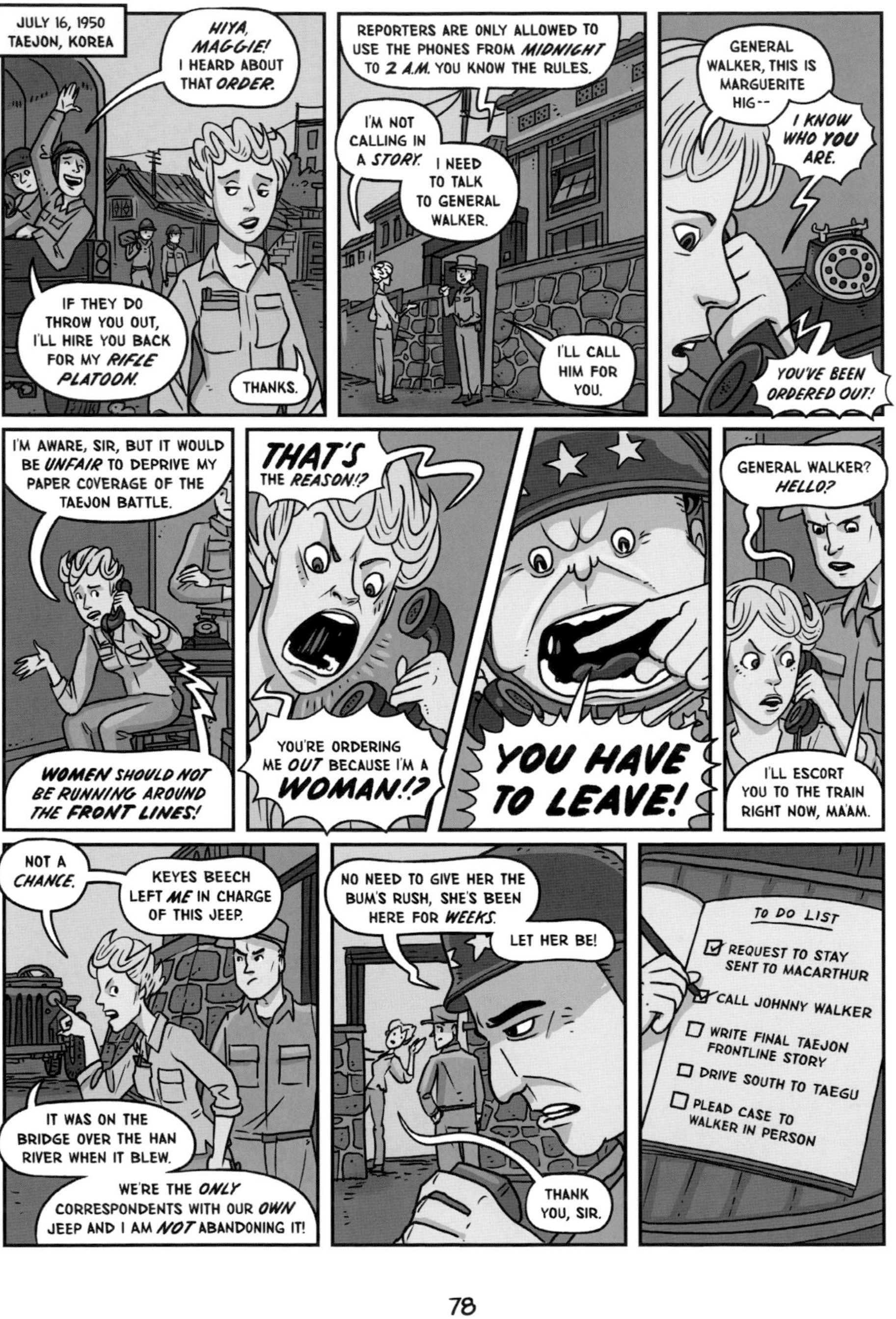
JULY 16, 1950
TAEJON, KOREA
HIYA, MAGGIE! I HEARD ABOUT THAT ORDER.
IF THEY DO THROW YOU OUT, I'LL HIRE YOU BACK FOR MY RIFLE PLATOON.
THANKS.
REPORTERS ARE ONLY ALLOWED TO USE THE PHONES FROM MIDNIGHT TO 2 A.M. YOU KNOW THE RULES.
I'M NOT CALLING IN A STORY.
I NEED TO TALK TO GENERAL WALKER.
I'LL CALL HIM FOR YOU.
GENERAL WALKER, THIS IS MARGUERITE HIG--
I KNOW WHO YOU ARE.
YOU'VE BEEN ORDERED OUT!
I'M AWARE, SIR, BUT IT WOULD BE UNFAIR TO DEPRIVE MY PAPER COVERAGE OF THE TAEJON BATTLE.
WOMEN SHOULD NOT BE RUNNING AROUND THE FRONT LINES!
THAT'S THE REASON!?
YOU'RE ORDERING ME OUT BECAUSE I'M A WOMAN!?
YOU HAVE TO LEAVE!
GENERAL WALKER? HELLO?
I'LL ESCORT YOU TO THE TRAIN RIGHT NOW, MA'AM.
NOT A CHANCE.
KEYES BEECH LEFT ME IN CHARGE OF THIS JEEP.
IT WAS ON THE BRIDGE OVER THE HAN RIVER WHEN IT BLEW.
WE'RE THE ONLY CORRESPONDENTS WITH OUR OWN JEEP AND I AM NOT ABANDONING IT!
NO NEED TO GIVE HER THE BUM'S RUSH, SHE'S BEEN HERE FOR WEEKS.
LET HER BE!
THANK YOU, SIR.
TO DO LIST
☑ REQUEST TO STAY SENT TO MACARTHUR
☑ CALL JOHNNY WALKER
☐ WRITE FINAL TAEJON FRONTLINE STORY
☐ DRIVE SOUTH TO TAEGU
☐ PLEAD CASE TO WALKER IN PERSON

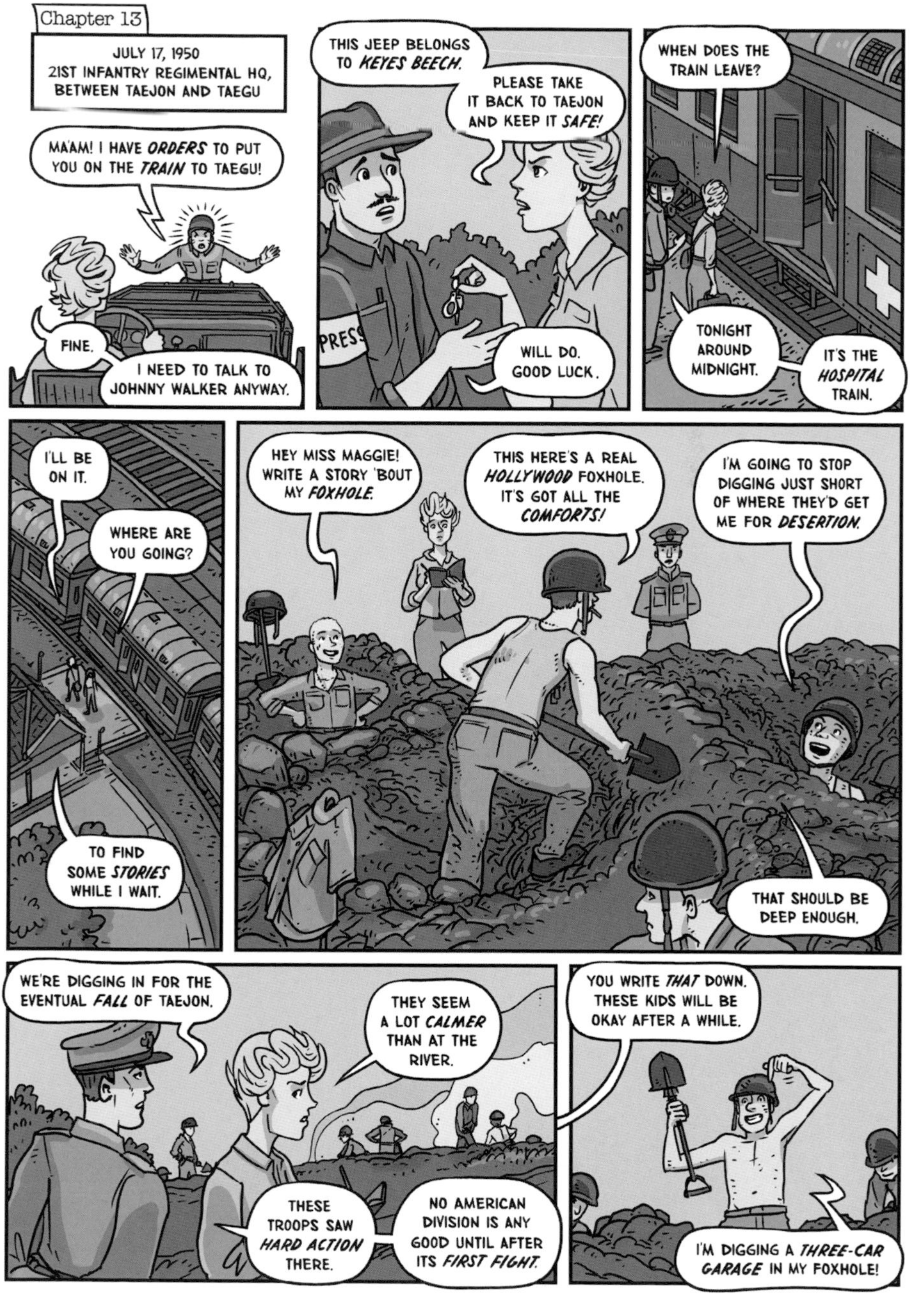
Chapter 13
JULY 17, 1950
21ST INFANTRY REGIMENTAL HQ, BETWEEN TAEJON AND TAEGU
MA'AM! I HAVE ORDERS TO PUT YOU ON THE TRAIN TO TAEGU!
FINE.
I NEED TO TALK TO JOHNNY WALKER ANYWAY.
THIS JEEP BELONGS TO KEYES BEECH.
PLEASE TAKE IT BACK TO TAEJON AND KEEP IT SAFE!
PRESS
WILL DO. GOOD LUCK.
WHEN DOES THE TRAIN LEAVE?
TONIGHT AROUND MIDNIGHT.
IT'S THE HOSPITAL TRAIN.
I'LL BE ON IT.
WHERE ARE YOU GOING?
TO FIND SOME STORIES WHILE I WAIT.
HEY MISS MAGGIE! WRITE A STORY 'BOUT MY FOXHOLE.
THIS HERE'S A REAL HOLLYWOOD FOXHOLE. IT'S GOT ALL THE COMFORTS!
I'M GOING TO STOP DIGGING JUST SHORT OF WHERE THEY'D GET ME FOR DESERTION.
THAT SHOULD BE DEEP ENOUGH.
WE'RE DIGGING IN FOR THE EVENTUAL FALL OF TAEJON.
THEY SEEM A LOT CALMER THAN AT THE RIVER.
THESE TROOPS SAW HARD ACTION THERE.
NO AMERICAN DIVISION IS ANY GOOD UNTIL AFTER ITS FIRST FIGHT.
YOU WRITE THAT DOWN. THESE KIDS WILL BE OKAY AFTER A WHILE.
I'M DIGGING A THREE-CAR GARAGE IN MY FOXHOLE!

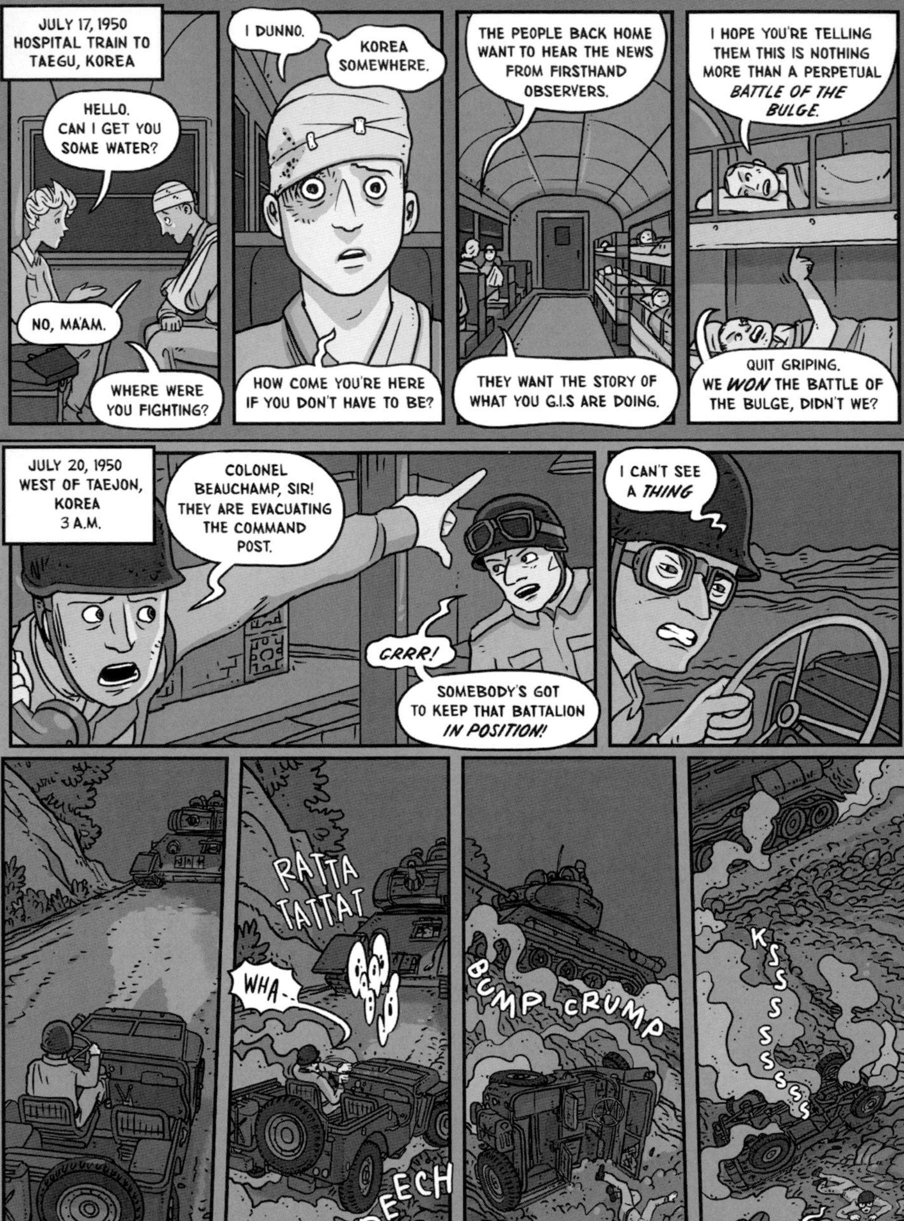
JULY 17, 1950
HOSPITAL TRAIN TO TAEGU, KOREA
HELLO. CAN I GET YOU SOME WATER?
NO, MA'AM.
WHERE WERE YOU FIGHTING?
I DUNNO.
KOREA SOMEWHERE.
HOW COME YOU'RE HERE IF YOU DON'T HAVE TO BE?
THE PEOPLE BACK HOME WANT TO HEAR THE NEWS FROM FIRSTHAND OBSERVERS.
THEY WANT THE STORY OF WHAT YOU G.I.S ARE DOING.
I HOPE YOU'RE TELLING THEM THIS IS NOTHING MORE THAN A PERPETUAL *BATTLE OF THE BULGE*.
QUIT GRIPING. WE *WON* THE BATTLE OF THE BULGE, DIDN'T WE?
JULY 20, 1950
WEST OF TAEJON, KOREA
3 A.M.
COLONEL BEAUCHAMP, SIR! THEY ARE EVACUATING THE COMMAND POST.
GRRR!
SOMEBODY'S GOT TO KEEP THAT BATTALION *IN POSITION!*
I CAN'T SEE A *THING*
RATTA TATTAT
WHA-
SCREECH
BUMP CRUMP
YAAAAAAA!
KSSSSSSS
I *HATE, HATE,* ***HATE*** THOSE TANKS.

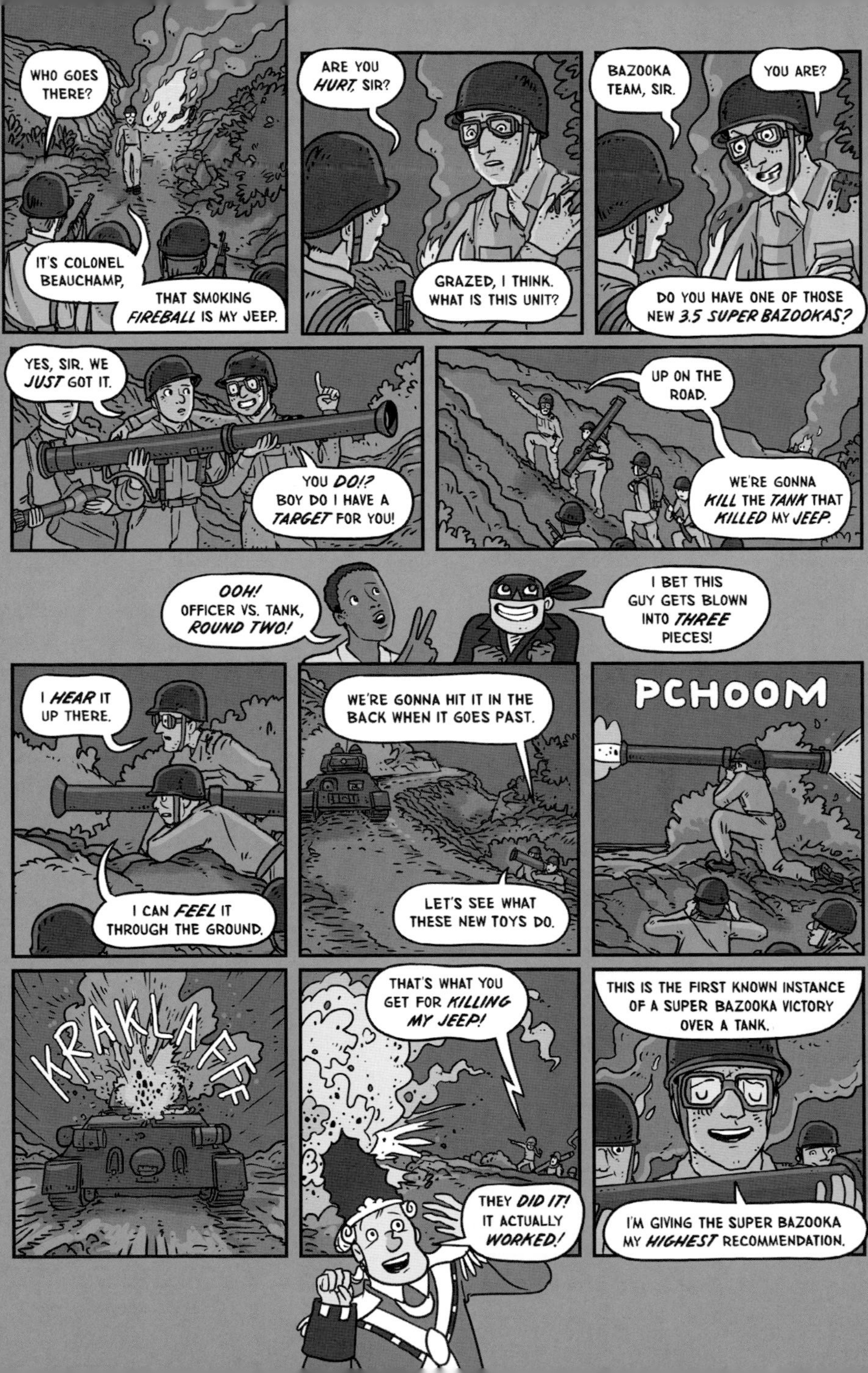
WHO GOES THERE?
IT'S COLONEL BEAUCHAMP,
THAT SMOKING *FIREBALL* IS MY JEEP.
ARE YOU *HURT,* SIR?
GRAZED, I THINK. WHAT IS THIS UNIT?
BAZOOKA TEAM, SIR.
YOU ARE?
DO YOU HAVE ONE OF THOSE NEW *3.5 SUPER BAZOOKAS?*
YES, SIR. WE *JUST* GOT IT.
YOU *DO!?* BOY DO I HAVE A *TARGET* FOR YOU!
UP ON THE ROAD.
WE'RE GONNA *KILL* THE *TANK* THAT *KILLED* MY *JEEP.*
OOH! OFFICER VS. TANK, *ROUND TWO!*
I BET THIS GUY GETS BLOWN INTO *THREE* PIECES!
I *HEAR* IT UP THERE.
I CAN *FEEL* IT THROUGH THE GROUND.
WE'RE GONNA HIT IT IN THE BACK WHEN IT GOES PAST.
LET'S SEE WHAT THESE NEW TOYS DO.
PCHOOM
KRAKLAFFF
THAT'S WHAT YOU GET FOR *KILLING MY JEEP!*
THEY *DID IT!* IT ACTUALLY *WORKED!*
THIS IS THE FIRST KNOWN INSTANCE OF A SUPER BAZOOKA VICTORY OVER A TANK.
I'M GIVING THE SUPER BAZOOKA MY *HIGHEST* RECOMMENDATION.

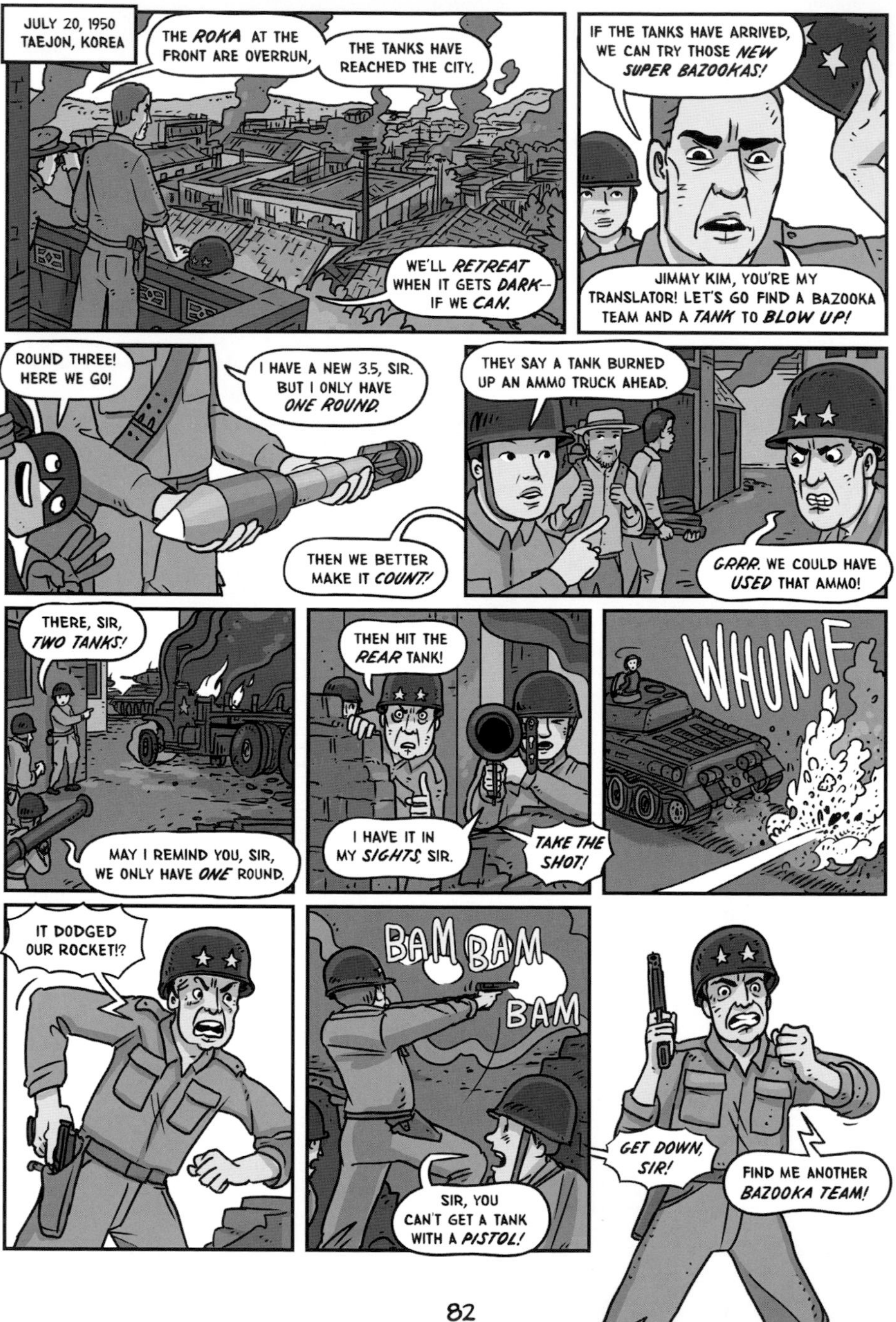
JULY 20, 1950
TAEJON, KOREA
THE ROKA AT THE FRONT ARE OVERRUN,
THE TANKS HAVE REACHED THE CITY.
WE'LL RETREAT WHEN IT GETS DARK-- IF WE CAN.
IF THE TANKS HAVE ARRIVED, WE CAN TRY THOSE NEW SUPER BAZOOKAS!
JIMMY KIM, YOU'RE MY TRANSLATOR! LET'S GO FIND A BAZOOKA TEAM AND A TANK TO BLOW UP!
ROUND THREE! HERE WE GO!
I HAVE A NEW 3.5, SIR. BUT I ONLY HAVE ONE ROUND.
THEN WE BETTER MAKE IT COUNT!
THEY SAY A TANK BURNED UP AN AMMO TRUCK AHEAD.
GRRR. WE COULD HAVE USED THAT AMMO!
THERE, SIR, TWO TANKS!
MAY I REMIND YOU, SIR, WE ONLY HAVE ONE ROUND.
THEN HIT THE REAR TANK!
I HAVE IT IN MY SIGHTS, SIR.
TAKE THE SHOT!
WHUMF
IT DODGED OUR ROCKET!?
BAM BAM
BAM
SIR, YOU CAN'T GET A TANK WITH A PISTOL!
GET DOWN, SIR!
FIND ME ANOTHER BAZOOKA TEAM!

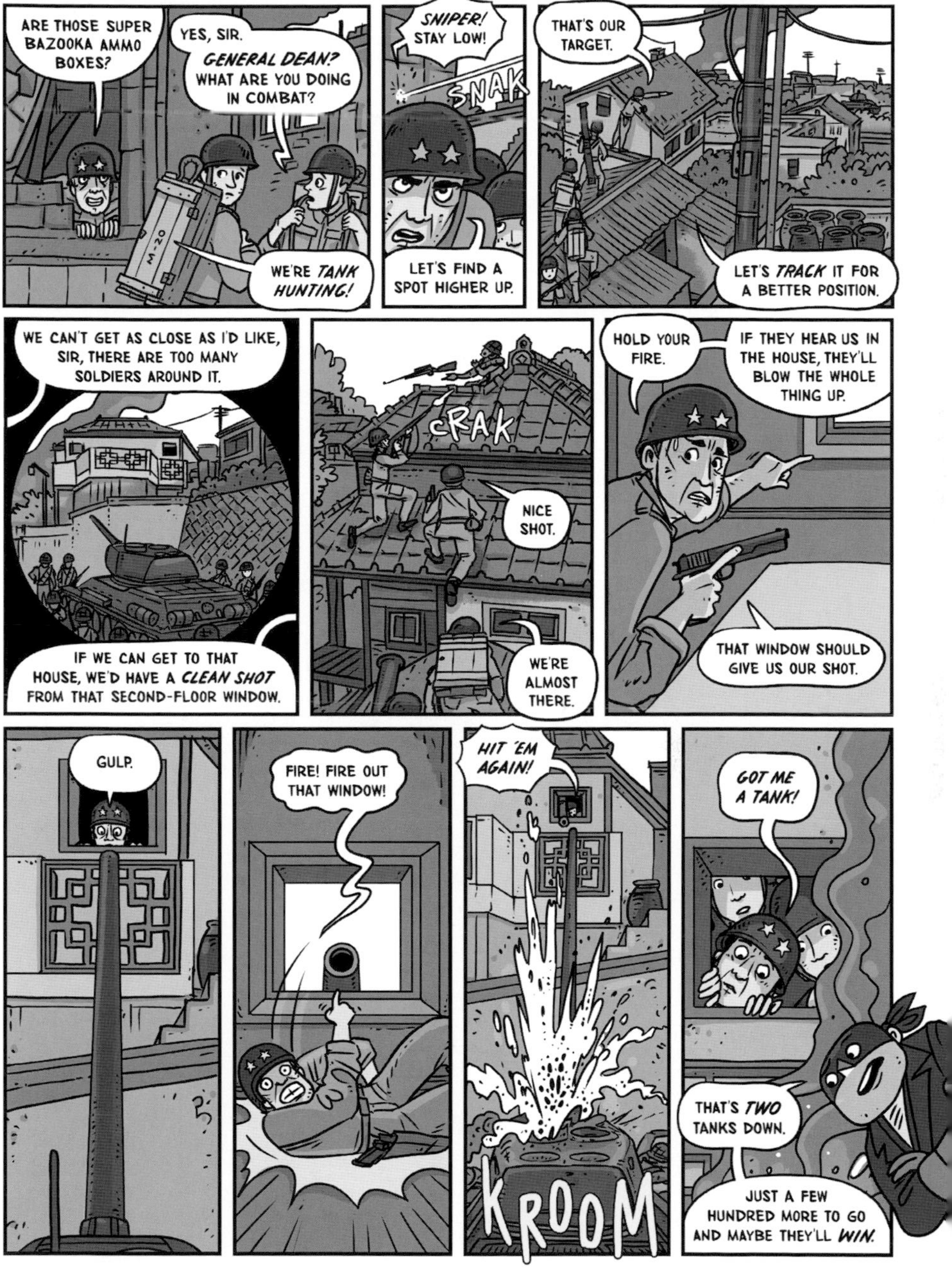
ARE THOSE SUPER BAZOOKA AMMO BOXES?
YES, SIR.
GENERAL DEAN? WHAT ARE YOU DOING IN COMBAT?
M-20
WE'RE TANK HUNTING!
SNIPER! STAY LOW!
SNAK
LET'S FIND A SPOT HIGHER UP.
THAT'S OUR TARGET.
LET'S TRACK IT FOR A BETTER POSITION.
WE CAN'T GET AS CLOSE AS I'D LIKE, SIR, THERE ARE TOO MANY SOLDIERS AROUND IT.
IF WE CAN GET TO THAT HOUSE, WE'D HAVE A CLEAN SHOT FROM THAT SECOND-FLOOR WINDOW.
CRAK
NICE SHOT.
WE'RE ALMOST THERE.
HOLD YOUR FIRE.
IF THEY HEAR US IN THE HOUSE, THEY'LL BLOW THE WHOLE THING UP.
THAT WINDOW SHOULD GIVE US OUR SHOT.
GULP.
FIRE! FIRE OUT THAT WINDOW!
HIT 'EM AGAIN!
KROOM
GOT ME A TANK!
THAT'S TWO TANKS DOWN.
JUST A FEW HUNDRED MORE TO GO AND MAYBE THEY'LL WIN.

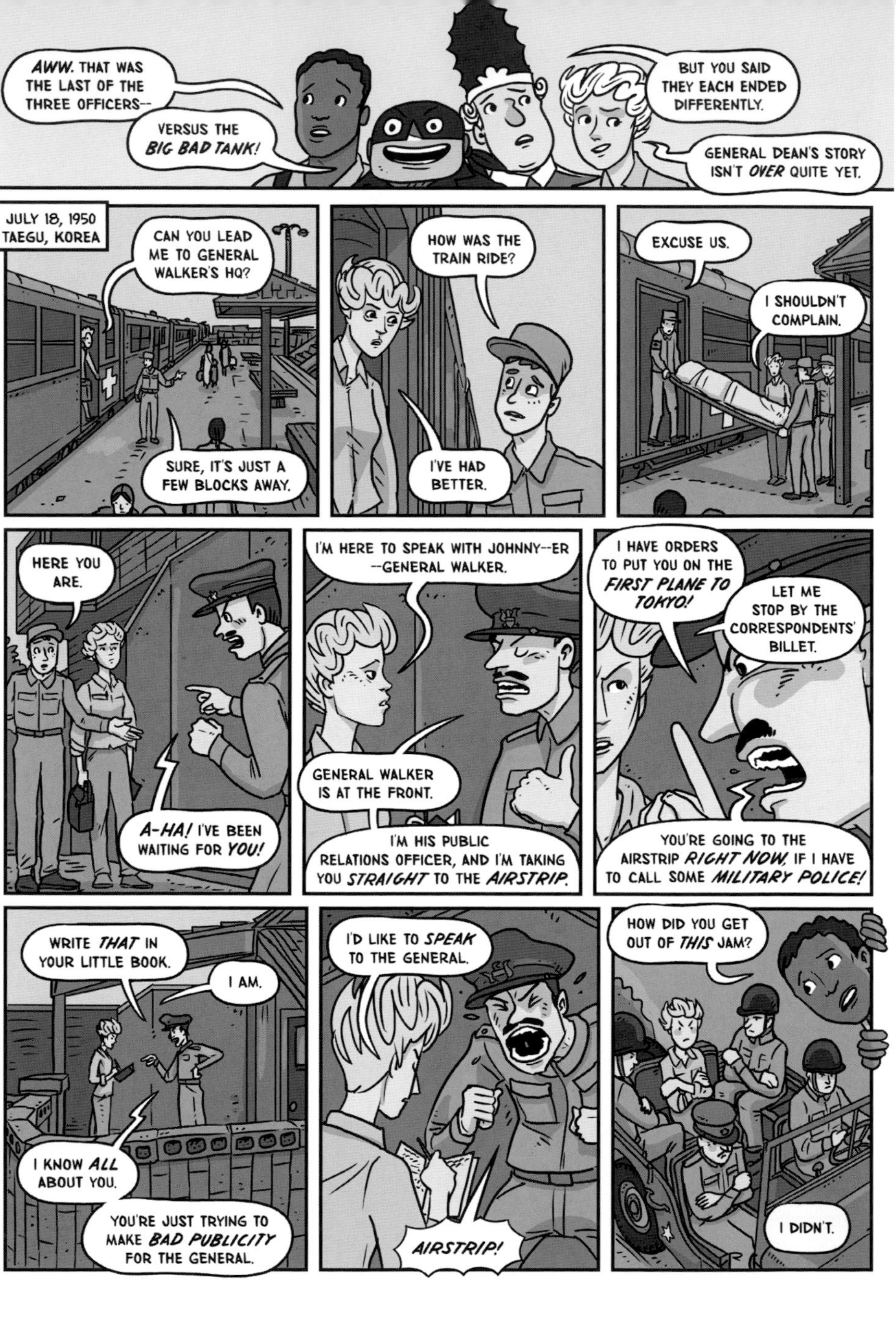
AWW. THAT WAS THE LAST OF THE THREE OFFICERS--
VERSUS THE BIG BAD TANK!
BUT YOU SAID THEY EACH ENDED DIFFERENTLY.
GENERAL DEAN'S STORY ISN'T OVER QUITE YET.
JULY 18, 1950 TAEGU, KOREA
CAN YOU LEAD ME TO GENERAL WALKER'S HQ?
SURE, IT'S JUST A FEW BLOCKS AWAY.
HOW WAS THE TRAIN RIDE?
I'VE HAD BETTER.
EXCUSE US.
I SHOULDN'T COMPLAIN.
HERE YOU ARE.
A-HA! I'VE BEEN WAITING FOR YOU!
I'M HERE TO SPEAK WITH JOHNNY--ER --GENERAL WALKER.
GENERAL WALKER IS AT THE FRONT.
I'M HIS PUBLIC RELATIONS OFFICER, AND I'M TAKING YOU STRAIGHT TO THE AIRSTRIP.
I HAVE ORDERS TO PUT YOU ON THE FIRST PLANE TO TOKYO!
LET ME STOP BY THE CORRESPONDENTS' BILLET.
YOU'RE GOING TO THE AIRSTRIP RIGHT NOW, IF I HAVE TO CALL SOME MILITARY POLICE!
WRITE THAT IN YOUR LITTLE BOOK.
I AM.
I KNOW ALL ABOUT YOU.
YOU'RE JUST TRYING TO MAKE BAD PUBLICITY FOR THE GENERAL.
I'D LIKE TO SPEAK TO THE GENERAL.
AIRSTRIP!
HOW DID YOU GET OUT OF THIS JAM?
I DIDN'T.

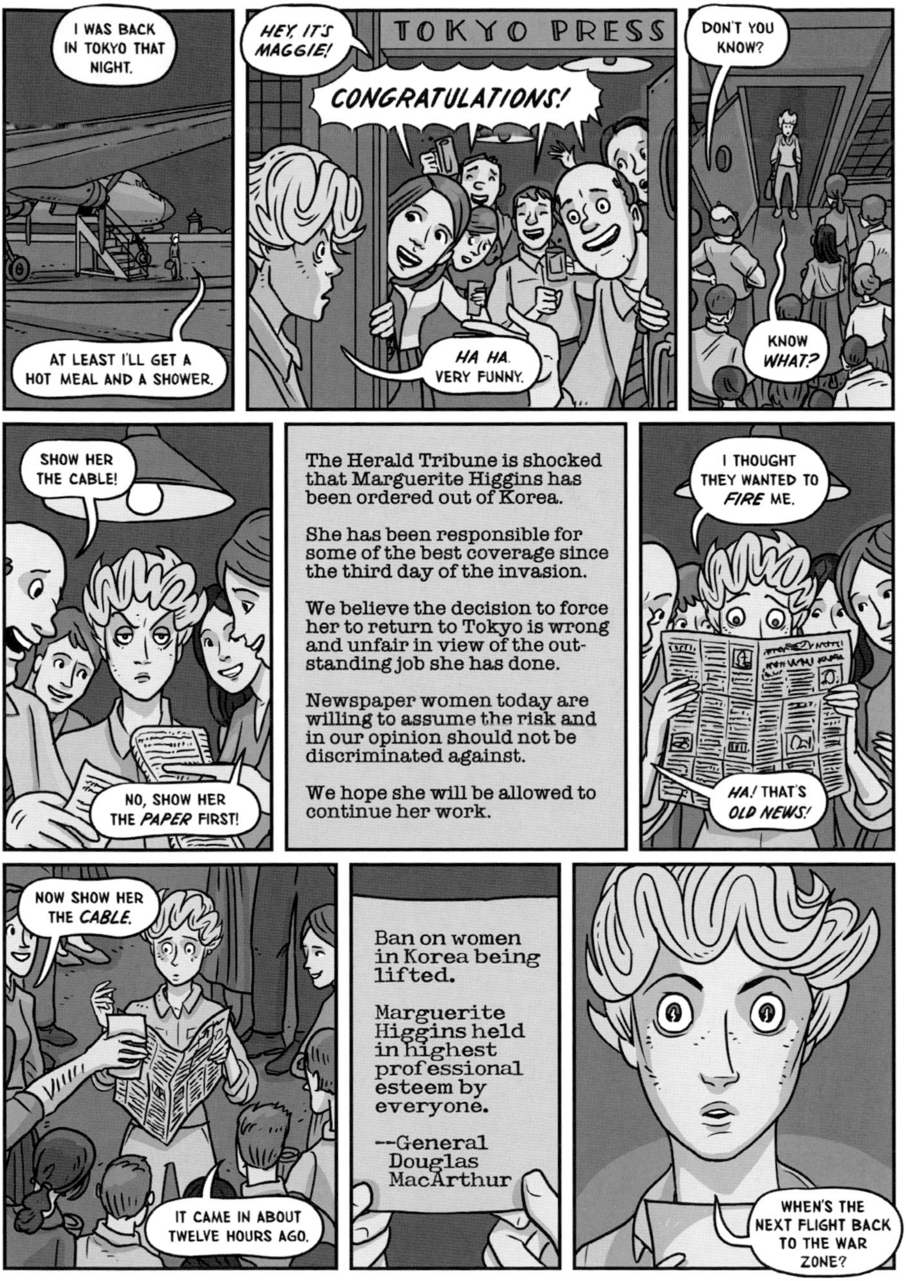
I WAS BACK IN TOKYO THAT NIGHT.
AT LEAST I'LL GET A HOT MEAL AND A SHOWER.
TOKYO PRESS
HEY, IT'S MAGGIE!
CONGRATULATIONS!
HA HA. VERY FUNNY.
DON'T YOU KNOW?
KNOW WHAT?
SHOW HER THE CABLE!
NO, SHOW HER THE PAPER FIRST!
The Herald Tribune is shocked that Marguerite Higgins has been ordered out of Korea.
She has been responsible for some of the best coverage since the third day of the invasion.
We believe the decision to force her to return to Tokyo is wrong and unfair in view of the outstanding job she has done.
Newspaper women today are willing to assume the risk and in our opinion should not be discriminated against.
We hope she will be allowed to continue her work.
I THOUGHT THEY WANTED TO FIRE ME.
HA! THAT'S OLD NEWS!
NOW SHOW HER THE CABLE.
IT CAME IN ABOUT TWELVE HOURS AGO.
Ban on women in Korea being lifted.
Marguerite Higgins held in highest professional esteem by everyone.
--General Douglas MacArthur
WHEN'S THE NEXT FLIGHT BACK TO THE WAR ZONE?

Chapter 14

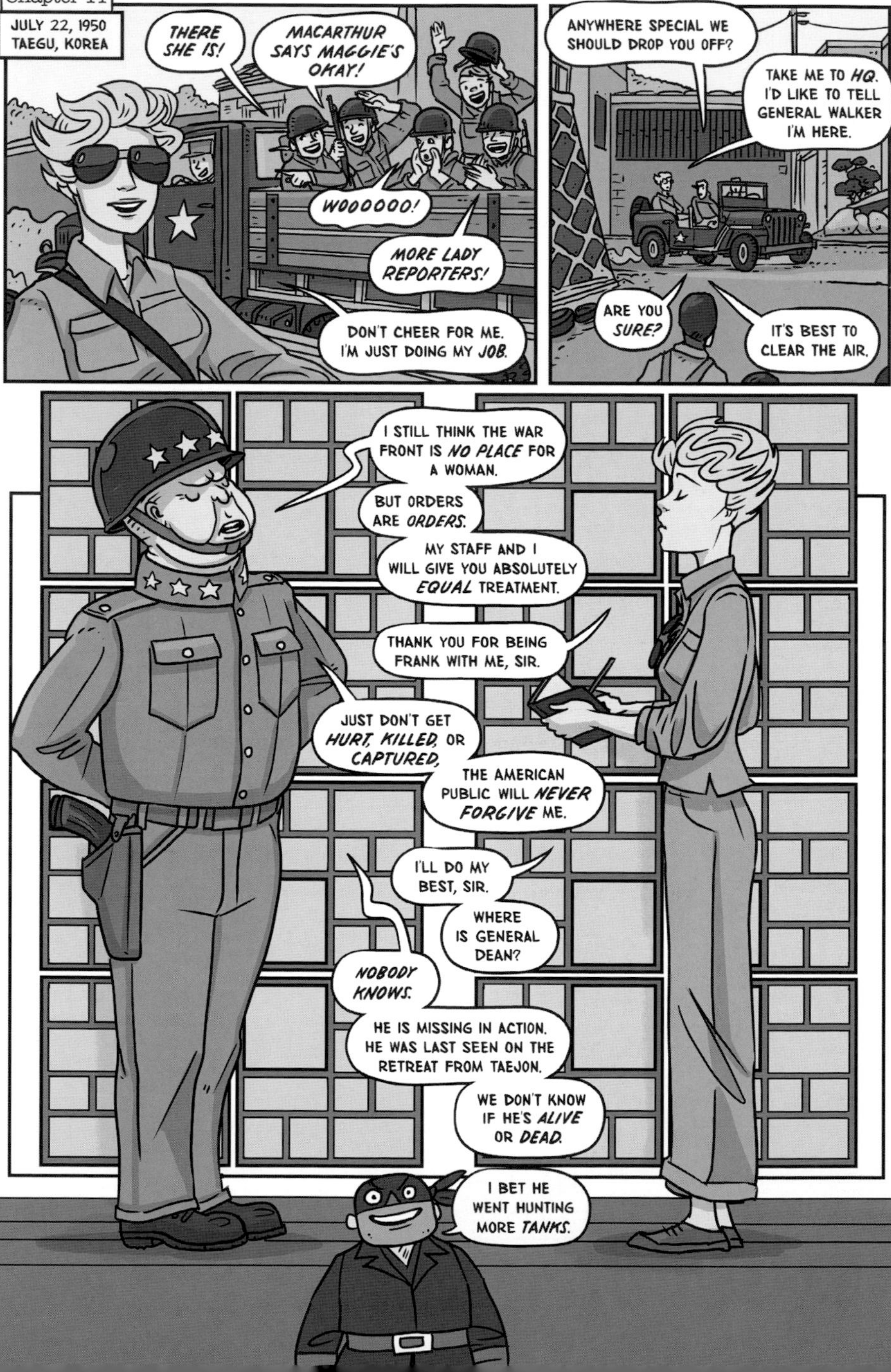
JULY 22, 1950 TAEGU, KOREA
THERE SHE IS!
MACARTHUR SAYS MAGGIE'S OKAY!
WOOOOOO!
MORE LADY REPORTERS!
DON'T CHEER FOR ME. I'M JUST DOING MY JOB.
ANYWHERE SPECIAL WE SHOULD DROP YOU OFF?
TAKE ME TO HQ. I'D LIKE TO TELL GENERAL WALKER I'M HERE.
ARE YOU SURE?
IT'S BEST TO CLEAR THE AIR.
I STILL THINK THE WAR FRONT IS NO PLACE FOR A WOMAN.
BUT ORDERS ARE ORDERS.
MY STAFF AND I WILL GIVE YOU ABSOLUTELY EQUAL TREATMENT.
THANK YOU FOR BEING FRANK WITH ME, SIR.
JUST DON'T GET HURT, KILLED, OR CAPTURED,
THE AMERICAN PUBLIC WILL NEVER FORGIVE ME.
I'LL DO MY BEST, SIR.
WHERE IS GENERAL DEAN?
NOBODY KNOWS.
HE IS MISSING IN ACTION. HE WAS LAST SEEN ON THE RETREAT FROM TAEJON.
WE DON'T KNOW IF HE'S ALIVE OR DEAD.
I BET HE WENT HUNTING MORE TANKS.

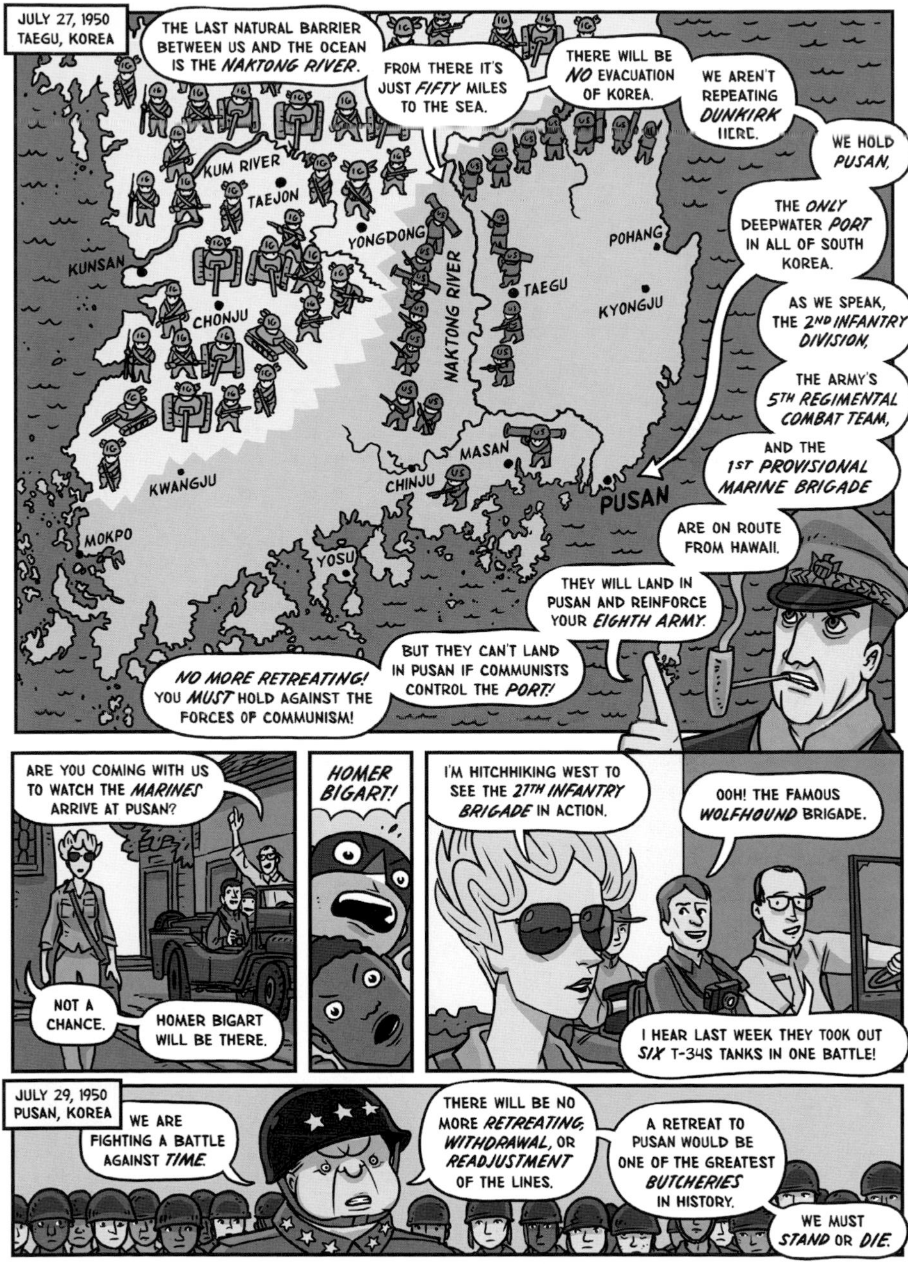
JULY 27, 1950
TAEGU, KOREA
THE LAST NATURAL BARRIER BETWEEN US AND THE OCEAN IS THE *NAKTONG RIVER*.
FROM THERE IT'S JUST *FIFTY* MILES TO THE SEA.
THERE WILL BE *NO* EVACUATION OF KOREA.
WE AREN'T REPEATING *DUNKIRK* HERE.
WE HOLD *PUSAN*,
THE *ONLY* DEEPWATER *PORT* IN ALL OF SOUTH KOREA.
AS WE SPEAK, THE 2ND *INFANTRY DIVISION*,
THE ARMY'S *5TH REGIMENTAL COMBAT TEAM*,
AND THE *1ST PROVISIONAL MARINE BRIGADE*
ARE ON ROUTE FROM HAWAII.
THEY WILL LAND IN PUSAN AND REINFORCE YOUR *EIGHTH ARMY*.
BUT THEY CAN'T LAND IN PUSAN IF COMMUNISTS CONTROL THE *PORT!*
NO MORE RETREATING! YOU *MUST* HOLD AGAINST THE FORCES OF COMMUNISM!
KUM RIVER
TAEJON
YONGDONG
KUNSAN
CHONJU
NAKTONG RIVER
POHANG
TAEGU
KYONGJU
MASAN
CHINJU
KWANGJU
PUSAN
MOKPO
YOSU
ARE YOU COMING WITH US TO WATCH THE *MARINES* ARRIVE AT PUSAN?
NOT A CHANCE.
HOMER BIGART WILL BE THERE.
HOMER BIGART!
I'M HITCHHIKING WEST TO SEE THE *27TH INFANTRY BRIGADE* IN ACTION.
OOH! THE FAMOUS *WOLFHOUND* BRIGADE.
I HEAR LAST WEEK THEY TOOK OUT *SIX* T-34S TANKS IN ONE BATTLE!
JULY 29, 1950
PUSAN, KOREA
WE ARE FIGHTING A BATTLE AGAINST *TIME*.
THERE WILL BE NO MORE *RETREATING*, *WITHDRAWAL*, OR *READJUSTMENT* OF THE LINES.
A RETREAT TO PUSAN WOULD BE ONE OF THE GREATEST *BUTCHERIES* IN HISTORY.
WE MUST *STAND* OR *DIE*.

Chapter 15

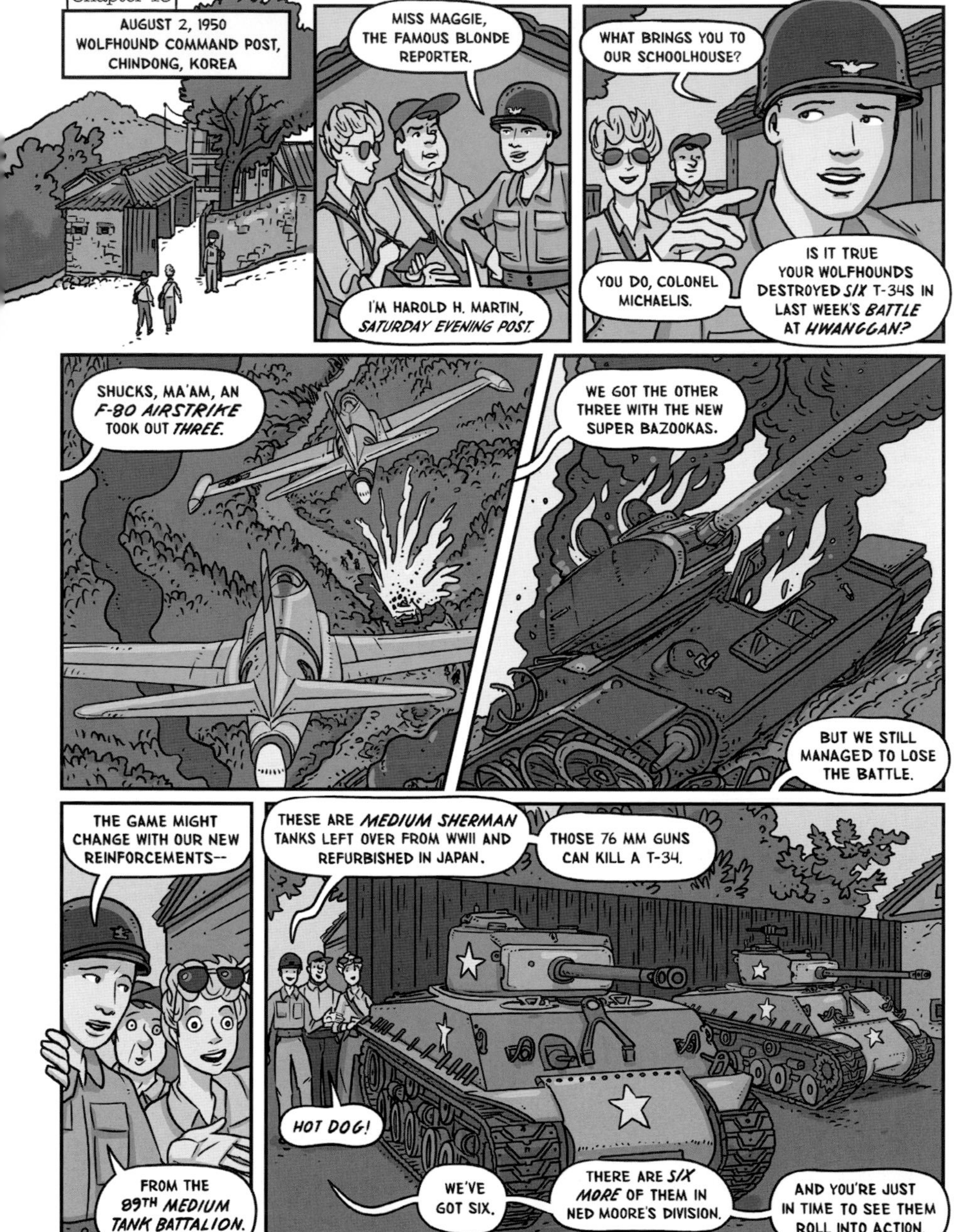
AUGUST 2, 1950
WOLFHOUND COMMAND POST,
CHINDONG, KOREA
MISS MAGGIE, THE FAMOUS BLONDE REPORTER.
I'M HAROLD H. MARTIN, *SATURDAY EVENING POST.*
WHAT BRINGS YOU TO OUR SCHOOLHOUSE?
YOU DO, COLONEL MICHAELIS.
IS IT TRUE YOUR WOLFHOUNDS DESTROYED *SIX* T-34S IN LAST WEEK'S *BATTLE* AT *HWANGGAN?*
SHUCKS, MA'AM, AN *F-80 AIRSTRIKE* TOOK OUT *THREE.*
WE GOT THE OTHER THREE WITH THE NEW SUPER BAZOOKAS.
BUT WE STILL MANAGED TO LOSE THE BATTLE.
THE GAME MIGHT CHANGE WITH OUR NEW REINFORCEMENTS--
FROM THE 89TH *MEDIUM TANK BATTALION.*
THESE ARE *MEDIUM SHERMAN* TANKS LEFT OVER FROM WWII AND REFURBISHED IN JAPAN.
THOSE 76 MM GUNS CAN KILL A T-34.
HOT DOG!
WE'VE GOT SIX.
THERE ARE *SIX MORE* OF THEM IN NED MOORE'S DIVISION.
AND YOU'RE JUST IN TIME TO SEE THEM ROLL INTO ACTION.

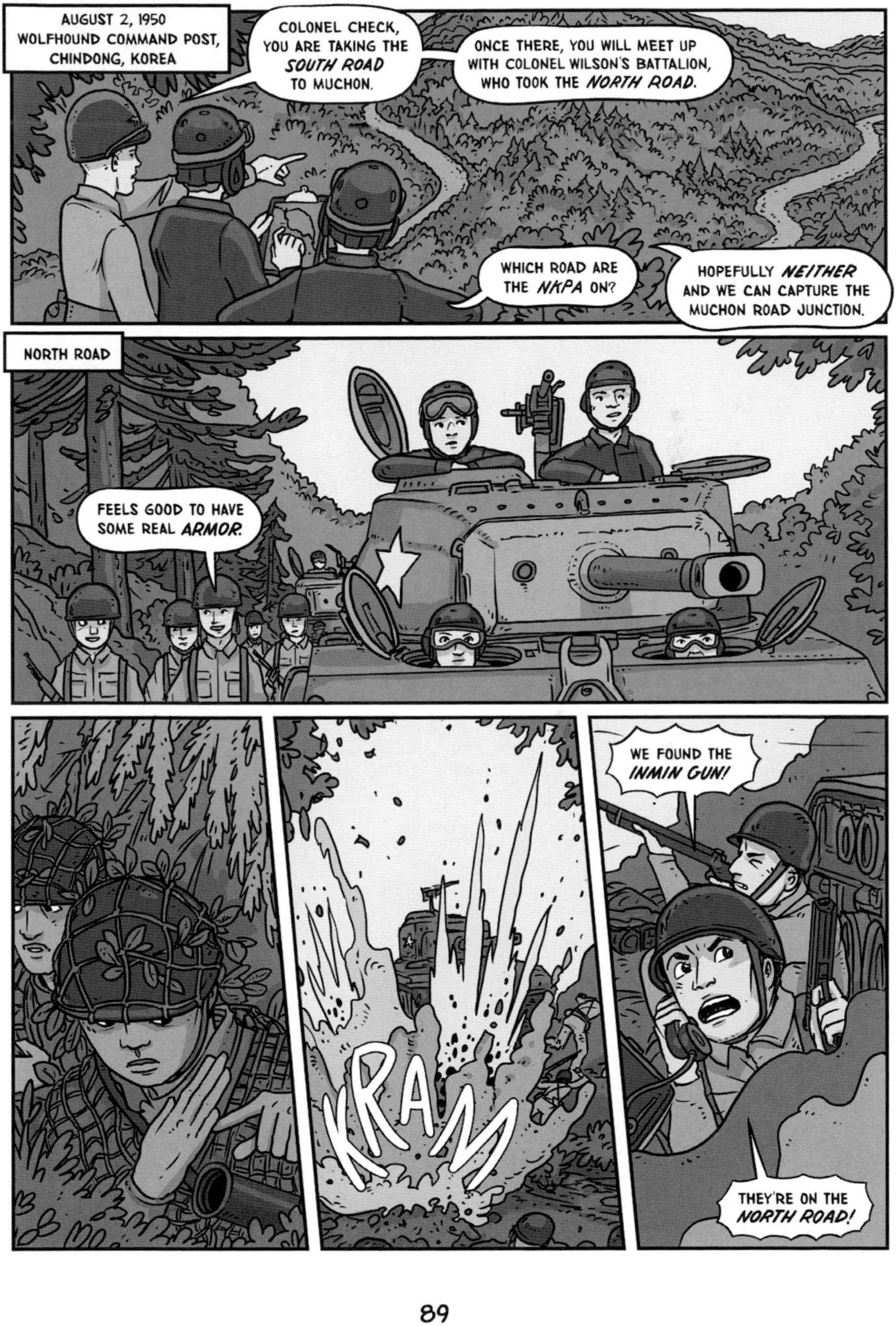
AUGUST 2, 1950
WOLFHOUND COMMAND POST,
CHINDONG, KOREA
COLONEL CHECK, YOU ARE TAKING THE *SOUTH ROAD* TO MUCHON.
ONCE THERE, YOU WILL MEET UP WITH COLONEL WILSON'S BATTALION, WHO TOOK THE *NORTH ROAD.*
WHICH ROAD ARE THE *NKPA* ON?
HOPEFULLY *NEITHER* AND WE CAN CAPTURE THE MUCHON ROAD JUNCTION.
NORTH ROAD
FEELS GOOD TO HAVE SOME REAL *ARMOR.*
KRAM
WE FOUND THE *INMIN GUN!*
THEY'RE ON THE *NORTH ROAD!*

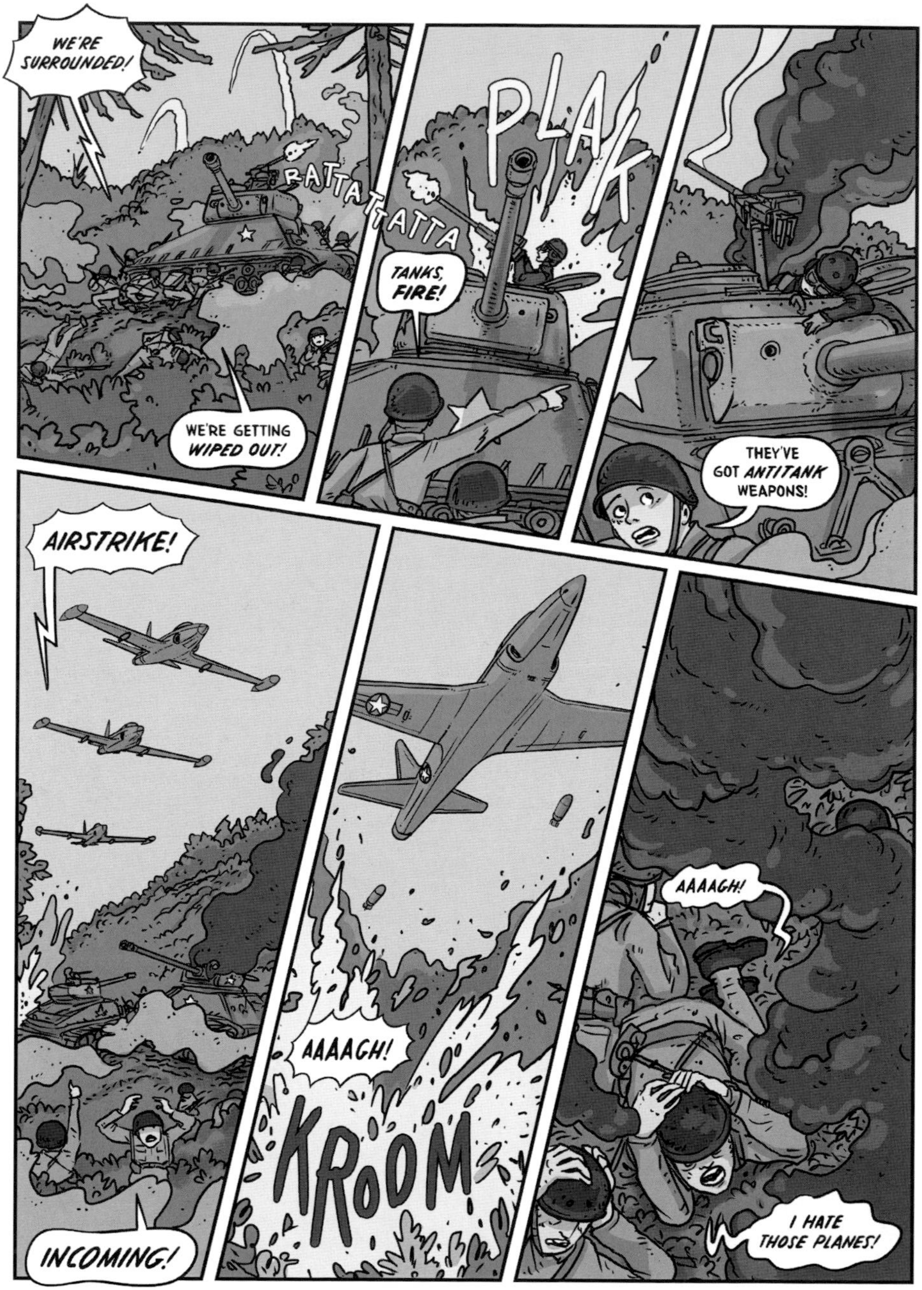
WE'RE SURROUNDED!
RATTATTATTA
WE'RE GETTING WIPED OUT!
PLAK
TANKS, FIRE!
THEY'VE GOT ANTITANK WEAPONS!
AIRSTRIKE!
INCOMING!
AAAAGH!
KROOM
AAAAGH!
I HATE THOSE PLANES!

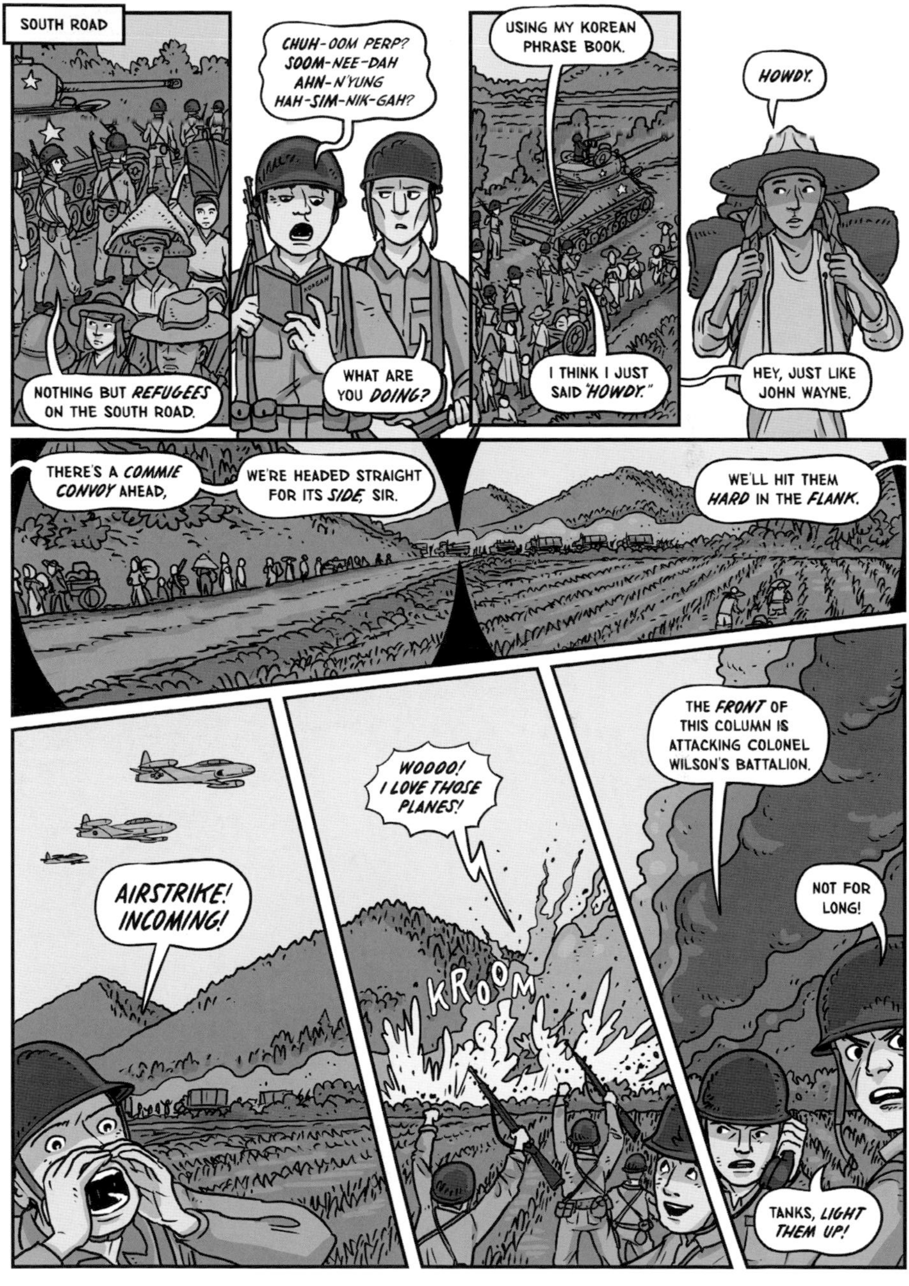
SOUTH ROAD
NOTHING BUT REFUGEES ON THE SOUTH ROAD.
CHUH-OOM PERP? SOOM-NEE-DAH AHN-N'YUNG HAH-SIM-NIK-GAH?
KOREAN
WHAT ARE YOU DOING?
USING MY KOREAN PHRASE BOOK.
I THINK I JUST SAID "HOWDY."
HOWDY.
HEY, JUST LIKE JOHN WAYNE.
THERE'S A COMMIE CONVOY AHEAD,
WE'RE HEADED STRAIGHT FOR ITS SIDE, SIR.
WE'LL HIT THEM HARD IN THE FLANK.
AIRSTRIKE! INCOMING!
WOOOO! I LOVE THOSE PLANES!
KROOM
THE FRONT OF THIS COLUMN IS ATTACKING COLONEL WILSON'S BATTALION.
NOT FOR LONG!
TANKS, LIGHT THEM UP!

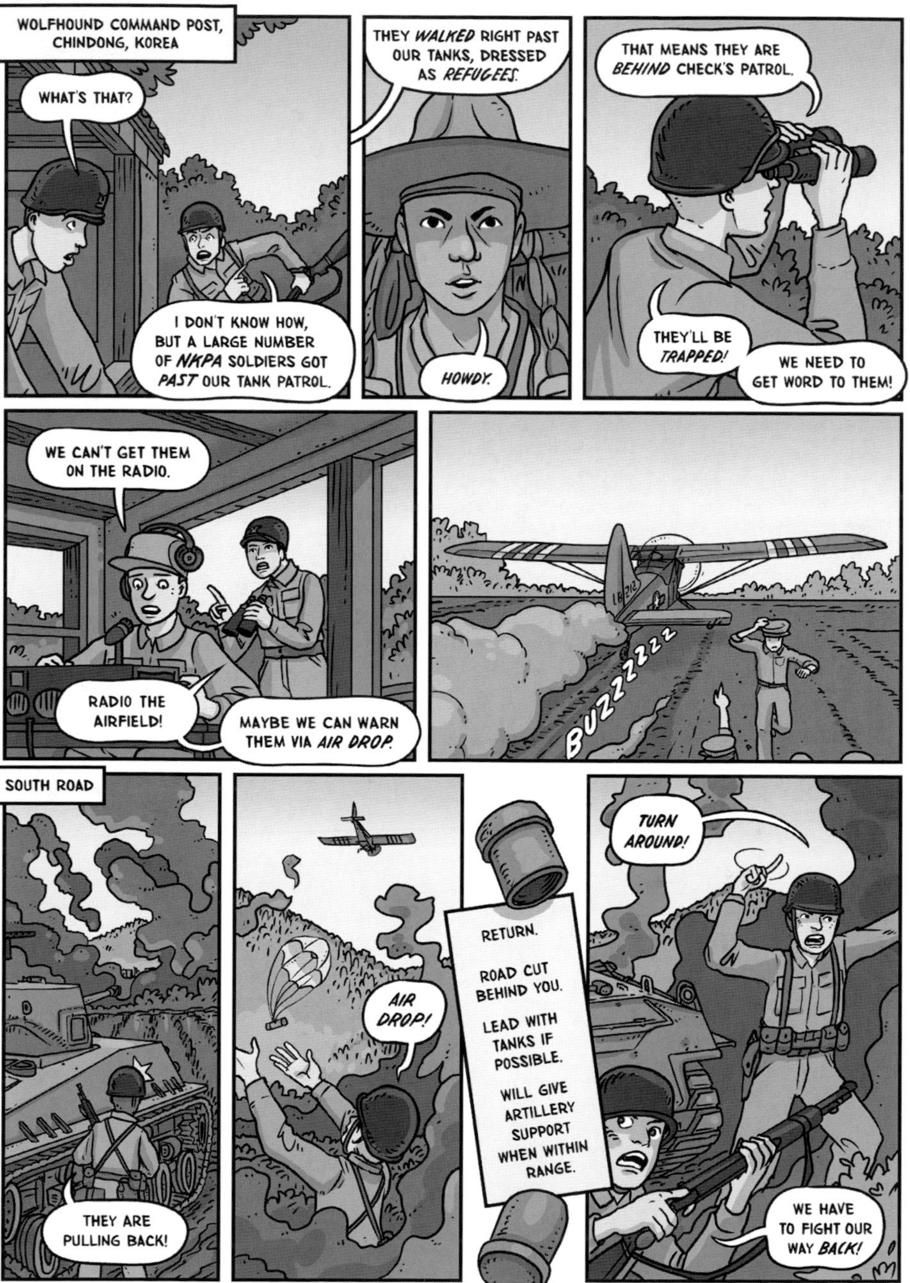
WOLFHOUND COMMAND POST, CHINDONG, KOREA
WHAT'S THAT?
I DON'T KNOW HOW, BUT A LARGE NUMBER OF NKPA SOLDIERS GOT PAST OUR TANK PATROL.
THEY WALKED RIGHT PAST OUR TANKS, DRESSED AS REFUGEES.
HOWDY.
THAT MEANS THEY ARE BEHIND CHECK'S PATROL.
THEY'LL BE TRAPPED!
WE NEED TO GET WORD TO THEM!
WE CAN'T GET THEM ON THE RADIO.
RADIO THE AIRFIELD!
MAYBE WE CAN WARN THEM VIA AIR DROP.
BUZZZZZZ
SOUTH ROAD
THEY ARE PULLING BACK!
AIR DROP!
RETURN.
ROAD CUT BEHIND YOU.
LEAD WITH TANKS IF POSSIBLE.
WILL GIVE ARTILLERY SUPPORT WHEN WITHIN RANGE.
TURN AROUND!
WE HAVE TO FIGHT OUR WAY BACK!

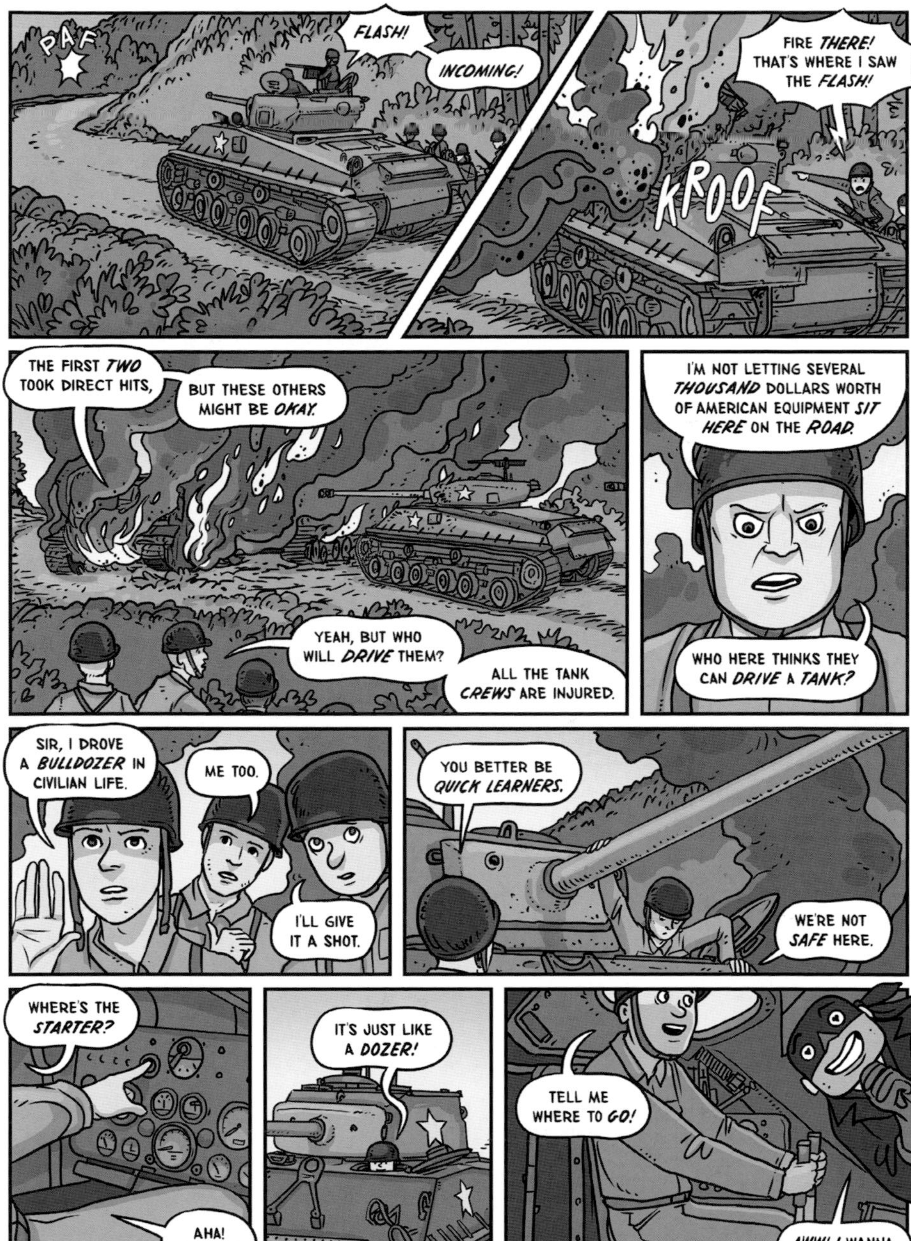
PAF
FLASH!
INCOMING!
FIRE THERE! THAT'S WHERE I SAW THE FLASH!
KROOF
THE FIRST TWO TOOK DIRECT HITS,
BUT THESE OTHERS MIGHT BE OKAY.
YEAH, BUT WHO WILL DRIVE THEM?
ALL THE TANK CREWS ARE INJURED.
I'M NOT LETTING SEVERAL THOUSAND DOLLARS WORTH OF AMERICAN EQUIPMENT SIT HERE ON THE ROAD.
WHO HERE THINKS THEY CAN DRIVE A TANK?
SIR, I DROVE A BULLDOZER IN CIVILIAN LIFE.
ME TOO.
I'LL GIVE IT A SHOT.
YOU BETTER BE QUICK LEARNERS.
WE'RE NOT SAFE HERE.
WHERE'S THE STARTER?
AHA! THAT'S IT.
IT'S JUST LIKE A DOZER!
TELL ME WHERE TO GO!
AWW! I WANNA DRIVE ONE!

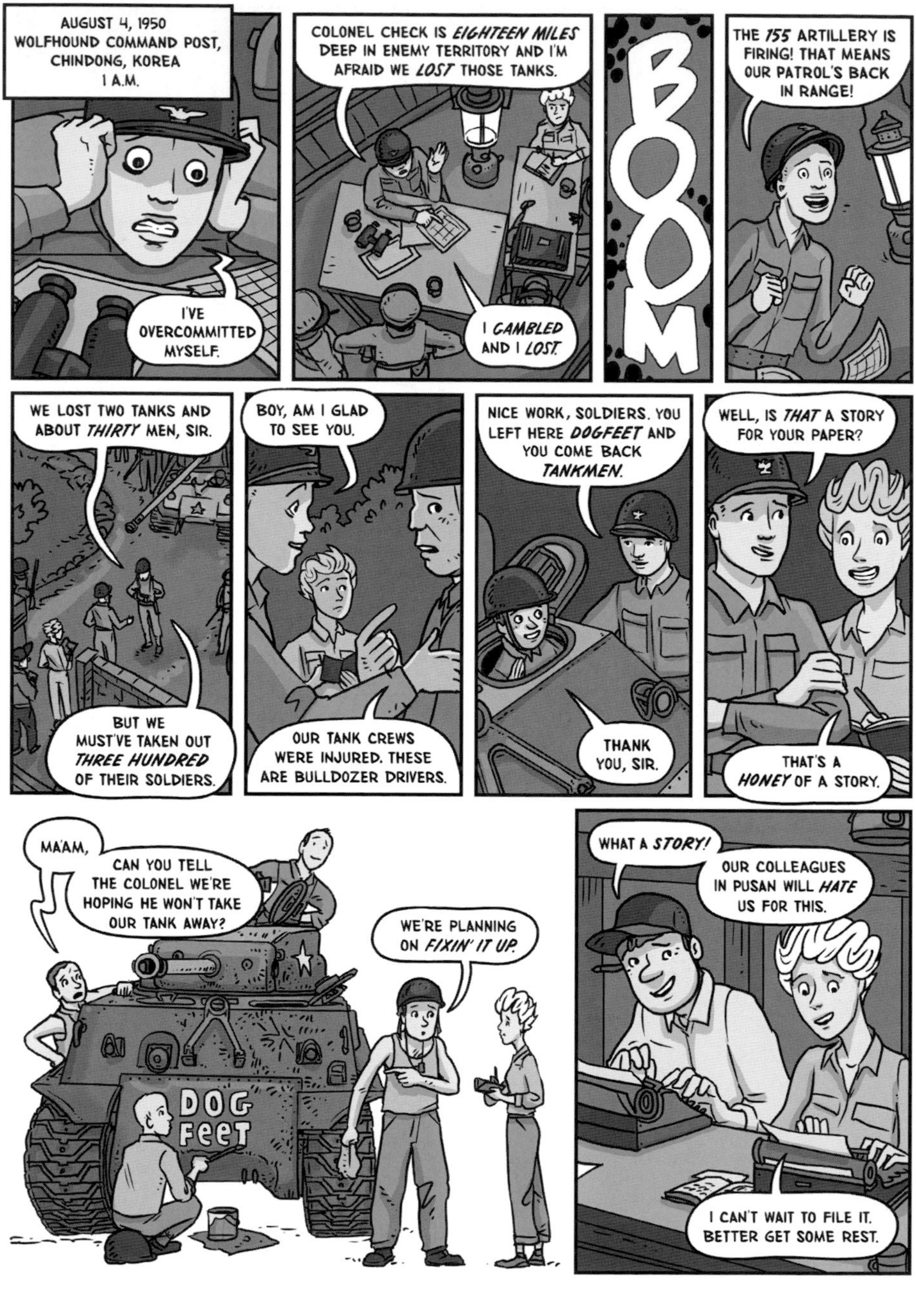
AUGUST 4, 1950
WOLFHOUND COMMAND POST, CHINDONG, KOREA
1 A.M.
I'VE OVERCOMMITTED MYSELF.
COLONEL CHECK IS *EIGHTEEN MILES* DEEP IN ENEMY TERRITORY AND I'M AFRAID WE *LOST* THOSE TANKS.
I *GAMBLED* AND I *LOST.*
BOOM
THE *155* ARTILLERY IS FIRING! THAT MEANS OUR PATROL'S BACK IN RANGE!
WE LOST TWO TANKS AND ABOUT *THIRTY* MEN, SIR.
BUT WE MUST'VE TAKEN OUT *THREE HUNDRED* OF THEIR SOLDIERS.
BOY, AM I GLAD TO SEE YOU.
OUR TANK CREWS WERE INJURED. THESE ARE BULLDOZER DRIVERS.
NICE WORK, SOLDIERS. YOU LEFT HERE *DOGFEET* AND YOU COME BACK *TANKMEN.*
THANK YOU, SIR.
WELL, IS *THAT* A STORY FOR YOUR PAPER?
THAT'S A *HONEY* OF A STORY.
MA'AM,
CAN YOU TELL THE COLONEL WE'RE HOPING HE WON'T TAKE OUR TANK AWAY?
WE'RE PLANNING ON *FIXIN' IT UP.*
DOG FEET
WHAT A *STORY!*
OUR COLLEAGUES IN PUSAN WILL *HATE* US FOR THIS.
I CAN'T WAIT TO FILE IT. BETTER GET SOME REST.

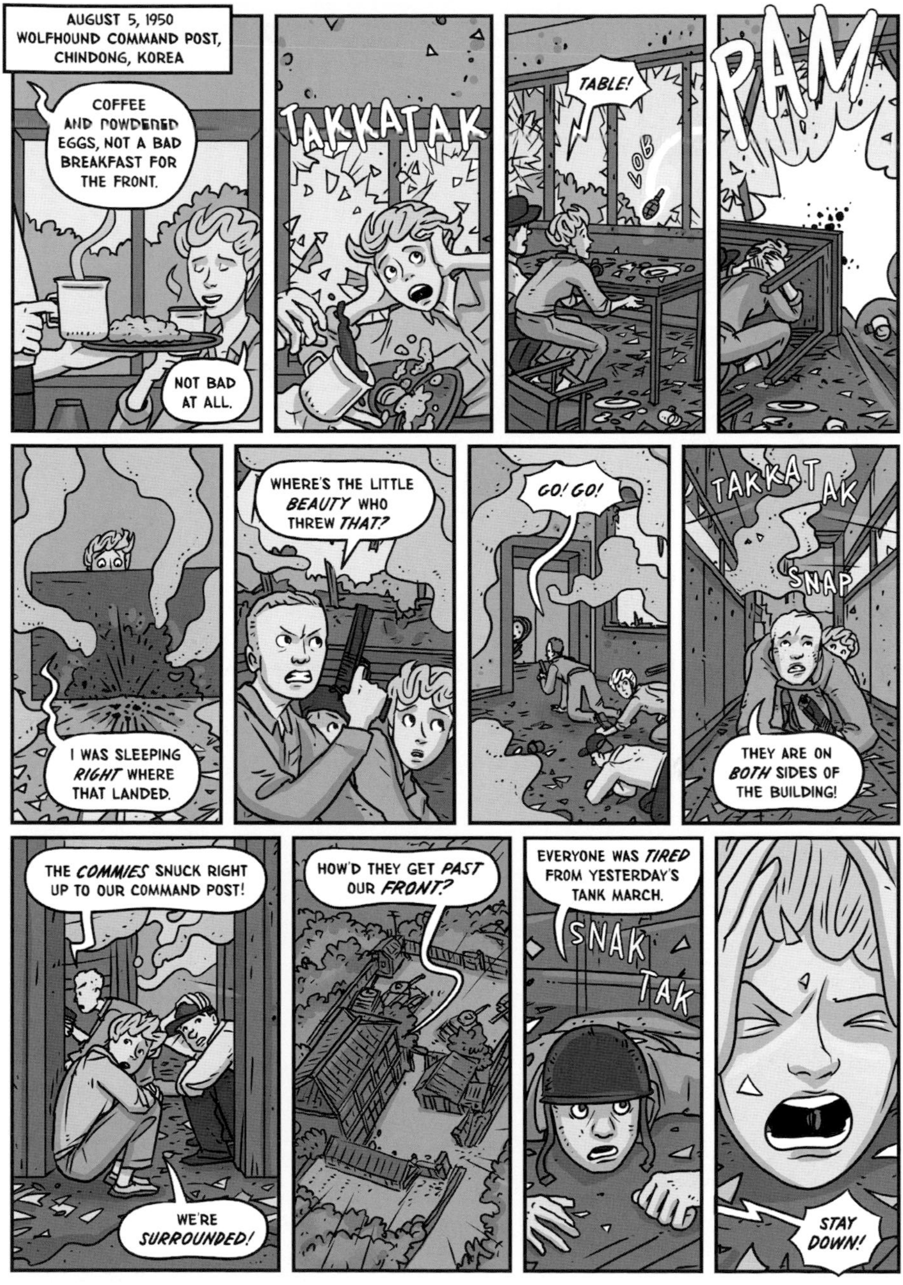
AUGUST 5, 1950
WOLFHOUND COMMAND POST,
CHINDONG, KOREA
COFFEE AND POWDERED EGGS, NOT A BAD BREAKFAST FOR THE FRONT.
NOT BAD AT ALL.
TAKKATAK
TABLE!
LOB
PAM
I WAS SLEEPING *RIGHT* WHERE THAT LANDED.
WHERE'S THE LITTLE *BEAUTY* WHO THREW *THAT?*
GO! GO!
TAKKATAK
SNAP
THEY ARE ON *BOTH* SIDES OF THE BUILDING!
THE *COMMIES* SNUCK RIGHT UP TO OUR COMMAND POST!
WE'RE *SURROUNDED!*
HOW'D THEY GET *PAST* OUR *FRONT?*
EVERYONE WAS *TIRED* FROM YESTERDAY'S TANK MARCH.
SNAK
TAK
STAY DOWN!

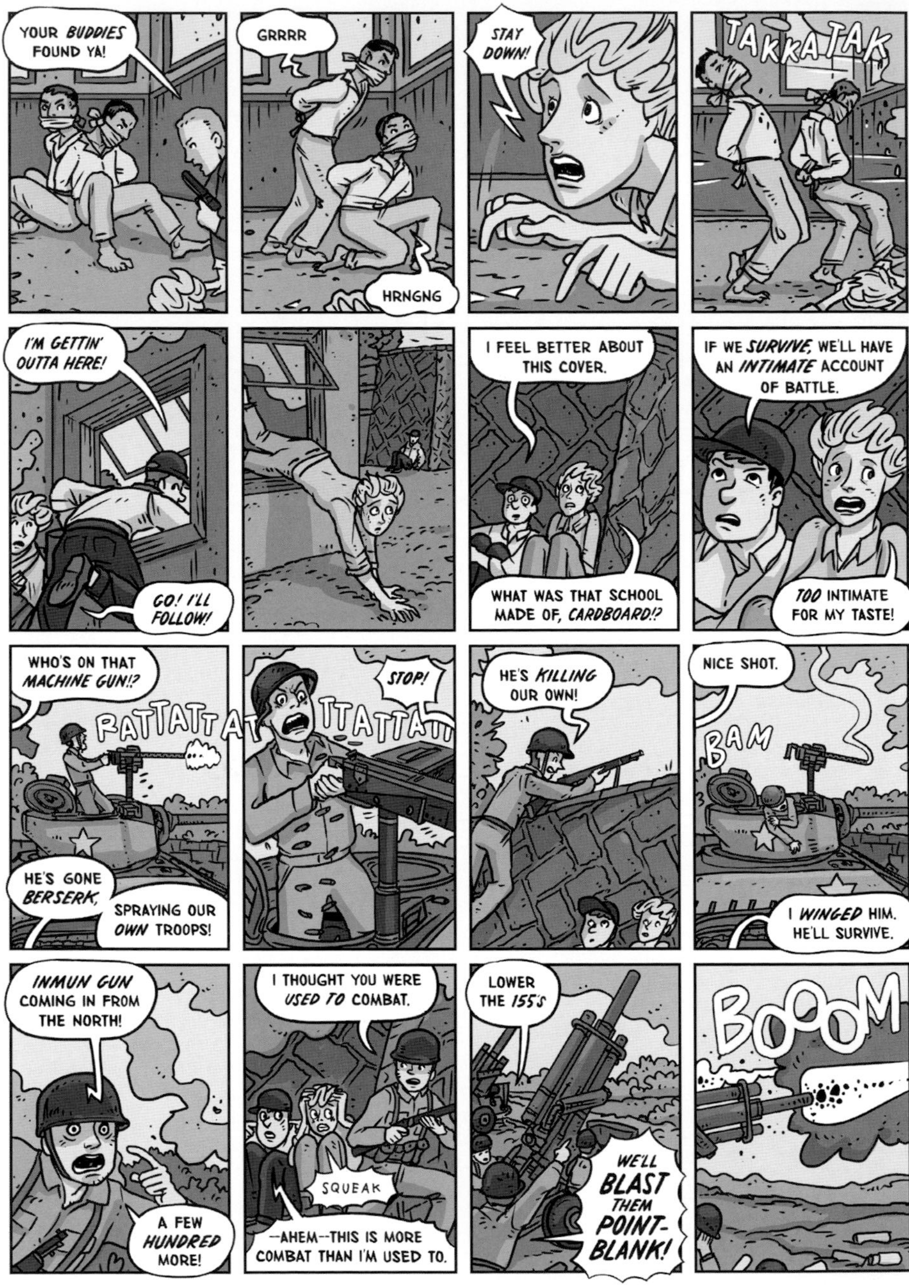
YOUR BUDDIES FOUND YA!
GRRRR
HRNGNG
STAY DOWN!
TAKKATAK
I'M GETTIN' OUTTA HERE!
GO! I'LL FOLLOW!
I FEEL BETTER ABOUT THIS COVER.
WHAT WAS THAT SCHOOL MADE OF, CARDBOARD!?
IF WE SURVIVE, WE'LL HAVE AN INTIMATE ACCOUNT OF BATTLE.
TOO INTIMATE FOR MY TASTE!
WHO'S ON THAT MACHINE GUN!?
RATTATTAT
HE'S GONE BERSERK,
SPRAYING OUR OWN TROOPS!
STOP!
TTATTATT
HE'S KILLING OUR OWN!
NICE SHOT.
BAM
I WINGED HIM. HE'LL SURVIVE.
INMUN GUN COMING IN FROM THE NORTH!
A FEW HUNDRED MORE!
I THOUGHT YOU WERE USED TO COMBAT.
SQUEAK
--AHEM--THIS IS MORE COMBAT THAN I'M USED TO.
LOWER THE 155'S
WE'LL BLAST THEM POINT-BLANK!
BOOOM

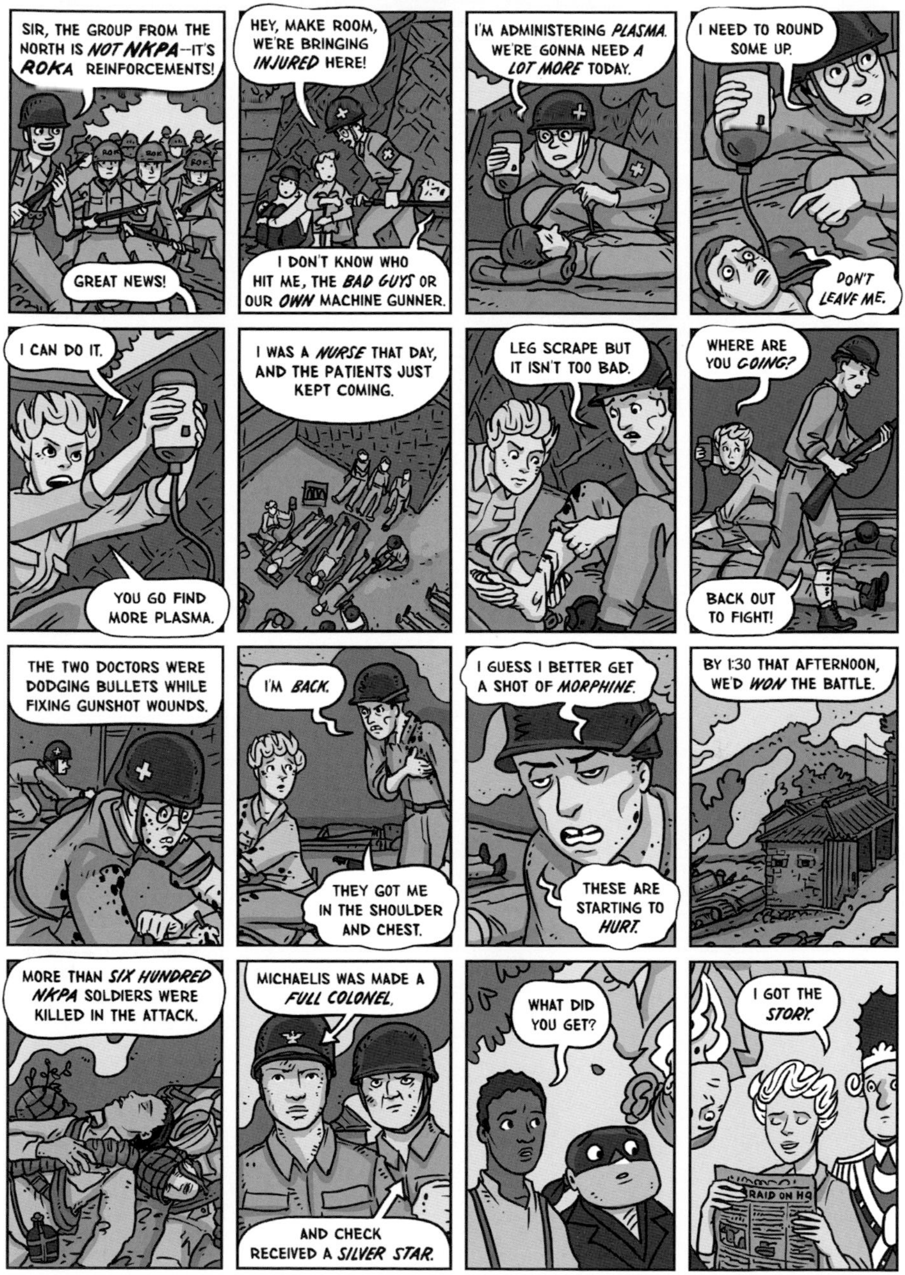
SIR, THE GROUP FROM THE NORTH IS *NOT NKPA*--IT'S *ROKA* REINFORCEMENTS!
ROK
GREAT NEWS!
HEY, MAKE ROOM, WE'RE BRINGING *INJURED* HERE!
I DON'T KNOW WHO HIT ME, THE *BAD GUYS* OR OUR *OWN* MACHINE GUNNER.
I'M ADMINISTERING *PLASMA*. WE'RE GONNA NEED *A LOT MORE* TODAY.
I NEED TO ROUND SOME UP.
DON'T *LEAVE ME*.
I CAN DO IT.
YOU GO FIND MORE PLASMA.
I WAS A *NURSE* THAT DAY, AND THE PATIENTS JUST KEPT COMING.
LEG SCRAPE BUT IT ISN'T TOO BAD.
WHERE ARE YOU *GOING?*
BACK OUT TO FIGHT!
THE TWO DOCTORS WERE DODGING BULLETS WHILE FIXING GUNSHOT WOUNDS.
I'M *BACK*.
THEY GOT ME IN THE SHOULDER AND CHEST.
I GUESS I BETTER GET A SHOT OF *MORPHINE*.
THESE ARE STARTING TO *HURT*.
BY 1:30 THAT AFTERNOON, WE'D *WON* THE BATTLE.
MORE THAN *SIX HUNDRED NKPA* SOLDIERS WERE KILLED IN THE ATTACK.
MICHAELIS WAS MADE A *FULL COLONEL*,
AND CHECK RECEIVED A *SILVER STAR*.
WHAT DID YOU GET?
I GOT THE *STORY*.
RAID ON HQ

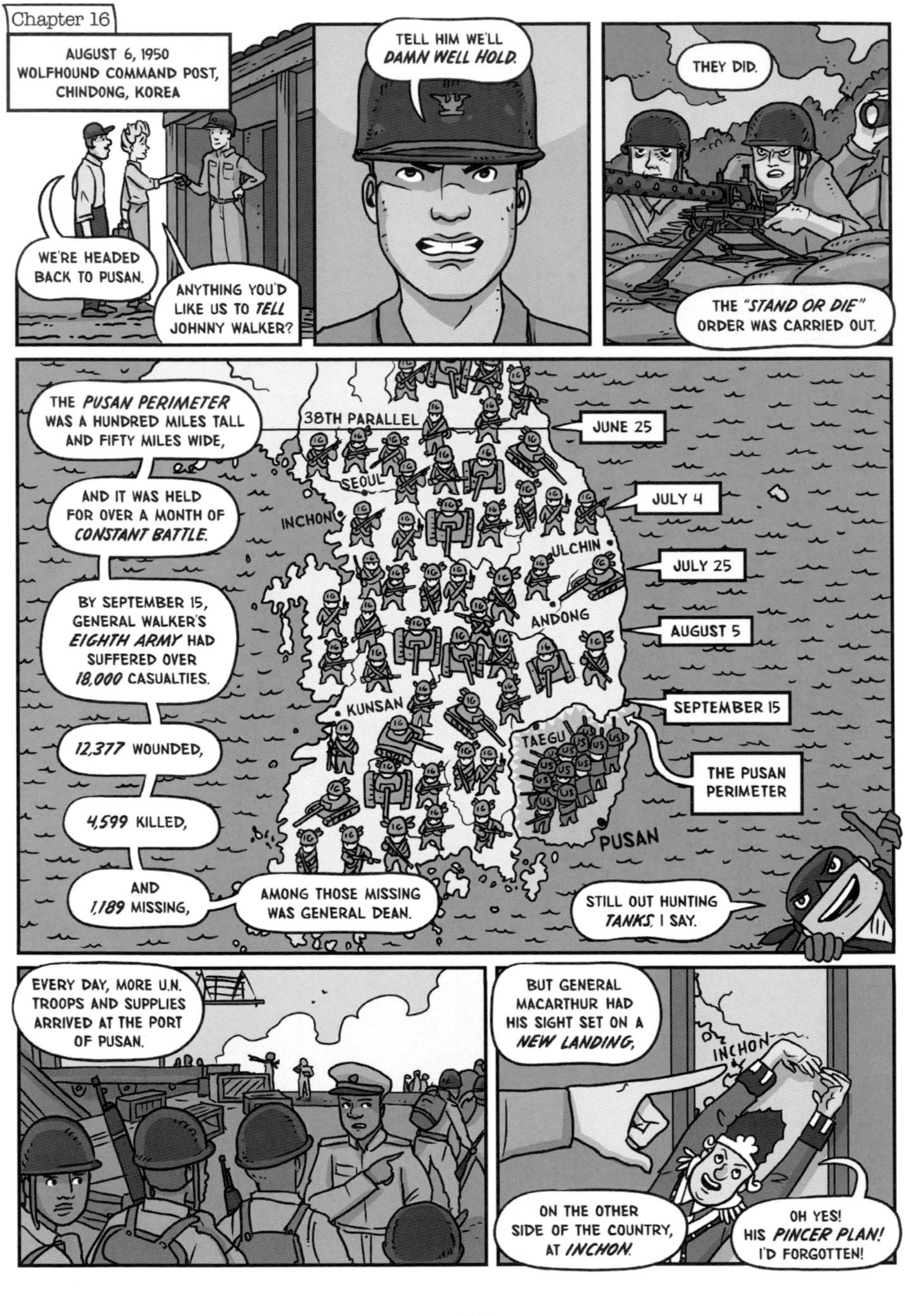
Chapter 16
AUGUST 6, 1950 WOLFHOUND COMMAND POST, CHINDONG, KOREA
WE'RE HEADED BACK TO PUSAN.
ANYTHING YOU'D LIKE US TO *TELL* JOHNNY WALKER?
TELL HIM WE'LL *DAMN WELL HOLD.*
THEY DID.
THE *"STAND OR DIE"* ORDER WAS CARRIED OUT.
THE *PUSAN PERIMETER* WAS A HUNDRED MILES TALL AND FIFTY MILES WIDE,
AND IT WAS HELD FOR OVER A MONTH OF *CONSTANT BATTLE.*
BY SEPTEMBER 15, GENERAL WALKER'S *EIGHTH ARMY* HAD SUFFERED OVER *18,000* CASUALTIES.
12,377 WOUNDED,
4,599 KILLED,
AND *1,189* MISSING,
AMONG THOSE MISSING WAS GENERAL DEAN.
38TH PARALLEL
SEOUL
INCHON
ULCHIN
ANDONG
KUNSAN
TAEGU
PUSAN
JUNE 25
JULY 4
JULY 25
AUGUST 5
SEPTEMBER 15
THE PUSAN PERIMETER
STILL OUT HUNTING *TANKS,* I SAY.
EVERY DAY, MORE U.N. TROOPS AND SUPPLIES ARRIVED AT THE PORT OF PUSAN.
BUT GENERAL MACARTHUR HAD HIS SIGHT SET ON A *NEW LANDING,*
INCHON
ON THE OTHER SIDE OF THE COUNTRY, AT *INCHON.*
OH YES! HIS *PINCER PLAN!* I'D FORGOTTEN!

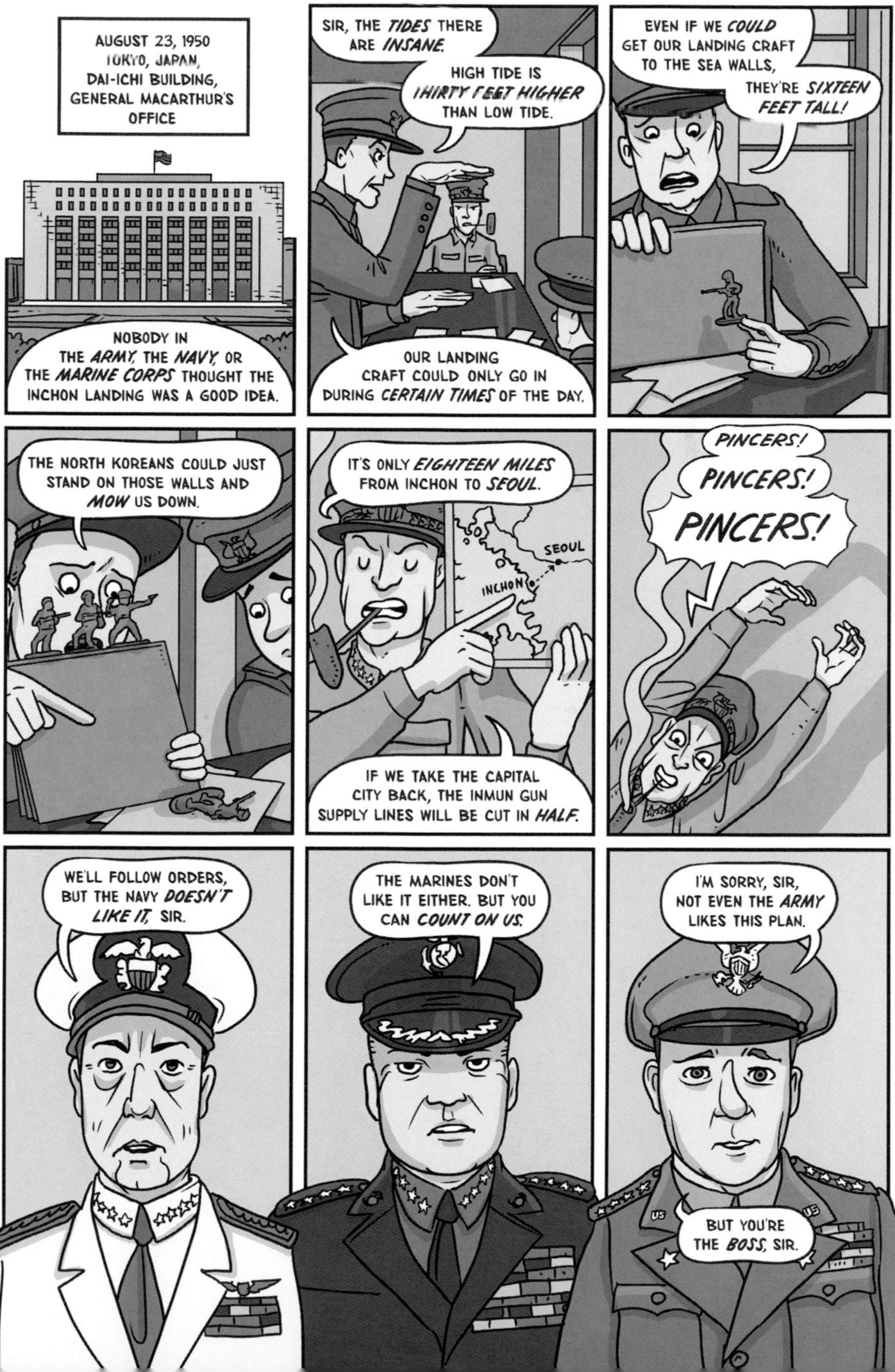
AUGUST 23, 1950
TOKYO, JAPAN,
DAI-ICHI BUILDING,
GENERAL MACARTHUR'S
OFFICE
NOBODY IN THE ARMY, THE NAVY, OR THE MARINE CORPS THOUGHT THE INCHON LANDING WAS A GOOD IDEA.
SIR, THE TIDES THERE ARE INSANE.
HIGH TIDE IS THIRTY FEET HIGHER THAN LOW TIDE.
OUR LANDING CRAFT COULD ONLY GO IN DURING CERTAIN TIMES OF THE DAY.
EVEN IF WE COULD GET OUR LANDING CRAFT TO THE SEA WALLS,
THEY'RE SIXTEEN FEET TALL!
THE NORTH KOREANS COULD JUST STAND ON THOSE WALLS AND MOW US DOWN.
IT'S ONLY EIGHTEEN MILES FROM INCHON TO SEOUL.
SEOUL
INCHON
IF WE TAKE THE CAPITAL CITY BACK, THE INMUN GUN SUPPLY LINES WILL BE CUT IN HALF.
PINCERS!
PINCERS!
PINCERS!
WE'LL FOLLOW ORDERS, BUT THE NAVY DOESN'T LIKE IT, SIR.
THE MARINES DON'T LIKE IT EITHER. BUT YOU CAN COUNT ON US.
I'M SORRY, SIR, NOT EVEN THE ARMY LIKES THIS PLAN.
BUT YOU'RE THE BOSS, SIR.

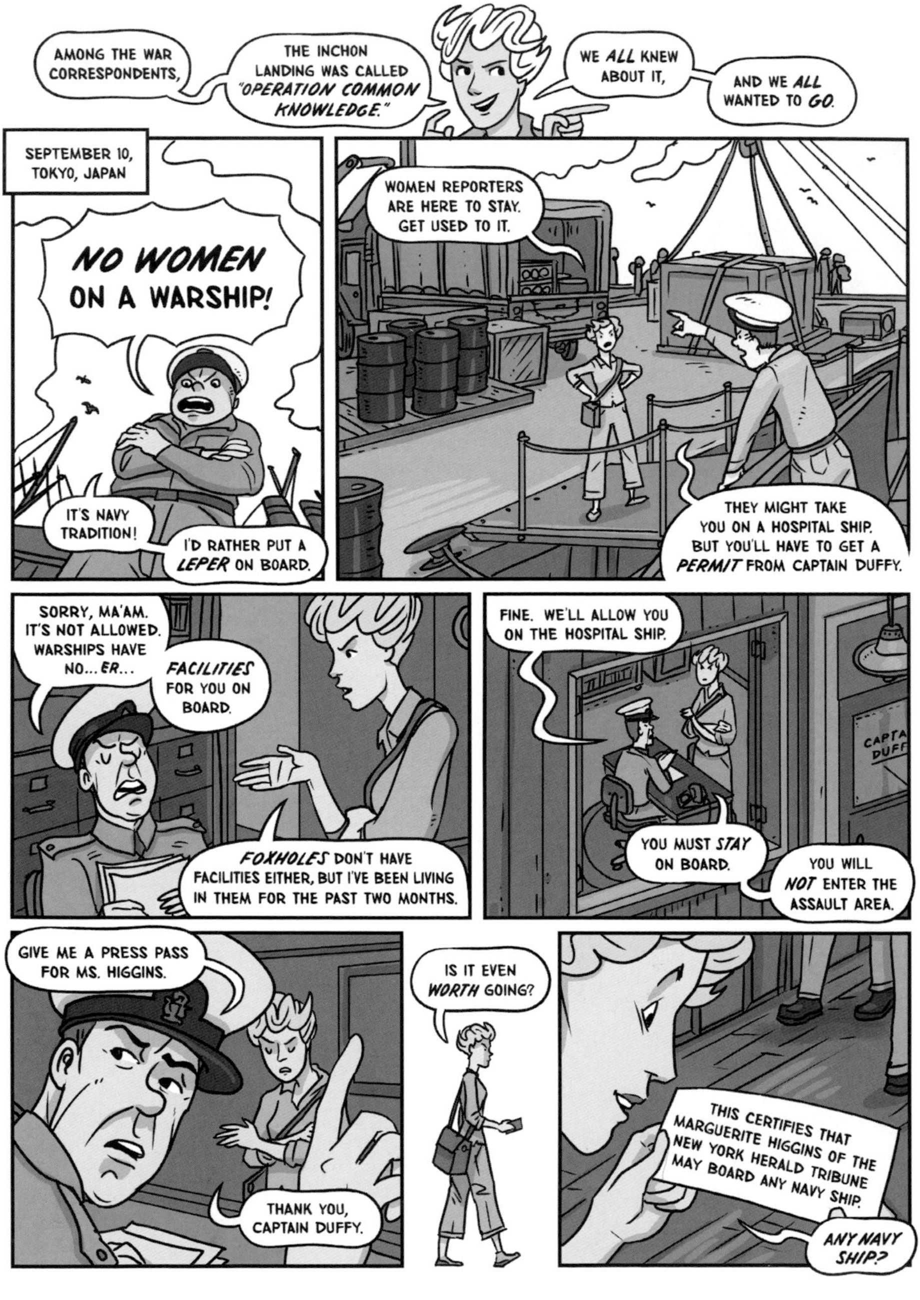
AMONG THE WAR CORRESPONDENTS,
THE INCHON LANDING WAS CALLED "OPERATION COMMON KNOWLEDGE."
WE ALL KNEW ABOUT IT,
AND WE ALL WANTED TO GO.
SEPTEMBER 10, TOKYO, JAPAN
NO WOMEN ON A WARSHIP!
IT'S NAVY TRADITION!
I'D RATHER PUT A LEPER ON BOARD.
WOMEN REPORTERS ARE HERE TO STAY. GET USED TO IT.
THEY MIGHT TAKE YOU ON A HOSPITAL SHIP. BUT YOU'LL HAVE TO GET A PERMIT FROM CAPTAIN DUFFY.
SORRY, MA'AM. IT'S NOT ALLOWED. WARSHIPS HAVE NO... ER...
FACILITIES FOR YOU ON BOARD.
FOXHOLES DON'T HAVE FACILITIES EITHER, BUT I'VE BEEN LIVING IN THEM FOR THE PAST TWO MONTHS.
FINE. WE'LL ALLOW YOU ON THE HOSPITAL SHIP.
YOU MUST STAY ON BOARD.
YOU WILL NOT ENTER THE ASSAULT AREA.
GIVE ME A PRESS PASS FOR MS. HIGGINS.
THANK YOU, CAPTAIN DUFFY.
IS IT EVEN WORTH GOING?
THIS CERTIFIES THAT MARGUERITE HIGGINS OF THE NEW YORK HERALD TRIBUNE MAY BOARD ANY NAVY SHIP.
ANY NAVY SHIP?

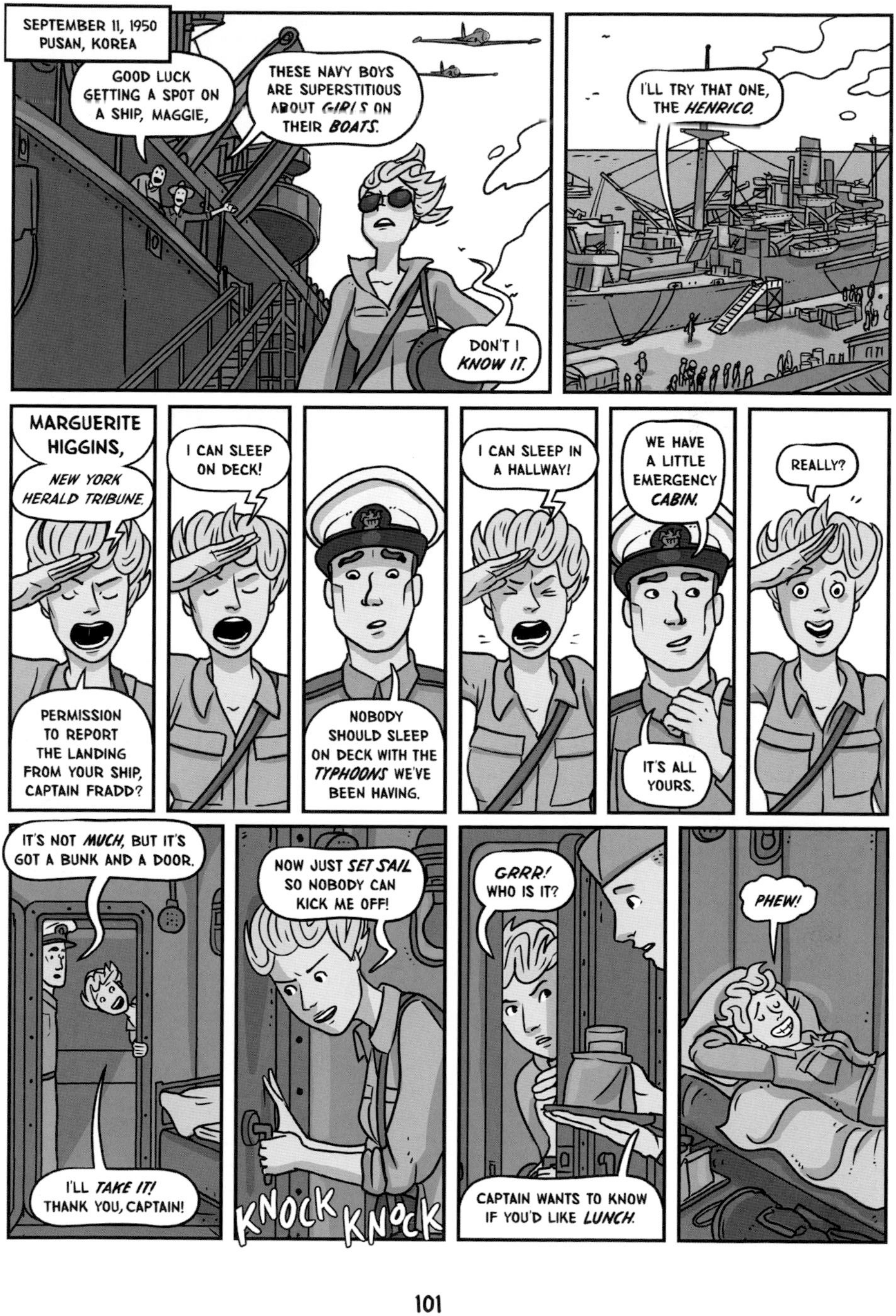

SEPTEMBER 11, 1950
PUSAN, KOREA
GOOD LUCK GETTING A SPOT ON A SHIP, MAGGIE,
THESE NAVY BOYS ARE SUPERSTITIOUS ABOUT *GIRLS* ON THEIR *BOATS*.
DON'T I *KNOW IT*.
I'LL TRY THAT ONE, THE *HENRICO*.
MARGUERITE HIGGINS,
NEW YORK HERALD TRIBUNE.
PERMISSION TO REPORT THE LANDING FROM YOUR SHIP, CAPTAIN FRADD?
I CAN SLEEP ON DECK!
NOBODY SHOULD SLEEP ON DECK WITH THE *TYPHOONS* WE'VE BEEN HAVING.
I CAN SLEEP IN A HALLWAY!
WE HAVE A LITTLE EMERGENCY *CABIN*.
IT'S ALL YOURS.
REALLY?
IT'S NOT *MUCH*, BUT IT'S GOT A BUNK AND A DOOR.
I'LL *TAKE IT!* THANK YOU, CAPTAIN!
NOW JUST *SET SAIL* SO NOBODY CAN KICK ME OFF!
KNOCK KNOCK
GRRR! WHO IS IT?
CAPTAIN WANTS TO KNOW IF YOU'D LIKE *LUNCH*.
PHEW!

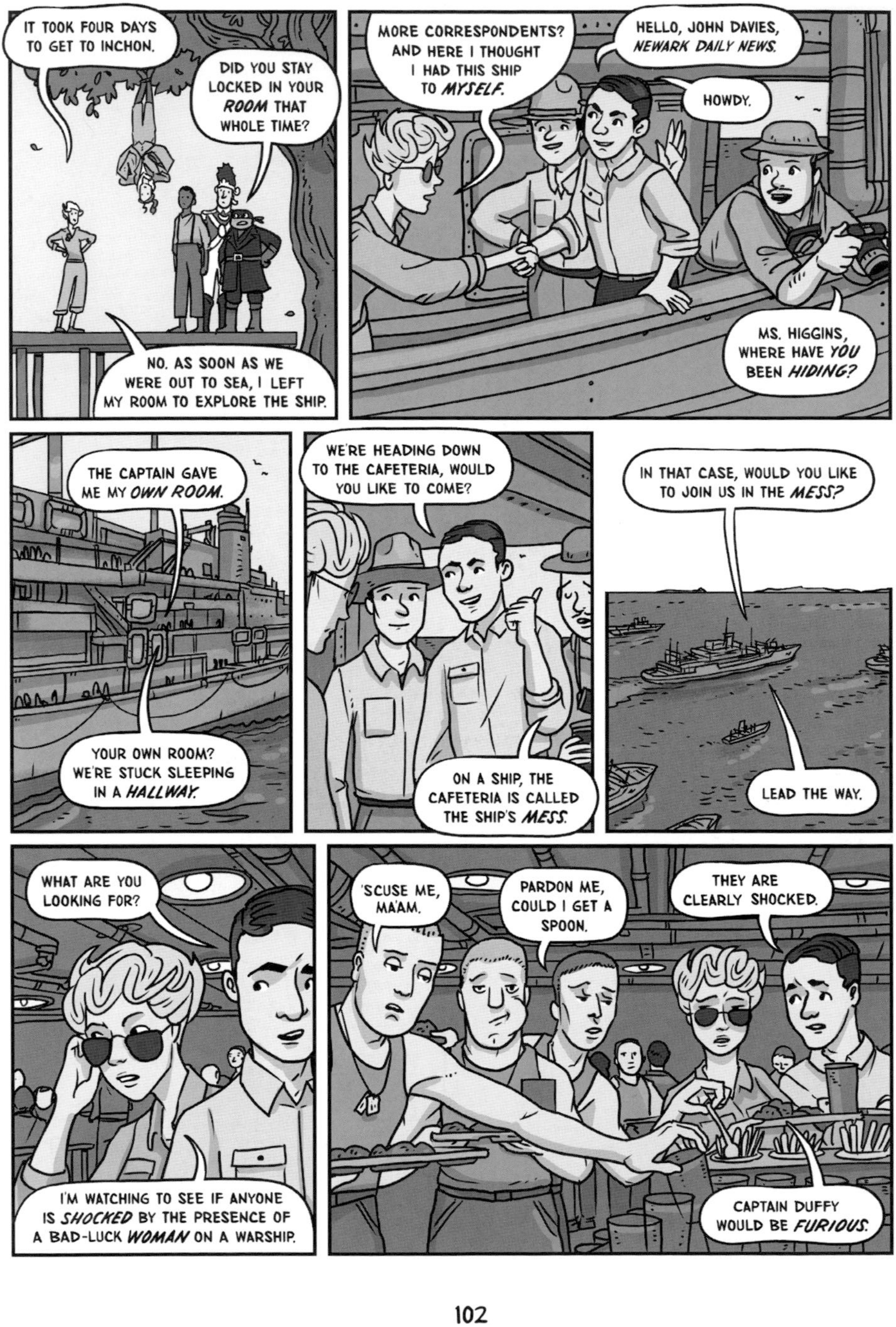
IT TOOK FOUR DAYS TO GET TO INCHON.
DID YOU STAY LOCKED IN YOUR *ROOM* THAT WHOLE TIME?
NO. AS SOON AS WE WERE OUT TO SEA, I LEFT MY ROOM TO EXPLORE THE SHIP.
MORE CORRESPONDENTS? AND HERE I THOUGHT I HAD THIS SHIP TO *MYSELF.*
HELLO, JOHN DAVIES, *NEWARK DAILY NEWS.*
HOWDY.
MS. HIGGINS, WHERE HAVE *YOU* BEEN *HIDING?*
THE CAPTAIN GAVE ME MY *OWN ROOM.*
YOUR OWN ROOM? WE'RE STUCK SLEEPING IN A *HALLWAY.*
WE'RE HEADING DOWN TO THE CAFETERIA, WOULD YOU LIKE TO COME?
ON A SHIP, THE CAFETERIA IS CALLED THE SHIP'S *MESS.*
IN THAT CASE, WOULD YOU LIKE TO JOIN US IN THE *MESS?*
LEAD THE WAY.
WHAT ARE YOU LOOKING FOR?
I'M WATCHING TO SEE IF ANYONE IS *SHOCKED* BY THE PRESENCE OF A BAD-LUCK *WOMAN* ON A WARSHIP.
'SCUSE ME, MA'AM.
PARDON ME, COULD I GET A SPOON.
THEY ARE CLEARLY SHOCKED.
CAPTAIN DUFFY WOULD BE *FURIOUS.*

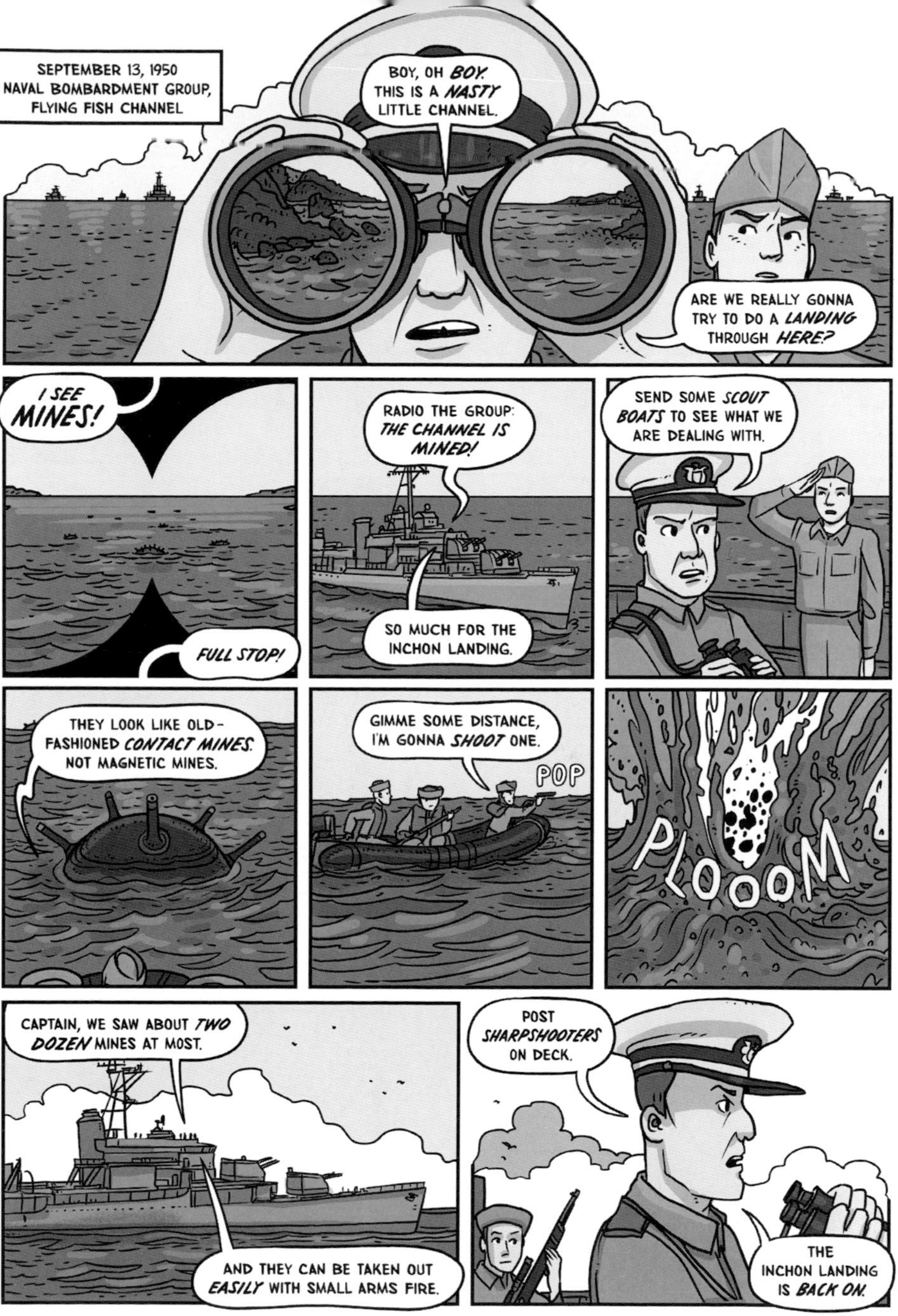
SEPTEMBER 13, 1950
NAVAL BOMBARDMENT GROUP,
FLYING FISH CHANNEL
BOY, OH BOY. THIS IS A NASTY LITTLE CHANNEL.
ARE WE REALLY GONNA TRY TO DO A LANDING THROUGH HERE?
I SEE MINES!
FULL STOP!
RADIO THE GROUP: THE CHANNEL IS MINED!
SO MUCH FOR THE INCHON LANDING.
SEND SOME SCOUT BOATS TO SEE WHAT WE ARE DEALING WITH.
THEY LOOK LIKE OLD-FASHIONED CONTACT MINES. NOT MAGNETIC MINES.
GIMME SOME DISTANCE, I'M GONNA SHOOT ONE.
POP
PLOOOM
CAPTAIN, WE SAW ABOUT TWO DOZEN MINES AT MOST.
AND THEY CAN BE TAKEN OUT EASILY WITH SMALL ARMS FIRE.
POST SHARPSHOOTERS ON DECK.
THE INCHON LANDING IS BACK ON.

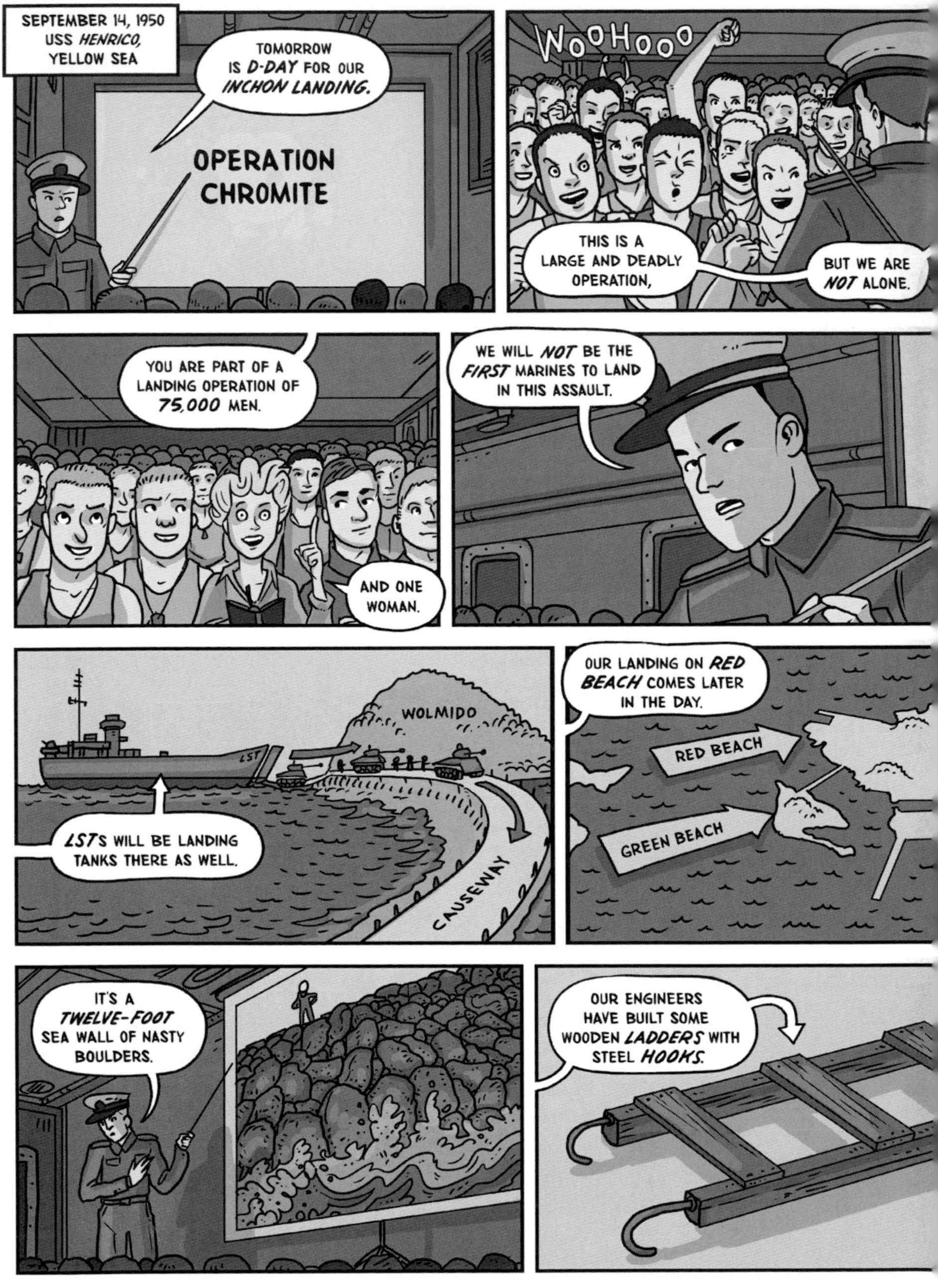
SEPTEMBER 14, 1950
USS *HENRICO*, YELLOW SEA
TOMORROW IS *D-DAY* FOR OUR *INCHON LANDING.*
OPERATION CHROMITE
WOOHOOO
THIS IS A LARGE AND DEADLY OPERATION,
BUT WE ARE *NOT* ALONE.
YOU ARE PART OF A LANDING OPERATION OF *75,000* MEN.
AND ONE WOMAN.
WE WILL *NOT* BE THE *FIRST* MARINES TO LAND IN THIS ASSAULT.
WOLMIDO
LST
*LST*S WILL BE LANDING TANKS THERE AS WELL.
CAUSEWAY
OUR LANDING ON *RED BEACH* COMES LATER IN THE DAY.
RED BEACH
GREEN BEACH
IT'S A *TWELVE-FOOT* SEA WALL OF NASTY BOULDERS.
OUR ENGINEERS HAVE BUILT SOME WOODEN *LADDERS* WITH STEEL *HOOKS*.

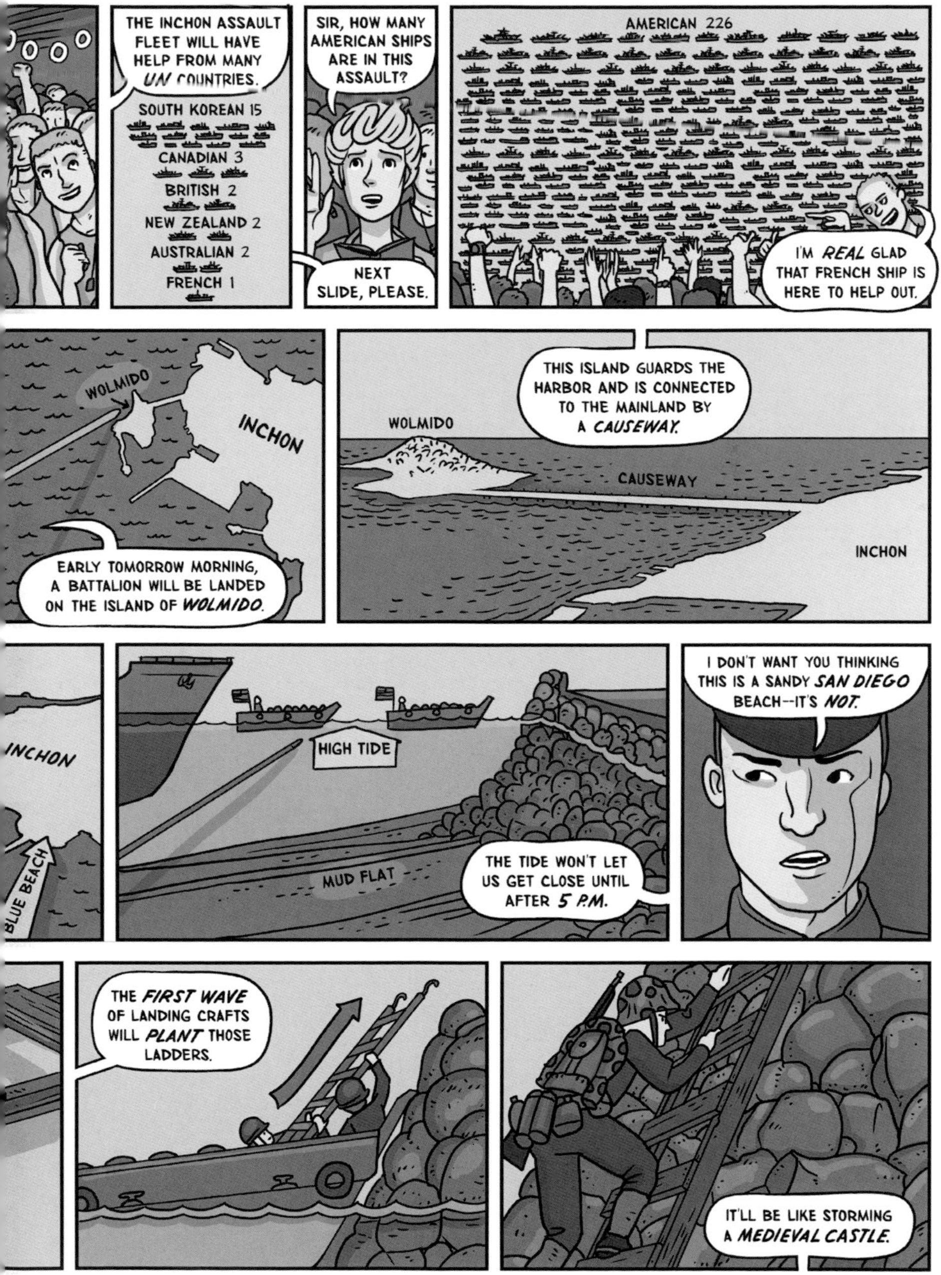
THE INCHON ASSAULT FLEET WILL HAVE HELP FROM MANY UN COUNTRIES.
SOUTH KOREAN 15
CANADIAN 3
BRITISH 2
NEW ZEALAND 2
AUSTRALIAN 2
FRENCH 1
SIR, HOW MANY AMERICAN SHIPS ARE IN THIS ASSAULT?
NEXT SLIDE, PLEASE.
AMERICAN 226
I'M REAL GLAD THAT FRENCH SHIP IS HERE TO HELP OUT.
WOLMIDO
INCHON
EARLY TOMORROW MORNING, A BATTALION WILL BE LANDED ON THE ISLAND OF WOLMIDO.
THIS ISLAND GUARDS THE HARBOR AND IS CONNECTED TO THE MAINLAND BY A CAUSEWAY.
WOLMIDO
CAUSEWAY
INCHON
INCHON
BLUE BEACH
HIGH TIDE
MUD FLAT
THE TIDE WON'T LET US GET CLOSE UNTIL AFTER 5 P.M.
I DON'T WANT YOU THINKING THIS IS A SANDY SAN DIEGO BEACH--IT'S NOT.
THE FIRST WAVE OF LANDING CRAFTS WILL PLANT THOSE LADDERS.
IT'LL BE LIKE STORMING A MEDIEVAL CASTLE.

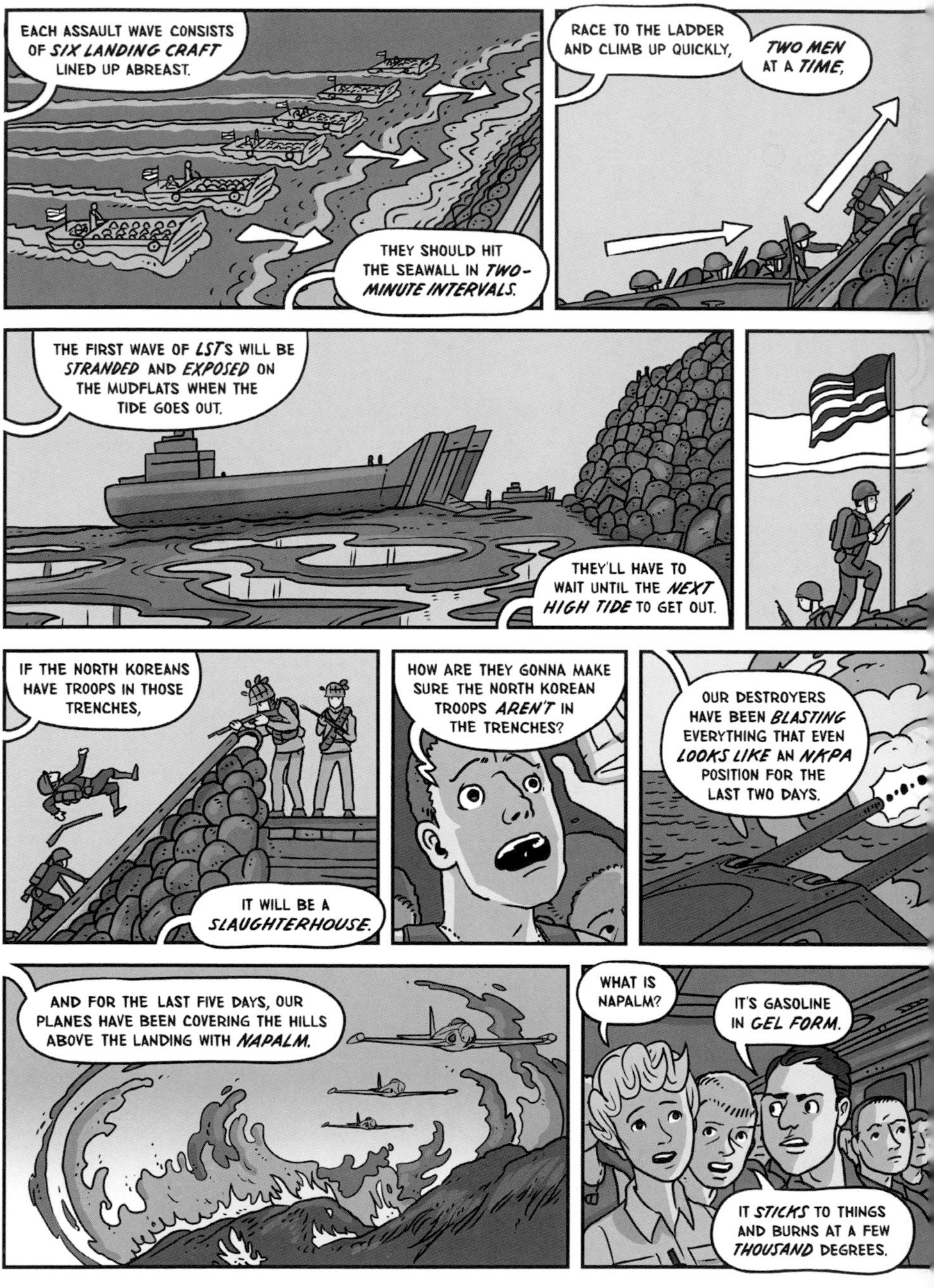
EACH ASSAULT WAVE CONSISTS OF SIX LANDING CRAFT LINED UP ABREAST.
THEY SHOULD HIT THE SEAWALL IN TWO-MINUTE INTERVALS.
RACE TO THE LADDER AND CLIMB UP QUICKLY,
TWO MEN AT A TIME,
THE FIRST WAVE OF LSTS WILL BE STRANDED AND EXPOSED ON THE MUDFLATS WHEN THE TIDE GOES OUT.
THEY'LL HAVE TO WAIT UNTIL THE NEXT HIGH TIDE TO GET OUT.
IF THE NORTH KOREANS HAVE TROOPS IN THOSE TRENCHES,
IT WILL BE A SLAUGHTERHOUSE.
HOW ARE THEY GONNA MAKE SURE THE NORTH KOREAN TROOPS AREN'T IN THE TRENCHES?
OUR DESTROYERS HAVE BEEN BLASTING EVERYTHING THAT EVEN LOOKS LIKE AN NKPA POSITION FOR THE LAST TWO DAYS.
AND FOR THE LAST FIVE DAYS, OUR PLANES HAVE BEEN COVERING THE HILLS ABOVE THE LANDING WITH NAPALM.
WHAT IS NAPALM?
IT'S GASOLINE IN GEL FORM.
IT STICKS TO THINGS AND BURNS AT A FEW THOUSAND DEGREES.

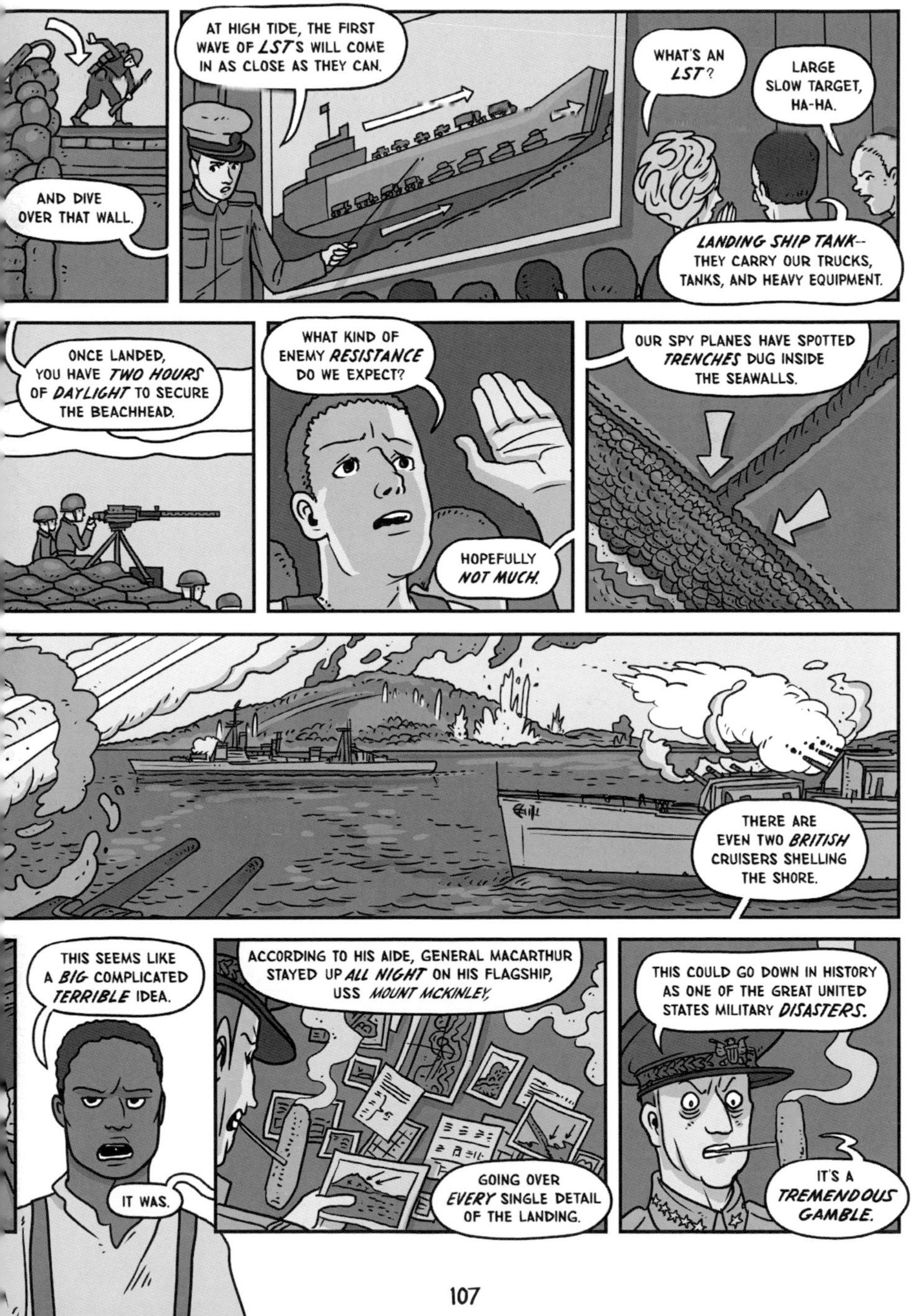
AND DIVE OVER THAT WALL.
AT HIGH TIDE, THE FIRST WAVE OF LSTS WILL COME IN AS CLOSE AS THEY CAN.
WHAT'S AN LST?
LARGE SLOW TARGET, HA-HA.
LANDING SHIP TANK-- THEY CARRY OUR TRUCKS, TANKS, AND HEAVY EQUIPMENT.
ONCE LANDED, YOU HAVE TWO HOURS OF DAYLIGHT TO SECURE THE BEACHHEAD.
WHAT KIND OF ENEMY RESISTANCE DO WE EXPECT?
HOPEFULLY NOT MUCH.
OUR SPY PLANES HAVE SPOTTED TRENCHES DUG INSIDE THE SEAWALLS.
THERE ARE EVEN TWO BRITISH CRUISERS SHELLING THE SHORE.
THIS SEEMS LIKE A BIG COMPLICATED TERRIBLE IDEA.
IT WAS.
ACCORDING TO HIS AIDE, GENERAL MACARTHUR STAYED UP ALL NIGHT ON HIS FLAGSHIP, USS MOUNT MCKINLEY,
GOING OVER EVERY SINGLE DETAIL OF THE LANDING.
THIS COULD GO DOWN IN HISTORY AS ONE OF THE GREAT UNITED STATES MILITARY DISASTERS.
IT'S A TREMENDOUS GAMBLE.

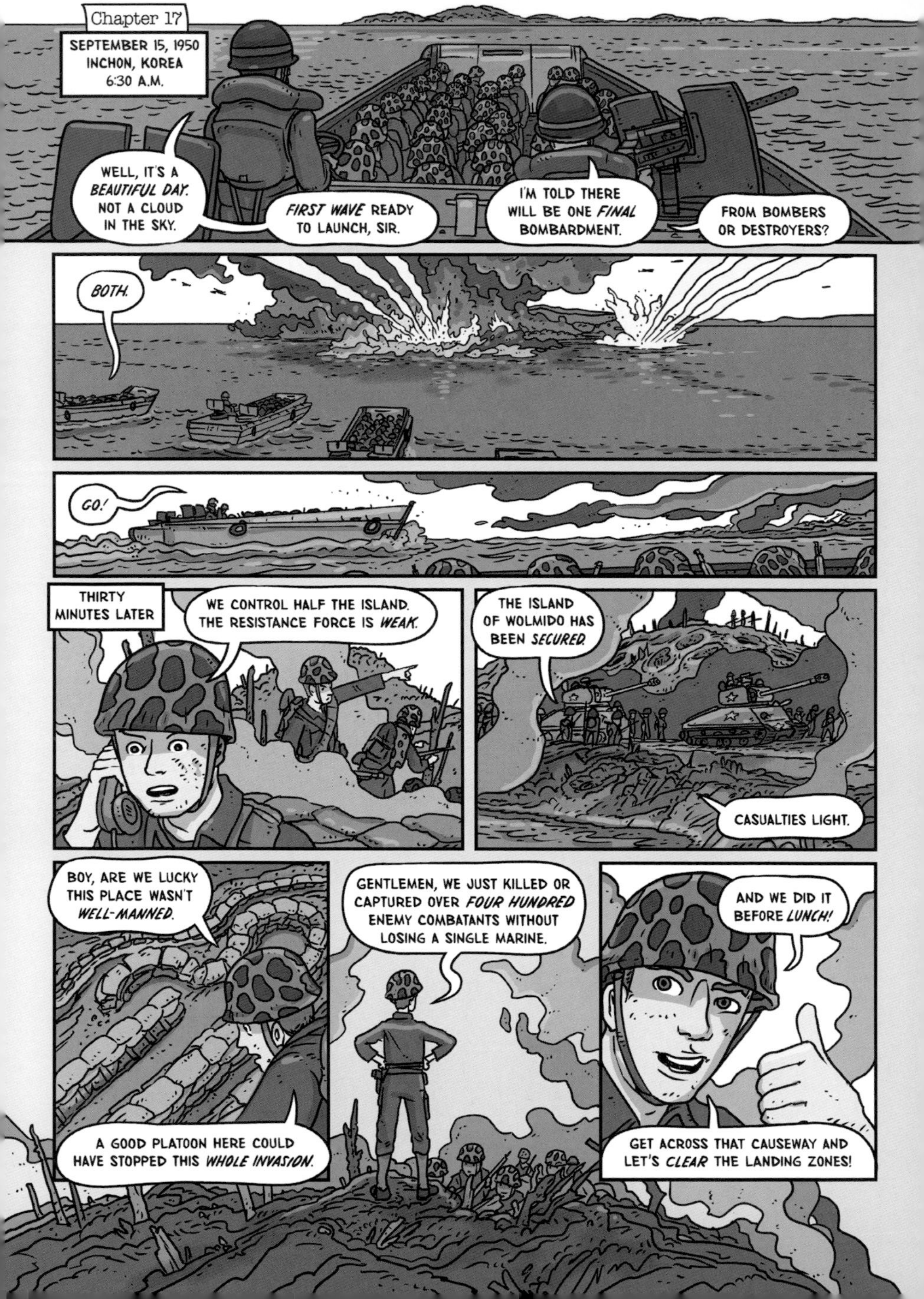
Chapter 17
SEPTEMBER 15, 1950 INCHON, KOREA 6:30 A.M.
WELL, IT'S A BEAUTIFUL DAY. NOT A CLOUD IN THE SKY.
FIRST WAVE READY TO LAUNCH, SIR.
I'M TOLD THERE WILL BE ONE FINAL BOMBARDMENT.
FROM BOMBERS OR DESTROYERS?
BOTH.
GO!
THIRTY MINUTES LATER
WE CONTROL HALF THE ISLAND. THE RESISTANCE FORCE IS WEAK.
THE ISLAND OF WOLMIDO HAS BEEN SECURED.
CASUALTIES LIGHT.
BOY, ARE WE LUCKY THIS PLACE WASN'T WELL-MANNED.
A GOOD PLATOON HERE COULD HAVE STOPPED THIS WHOLE INVASION.
GENTLEMEN, WE JUST KILLED OR CAPTURED OVER FOUR HUNDRED ENEMY COMBATANTS WITHOUT LOSING A SINGLE MARINE.
AND WE DID IT BEFORE LUNCH!
GET ACROSS THAT CAUSEWAY AND LET'S CLEAR THE LANDING ZONES!

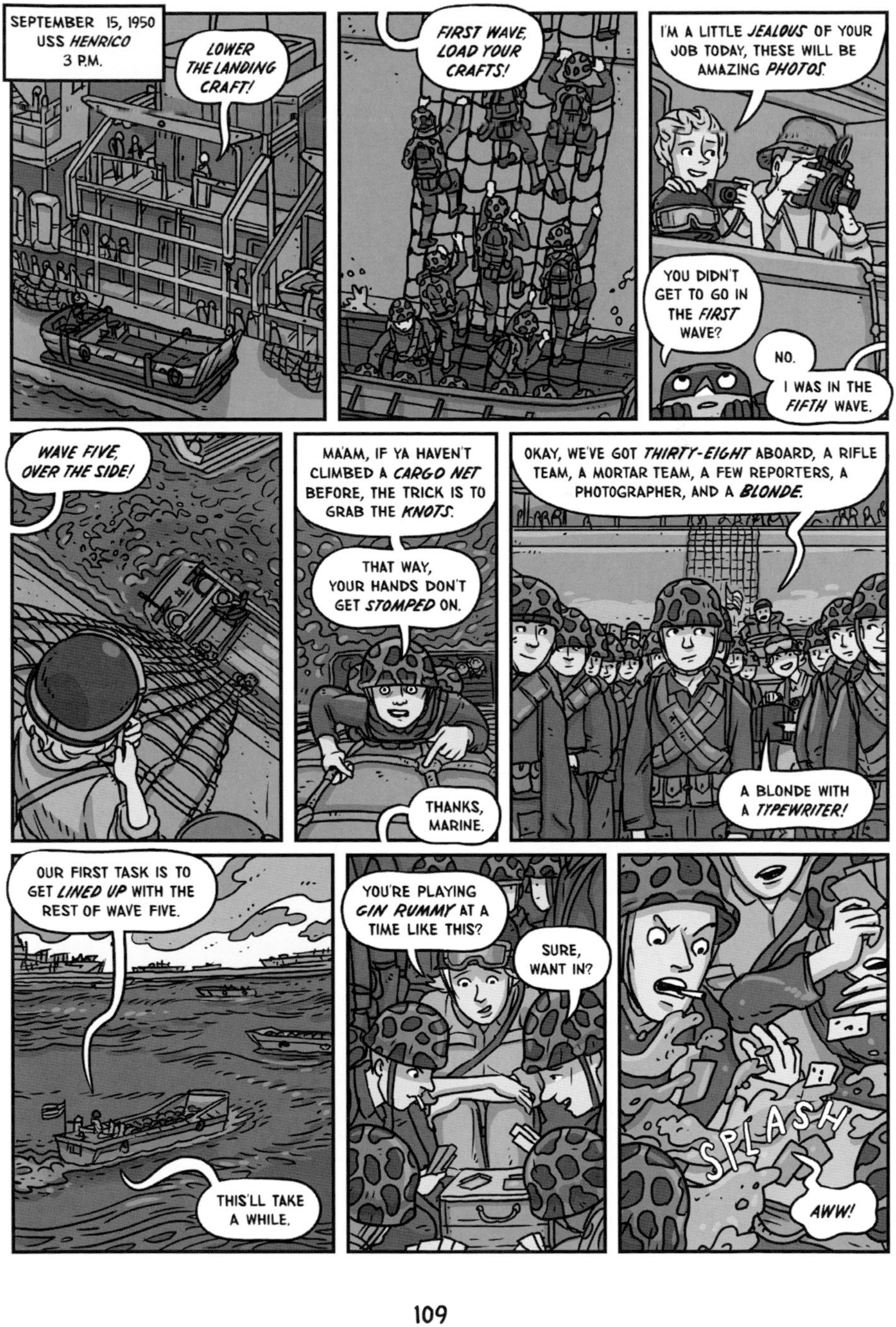
SEPTEMBER 15, 1950
USS *HENRICO*
3 P.M.
LOWER THE LANDING CRAFT!
FIRST WAVE, LOAD YOUR CRAFTS!
I'M A LITTLE *JEALOUS* OF YOUR JOB TODAY, THESE WILL BE AMAZING *PHOTOS*.
YOU DIDN'T GET TO GO IN THE *FIRST* WAVE?
NO.
I WAS IN THE *FIFTH* WAVE.
WAVE FIVE, OVER THE SIDE!
MA'AM, IF YA HAVEN'T CLIMBED A *CARGO NET* BEFORE, THE TRICK IS TO GRAB THE *KNOTS*.
THAT WAY, YOUR HANDS DON'T GET *STOMPED* ON.
THANKS, MARINE.
OKAY, WE'VE GOT *THIRTY-EIGHT* ABOARD, A RIFLE TEAM, A MORTAR TEAM, A FEW REPORTERS, A PHOTOGRAPHER, AND A *BLONDE*.
A BLONDE WITH A *TYPEWRITER!*
OUR FIRST TASK IS TO GET *LINED UP* WITH THE REST OF WAVE FIVE.
THIS'LL TAKE A WHILE.
YOU'RE PLAYING *GIN RUMMY* AT A TIME LIKE THIS?
SURE, WANT IN?
SPLASH
AWW!

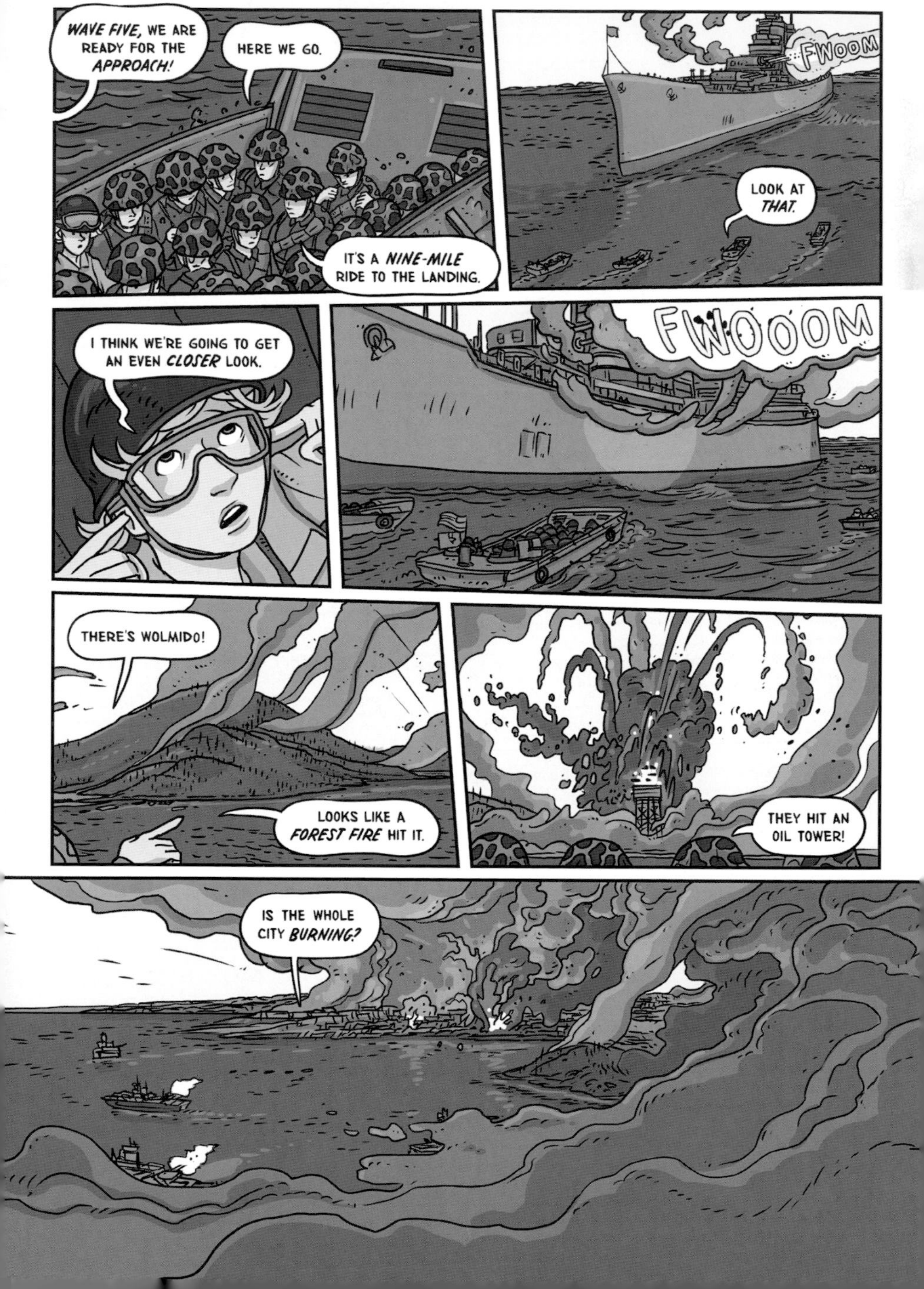
WAVE FIVE, WE ARE READY FOR THE APPROACH!
HERE WE GO.
IT'S A NINE-MILE RIDE TO THE LANDING.
FWOOM
LOOK AT THAT.
I THINK WE'RE GOING TO GET AN EVEN CLOSER LOOK.
FWOOOM
THERE'S WOLMIDO!
LOOKS LIKE A FOREST FIRE HIT IT.
THEY HIT AN OIL TOWER!
IS THE WHOLE CITY BURNING?

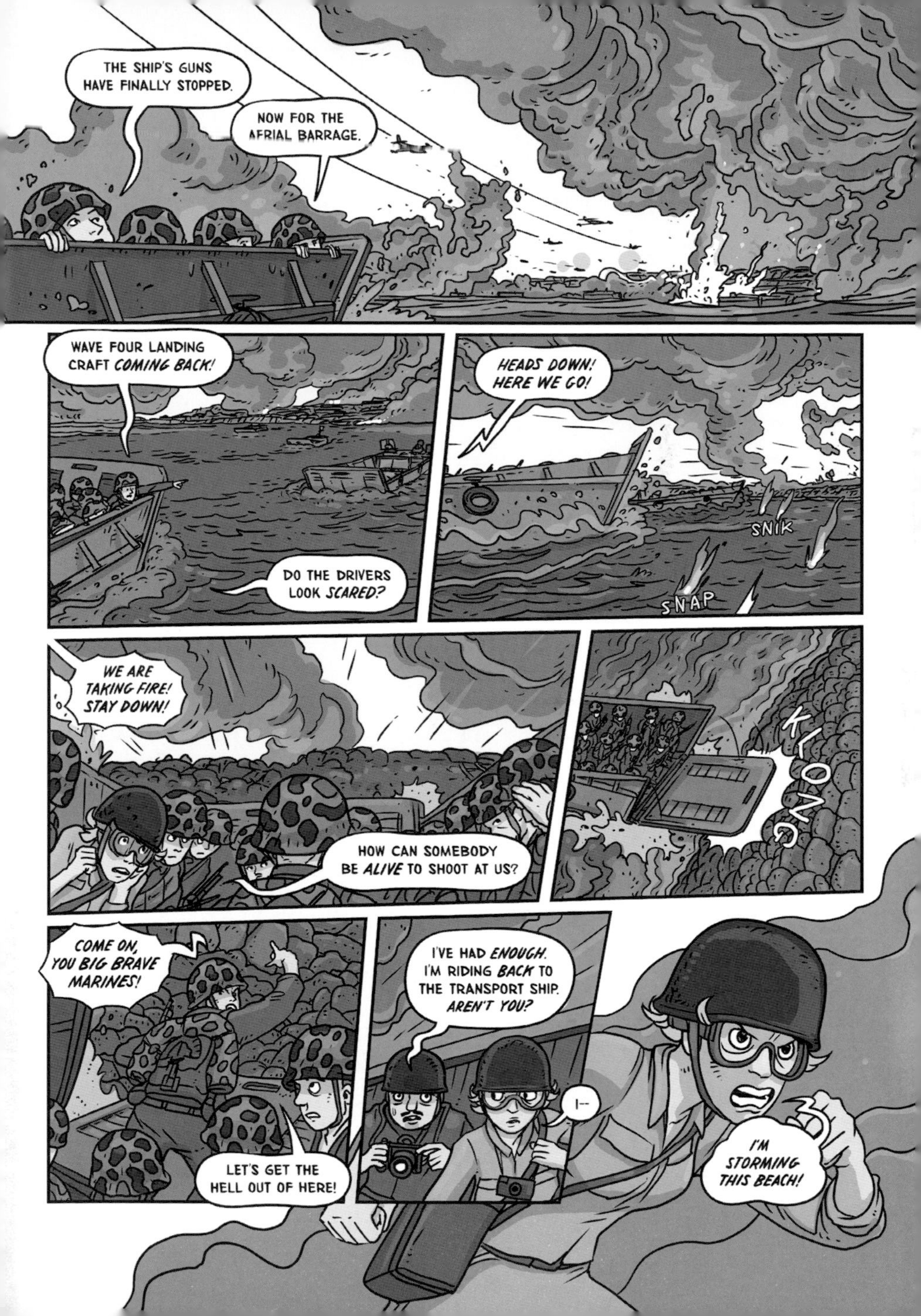
THE SHIP'S GUNS HAVE FINALLY STOPPED.
NOW FOR THE AERIAL BARRAGE.
WAVE FOUR LANDING CRAFT COMING BACK!
DO THE DRIVERS LOOK SCARED?
HEADS DOWN! HERE WE GO!
SNIK
SNAP
WE ARE TAKING FIRE! STAY DOWN!
HOW CAN SOMEBODY BE ALIVE TO SHOOT AT US?
KLONG
COME ON, YOU BIG BRAVE MARINES!
LET'S GET THE HELL OUT OF HERE!
I'VE HAD ENOUGH. I'M RIDING BACK TO THE TRANSPORT SHIP. AREN'T YOU?
I--
I'M STORMING THIS BEACH!

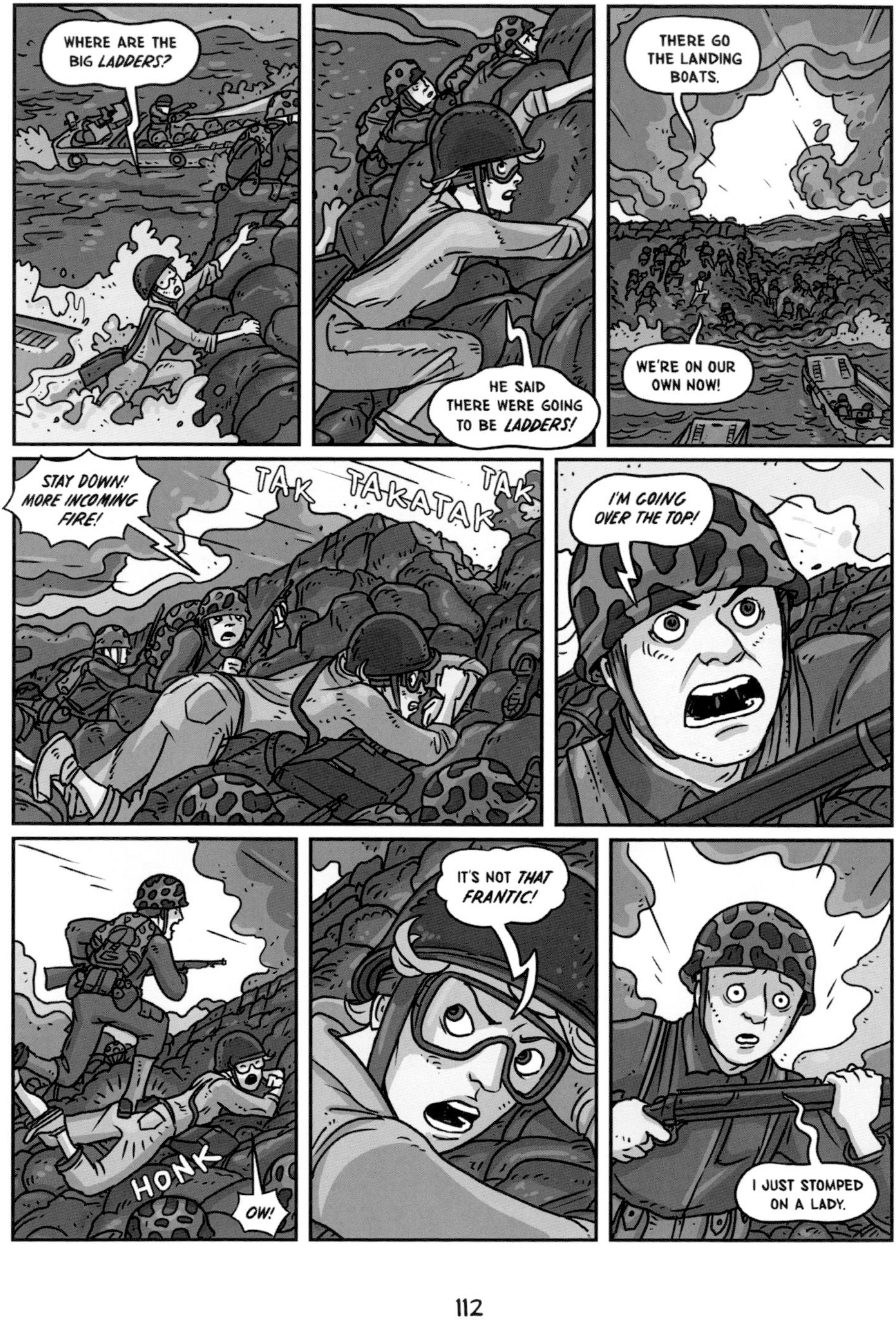
WHERE ARE THE BIG *LADDERS?*
HE SAID THERE WERE GOING TO BE *LADDERS!*
THERE GO THE LANDING BOATS.
WE'RE ON OUR OWN NOW!
STAY DOWN! MORE INCOMING FIRE!
TAK TAKATAK TAK
I'M GOING OVER THE TOP!
HONK
OW!
IT'S NOT *THAT FRANTIC!*
I JUST STOMPED ON A LADY.

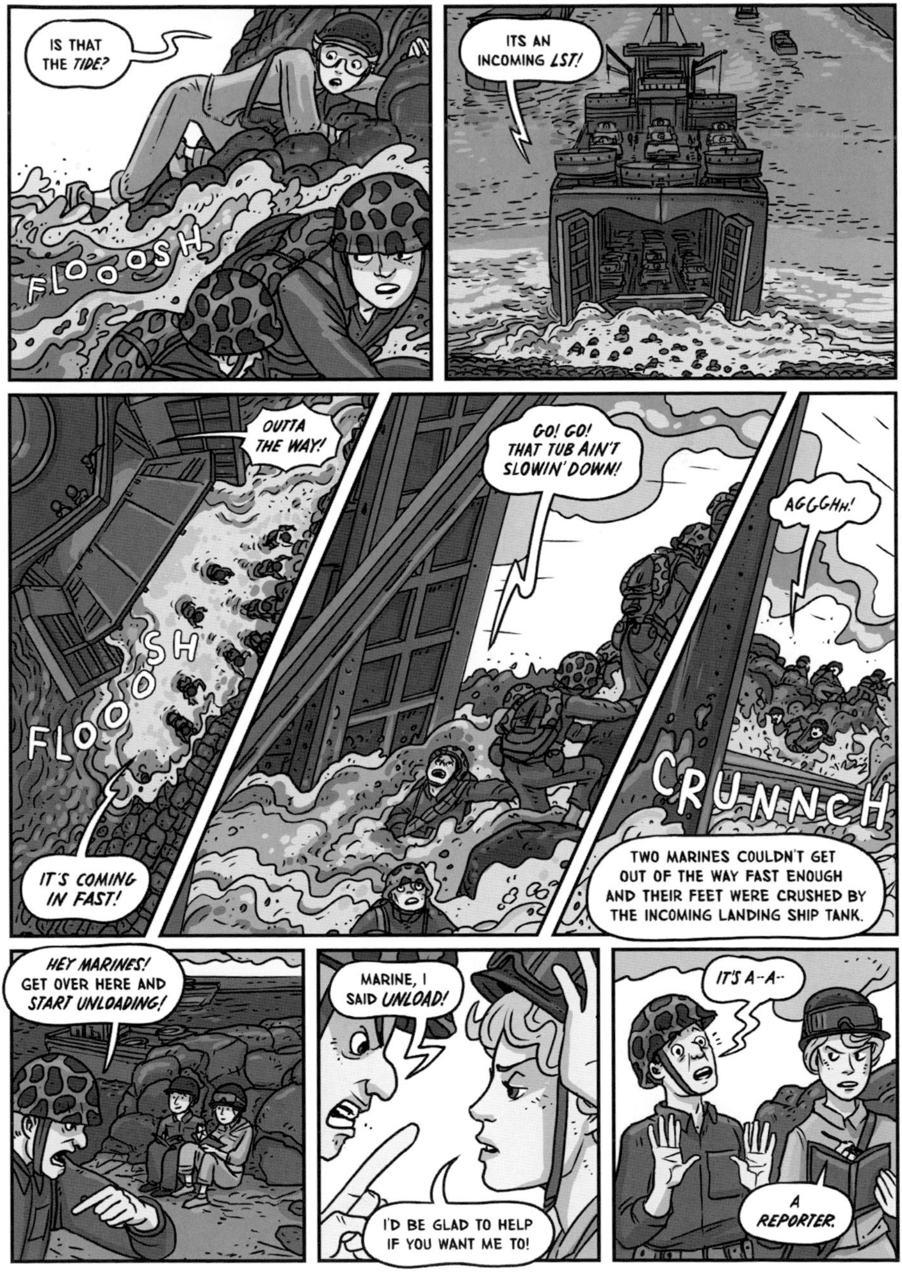
IS THAT THE *TIDE?*
FLOOOSH
ITS AN INCOMING *LST!*
OUTTA THE WAY!
FLOOOSH
IT'S COMING IN FAST!
GO! GO! THAT TUB AIN'T SLOWIN' DOWN!
AGGGHH!
CRUNNCH
TWO MARINES COULDN'T GET OUT OF THE WAY FAST ENOUGH AND THEIR FEET WERE CRUSHED BY THE INCOMING LANDING SHIP TANK.
HEY MARINES! GET OVER HERE AND *START UNLOADING!*
MARINE, I SAID *UNLOAD!*
I'D BE GLAD TO HELP IF YOU WANT ME TO!
IT'S A--A--
A *REPORTER.*

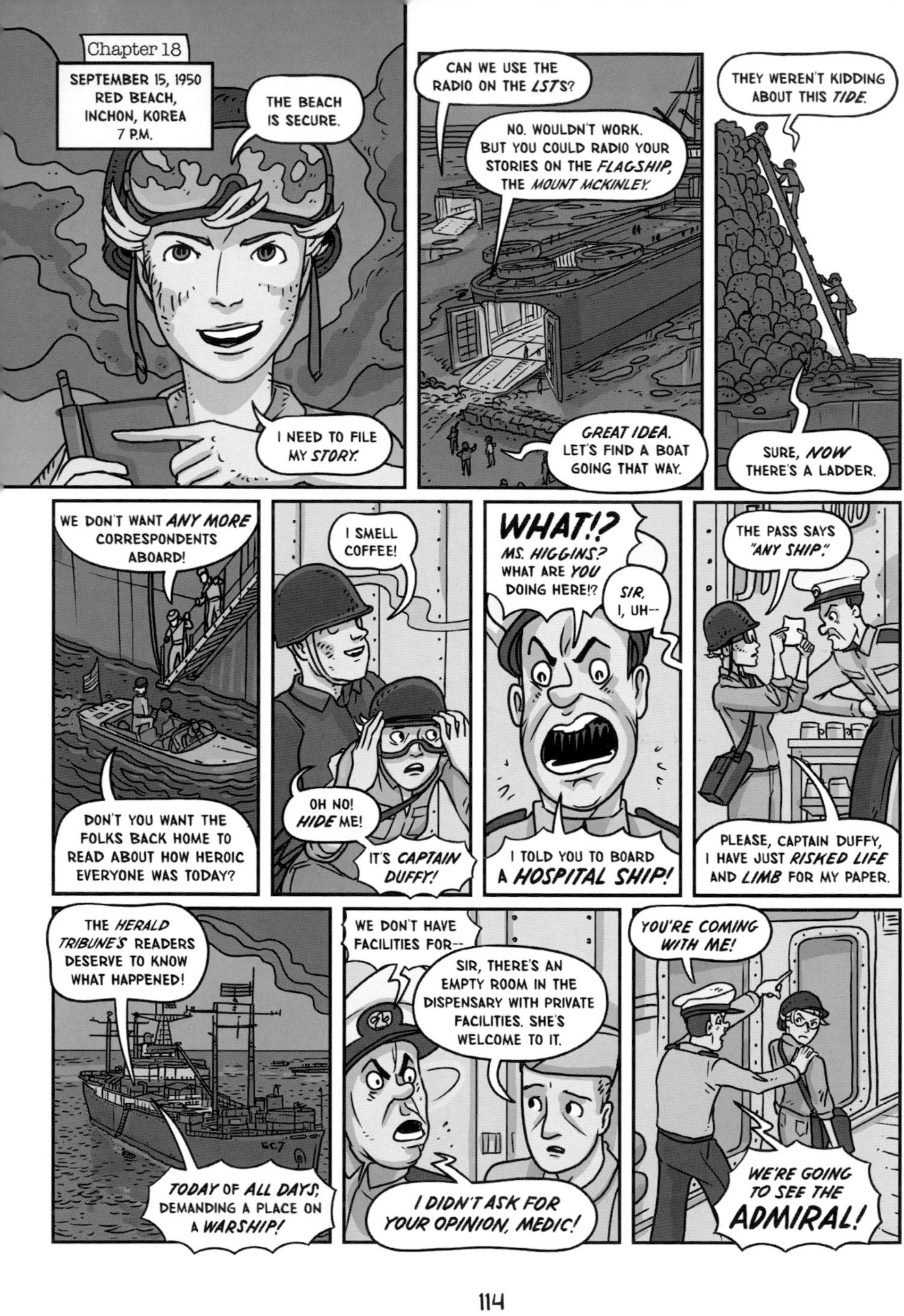
Chapter 18
SEPTEMBER 15, 1950
RED BEACH,
INCHON, KOREA
7 P.M.
THE BEACH IS SECURE.
I NEED TO FILE MY *STORY.*
CAN WE USE THE RADIO ON THE *LSTS*?
NO. WOULDN'T WORK. BUT YOU COULD RADIO YOUR STORIES ON THE *FLAGSHIP*, THE *MOUNT MCKINLEY.*
GREAT IDEA. LET'S FIND A BOAT GOING THAT WAY.
THEY WEREN'T KIDDING ABOUT THIS *TIDE.*
SURE, *NOW* THERE'S A LADDER.
WE DON'T WANT *ANY MORE* CORRESPONDENTS ABOARD!
DON'T YOU WANT THE FOLKS BACK HOME TO READ ABOUT HOW HEROIC EVERYONE WAS TODAY?
I SMELL COFFEE!
OH NO! *HIDE* ME!
IT'S *CAPTAIN DUFFY!*
WHAT!?
MS. HIGGINS? WHAT ARE *YOU* DOING HERE!?
SIR, I, UH--
I TOLD YOU TO BOARD A *HOSPITAL SHIP!*
THE PASS SAYS *"ANY SHIP."*
PLEASE, CAPTAIN DUFFY, I HAVE JUST *RISKED LIFE* AND *LIMB* FOR MY PAPER.
THE *HERALD TRIBUNE'S* READERS DESERVE TO KNOW WHAT HAPPENED!
TODAY OF *ALL DAYS*, DEMANDING A PLACE ON A *WARSHIP!*
WE DON'T HAVE FACILITIES FOR--
SIR, THERE'S AN EMPTY ROOM IN THE DISPENSARY WITH PRIVATE FACILITIES. SHE'S WELCOME TO IT.
I DIDN'T ASK FOR YOUR OPINION, MEDIC!
YOU'RE COMING WITH ME!
WE'RE GOING TO SEE THE **ADMIRAL!**

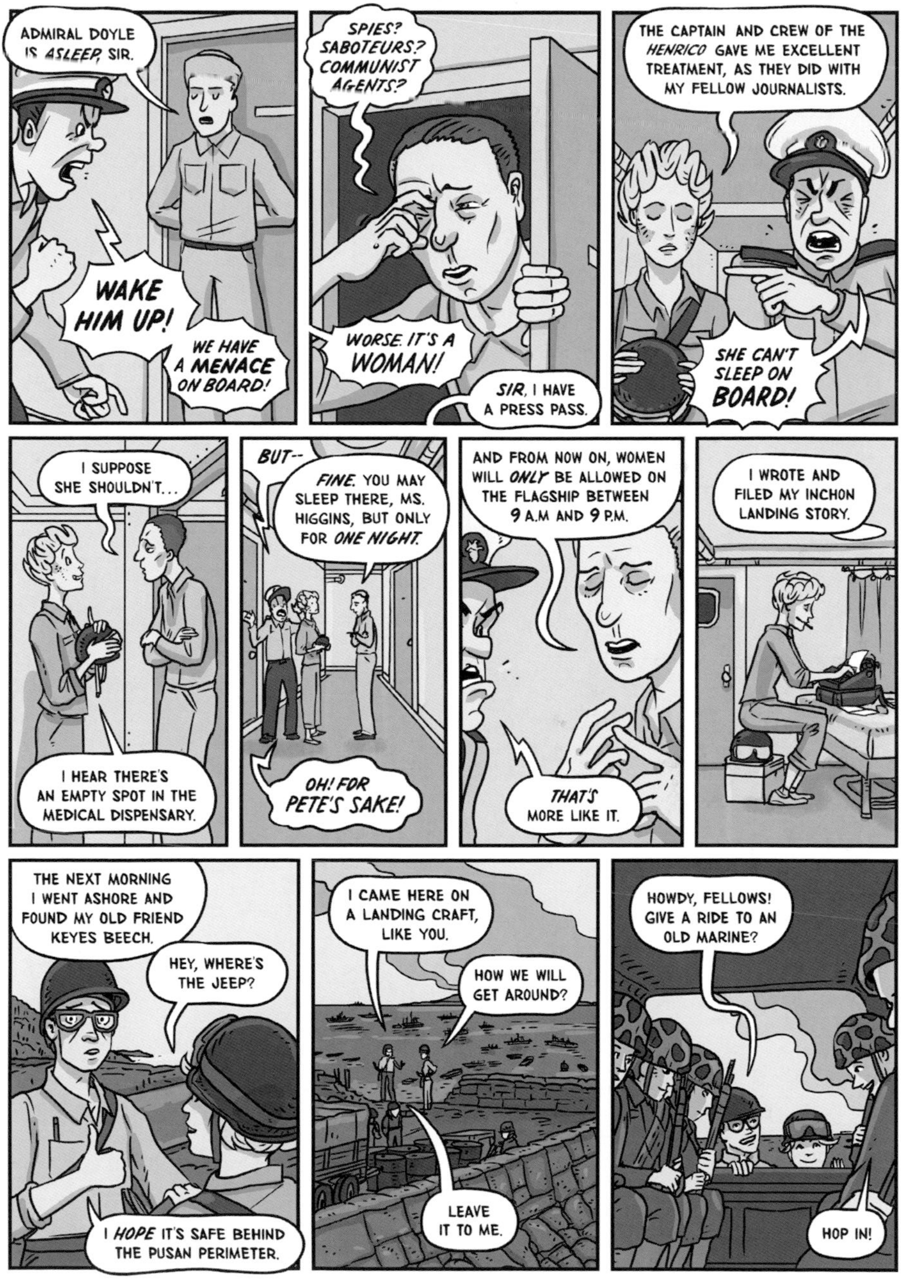
ADMIRAL DOYLE IS ASLEEP, SIR.
WAKE HIM UP!
WE HAVE A MENACE ON BOARD!
SPIES? SABOTEURS? COMMUNIST AGENTS?
WORSE. IT'S A WOMAN!
SIR, I HAVE A PRESS PASS.
THE CAPTAIN AND CREW OF THE HENRICO GAVE ME EXCELLENT TREATMENT, AS THEY DID WITH MY FELLOW JOURNALISTS.
SHE CAN'T SLEEP ON BOARD!
I SUPPOSE SHE SHOULDN'T...
I HEAR THERE'S AN EMPTY SPOT IN THE MEDICAL DISPENSARY.
BUT--
FINE. YOU MAY SLEEP THERE, MS. HIGGINS, BUT ONLY FOR ONE NIGHT.
OH! FOR PETE'S SAKE!
AND FROM NOW ON, WOMEN WILL ONLY BE ALLOWED ON THE FLAGSHIP BETWEEN 9 A.M AND 9 P.M.
THAT'S MORE LIKE IT.
I WROTE AND FILED MY INCHON LANDING STORY.
THE NEXT MORNING I WENT ASHORE AND FOUND MY OLD FRIEND KEYES BEECH.
HEY, WHERE'S THE JEEP?
I HOPE IT'S SAFE BEHIND THE PUSAN PERIMETER.
I CAME HERE ON A LANDING CRAFT, LIKE YOU.
HOW WE WILL GET AROUND?
LEAVE IT TO ME.
HOWDY, FELLOWS! GIVE A RIDE TO AN OLD MARINE?
HOP IN!

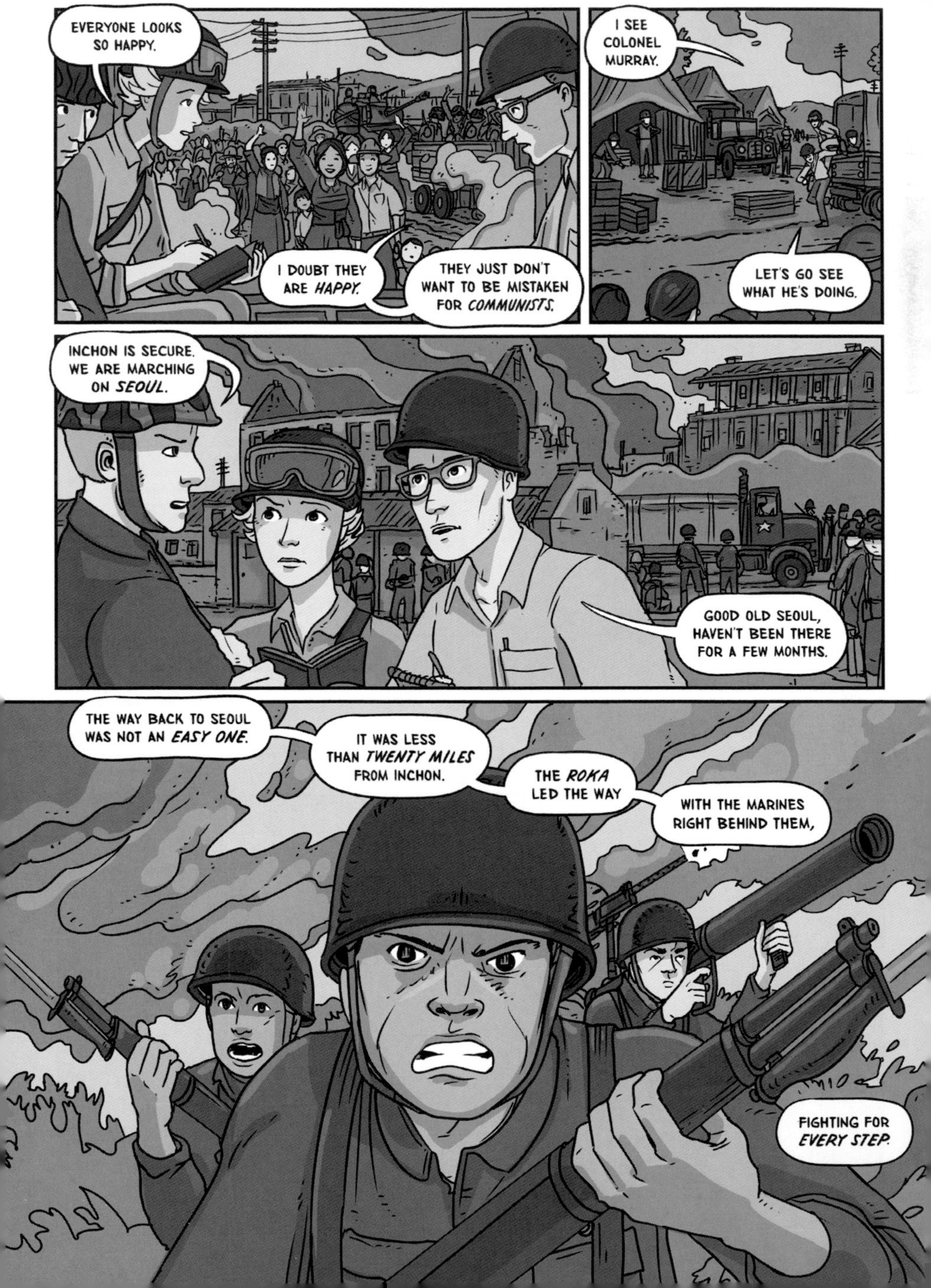
EVERYONE LOOKS SO HAPPY.
I DOUBT THEY ARE *HAPPY.*
THEY JUST DON'T WANT TO BE MISTAKEN FOR *COMMUNISTS.*
I SEE COLONEL MURRAY.
LET'S GO SEE WHAT HE'S DOING.
INCHON IS SECURE. WE ARE MARCHING ON *SEOUL*.
GOOD OLD SEOUL, HAVEN'T BEEN THERE FOR A FEW MONTHS.
THE WAY BACK TO SEOUL WAS NOT AN *EASY ONE*.
IT WAS LESS THAN *TWENTY MILES* FROM INCHON.
THE *ROKA* LED THE WAY
WITH THE MARINES RIGHT BEHIND THEM,
FIGHTING FOR *EVERY STEP.*

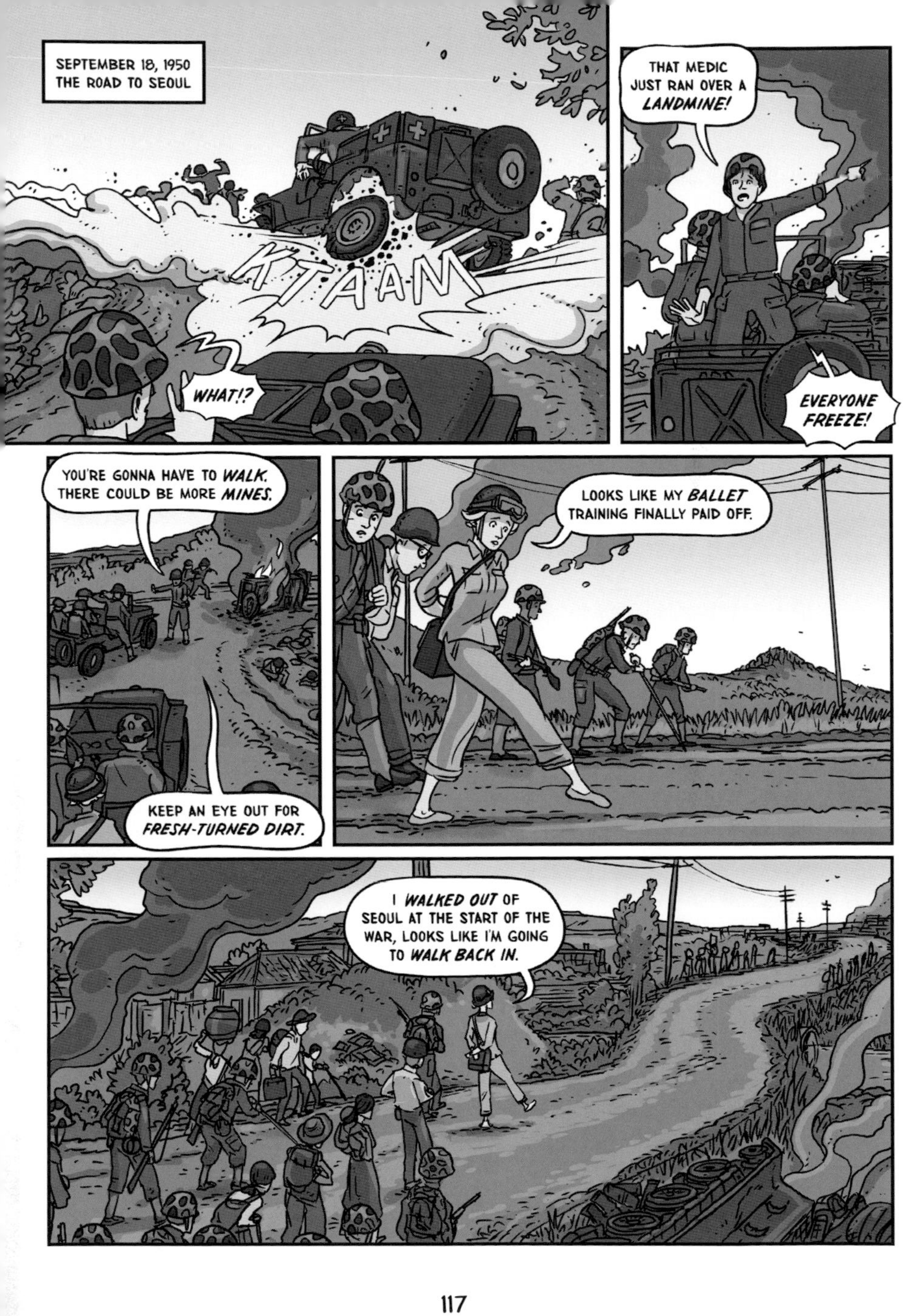
SEPTEMBER 18, 1950
THE ROAD TO SEOUL
KTAAM
WHAT!?
THAT MEDIC JUST RAN OVER A LANDMINE!
EVERYONE FREEZE!
YOU'RE GONNA HAVE TO WALK. THERE COULD BE MORE MINES.
KEEP AN EYE OUT FOR FRESH-TURNED DIRT.
LOOKS LIKE MY BALLET TRAINING FINALLY PAID OFF.
I WALKED OUT OF SEOUL AT THE START OF THE WAR, LOOKS LIKE I'M GOING TO WALK BACK IN.

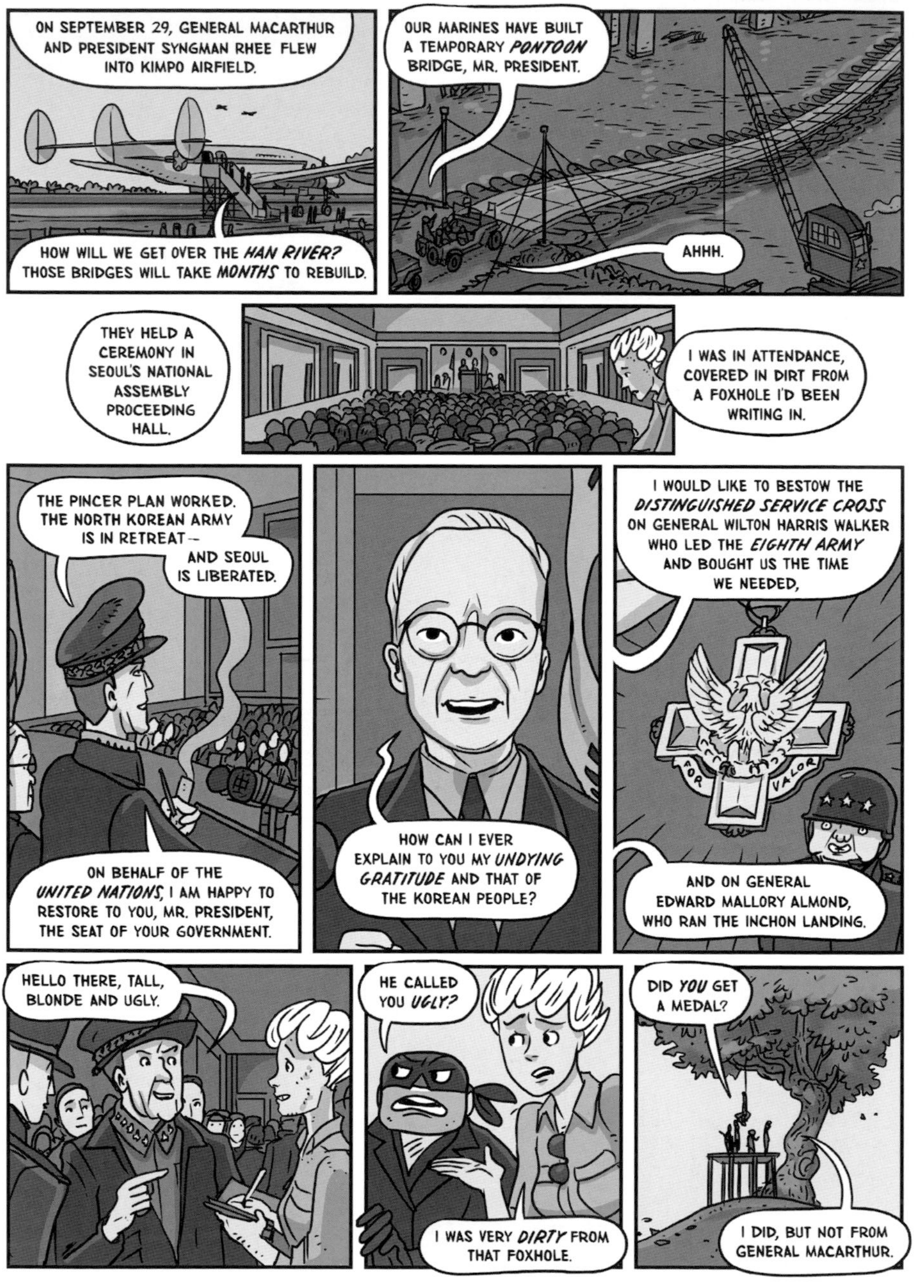
ON SEPTEMBER 29, GENERAL MACARTHUR AND PRESIDENT SYNGMAN RHEE FLEW INTO KIMPO AIRFIELD.
HOW WILL WE GET OVER THE HAN RIVER? THOSE BRIDGES WILL TAKE MONTHS TO REBUILD.
OUR MARINES HAVE BUILT A TEMPORARY PONTOON BRIDGE, MR. PRESIDENT.
AHHH.
THEY HELD A CEREMONY IN SEOUL'S NATIONAL ASSEMBLY PROCEEDING HALL.
I WAS IN ATTENDANCE, COVERED IN DIRT FROM A FOXHOLE I'D BEEN WRITING IN.
THE PINCER PLAN WORKED. THE NORTH KOREAN ARMY IS IN RETREAT—
AND SEOUL IS LIBERATED.
ON BEHALF OF THE UNITED NATIONS, I AM HAPPY TO RESTORE TO YOU, MR. PRESIDENT, THE SEAT OF YOUR GOVERNMENT.
HOW CAN I EVER EXPLAIN TO YOU MY UNDYING GRATITUDE AND THAT OF THE KOREAN PEOPLE?
I WOULD LIKE TO BESTOW THE DISTINGUISHED SERVICE CROSS ON GENERAL WILTON HARRIS WALKER WHO LED THE EIGHTH ARMY AND BOUGHT US THE TIME WE NEEDED,
FOR VALOR
AND ON GENERAL EDWARD MALLORY ALMOND, WHO RAN THE INCHON LANDING.
HELLO THERE, TALL, BLONDE AND UGLY.
HE CALLED YOU UGLY?
I WAS VERY DIRTY FROM THAT FOXHOLE.
DID YOU GET A MEDAL?
I DID, BUT NOT FROM GENERAL MACARTHUR.

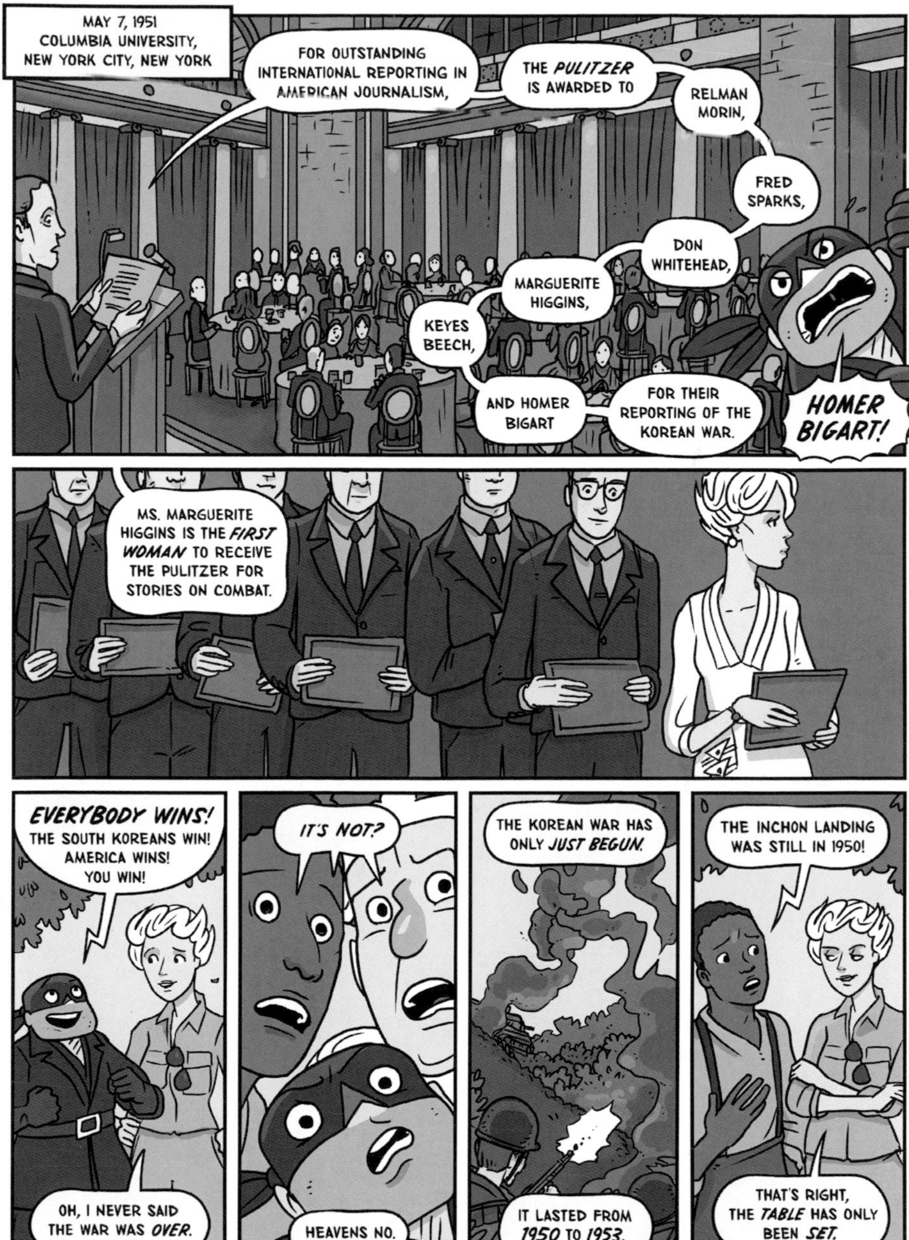
MAY 7, 1951
COLUMBIA UNIVERSITY, NEW YORK CITY, NEW YORK
FOR OUTSTANDING INTERNATIONAL REPORTING IN AMERICAN JOURNALISM,
THE *PULITZER* IS AWARDED TO
RELMAN MORIN,
FRED SPARKS,
DON WHITEHEAD,
MARGUERITE HIGGINS,
KEYES BEECH,
AND HOMER BIGART
FOR THEIR REPORTING OF THE KOREAN WAR.
HOMER BIGART!
MS. MARGUERITE HIGGINS IS THE *FIRST WOMAN* TO RECEIVE THE PULITZER FOR STORIES ON COMBAT.
EVERYBODY WINS! THE SOUTH KOREANS WIN! AMERICA WINS! YOU WIN!
OH, I NEVER SAID THE WAR WAS *OVER*.
IT'S NOT?
HEAVENS NO.
THE KOREAN WAR HAS ONLY *JUST BEGUN*.
IT LASTED FROM *1950* TO *1953*.
THE INCHON LANDING WAS STILL IN 1950!
THAT'S RIGHT, THE *TABLE* HAS ONLY BEEN *SET*.

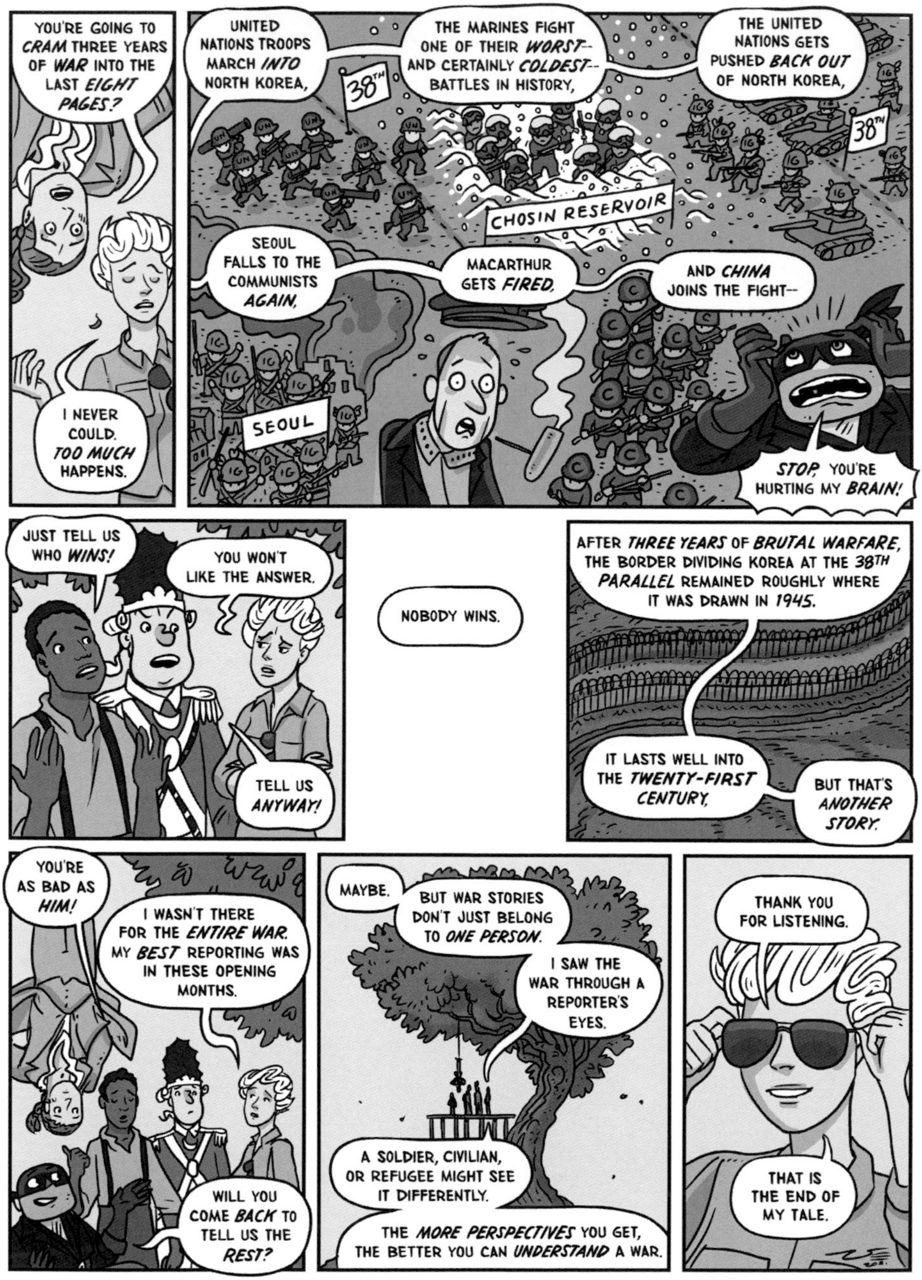

YOU'RE GOING TO CRAM THREE YEARS OF WAR INTO THE LAST EIGHT PAGES?
UNITED NATIONS TROOPS MARCH INTO NORTH KOREA,
THE MARINES FIGHT ONE OF THEIR WORST-- AND CERTAINLY COLDEST-- BATTLES IN HISTORY,
THE UNITED NATIONS GETS PUSHED BACK OUT OF NORTH KOREA,
38TH
UN
CHOSIN RESERVOIR
IG
SEOUL FALLS TO THE COMMUNISTS AGAIN,
MACARTHUR GETS FIRED,
AND CHINA JOINS THE FIGHT--
C
SEOUL
I NEVER COULD. TOO MUCH HAPPENS.
STOP, YOU'RE HURTING MY BRAIN!
JUST TELL US WHO WINS!
YOU WON'T LIKE THE ANSWER.
TELL US ANYWAY!
NOBODY WINS.
AFTER THREE YEARS OF BRUTAL WARFARE, THE BORDER DIVIDING KOREA AT THE 38TH PARALLEL REMAINED ROUGHLY WHERE IT WAS DRAWN IN 1945.
IT LASTS WELL INTO THE TWENTY-FIRST CENTURY,
BUT THAT'S ANOTHER STORY.
YOU'RE AS BAD AS HIM!
I WASN'T THERE FOR THE ENTIRE WAR. MY BEST REPORTING WAS IN THESE OPENING MONTHS.
WILL YOU COME BACK TO TELL US THE REST?
MAYBE.
BUT WAR STORIES DON'T JUST BELONG TO ONE PERSON.
I SAW THE WAR THROUGH A REPORTER'S EYES.
A SOLDIER, CIVILIAN, OR REFUGEE MIGHT SEE IT DIFFERENTLY.
THE MORE PERSPECTIVES YOU GET, THE BETTER YOU CAN UNDERSTAND A WAR.
THANK YOU FOR LISTENING.
THAT IS THE END OF MY TALE.

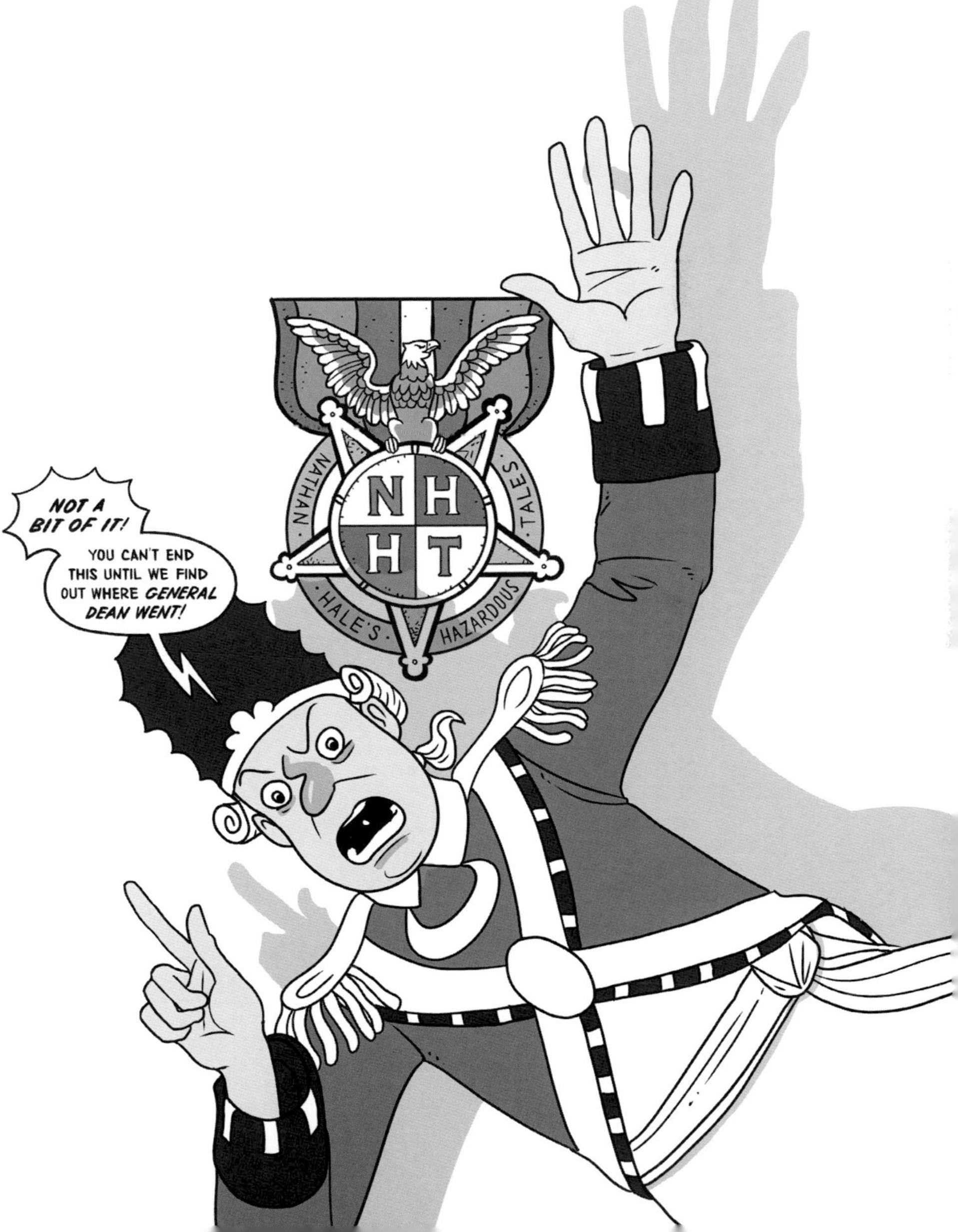
NATHAN HALE'S HAZARDOUS TALES
NH HT
NOT A BIT OF IT!
YOU CAN'T END THIS UNTIL WE FIND OUT WHERE GENERAL DEAN WENT!

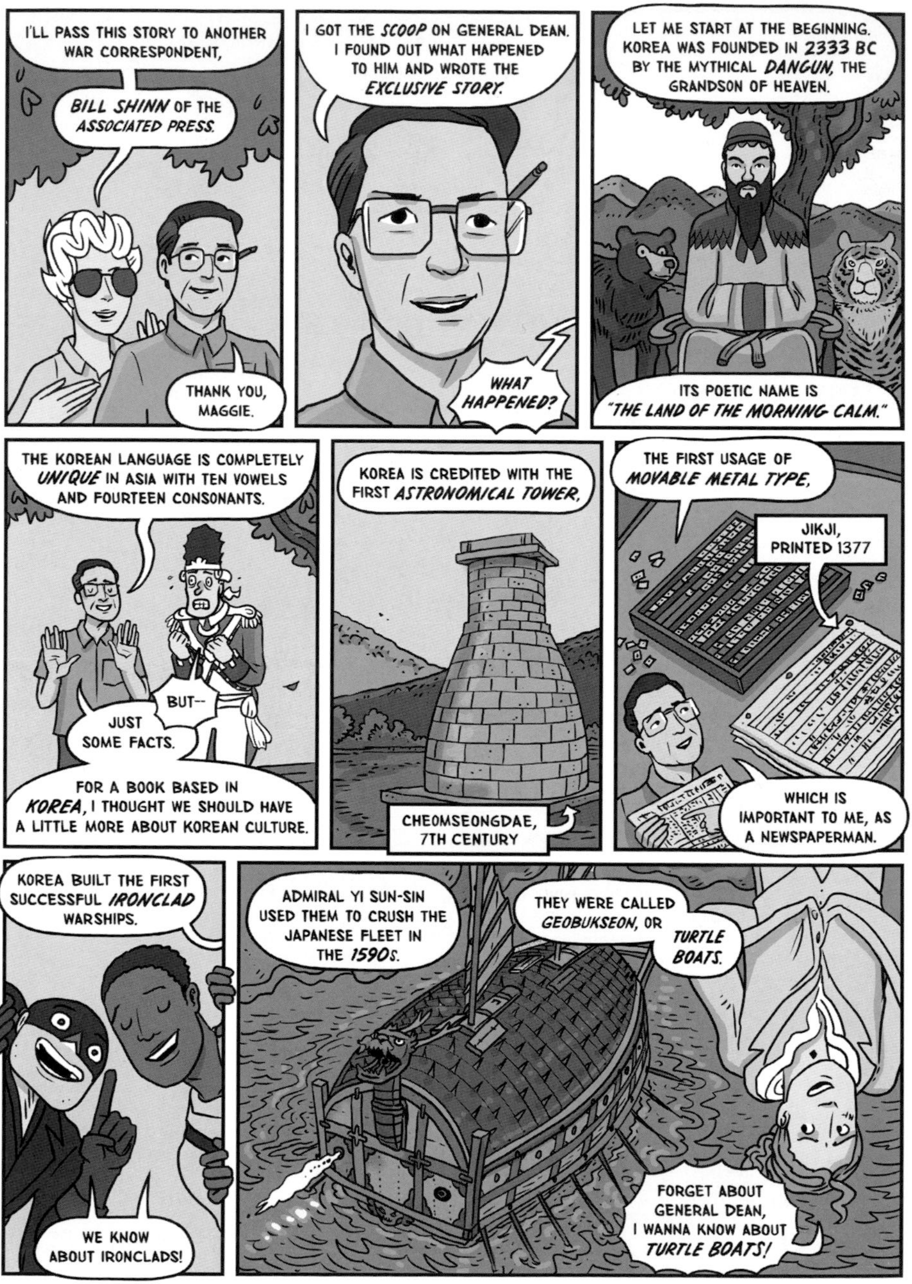
I'LL PASS THIS STORY TO ANOTHER WAR CORRESPONDENT,
BILL SHINN OF THE ASSOCIATED PRESS.
THANK YOU, MAGGIE.
I GOT THE SCOOP ON GENERAL DEAN. I FOUND OUT WHAT HAPPENED TO HIM AND WROTE THE EXCLUSIVE STORY.
WHAT HAPPENED?
LET ME START AT THE BEGINNING. KOREA WAS FOUNDED IN 2333 BC BY THE MYTHICAL DANGUN, THE GRANDSON OF HEAVEN.
ITS POETIC NAME IS "THE LAND OF THE MORNING CALM."
THE KOREAN LANGUAGE IS COMPLETELY UNIQUE IN ASIA WITH TEN VOWELS AND FOURTEEN CONSONANTS.
BUT--
JUST SOME FACTS.
FOR A BOOK BASED IN KOREA, I THOUGHT WE SHOULD HAVE A LITTLE MORE ABOUT KOREAN CULTURE.
KOREA IS CREDITED WITH THE FIRST ASTRONOMICAL TOWER,
CHEOMSEONGDAE, 7TH CENTURY
THE FIRST USAGE OF MOVABLE METAL TYPE,
JIKJI, PRINTED 1377
WHICH IS IMPORTANT TO ME, AS A NEWSPAPERMAN.
KOREA BUILT THE FIRST SUCCESSFUL IRONCLAD WARSHIPS.
WE KNOW ABOUT IRONCLADS!
ADMIRAL YI SUN-SIN USED THEM TO CRUSH THE JAPANESE FLEET IN THE 1590S.
THEY WERE CALLED GEOBUKSEON, OR TURTLE BOATS.
FORGET ABOUT GENERAL DEAN, I WANNA KNOW ABOUT TURTLE BOATS!

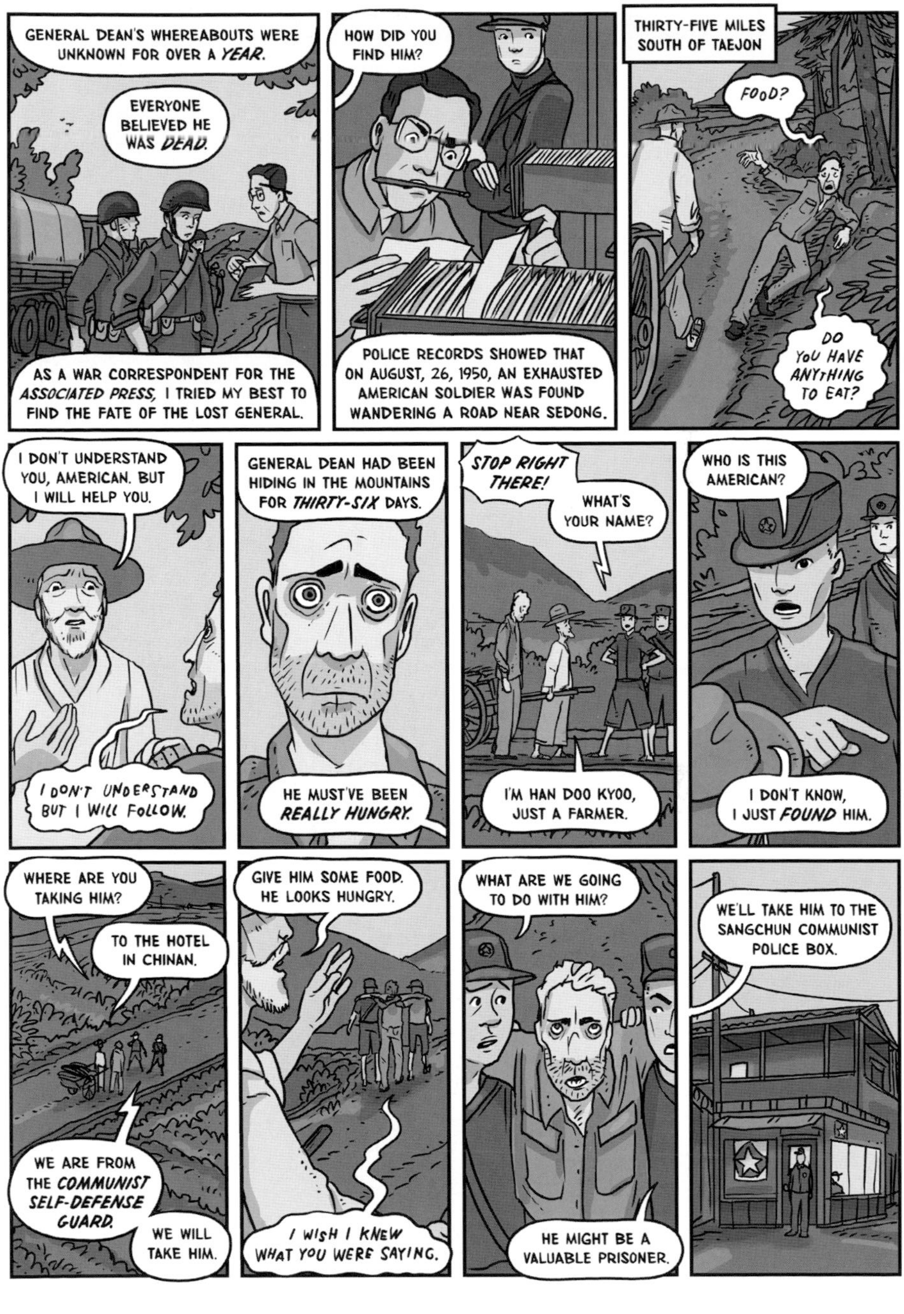
GENERAL DEAN'S WHEREABOUTS WERE UNKNOWN FOR OVER A *YEAR*.
EVERYONE BELIEVED HE WAS *DEAD*.
AS A WAR CORRESPONDENT FOR THE *ASSOCIATED PRESS*, I TRIED MY BEST TO FIND THE FATE OF THE LOST GENERAL.
HOW DID YOU FIND HIM?
POLICE RECORDS SHOWED THAT ON AUGUST, 26, 1950, AN EXHAUSTED AMERICAN SOLDIER WAS FOUND WANDERING A ROAD NEAR SEDONG.
THIRTY-FIVE MILES SOUTH OF TAEJON
FOOD?
DO YOU HAVE ANYTHING TO EAT?
I DON'T UNDERSTAND YOU, AMERICAN. BUT I WILL HELP YOU.
I DON'T UNDERSTAND BUT I WILL FOLLOW.
GENERAL DEAN HAD BEEN HIDING IN THE MOUNTAINS FOR *THIRTY-SIX* DAYS.
HE MUST'VE BEEN *REALLY HUNGRY*.
STOP RIGHT THERE!
WHAT'S YOUR NAME?
I'M HAN DOO KYOO, JUST A FARMER.
WHO IS THIS AMERICAN?
I DON'T KNOW, I JUST *FOUND* HIM.
WHERE ARE YOU TAKING HIM?
TO THE HOTEL IN CHINAN.
WE ARE FROM THE *COMMUNIST SELF-DEFENSE GUARD*.
WE WILL TAKE HIM.
GIVE HIM SOME FOOD. HE LOOKS HUNGRY.
I WISH I KNEW WHAT YOU WERE SAYING.
WHAT ARE WE GOING TO DO WITH HIM?
HE MIGHT BE A VALUABLE PRISONER.
WE'LL TAKE HIM TO THE SANGCHUN COMMUNIST POLICE BOX.

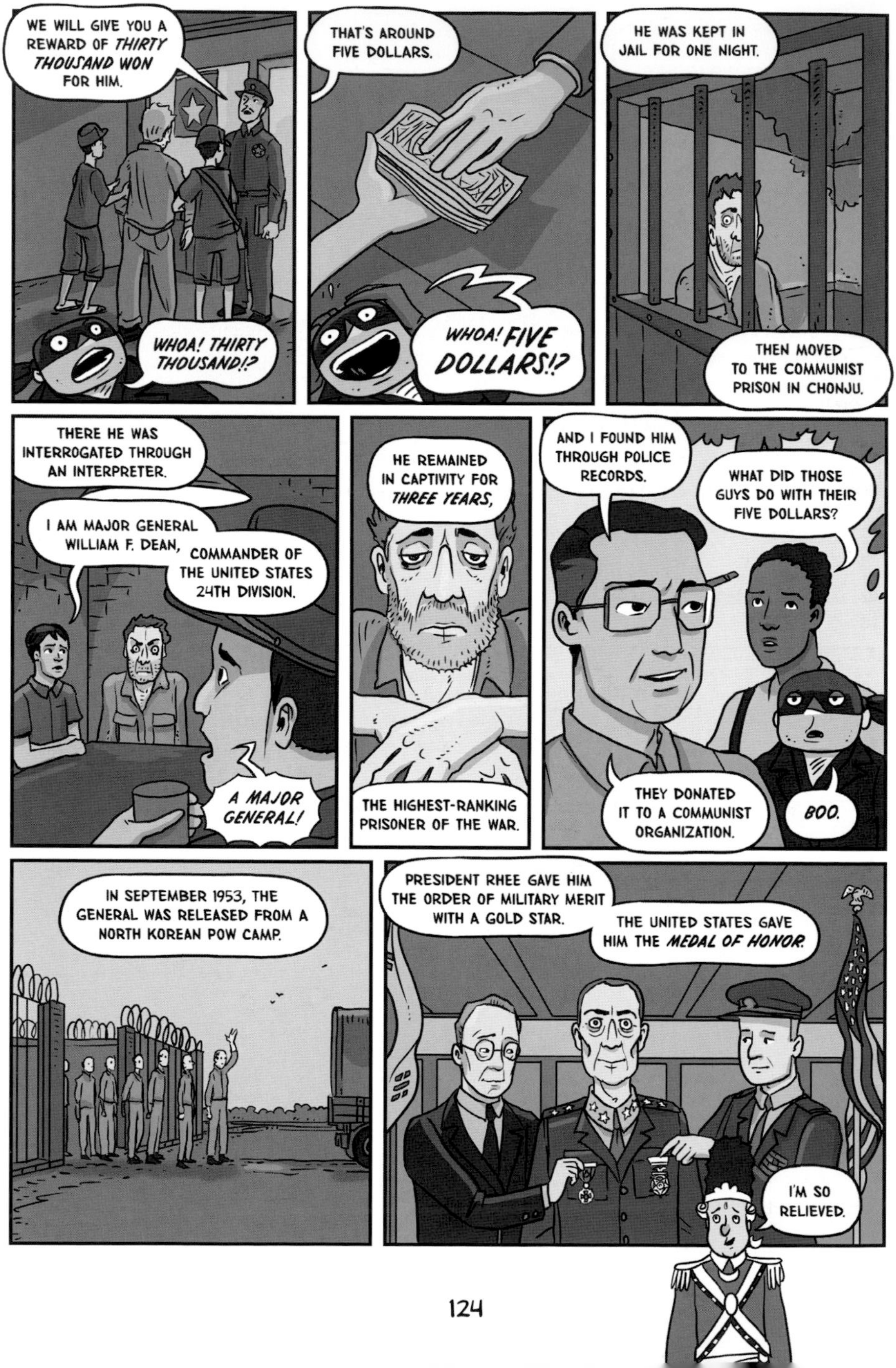
WE WILL GIVE YOU A REWARD OF *THIRTY THOUSAND WON* FOR HIM.
WHOA! THIRTY THOUSAND!?
THAT'S AROUND FIVE DOLLARS.
WHOA! FIVE DOLLARS!?
HE WAS KEPT IN JAIL FOR ONE NIGHT.
THEN MOVED TO THE COMMUNIST PRISON IN CHONJU.
THERE HE WAS INTERROGATED THROUGH AN INTERPRETER.
I AM MAJOR GENERAL WILLIAM F. DEAN,
COMMANDER OF THE UNITED STATES 24TH DIVISION.
A MAJOR GENERAL!
HE REMAINED IN CAPTIVITY FOR *THREE YEARS,*
THE HIGHEST-RANKING PRISONER OF THE WAR.
AND I FOUND HIM THROUGH POLICE RECORDS.
WHAT DID THOSE GUYS DO WITH THEIR FIVE DOLLARS?
THEY DONATED IT TO A COMMUNIST ORGANIZATION.
BOO.
IN SEPTEMBER 1953, THE GENERAL WAS RELEASED FROM A NORTH KOREAN POW CAMP.
PRESIDENT RHEE GAVE HIM THE ORDER OF MILITARY MERIT WITH A GOLD STAR.
THE UNITED STATES GAVE HIM THE *MEDAL OF HONOR.*
I'M SO RELIEVED.

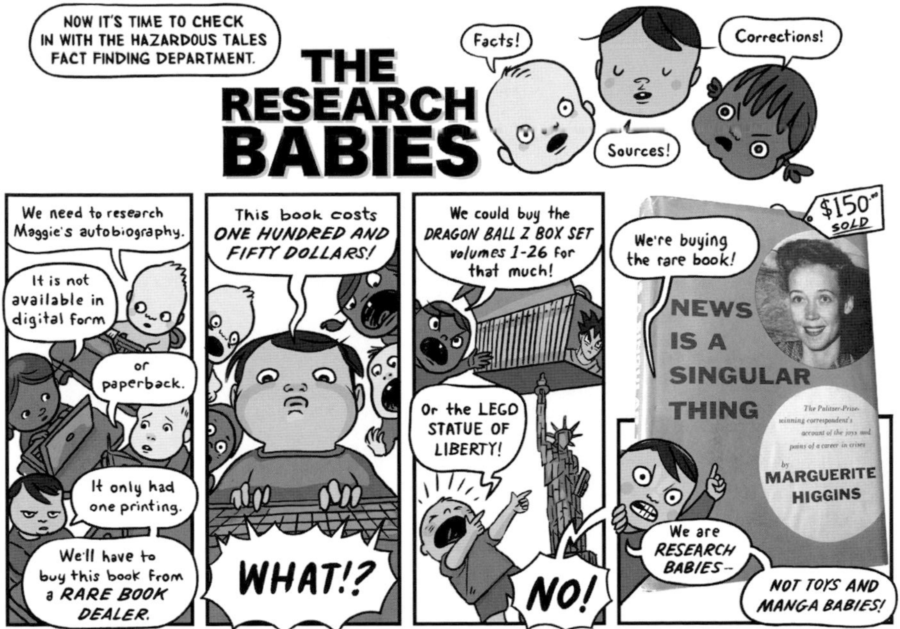
NOW IT'S TIME TO CHECK IN WITH THE HAZARDOUS TALES FACT FINDING DEPARTMENT.
THE RESEARCH BABIES
Facts!
Sources!
Corrections!
We need to research Maggie's autobiography.
It is not available in digital form
or paperback.
It only had one printing.
We'll have to buy this book from a RARE BOOK DEALER.
This book costs ONE HUNDRED AND FIFTY DOLLARS!
WHAT!?
We could buy the DRAGON BALL Z BOX SET volumes 1-26 for that much!
Or the LEGO STATUE OF LIBERTY!
NO!
$150.00 SOLD
We're buying the rare book!
NEWS IS A SINGULAR THING
The Pulitzer-Prize-winning correspondent's account of the joys and pains of a career in crises
by MARGUERITE HIGGINS
We are RESEARCH BABIES--
NOT TOYS AND MANGA BABIES!

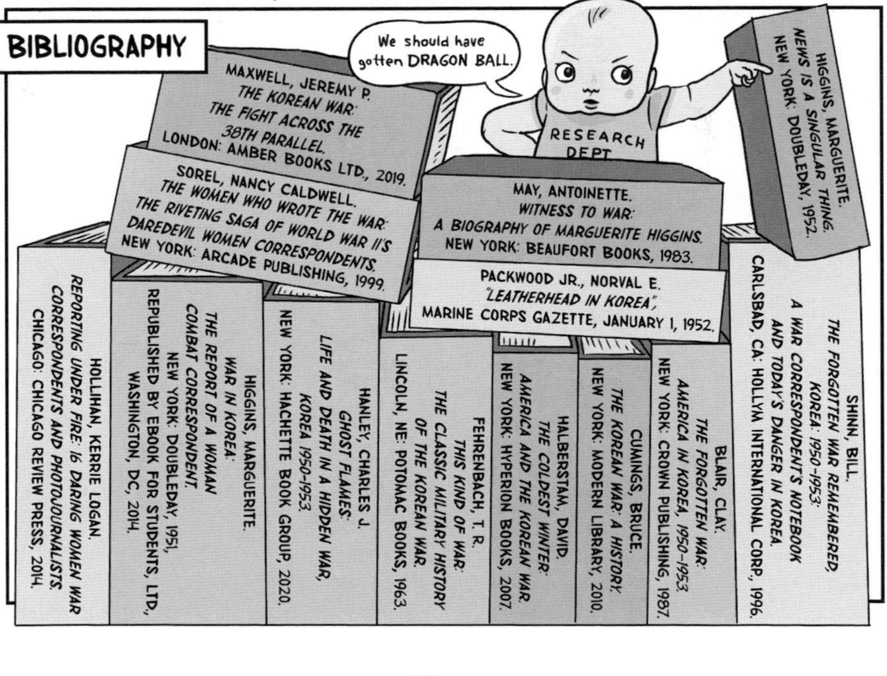
BIBLIOGRAPHY
We should have gotten DRAGON BALL.
RESEARCH DEPT
MAXWELL, JEREMY P. THE KOREAN WAR: THE FIGHT ACROSS THE 38TH PARALLEL. LONDON: AMBER BOOKS LTD., 2019.
SOREL, NANCY CALDWELL. THE WOMEN WHO WROTE THE WAR: THE RIVETING SAGA OF WORLD WAR II'S DAREDEVIL WOMEN CORRESPONDENTS. NEW YORK: ARCADE PUBLISHING, 1999.
MAY, ANTOINETTE. WITNESS TO WAR: A BIOGRAPHY OF MARGUERITE HIGGINS. NEW YORK: BEAUFORT BOOKS, 1983.
PACKWOOD JR., NORVAL E. "LEATHERHEAD IN KOREA", MARINE CORPS GAZETTE, JANUARY 1, 1952.
HIGGINS, MARGUERITE. NEWS IS A SINGULAR THING. NEW YORK: DOUBLEDAY, 1952.
HOLLIHAN, KERRIE LOGAN. REPORTING UNDER FIRE: 16 DARING WOMEN WAR CORRESPONDENTS AND PHOTOJOURNALISTS. CHICAGO: CHICAGO REVIEW PRESS, 2014.
HIGGINS, MARGUERITE. WAR IN KOREA: THE REPORT OF A WOMAN COMBAT CORRESPONDENT. NEW YORK: DOUBLEDAY, 1951, REPUBLISHED BY EBOOK FOR STUDENTS, LTD., WASHINGTON, DC, 2014.
HANLEY, CHARLES J. GHOST FLAMES: LIFE AND DEATH IN A HIDDEN WAR, KOREA 1950-1953. NEW YORK: HACHETTE BOOK GROUP, 2020.
FEHRENBACH, T. R. THIS KIND OF WAR: THE CLASSIC MILITARY HISTORY OF THE KOREAN WAR. LINCOLN, NE: POTOMAC BOOKS, 1963.
HALBERSTAM, DAVID. THE COLDEST WINTER: AMERICA AND THE KOREAN WAR. NEW YORK: HYPERION BOOKS, 2007.
CUMINGS, BRUCE. THE KOREAN WAR: A HISTORY. NEW YORK: MODERN LIBRARY, 2010.
BLAIR, CLAY. THE FORGOTTEN WAR: AMERICA IN KOREA, 1950-1953. NEW YORK: CROWN PUBLISHING, 1987.
SHINN, BILL. THE FORGOTTEN WAR REMEMBERED, KOREA: 1950-1953: A WAR CORRESPONDENT'S NOTEBOOK AND TODAY'S DANGER IN KOREA. CARLSBAD, CA: HOLLYM INTERNATIONAL CORP., 1996.

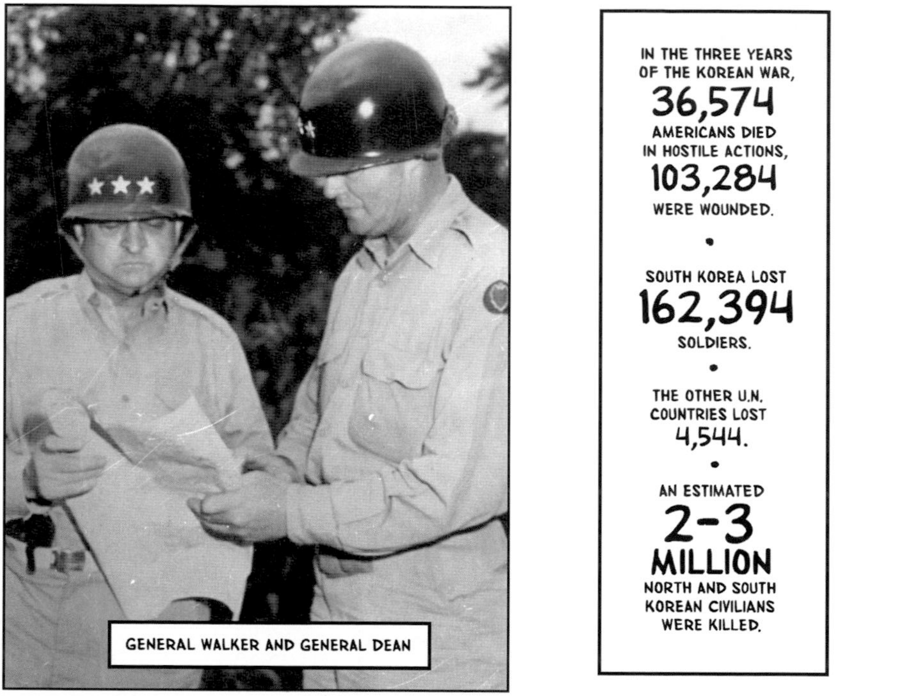

GENERAL WALKER AND GENERAL DEAN

IN THE THREE YEARS OF THE KOREAN WAR,

36,574

AMERICANS DIED IN HOSTILE ACTIONS,

103,284

WERE WOUNDED.

•

SOUTH KOREA LOST

162,394

SOLDIERS.

•

THE OTHER U.N. COUNTRIES LOST 4,544.

•

AN ESTIMATED

2-3 MILLION

NORTH AND SOUTH KOREAN CIVILIANS WERE KILLED.

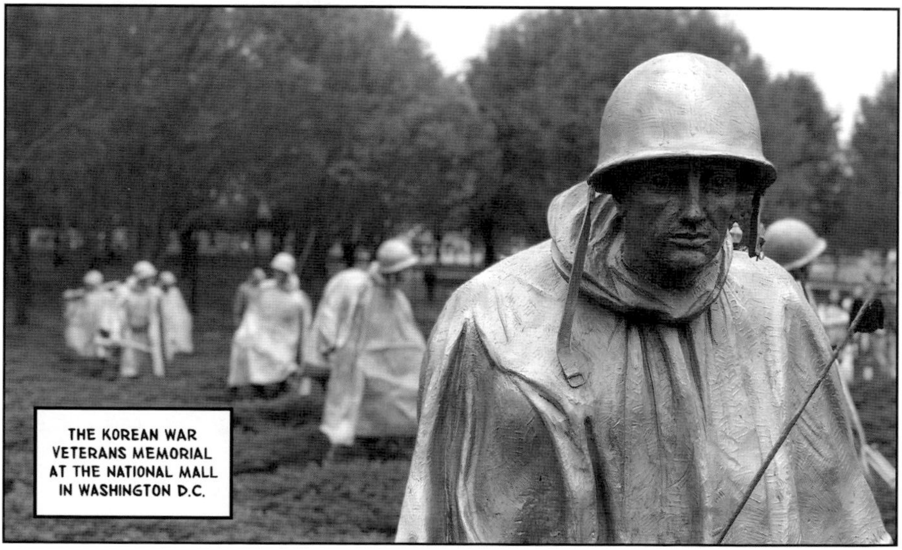

THE KOREAN WAR VETERANS MEMORIAL AT THE NATIONAL MALL IN WASHINGTON D.C.

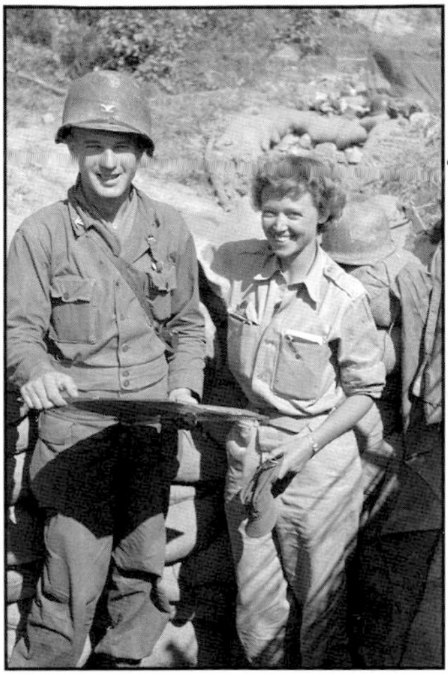

MAGGIE WITH COLONEL MICHAELIS AT WOLFHOUND HEADQUARTERS

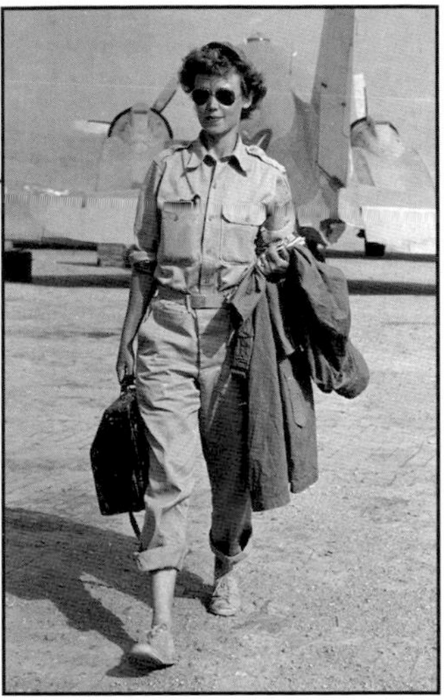

MAGGIE AND HER TYPEWRITER

BOTH OF THESE PHOTOS WERE SHOT BY CARL MYDANS

MAGGIE AND GENERAL DOUGLAS MACARTHUR

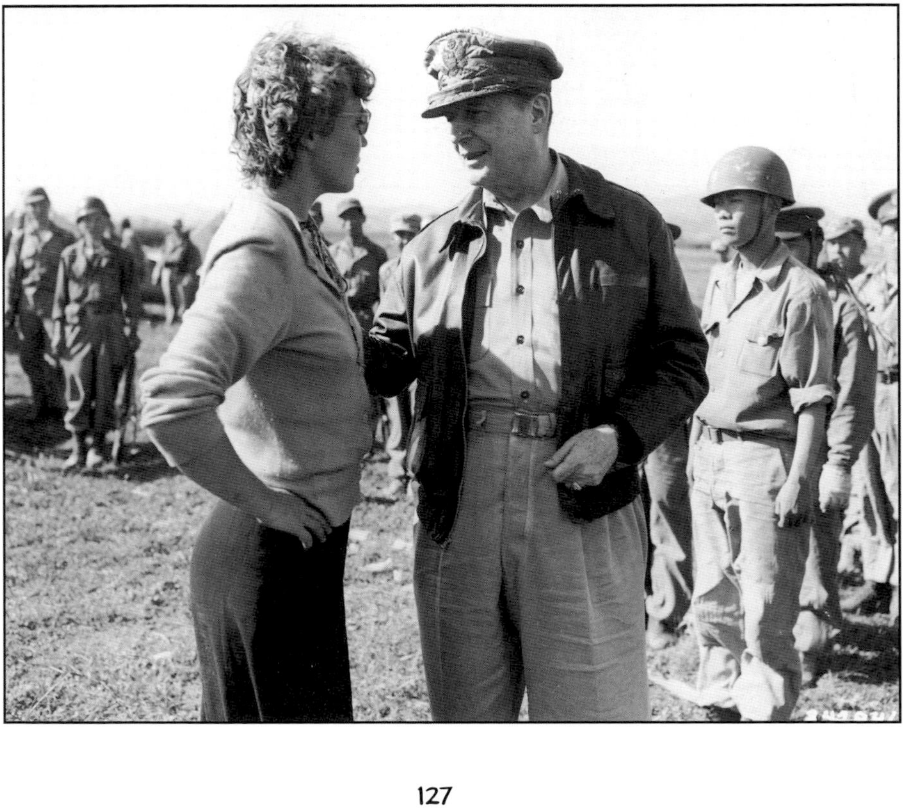

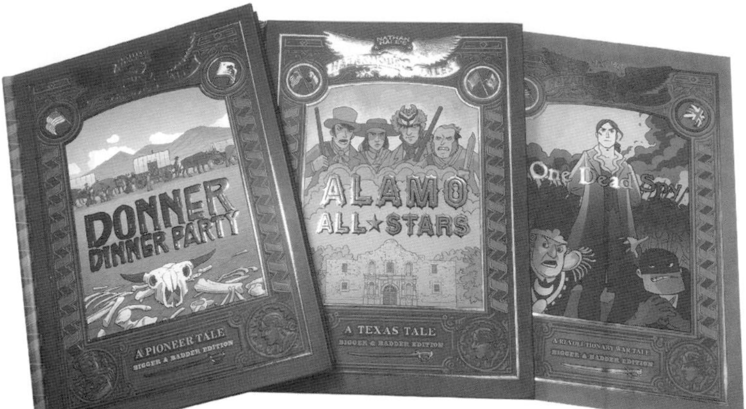
DONNER DINNER PARTY
A PIONEER TALE
BIGGER & BADDER EDITION
ALAMO ALL★STARS
A TEXAS TALE
BIGGER & BADDER EDITION
One Dead Spy
BIGGER & BADDER EDITION

THE BIGGER & BADDER EDITIONS
EACH WITH SIXTEEN BONUS PAGES OF MINI COMICS!

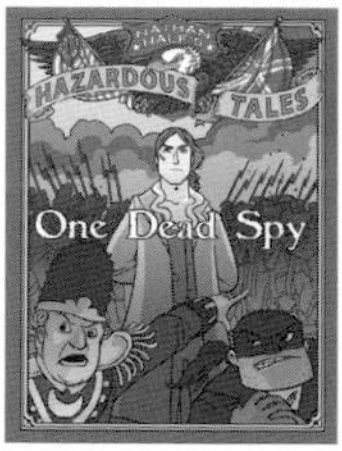
NATHAN HALE'S
HAZARDOUS TALES
One Dead Spy
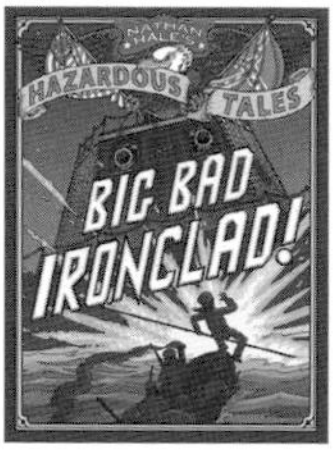
NATHAN HALE'S
HAZARDOUS TALES
BIG BAD IRONCLAD!
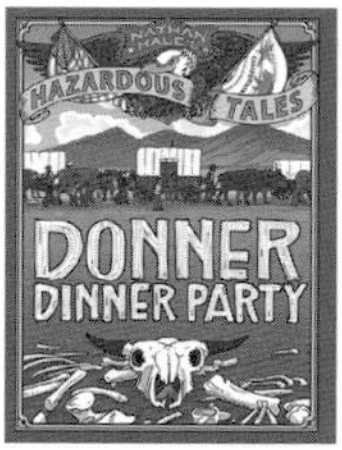
NATHAN HALE'S
HAZARDOUS TALES
DONNER DINNER PARTY
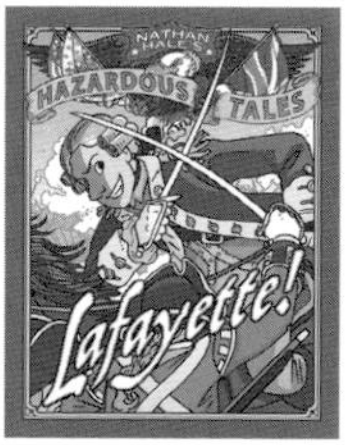
NATHAN HALE'S
HAZARDOUS TALES
Lafayette!
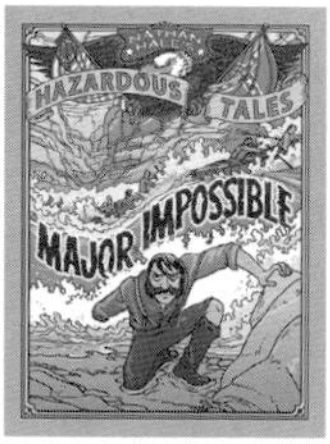
NATHAN HALE'S
HAZARDOUS TALES
MAJOR IMPOSSIBLE
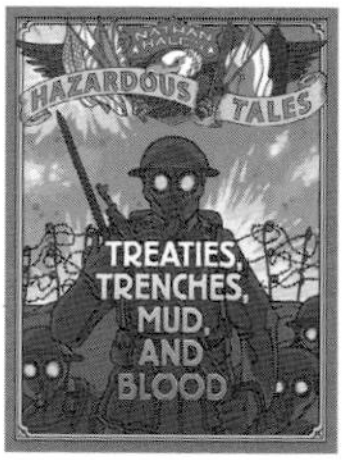
NATHAN HALE'S
HAZARDOUS TALES
TREATIES, TRENCHES, MUD, AND BLOOD
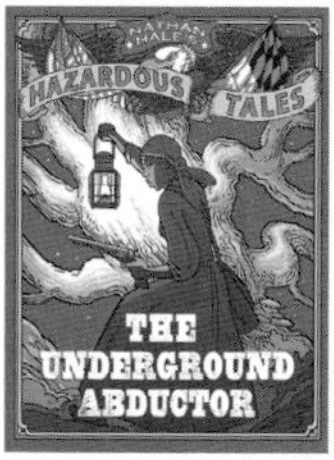
NATHAN HALE'S
HAZARDOUS TALES
THE UNDERGROUND ABDUCTOR
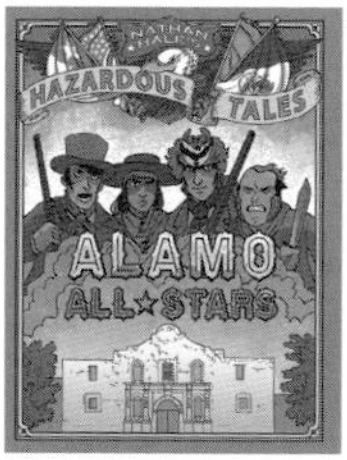
NATHAN HALE'S
HAZARDOUS TALES
ALAMO ALL★STARS
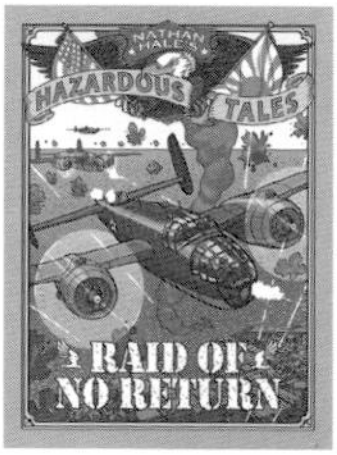
NATHAN HALE'S
HAZARDOUS TALES
RAID OF NO RETURN
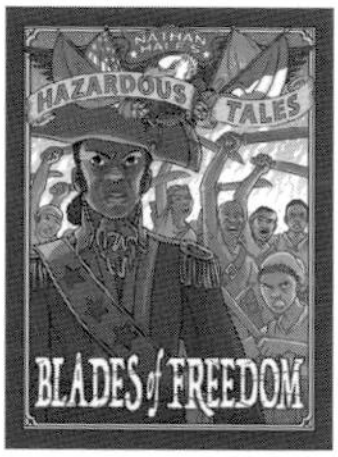
NATHAN HALE'S
HAZARDOUS TALES
BLADES of FREEDOM

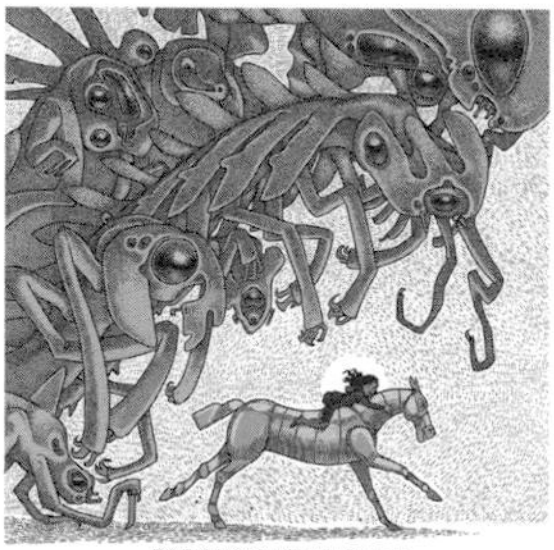
BY THE NEW YORK TIMES BESTSELLING AUTHOR
NATHAN HALE
ONE TRICK PONY

TAKE A BREAK FROM HISTORY
WITH SCIENCE-FICTION THRILLS
IN *ONE TRICK PONY* AND
APOCALYPSE TACO!

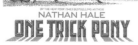

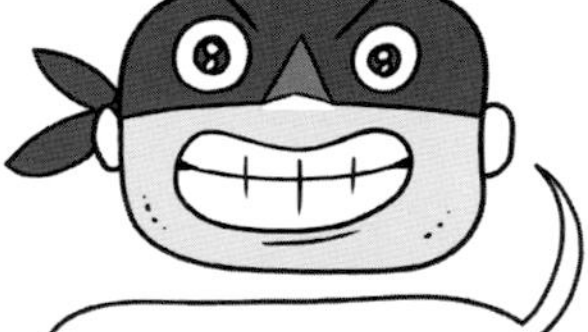
ONE THOUSAND FIVE HUNDRED AND EIGHTY-FOUR PAGES OF CARTOON CALAMITIES!

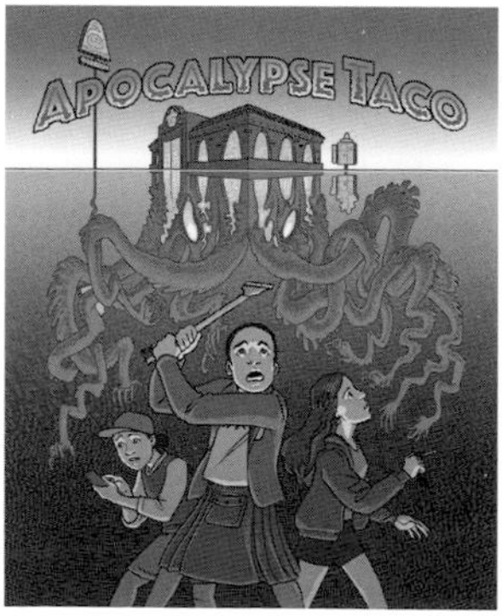
APOCALYPSE TACO

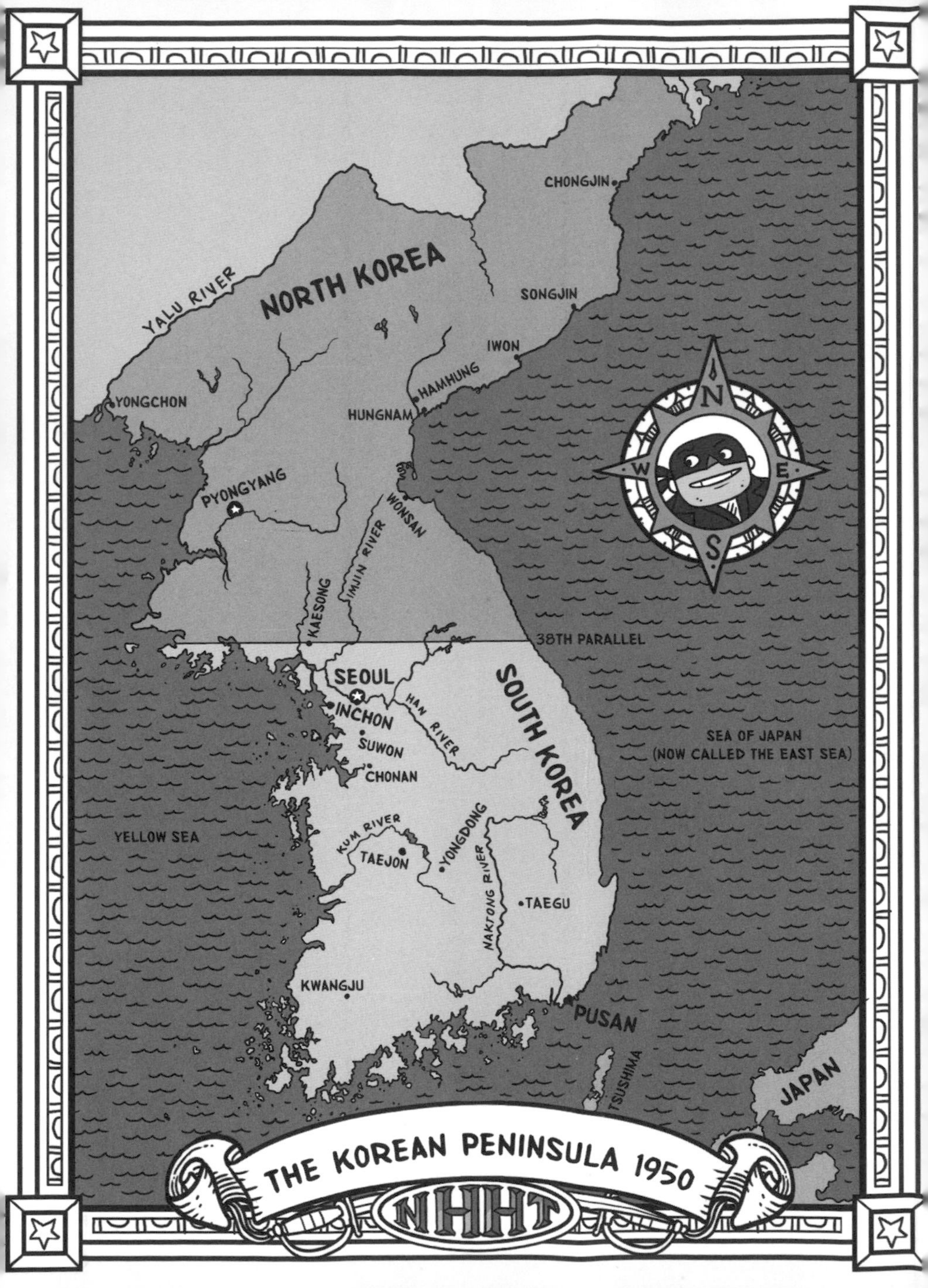
NORTH KOREA
YALU RIVER
CHONGJIN
SONGJIN
IWON
HAMHUNG
HUNGNAM
YONGCHON
PYONGYANG
WONSAN
IMJIN RIVER
KAESONG
38TH PARALLEL
SEOUL
INCHON
SUWON
CHONAN
HAN RIVER
SOUTH KOREA
SEA OF JAPAN
(NOW CALLED THE EAST SEA)
YELLOW SEA
KUM RIVER
TAEJON
YONGDONG
NAKTONG RIVER
TAEGU
KWANGJU
PUSAN
TSUSHIMA
JAPAN
N
W
E
S
THE KOREAN PENINSULA 1950
NHHT